Explanation and Progress in Security Studies

Bridging Theoretical Divides in International Relations

Fred Chernoff

Stanford Security Studies, An Imprint of Stanford University Press
Stanford, California

Stanford University Press
Stanford, California

Printed in the United States of America on acid-free, archival-quality paper

Library of Congress Cataloging-in-Publication Data

Chernoff, Fred, author.
Explanation and progress in security studies : bridging theoretical divides in international relations / Fred Chernoff.
pages cm
Includes bibliographical references and index.
ISBN 978-0-8047-9095-6 (cloth : alk. paper) — ISBN 978-0-8047-9226-4 (pbk. : alk. paper)
1. International relations—Methodology. 2. International relations—Philosophy. 3. Security, International. 4. Explanation. I. Title.
JZ1305.C439 2014
327.101—dc23

2014010075

ISBN 978-0-8047-9229-5 (electronic)

Typeset by Newgen in 10/14 Minion

Contents

Preface vii

Introduction 1

1 Traditions of Explanation and the Idea of Scientific Progress 8

2 Explanation in the Natural and Social Sciences 34

3 The Nuclear Proliferation Debate: Why Do States Build Nuclear Weapons? 62

4 The Balance-of-Power Debate: Why Do States Form Alliances? 123

5 The Democratic Peace Debate: Why Do Democracies Act the Way They Do? 181

6 Analysis, Alternatives, Conclusion 241

Notes 271

References 285

Index 303

Preface

DOES THE STUDY of international relations (IR) and security lead to knowledge? If so, why has there not been more progress in the ways that we ordinarily associate with the natural sciences? Progress has several elements, including the cumulation of knowledge over time, predictiveness, and, when disputes arise, patterns of approach-to-consensus on the best theoretical explanation. This book asks about scientific progress by focusing specifically on the latter, approach-to-consensus.

A clear obstacle to this sort of progress in the social sciences is that, for disputing scholars to approach a consensus, some of the disputants will have to accept that they were wrong. Given that academics, no less than civilians, would rather be right all the time, a crucial question is whether, at some point after sufficient debate, one side will be shown to have the better answer, or whether those on all sides of an issue can just continue to insist that they're right. In other words, is there a point at which social scientists ever have to admit that they're wrong?

Some of the central questions in IR and security studies have been debated for centuries without agreement as to the best answer. In contrast, natural scientists over time come to agree on facts and explanations; we do not find natural scientists continuing to claim that fire is better explained by phlogiston than oxidation or that Earth is flat rather than oblate ellipsoidal. One of the reasons we regard the natural sciences as producing genuine knowledge is the very fact that those on the losing sides of the debates eventually adopt the winning position, or at the very least, cease claiming that they were right. Although this pattern of approach-to-consensus is not the norm in IR and most social sciences, it is important to know if it is at least possible, with some improvements, to approximate more closely the natural sciences. To that end, this book asks, Is it possible that one of the reasons consensus explanations have been so hard to come by in security studies is that researchers evaluate their explanations using criteria different from that of their opponents? If so, then we must ask, Is it possible that closer attention to which criteria scholars use will improve scholars' ability to engage directly with one another and to reach agreement on the best explanatory answers? The chapters that follow argue for an affirmative answer to both questions.

This book defends three closely related observations. First, natural scientists have recourse to a variety of criteria of evaluation when they argue about which explanatory theory is best (Chapter 2). Second, within criteria that are generally accepted in the natural sciences, there are disagreements among scientists and philosophers as to which criteria are more important than which others (Chapter 2). Third, in advancing their positions, security studies authors rarely identify the criteria they use, and they never identify the criteria their opponents use (Chapters 3–5). From these building blocks, the book argues that if scholars were to adopt the practice of explicitly acknowledging the criteria they use to advance their explanatory answers, significant improvements would be possible in their ability to move toward the best available explanations.

An inquiry into whether the study of international security produces genuine "knowledge," and whether that knowledge advances over time, has consequences for policy as well as theory. The ability to develop better explanations of international politics provides us with an enhanced ability to identify which causal factors are most strongly connected to which effects. This is essential for effective policy making, since policies based on flawed or inadequate understandings of key connections are unlikely to bring about the hoped-for outcomes. Furthermore, if current methods of study do not produce real knowledge, then it is important to explore whether there are better ways to go about studying IR.

I am fortunate to have had, and am happy to acknowledge, considerable help in the course of writing this book. John Vasquez of the University of Illinois, Jack Levy of Rutgers University, and Jim Wirtz of the Naval Postgraduate School made very helpful suggestions when this project was taking shape. Ewan Harrison of Rutgers provided generous feedback on a near-final draft. Several discussants and co-panelists at International Studies Association conferences over the past four years, as well as regulars at the weekly Yale IR seminar series, provided ideas on research design. As always, I am grateful to Bruce Russett, who long ago formed for me, and consistently continues to exemplify, the ideal of the knowledge-seeking social scientist. The generosity of Colgate University allowed me leave during the course of this project, and Colgate IR colleagues, notably Ed Fogarty and—going back to graduate school days—Al Yee, have provided stimulating intellectual discourse. The libraries of the Yale Club of New York and the City University of New York Graduate Center were, once again, cooperative and hospitable. Geoffrey Burn of Stanford University Press offered constructive advice on the original prospectus, waited patiently for the completion of the full manuscript, and has been thoroughly supportive throughout. Reviewers for the press made recommendations that improved the final product. A number of Colgate research assistants were valuable. Sarah Titcomb helped collect materials for the rankings of the books and articles in each area of debate. Amy Basu, Annie Hines, Kelsey Paustis, and Elizabeth Sadler proofread early drafts of several chapters. Keith England and Albert Naïm provided much help with references. And Ashley Hill, now at Princeton, read through, and offered advice on, the entire manuscript.

My young goddaughters, Sofie and Josie Song, provide on-demand joy and inspiration. Thanks also to Christina H. for enriching The Many, and for her enthusiasm in sharing the good news of the completion of this project. I appreciate the encouragement of my family, Myrna and Marshall Barth and K. Nastassja Chernoff and cousins, especially Syvia Lady Dhenin; and most of all, my late parents, Naomi and Romo Chernoff—the latter of whom radiated his unique energy for fully one hundred years—from Nicholas the Second to the Obama second term. Finally, I want to thank Vida Behn Chernoff and her small support staff of Montmorency J. and MiaMaria for the wonderful difference they have made in my life.

Grateful for the body of work he created, fortunate to have crossed paths with him the times I did, inspired by the genuine greatness that he achieved—to the memory of PSH.

Explanation and Progress in Security Studies

INTRODUCTION

1. THE CENTRAL QUESTION—WHY HAS THERE BEEN SO LITTLE PROGRESS IN SECURITY STUDIES?

Why do many debates in security studies and international relations (IR) go on for decades, even centuries, without moving toward resolutions or agreements on the best explanation? Is there a way to improve the ability of IR and security scholars to make progress in finding the best explanation for the events and processes we study? This book tries to find at least one factor that will help answer the first question, and it uses that to suggest a change in the way that scholars advance their own positions and engage their rivals' views. The proposed change is a modest one, but it has the potential to make a significant difference in the way debates progress.

If policy choices are to have a chance of accomplishing their intended purposes, then it is of paramount importance for decision makers to draw on the best possible theoretical understanding available (Walt 1998). If a policy is based on a flawed theory, it will succeed only by luck. If scholarly debate is in disarray, arriving at the best policy choices—which sometimes are matters of war and peace—will be difficult for decision makers. This book looks at what might be more effective ways that scholars can reach conclusions about the best theory.

The natural sciences manage to progress over time, no matter how *progress* is defined. From time to time natural scientists have to debate a new theory. In those instances, the history of science shows that scientists eventually move toward agreement on the best theoretical explanation. Of course, what the natural sciences study is very different from the human affairs and relationships that the social sciences study. But since both claim to produce knowledge, it is worth considering whether social scientists may be able to make more progress if they were to apply some aspects of natural scientists' methods. Thus, this book begins by considering the possibility that some aspects of what natural scientists do that enables them to make intellectual progress and build structures of knowledge might be applicable to the social sciences.

Perhaps what the natural sciences have that IR and security studies lack is a set of well-established criteria that are used to evaluate theoretical explanations. And if that is so, then an increased degree of clarity on criteria will enable authors to deal more directly with, and to respond to, one another's explanatory arguments. Success in dealing directly with opposing arguments could lead to greater success in finding the best explanations. No studies of IR have previously explored whether the use of different explanatory criteria may be one of the reasons that debates do not more often move toward resolution. The book thus investigates the hypothesis that progress in security studies has been slowed because of different scholars' use of different notions of explanation and different criteria of explanatory superiority.

To answer the central question of whether divergent uses of criteria inhibit agreement and progress, this book must address several prior questions, including the following: What do political scientists *actually do* when they claim to be "explaining"? And what is it about one explanation that leads scholars to regard it as superior to its rivals? The book begins by examining the core differences in debates over what science is and how it should ideally be conducted. Some authors who examine scientific practice focus on the descriptive task of finding out what scientists in fact do. Others focus on the prescriptive task of what makes empirical knowledge valid, true, useful, and/or reliable, since they develop principles about how scientific inquiry should be conducted. Chapter 1 offers a discussion of the relationship between the two. It asks whether improvements in explanatory practice must take account of existing practices, however justifiable or deficient they may be. The book does not assume that there is a single, univocal meaning that IR theorists attach to the term *explanation*; rather, it aims to determine which meaning(s) is used in the field.

Anyone who offers an explanation in security studies or IR should be able to specify what he or she means by that term and which factors or criteria qualify an explanation as a good one, even though books and journal articles in IR do not often present explicit definitions. The literature on IR methodology and metatheory offers several competing accounts of *explanation*. Because authors of substantive work in IR rarely identify any of these as the basis for their approaches, the foundation for each approach remains implicit rather than explicit. While not minimizing the difficulty and fallibility of the task, this book attempts to identify the implicit ideas of explanation and good explanation in the writings of security studies scholars.

Further, the book attempts to determine how authors judge good explanations by examining three of the core debates in security studies: (1) Why do states pursue policies of nuclear proliferation? (2) Why do states choose to form the alliances they do, especially with regard to the role of power balancing? (3) And why do liberal democratic states behave the way they do toward other liberal democracies? The descriptive element of the book will select ten to twelve of the most influential and widely cited works on each of the three questions and will examine them with an eye toward extracting, as well as is possible, the notion or notions of explanation embodied in each. This requires a good deal of interpretation for most of the publications included. The initial goal was to find the ten most influential works. But since the ranking process was not purely formulaic or mechanical, and since some works ranked quite closely, there was an attempt to avoid an arbitrary cutoff point. In the alliance formation debate, two works ranked very close together; rather than choose one arbitrarily, both were included. In the democratic peace debate, three ranked so closely that all were included, for a total of twelve.

This book begins with the presumption that there is merit in Thomas Kuhn's (1970) view of how scientists come to learn how to conduct inquiry; that is, scientists in a particular question area conduct research in ways that fit with the paradigm or disciplinary matrix in which they were trained. They are taught which works are the key works, or "exemplars," in the field. As they enter a field, researchers absorb both the substantive theories and the implicit standards of how to contribute to the debate. From these works they learn what constitutes good defense of a theory, what kinds of evidence are expected, what kinds of mathematical or logical methods are appropriate, and so on. Students internalize the methods and assumptions of exemplar works and then carry them forward in their own studies. If this account is correct, then it will be useful to look at works that appear to be such exemplars of high-quality security studies.

2. POSSIBLE ANSWERS

Is there a unified concept of good explanation—or best available explanation—used by political scientists in the field of security studies, and thus a single set of criteria by which they choose explanatory theories? There are three possible answers. First, we may find that there is a clear notion of good explanation that spans the various discourses in security studies with a consistent set of criteria used by all. A second is that we may find that each of the substantive debate areas has a unified notion and unified set of criteria that are used by all authors in that debate, but those differ from one debate to another—perhaps because of systematic differences arising from methodological peculiarities of each area (e.g., proliferation studies tend to be small-*N* and others tend to be large-*N*). Third, we may find that there is no unified notion of explanation or pattern of criteria at all; in this case, different authors within a single debate area use different notions of explanation and/or different criteria of explanatory superiority. This book argues for the third, which in turn raises the question of whether divergences in the criteria do or do not have an effect on the differences in the explanations offered by different theoretical schools.

3. EVIDENCE

Just what sort of evidence reveals how security studies authors judge which explanation is best? A survey of works in security studies that focuses on what the authors mean by "good explanation" would do the job. A comprehensive survey of all major journals and presses would tell us how the term is used, but it is too large a project to be practical. A much smaller survey will suffice, if it contains the most widely read, widely assigned, and widely cited works, since such works must embody the one (or several) most entrenched notion(s) of explanation. If those works did not use the term in these well-understood ways, they would be unlikely to reach the status of most often read, assigned, and cited. In fact, if there were a difference in the meaning used by the most widely read works and the less influential works, we would discover an interesting paradox, and possibly a counterexample to Kuhn's view of how new researchers learn how to conduct inquiry in a particular field. But because of both the low probability that there is such a split and the limitations of space, this study confines itself to ten-to-twelve published works in each of the three question areas, and so will not explore the popular-obscure divide.

Discounting the small probability that there is a divergence between the influential and obscure works, we may expect that ten to twelve works in each area are enough to show either that there are wide discrepancies in what authors mean by *explanation* or that there is convergence on a specific meaning—and if the latter, what the meaning is. The highest-profile works both reflect what the field does in the way of scholarship and shape how those who are currently being trained for professional academic careers understand the concept. That is, the most widely read, cited, and assigned works convey the idea or meaning of *explanation* to the next generation of scholars. As noted already, Kuhn's account of the history of the natural sciences includes an analysis of how key methodological ideas are conveyed from one generation to the next. The ways these exemplar works convey core questions and methods in the field is discussed in Chapter 1.

4. EXEMPLAR WORKS

The research design of this book requires, as just noted, the identification of a set of works that manifests the concept (or a concept) of explanation, as it is currently understood in security studies, which also transmits the understanding to the next group of students in the field. The selection of works is based on three sorts of considerations. One consideration is a survey of the most cited articles in the five key academic journals that cover international security issues. Two of these are general scholarly journals of IR, namely *International Organization* and *International Studies Quarterly*, and the other three are the most prominent journals that focus specifically on security-oriented issues, namely *International Security*, *Journal of Conflict Resolution*, and *Security Studies*. A second source is a survey of editors of the top twenty IR journals (as rated by the most recent *Teaching, Research, and International Policy*, or *TRIP*, survey of scholars in the field of IR at the time the research design was finalized; see Jordan et al. [2009]). These individuals have unique advantages in gaining a sense of which journal articles and books are the most influential in the three issue areas. The third source is graduate syllabi from courses that deal with international security affairs in the major graduate programs, that is, the institutions most likely to produce the next generation of publishing scholars. The top twenty institutions, as ranked by the *TRIP* study (Jordan et al. 2009), were contacted and asked to provide course syllabi and reading lists in the fields covered. Approximately fifty course syllabi were collected. Of the three methods used to select works, only the inspection of course syllabi targets books as opposed to journal articles. So there was an additional effort to balance books with journal articles. However, some of the books that appeared had been summarized in widely read journal articles prior to their publication. So the notion of explanation of those articles that are analyzed in this book was checked against the notion in the same authors' books for any discrepancies.

The works on course syllabi were evaluated for their prominence by counting them only once for appearing on a given syllabus; works that were assigned at different points for the same course were still counted only once. Works that were listed as "recommended" were not counted. Works authored by the course instructors were excluded from consideration for that syllabus. In a few cases, a specific author was frequently assigned, but there was no single work by that author; rather, there were several different works assigned with more or less equal frequency. Because, in those cases, each author's concept of explanation would thus seem to be an important one in transmitting the notion to current students, an effort was made to be sure that one of the author's works appeared on the list of publications surveyed.

Some authors published multiple works in the same substantive area in which they advanced or refined their arguments. For example, in the case of democratic peace, there are multiple works by Farber and Gowa, by Doyle, and by Russett and his various coauthors. Since these did not generally constitute independent positions and did not represent an expansion of the range of concepts of or criteria for explanation, the set of works is considered together as constituting a single position, and one of the works is emphasized in the descriptive analysis. Most attention in the analyses in Chapters 3–5 emphasizes the most prominent of the works, although references to others on the same topic by the same author are referred to when appropriate.

5. STRUCTURE OF THE BOOK

This book proceeds in several parts. First, in Chapter 1 it poses the central question of the study, asking whether progress in some areas of security study is slowed by scholars' failure to use similar criteria in assessing their arguments in favor of competing explanations. It then considers whether such a question can be answered in view of the complex relationship between describing epistemic norms and prescribing new norms in the natural sciences, examines the two traditions of inquiry in IR, and briefly discusses the notion of progress. Second, in Chapter 2, the book examines some of the most serious and widely debated efforts to analyze the notion of explanation and the criteria regarded as showing that one explanation is best. Third, in Chapters 3–5, the book surveys the prominent mainstream works in three selected topical areas of security studies—nuclear proliferation, alliance formation, and democratic peace—and seeks to identify common features, criteria, and patterns of progress. Finally, in Chapter 6, the book offers a broader look at the data in a way that connects the three debates with the notion of progress in social science knowledge. It concludes with an examination of possible alternative answers to the central question, some caveats, and recommendations for improving research in a way that will open up more opportunities for progress and approach-to-consensus about "best explanations" in security studies.

This book focuses on "explanation" in empirical-explanatory debates in security studies. As a field, IR encompasses question areas in various other subfields, such as international political economy, international law, and international organization. Furthermore, even within security studies there are different sorts of question areas, and some of the questions within these areas are primarily moral-normative, such as, when is the use of force justified? (For a discussion of the distinction between statements with "primarily" factual versus evaluative content, see Chernoff [2005, 18–19, 41].) No claim is made here that the analysis and conclusion of Chapter 6 apply beyond empirical-explanatory debates in security studies. There are prima facie reasons to suspect that there are differences, and generalization beyond security studies would require additional case studies. But in debates that are primarily empirical-explanatory, the recommended focus on identifying the criteria that one's study relies on could significantly enhance the possibility of progress.

1 TRADITIONS OF EXPLANATION AND THE IDEA OF SCIENTIFIC PROGRESS

THIS BOOK SEEKS to determine whether divergent uses of criteria have slowed movement toward consensus explanations in security studies. The central question of this study is whether to accept the hypothesis H_1, ***that progress in security studies has been slowed because different scholars use of different notions of explanation or different criteria of explanatory superiority.*** The study also considers a directly related second hypothesis, H_2, ***that if progress occurs, then contending explanatory schools use similar criteria.***

In the course of finding answers, it will be necessary to see what exactly security studies authors are in fact trying to do when they offer explanations that are better than their rivals, and thus constitute "progress" over them. To succeed in these tasks, it is necessary to understand what international relations (IR) authors mean by the terms *progress* and *explanation.* This chapter offers a brief sketch of some of the important ideas about how progress is understood by some of the major philosophers of science in the past century, and explanation is the subject of the next chapter. This chapter begins the effort of answering the central question of why progress has been so slow by considering arguments for, and criticisms of, the effort to turn IR into a science. To understand the explanatory goals of these efforts, we must consider the overall goals and methods advocated by proponents and critics of the behavioral-quantitative approach to IR.

1. DEVELOPMENT OF IR THEORY AND APPROPRIATE METHODS

People in many cultures have been studying IR for centuries. Some claim to have discovered persistent patterns and even social science laws. Around 430 BCE

Sun Tzu developed a set of principles based on observations of multiple cases, from which he derived regularities in the decisions of military leaders. He identified which politico-military methods were successful and which were not, and he then concluded which among them should be adopted. He confidently announced that whoever followed his strategic principles would be victorious, and whoever failed to heed them would be vanquished. Over the centuries, studies of IR have come to include many different topics and questions—examples include the relationship between trade and national wealth; the nature, effectiveness, and possibilities of international law; and the effects of different forms and structures of international institutions. But throughout the centuries, center stage has gone to concerns about the causes and consequences of war, and to identifying the factors that lead to victory once war has begun.

As the behavioral movement in the social sciences gained momentum in the 1950s and 1960s, IR scholars collaborated to construct what has become an enormous database, the well-known Correlates of War. As its name indicates, the project focuses on factors that theorists have associated, rightly or wrongly, with the onset of war. The core mission of the project has been to gain a greater understanding of war. While some expected that the quantitative study of IR would eventually dominate the entire field, many other approaches have persisted, including philosophical and legal studies. More recently, IR scholars have applied rational choice and game theory as they try to explain the actions of states.

No single method or methodology has come to dominate the field. Today there are frequent pleas for "methodological pluralism." Many who write on the subject of methods and make explicit recommendations are almost universally in favor of pluralism; they oppose the goal of finding the one ideal, all-purpose approach that alone has the potential to add to our knowledge and understanding of IR. The present study seeks to identify what sort of concept of explanation is used in security studies by examining the efforts to explain nuclear proliferation, alliance formation, and the relationship between democracy and peace.

2. THREE CENTRAL ISSUES IN SECURITY STUDIES

The study of IR has historically focused on questions of war, peace, and security. The contemporary field of security studies has a number of "most studied" issues, one of which is the presence of nuclear weapons. Two specific questions about nuclear arms have gained the most attention. The first concerns causes—

why do states become nuclear weapons states?—and is primarily explanatory. The second concerns consequences—how will stability and warfare be affected if more states acquire nuclear weapons?—and is principally about predictions. The emphasis of this book on questions of explanation leads us to focus on the first. The earliest states to acquire nuclear weapons, the United States and Soviet Union in the 1940s, and the United Kingdom, France, and China in the 1950s and early 1960s, were largely seen as doing so for security reasons, which realist theories were able to explain. However, as more states pursued nuclear weapons and a new factor entered the calculations of states, namely the nuclear Non-Proliferation Treaty (NPT), a wider-ranging debate emerged on why various additional states would want to build nuclear weapons and why various others would resist. Even some of the reasons that the first five nuclear weapons states chose to "go nuclear" came to be reexamined. Chapter 3 outlines the theoretical background of the contemporary debate and surveys the most influential works of the past several decades.

Another major issue that has been studied for centuries, and is still a major focus of debate, is how and why alliances form as they do. The most common explanations over the centuries have been tied to the realist concept of the balance of power. There are several versions of so-called balance-of-power theory. However, realist views have been challenged by liberals and constructivists, who deny that states, intentionally or unintentionally, seek power balances. In recent decades traditional balance-of-power explanations have also been challenged by arguments that states seek to balance in other ways that do not directly involve the balancing of power or capabilities. Chapter 4 examines the history of the debate and the current state of movement toward consensus on at least certain empirical claims.

A third important area that has risen in prominence in the past quarter century is sometimes called democratic peace (DP) studies. The key claim at issue here is that democracies are somehow different from other sorts of states, and they are most especially different in the way they deal with one another. Realists of course claim that power arrangements determine the stability or instability of international systems and that the maximization of power drives the behavior of states, no matter what sort of internal regimes they have. This fundamental realist claim would be undercut if it were shown that the behavior of democratic states is better explained by reference to the democratic nature of their governance structures. At the end of the eighteenth century Kant argued on theoretical grounds that a world of liberal democracies—specifically "republics"—would be a world at peace, given certain other conditions. Nearly two centuries later a vigorous debate emerged, with realists energetically attacking those who argued that the liberal democratic nature of some states affected their behavior, especially their behavior toward other liberal democracies. Chapter 5 examines the most influential works on both sides of this question from the 1970s onward.

3. NORMATIVE AND DESCRIPTIVE INQUIRY

Philosophers of science develop accounts of science by taking some cases of theory change as clear-cut instances of progress or advancement: oxidation over phlogiston, Newton over Ptolemy, Harvey over Galen. Anyone who sought to argue that Newton's theory was not an advance over Ptolemy would have to make a spectacularly original and persuasive argument (see Feyerabend 1975). These universally acknowledged cases of scientific progress may be so widely accepted as such because there are in fact many respects, not just one, in which the new theory was superior to the old. In other instances in the history of science, some newly proposed changes (e.g., when a theory's entia moved away from "observability") have sparked major debates as to whether they truly constituted progress. This leads to the question of which respects are more important than which other respects to produce genuine progress.

If the social sciences can be improved, then the process will most likely proceed in a way similar to that in the natural sciences, that is, only in a piecemeal way that combines interaction between descriptive and prescriptive (or epistemic-normative) elements. Some think that the sciences, whether natural or social, can be improved by a purely normative approach, in which ideas about legitimate knowledge guide the argument. Others hold that the success of science is itself the normative justification of its character and thus argue that the methods and progress of the sciences must be purely descriptive, aiming to identify key or essential practices, which, because they are scientific practices, are justifiable. But there are flaws with arguments for either of the pure approaches (Bohman 1993).

The social sciences are different from the natural sciences in many significant ways. Hashing out the exact relationship between them is one of the most important areas of the philosophy of the social sciences. Theorists in IR and elsewhere hold divergent views on the character and methods of the social sciences and their relation to those of the natural sciences. But there are some parallels, and there are some areas in which there is a good deal of agreement about how theories are developed and debated within specific disciplines. One philosophical strategy is to identify practices that are both historically represented and normatively justifiable.

Many philosophers of science make clear that description plays an important role in their normative analyses. Kuhn (1970, 207) notes that his efforts to understand science "repeatedly pass back and forth between the descriptive and the normative modes." He acknowledges that the reasoning he uses is circular, but he defends it by arguing that it does not produce a vicious circle. The present study allows for a dialogue between normative arguments about the nature of knowledge and practical arguments about how those norms are pursued by social scientists; it proceeds by examining specific works in the three security studies questions of nuclear proliferation, alliance formation, and democratic peace. It looks descriptively at how security studies scholars offer explanations and, on the basis of the observations it offers in Chapter 6, proposes some simple prescriptions for improving social scientific practice.

4. KUHN AND THE SOCIAL SCIENCES

Most social sciences, according to Kuhn, lack a single paradigm that dominates any particular generation of scholarship. Kuhn (1970, 21) views all sciences as maturing slowly and does not see them as having any clear threshold at which they move from immature to mature. Kuhn does not regard any of the social sciences as having reached maturity, although in his view economics has come the farthest. In social sciences like political science, sociology, and IR there are distinct and competing research traditions; there is no single, dominant paradigm. These disciplines have some parallels to the pre-Newtonian study of optics, which had no single, dominant paradigm about the nature of light. There were competing views. Some held light to consist in particles; some, a modification of the illuminated body; and some, an emanation from the eye. While there have been different theories since then—from corpuscular to wave to photon—one or another paradigm has dominated each generation. Each group emphasized tests that lent weight to its own particular theory.

International relations has long had competing theoretical traditions that seek to explain international behavior, and each has its preferred supporting case studies. Each of the approaches or research traditions in IR has its exemplar works, published in major journals or by major academic presses, which indicate what peer reviewers in that tradition regard as good social science that offers proper explanations. There are also specific works that have such a high profile that they are cited widely by other authors and find their way onto graduate school course syllabi, where they serve as models for the next generation of scholars. Kuhn argues that the exemplar works in physics are exemplars not for the entire field but rather for specific problem traditions, such as optics, mechanics, hydraulics, and the like. Thus, in international security studies, it seems reasonable to start with the belief that there are exemplar works in areas like those examined here: nuclear proliferation, alliance formation, and democratic peace studies.

According to Kuhn, in mature sciences revolutions occur from time to time. But in between the revolutions there are long periods of stability, or "normal science," during which each scientific field is unified by a universally (or nearly universally) accepted dominant paradigm. One of the advantages of debates in mature sciences under a unifying paradigm is that each researcher does not have the burden of having to explain every important methodological or theoretical concept that he or she uses. Kuhn (1970, 19–20) says, "When the individual scientist can take a paradigm for granted, he need no longer, in his major works, attempt to build his field anew, starting from first principles and justifying the use of each concept introduced. That can be left to the writers of textbooks." Natural scientists' ability to take these notions of method for granted allows them to put more energy into building on what is thus far accepted in their fields and to add to the accumulated experimental evidence that allows for scientific progress. In specific substantive works in IR, security scholars rarely define any of the key methodological concepts, including explanation. While this appears to parallel what we find in the natural sciences, most IR scholars nevertheless see themselves as operating within one or another of competing research traditions; at least they seem to have no trouble self-identifying when asked to do so (see Jordan et al. 2009).

One of Kuhn's contributions is an account of how scientists come to learn what science is and, in particular, what good science is. He says that scientists undergo education and "professional initiation" that is "unparalleled in most other fields" (Kuhn 1970, 177). In Kuhn's view, "some examples of actual scientific practice—examples which include law, theory, application, and instrumentation together—provide models from which spring particular coherent traditions of scientific research" (1970, 10). As just noted, prior to the relatively recent advent of textbooks, scientists were given important works to read that were regarded as examples of high-quality work in their fields. Kuhn says,

"Many of the classics of science . . . did what textbooks do today. In physics, classics, such as Aristotle's *Physica*, Ptolemy's *Almagest*, Newton's *Principia* and *Optiks* . . . and many other works served for a time implicitly to define the legitimate problems and methods of a research field for succeeding generations of practitioners" (1970, 10).

The most respected works in each problem area instructed students explicitly about the solutions to specific scientific problems, but also implicitly about the proper way to carry out scientific research. Such classic works provide the sort of "concrete achievement" that Kuhn argues is "a locus of professional commitment, prior to the various concepts, laws, theories, and points of view that may be abstracted from it" (1970, 11). The parallel with IR is a strong one, as graduate courses in security studies similarly avoid textbooks to introduce students to core debates and rely instead on the works of major contemporary authors. Kuhn notes that the classic works in a field contain rules of method, but such rules are typically implicit. Hence, it is not always easy to state precisely what those rules are. He says, "The determination of shared paradigms is not, however, the determination of shared rules. That demands a second step" (1970, 43). The search for rules "is more difficult than the search for paradigms" when the latter is conceived simply as examples (1970, 43).

The research design of the present study is structured in part by drawing on Kuhn's view of how classic scientific publications implicitly define methods and key concepts, including what is to count as a compelling scientific argument or good explanation. One may object to the use of Kuhn here on at least three grounds. First, Kuhn was talking about the natural and not social sciences, the social sciences do not exhibit the same patterns of inquiry and the transmission of proper methods of inquiry, and Kuhn's account even of the natural sciences is highly contested. But the controversial philosophical elements of Kuhn's view, especially his "incommensurability thesis" (see Section 9 in this chapter), need not be addressed to make use of the insights of his well-founded and much less contested view of how scientists are educated and socialized.

Second, one might object that the social sciences are divided by theoretical, methodological, and ideological tradition in a way that the natural sciences are not. But cleavages can occur in the natural sciences, at least for a time. Kuhn says, "There are schools in the sciences, communities, that is, which approach the same subject matter from incompatible viewpoints" (1970, 177). He immediately adds, "But . . . their competition is usually quickly ended" (1970, 177). The difference between the social and natural sciences in this regard is one of degree rather than kind. Natural scientists usually come to agreement on these disputes, whereas the same cannot be said for social scientists.

And third, one might object that since Kuhn is talking about the natural sciences, where each problem area is typically dominated by a paradigm, at least in all normal or "nonrevolutionary" periods, his views cannot be exported to social sciences like IR in which there is no single, dominant paradigm most, or even much, of the time. This objection disappears, however, when we remember that Kuhn believes that the natural sciences, including physical sciences like astronomy, mechanics, optics, and so on, operated before there was any single dominant paradigm—indeed through their entire histories prior to Newton—yet they were genuine sciences. To return to the example of optics just mentioned, Kuhn says, "No period between remote antiquity and the end of the seventeenth century exhibited a single, generally accepted view about the nature of light. Instead there were a number of competing schools and subschools" (1970, 12). Kuhn concludes that even though what was accomplished may or may not be regarded as "something less than science," still, "the practitioners were scientists" (1970, 13).

Overall, there is solid justification to make use of Kuhn's view of how scholars come to learn what is a good explanation. He says that in the social sciences the process of transmitting what each field is and what the methodological rules are is similar to pre-Newtonian natural science. Kuhn adds, "Even at the undergraduate level some 'classics' of the field" are assigned that teach both the methods of each paradigm and the competing paradigms and solutions (1970, 165). This is true, at least at the graduate level, in security studies. In the social sciences each intellectual or theoretical tradition has its own classics, and each problem area has important works. Given Kuhn's understanding of how scientific knowledge is produced, it would seem that, for better or worse, political scientists learn much of what they come to see as "the right way" to answer questions, solve problems, and explain phenomena by carefully reading and analyzing important works in their own fields and subfields. The present study takes this notion seriously and inquires into the concept of explanation employed by prominent authors in the three subject areas this book investigates: nuclear proliferation, alliance formation, and democratic peace.

5. THE SCIENTIFIC-CAUSAL TRADITION

The doctrine of naturalism in the philosophy of the social sciences holds that that social inquiry can legitimately be modeled on the methods of the natural sciences. But naturalism will always be limited by the fact that, on any account, the social sciences differ from natural sciences, which entails that any strict parallel will fail at some point. So we must ask, how far, if at all, can a parallel be drawn? And do the limitations on the parallels undermine naturalism?

Origins

The causal tradition in social science has its origins in the sixteenth century and was developed by thinkers like Bacon and Hobbes. In that period the scientific-causal approach was applied to both the natural world and the social world, and has been adopted in one form or another by most scholars since then. The two broad traditions in Western philosophy that developed—realism and anti-realist empiricism—came to view "explanation" in different ways. For realists a good explanation is one that provides us with, among other things, true statements. For empiricists (such as instrumentalists, operationalists, and conventionalists) a good explanation is one that allows us to order our experience and produce accurate predictions. Empiricist philosophers typically see explanations as fundamentally about some aspect of human knowledge, however "knowledge" may be conceived, whereas realist philosophers see it as fundamentally about the nature of the world. In recent decades other accounts have argued that "explanation" is constituted by the creation of a psychological state in the minds of investigators, and that it is essentially a process of communication among scientific investigators.

Many empiricist thinkers regarded the explanation of a phenomenon essentially as a process of identifying observable correlates and causes. However, in modern physics the role of postulated unobservable entities, like subatomic particles, became so significant that many philosophers came to separate the literal truth of statements that occur within an explanation from the ability of the statements to explain. In their view it was impossible to claim the same sort of certainty for statements about electrons as it was for statements about trees and stones. Subatomic theory is one of the important cases that led philosophers to shift their normative views of what scientists should do to take fuller account of actual developments in scientific theorizing.

The Core Scientific Issues of the Twentieth Century

The philosophers and philosopher-scientists at the beginning of the twentieth century, noted earlier, were interested in how science contributes to human knowledge, which was why they sought to discover the nature of knowledge and its rational justification. They were especially interested in developing justifications that do not go beyond the limitations implied by Hume's critiques of induction and causation, which meant that they did not treat the development of laws and theories as arising inductively from individual instances. They saw considerable appeal in the so-called covering law model of scientific explanation, formalized by Carl Hempel (1945) in the 1940s, since it offers what claims to be an account of how science can explain without introducing an inductive component.

Karl Popper developed a very different way to circumvent the use of inductive reasoning, namely the "methodology of falsificationism." Popper first published the *Logic of Scientific Discovery* (*Logik der Forschung*) in 1935. His book *Conjectures and Refutations* (1965) was a further major statement of his position. He continued to develop his ideas on this and other topics throughout the remainder of the twentieth century. Popper intended his work as a critique of the logical positivists, who sought a criterion of *meaningfulness* capable of separating significant laws of physics, chemistry, and sociology from meaningless statements of metaphysics and speculative philosophy. Popper sought instead the demarcation between science and non-science. For Popper the demarcation was not merely descriptive; it would also show which disciplines contain statements whose nature is capable of leading to truth or truth-likeness, that is, "verisimilitude." Although Popper's criterion of falsifiability was prescriptive, it was drawn much more from an examination of actual scientific theories. Falsificationism has been compelling to many philosophers and scientists because of its fidelity to the goal of avoiding induction, which it does by depicting theories as having the capacity to be conclusively refuted but not the capacity to be conclusively proved true.

Some have argued that philosophers' efforts to develop an account of science that circumvents inductive reasoning fails because such philosophers inevitably "smuggle in" induction when they claim that general laws are part of scientific procedure; critics argue that general laws, whether acknowledged or not, arise from inductive reasoning. But Popper, Hempel, and others dismiss this criticism by claiming that the ways in which laws come about historically have nothing to do with their justification, the logic of science, or the epistemic security of scientific findings. The laws might come to scientists from inductive insights or any other source of inspiration, including dreams. How they arise may be of interest to psychologists, but not to philosophers, who are properly concerned only with the procedures employed in assessing proposed laws before they are accepted. Popper and many of his contemporaries thus distinguished "the context of justification" from the "context of discovery." Only the former is subject to philosophical scrutiny.

Critics

Traditional empiricism (logical positivism, logical empiricism, and Popperian falsificationism) came under sustained attack by a wave of critics beginning in the late 1950s, which led to a reevaluation of many empiricist views of science. The works of Wilfred Sellars (1956), N. R. Hanson (1961), Thomas Kuhn (1970, first published in 1962), and Paul Feyerabend (1975) formed much of the core of this movement. Among the targets of their attacks were the methods of rational reconstruction and normative critique of science. Kuhn and Feyerabend were especially forceful in arguing that what scientists in fact do is more central to the task of the outsider studying science. Kuhn made claims about the nature of research and, as discussed earlier, distinguishes periods of "normal" from periods of "revolutionary" science. These claims are descriptive and explanatory rather than prescriptive and normative. Even in the moderated form of his starker original 1962 argument, Kuhn (1970, 199) maintained that what is important about his concept of scientific revolutions is that scientists' arguments supporting new paradigms are not justified entirely on rational (logical, mathematical, or observational) grounds. And in the philosophy of the social sciences the application of naturalist-inspired empiricism also produced a throng of harsh critics at that time, most of whom advocated social research in the "interpretive" or "hermeneutic" tradition.

6. THE INTERPRETIVE TRADITION

Authors in the interpretive, anti-naturalist approach reject the idea that the study of the social world should be modeled on the study of the natural world. They offer several lines of argument for this conclusion. One sort of argument builds on the claim that human behavior is based on intentions, whereas the behavior of physical objects like asteroids or electrons is not. A second begins with the claim that human behavior essentially conveys meaning to other human beings, which is again fundamentally different from the behavior of the objects studied by natural scientists, and especially by physical scientists. Only institutions and sets of rules can imbue actions with meaning; that is, actions only come to constitute the domain of the social scientist, as opposed to the study of the human heart beating or the blink reflex, because the actions are performed in a context in which there are shared understandings of rules and social institutions. And a third is that humans have free will, which allows them to choose to deviate from whatever "scientific laws" social theorists claim to have identified. These scholars argue that the study of the social world bears much closer similarity to the study of language than to the study of nature. A statement of remorse is just that (i.e., *constitutes* a statement of remorse), only because the speaker and hearer share a common framework of rules governing which sounds or written signs carry which particular meanings. Both social behavior and language are systems of symbols that convey meaning and lead to little, if any, predictive knowledge. Along those lines, social scientists in the noncausal tradition argue that the social action of signing a treaty or paying cash for a purchase in a shop is *that particular action* because many people share a set of rules about what is signified by authoritative roles (e.g., head of state) and rules (e.g., those of international law), and share common understandings (e.g., in the case of cash currency, of the trading value associated with certain rectangular pieces of colored paper bearing pictures of heads of state).

The origin of the interpretive approach to social action stems from the hermeneutic study of Scripture in which theologians debated the meaning of sacred texts. In these debates scholars asked how one should decide which among the competing interpretations is the one that conveys the true meaning of the text. Various interpretive methods were developed, such as searching for consistency, coherence, and so on. These allowed hermeneutists to begin to claim that the meaning of all intentional human actions, including painting, sculpture, music, and the like, could be understood properly only by applying the interpretive principles of hermeneutics. Eventually some scholars extended the scope of actions that should be studied in this way to include political acts.

Interpretivists reject any form of linear, causal scientific methods because of the inherent circularity of social enquiry. Interpretivist scholars see many forms of circularity; one of the most commonly identified is the hermeneutic circle, according to which one needs a framework of interpretation to make sense of a particular action, and one needs to know the meaning of particular actions to formulate an interpretive framework.[1]

When we look at the actions of individual leaders in declaring wars or signing treaties, when we examine past behavior, we can never know exactly why they did what they did. Our search for the reasons a particular leader made a certain decision is much like our search for the meaning of a text, since the author of the text has already composed it before we read and analyze it. The author of the text and the author of the action may not be available to answer our queries about the meaning of the text or reason for the action. Even if they were available, they might offer deceptive or evasive answers, or they might have forgotten what was in their thoughts at the time of the composition of the text or the decision to act. Thus, hermeneutists argue, the parallel holds.

Winch's *The Idea of a Social Science*

It is clear that interpretivists' conception of how language works and how it is connected to the world are central to how they understand the proper methods of studying the social world. The most influential statement of the interpretive approach is found in Peter Winch's (1958) classic work, *The Idea of a Social Science*. Winch's conception of language, deriving clearly from Wittgenstein's *Philosophical Investigations* (1953), plays a central role in his view of how the social world may be studied. According to that view, language very much constructs the world in which humans live. Investigators cannot, contrary to dominant views of science, focus on theory-neutral experience and formulate laws and theories, because much of what investigators experience results from their previous experience and education, including their language acquisition. The language that people have available to them significantly shapes the world available for them to experience. For example, a professor of biochemistry and her five-year-old child actually experience different things when they peer through a microscope at a slide of human tissue because the child does not have language to express the scientist's experience of "seeing" the cell nucleus, mitochondria, cell membranes, and so on.

Winch (1958, 23) rejects the dominant naturalist form of social science. He believes that it is essential for social inquiry that the inquirer come to understand the values and points of view of those whose actions are to be explained: "A man's social relations with his fellows are permeated with his ideas about reality. Indeed, 'permeated' is hardly a strong enough word: social relations are expressions of ideas about reality" (1958, 23). One could not give anything beyond a "superficial account" of a monk's relations with fellow monks and his relations with laypersons "without taking into account the religious ideas around which the monk's life revolves" (1958, 23). Social science naturalists may, however, agree that what they seek is external, observable behavior, which, in the interpretivist's sense, is a "surface" or "superficial" account.

An interpretivist follower might take one aspect of Winch's Wittgensteinian position even further by arguing that a linear understanding of our reasoning is impossible on an even deeper level because the use of language itself involves a circularity, or at least a regress. As just noted, Wittgenstein (1953) holds that our experience depends upon what we have learned, including the language and vocabulary we have learned. But the learning and use of language themselves involve circularities, since, when we learn to use a word, we learn to follow the rule of applying that word in the same sorts of circumstances. There will be circumstances in which the word may be correctly applied and others in which it may be incorrectly applied.

Winch holds that empiricists in the philosophy of science overstate the role of observation in the social sciences and underestimate the role of a priori conceptual analysis. He argues that the traditional empiricist critique of causality underestimates the role of a priori reasoning in trying to conceive of the possibility that the order of nature undergoes a radical change; conceptual analysis is not a posteriori but rather involves issues of what it makes sense to say. Such conceptual analysis is, at bottom, a priori (1958, 71–72). While one may disagree with much of Winch's position on the fundamentally nonnaturalist and interpretivist character of social science, he nevertheless makes a strong case for the claim that there is a distinct role for philosophical enquiry that encompasses conceptual analysis and a priori reasoning.

Rules

It is of their essence for rules to be public. Wittgenstein argues against the possibility of a purely private language that is devised by a solitary person who has no contact with others because language is entirely rule based and rule generated, and there can be no purely private rules. His reasoning is that rules are rules only if there is a way to follow them, and we can conceive of a rule having a method for following it only if we can conceive of ways to fail to follow it. This is a result of conceptual analysis of "rules" rather than a result of observations of isolated individuals who have sought to create private rules or private languages. Rules, for Wittgenstein and Winch, are by their very nature public. And all public, that is, social, action is rule governed.

One further dilemma we encounter as we look into the nature of various scientific concepts stems from the relationship between normative and descriptive analysis discussed earlier. If we know what an explanation is in ordinary discourse, we may ask whether a scientific explanation must be of the same sort in order to be an explanation. The positive argument is that we know from ordinary discourse what it means for something to be an explanation, and if a scientific explanation does something other than "explain," then it is something other than an explanation. The contrasting view is that a scientific explanation may indeed do something different from an ordinary explanation in virtue of the fact that a body of scientific knowledge progresses because scientific method refines and improves upon our prescientific ways of acquiring knowledge. Science has to improve upon our traditional or folk understanding of what an explanation is in order to lead to new and deeper knowledge.

MacIntyre's Interpretivist Critique of Winch

Winch's view that all social action is rule governed has been challenged by Alasdair MacIntyre, who argues that Winch's view confuses different meanings of "rule." MacIntyre (1970, 20) says, "A distinction may be made between those rules which agents in a given society sincerely profess to follow and to which their actions may in fact conform, but which do not in fact direct their actions, and those rules which, whether they profess to follow them or not, do in fact guide their acts by providing them with reasons and motives for acting in one way rather than another."

Moreover, the sorts of rules that guide a chess player to choose one among several permissible moves are quite different from the rules that limit the range of choices a mental patient has in a psychiatric ward (MacIntyre 1970, 22). In terms of the depth of analysis available to the social scientists, we may explain the actions of people or institutions by reference to their own conceptions of what they are doing or by claiming there is a "deeper" level of the reality of their action, to which the actors themselves may not have access. MacIntyre points out that Winch says that all social action is meaningful and is thus rule governed. The only actions that Winch says are exceptions are those of someone who is "berserk." An action, according to Winch, is rule governed when one can say that the action either follows or violates the rule, that is, when there is a right way and a wrong way to perform the action. But MacIntyre (1971, 211–29) says that with many social actions, such as smoking a cigar or going for a walk, there is no right way and wrong way to perform them.

MacIntyre also contests Winch's claim that the key to the social scientist's analysis of the social actor's action is the latter's self-conception of that action in terms of the way the social actor envisions the rule the actor is following. MacIntyre argues the contrary position by considering the venerable example of post-hypnotic suggestion; someone under hypnosis is instructed to perform action x on occasions of type y. When the social scientist asks, on a y-type occasion, why the subject performed x, the subject will give an answer that may not touch on the real reason or cause of the performance of x. A similar "deeper" grounding for human action is necessary to make sense of certain social science concepts.[2]

The standard objection to the idea that reasons can be regarded as having causal status is that in causal relationships the cause and the effect are related contingently and so must be able to be conceived of without reference to each other; the idea of a stone at rest is not part of, and does not contain, the idea of a stone falling. But the concepts of human causes and effects are different. Two people may perform an identical act, such as putting a knife into a man lying in the street and pulling from that man an internal organ, such as his appendix. But the two identical behaviors are "different actions" if the intentions are different; for example, if one person is a sadist who enjoys inflicting pain and the other is a surgeon who determined by a quick examination that the man was suffering a severe bout of appendicitis. What makes one act assault and the other emergency surgery is the intention of the agent performing it; this is not contingently related to the act but is an intrinsic part of the phenomenon itself. (We might even hypothesize that the individual wields the knife in exactly the same places and ways, purely by coincidence, as the surgeon.) Thus, the motivating "cause" of the action is *part of* what makes the behavioral "effect-act" the act that it is. The reason for the action is, according to interpretivists, internal to the action and conceptually related to it. But MacIntyre argues that outside observers may well be able to identify the agent's possessing the reason for the action independently of the way in which they identify the agent's performance of the action. This, MacIntyre believes, is enough to count reasons as causes.[3]

7. ASSUMPTIONS AND STARTING POINTS

If the central hypothesis of this book, H_1, is right, then many security studies authors pay too little attention to criteria of explanatory superiority. It is, then, logical to ask, how much metatheory and methodology is enough? The answer will depend upon the nature of the claims being advanced and the nature of the intended audience.

Starting Points Are Unavoidable

Every study must start at a starting point, and assumptions must be made. Some of the starting points will be at the metatheory level. It may be possible to defend rather than assume some such propositions, but it will not be possible to defend every one of them. And each assumption an author makes will allow readers who do not accept that assumption to dismiss the argument based on them, and this absolves those who reject the assumption of the responsibility to regard the argument as rationally compelling. In general, then, the fewer assumptions required, the better. In Chapter 6 we return to the question of starting points and the role of metatheoretical assumptions. For the moment we identify only some of the important assumptions of this study.

Methodological Pluralism

One assumption of this book is that different types of question are posed in IR, and the most appropriate methods of argument to answer them depend on the type of question. Naturalist approaches are most appropriate for many, but not all, questions in IR and security studies. This form of methodological pluralism is an assumption of this study. It is not defended here, but arguments for it have been offered elsewhere (Chernoff 2005, 2007b, 2009). This book, rather, has identified three major questions in security studies and has formulated a set of criteria for selecting the key works in those debates.

The Notion of Progress in the Social Sciences Is Coherent

This book draws on the belief that naturalism is justifiable, that progress is important for the social sciences, and that progress can be gauged by agreement and disagreement, among other things, in an area of enquiry. The fact that there has been progress in the democratic dyad debate (argued in Chapter 5; see also Chernoff 2004) is powerful evidence that the notion has coherent application to IR. With regard to naturalism, all thirty-three works analyzed in this study adopt some form of naturalism in that they make use of broad parallels to the empirical methods of the natural sciences. While the present author has discussed and defended a version of naturalism elsewhere (Chernoff 2005), no such defense is offered here.

Socialization of Authors into Scholarly Debates

This book assumes a generally Kuhnian understanding (see Section 4 of this chapter) of how debates in empirical inquiry proceed, and of how new entrants in those debates come to understand the outlines of the contending schools and the acceptable methods of study in the field. New entrants into a field read the works that they are told are the key or seminal works in that field. The methods of argument and inference are "internalized" by scholars as exemplars in the field.

An understanding of scholarship-socialization along these lines requires that there are "key works" in a field or debate and that there are ways to identify those works. The standards used in this book for selecting works to be included as "most influential," as described in the introduction, involved numbers of citations, surveys of editors of major journals, and reading lists of security studies courses in top doctoral programs in the United States. But it was rather surprising that none of the top ten or twelve works was of an interpretivist nature. This reflects the high scores that certain journals in security studies were accorded on the *Teaching, Research, and International Policy (TRIP)* survey (Jordan et al. 2009), and, of course, it reflects the decision to focus on graduate-level reading lists at US universities. The latter poses limitations on the scope of the conclusions the study reaches but does not diminish their power within the context of the US debate, which helps to define the scope of the debate. One could propose using US and UK graduate programs, or all programs around the globe. While many of the works included here would still be included, probably even at the top of the "influence" pyramid, there would be some differences in the choices made. This study does not claim that there is greater legitimacy in the chosen focus than in other possible foci, but a choice one way or the other is required, and that choice, whatever it is, relativizes the results that follow that choice.[4]

Domain Specification

This study requires that the notion of debate is defined in a specific enough way so that the reader can clearly distinguish the evidence that would count from the evidence that would not count. This is related to the metatheoretical proposition, accepted by many philosophers of science, as well as by Waltz (1979), that any explanation or theory must set out what the scope of its domain is; it must state clearly which phenomena fall within the scope of what it claims to explain and which do not. This book identified what falls within its scope by providing three conditions. Within that understanding, empirical examination of published works is required to identify the contending schools, methods of argument used in those schools, and overall contours of the debates. With regard to the broad outlines, this study makes the conventional choice to include US graduate programs training IR scholars among the three measures.

8. NONEXPLANATORY GOALS OF INQUIRY

This book seeks to identify (1) what authors in security studies are trying to accomplish when they say that they are offering explanations; (2) whether there are implicit differences in different authors' explanatory goals, which would lead them to miss one another's arguments and critiques; and (3) whether there are ways to solve any problems identified in performing the two preceding tasks. We must compare only authors who claim to be offering explanations. Some authors do not say that they are developing explanations. They may say that their goal is to provide understandings, analyses, descriptions, or predictions. It is also possible that some authors regard these things as valuable as part of, or as an indicator of, an explanation. In any case, it would be unfair to criticize authors for failing to adhere to the canon of good explanation if they are not claiming to explain. Thus, the works that are considered in Chapters 3–5 are ones in which the authors say explicitly that they are offering explanations.

Some authors draw a distinction between *explanation* and *understanding*. But it is worth noting that such a distinction does not arise from, and is not consistent with, ordinary usage. In their popular textbook, Hollis and Smith (1991) follow Weber's (1947) and Von Wright's (1971) distinction between the German terms *Erklären* and *Verstehen*. Hollis and Smith are careful to use the terms *explanation* for the former (scientific-causal) and *understanding* for the latter (interpretive-hermeneutic). However, ordinary English usage does not distinguish these two terms in this way. Even philosophers of social science do not usually hold to this distinction between the terms. They often talk about how interpretive scholars *explain* behavior in terms of reasons or roles, which gives us a way of *understanding* action but may not be taken as having causal efficacy. They typically use the two terms in a way that links them rather than sets them against each other. While Hollis and Smith's separation of the two terms is useful and makes their presentation easier to follow once the reader catches on to their language, it is not entirely helpful for the purposes of the present book, which seeks to describe and analyze the way IR scholars in fact talk about their efforts to develop explanations. The present book, then, leaves open the question of the usage of the terms *explanation* and *understanding* so as to be able to apply them in whatever ways the various authors intend.

Two other nonexplanatory goals of social inquiry are analysis and prediction. The term *analysis* has a quite specific meaning, which is to break things into their component parts, and perhaps to break them down to their irreducible or "un-analyzable" component parts. This is typically how natural scientists use the term and how dictionaries define it. However, it seems that when the term is used in typical social science parlance, it may mean "to clarify" or "make more understandable," without the specific denotation of breaking into parts. The term *account* is used in a very broad and nonspecific way. It can mean virtually anything along the lines of "adding to our knowledge of."

A prediction is a statement about what will or may happen in the future. Offering compelling arguments about if and how prediction is possible requires a definition of the term that captures the way the term is used in the social sciences.[5] This is important to note because many authors regard prediction as a goal in the social and natural sciences. And security studies scholars often seek to use explanations to predict what will happen. One might predict, for example, that if regional power A acquires nuclear weapons, then neighbors B and C, which meet various conditions, will do so soon thereafter. The concept of a prediction is fairly clear, although political scientists (and philosophers of social science who argue that prediction is impossible in the social world) sometimes commit a straw-man fallacy as they shift the meaning of *prediction* in such a way as to raise the bar for what will officially count as a prediction. The higher they set the bar, the easier it is for critics of predictive IR to show that reaching the bar is impossible.

Some have argued that science does not properly seek explanations. This view was advanced at the turn of the previous century by a number of empiricist physicists and philosophers, such as Pierre Duhem (1954, 7), who said, "A physical theory is not an explanation. It is a system of mathematical propositions deduced from a small number of principles, which aim to represent as simply, as completely, and as exactly as possible a set of experimental laws." For Duhem, "To explain . . . is to strip the reality of the appearances covering it like a veil, in order to see the bare reality itself" (1954, 19). The role of science is to order observations and experience; explanation is something that philosophy or metaphysics does. Others have added that while science provides theories and sets of laws, the explanation of those laws or phenomena explained is a matter of the scientist becoming comfortable or familiar with the content of the theory. In their view there is nothing in science proper that we could call "explanation." This is a matter of biography rather than science or philosophy. In the social sciences there has been much greater reluctance to see theorizing in any substantive area as divorced from explanation. In contrast, for Hempel (1965) and other antirealists, explaining does help science to do the things it should do, especially providing greater predictive capacity and control over future experience.

The concept of explanation has been understood in different ways in the past century or so. Traditionally it was regarded as essentially the identification of causes. In the contemporary literature an explanation is variously regarded as a logical statement or argument, a means of communication, and an answer to a question. The various usages and differences are the subject of Chapter 2.

9. PROGRESS AND STALEMATE

Progress in the Natural Sciences

The notion of progress implies that whatever is progressing is moving to a "better" state from one that is inferior in specifiable ways. As such, the concept is a normative one. Attempts to remove the normative element from the concept of progress have had limited success. Even Kuhn (1970, 162), despite his claim of incommensurability, acknowledges that, in general, people define an area of inquiry as scientific so long as it is one "in which progress is marked." Indeed, philosophers of natural science regard the concept of progress, as much as any feature, as a hallmark of genuine science. The centrality of progress to the standard notion of science may be seen by imagining how hard it would be to make sense of someone claiming to introduce a new scientific area of inquiry that admittedly was incapable of progress or knowledge cumulation.

Most major figures in the history of modern philosophy, from Bacon and Descartes onward, believed that human knowledge of the natural world (and beyond) could be indefinitely extended by the application of proper reasoning and methods. Later thinkers, such as Kant, Hegel, Marx, and their followers, continued to argue for optimistic views of the capabilities of the human mind and the ability of modern science to extend our grasp of, and potential control over, the world around us. Science has changed over the centuries, not only in the content and scope of its theories but also in the most widely practiced and respected methods. Newton and other leading figures in early modern science believed that what they were doing was methodologically different from anything that had been done before. The new inductivist methods they developed ultimately came to be doubted, most notably because of Hume's attacks on claims of scientific certainty gained by causal and inductive reasoning. In the nineteenth century this approach finally gave way to new methodological principles, especially the hypothetico-deductive method.

The extraordinary advances of twentieth-century science led philosophers to focus on identifying what is distinctive about scientific knowledge. This attention produced extensive debates on all aspects of science. Because these philosophers carried out such thorough investigations of methodology, virtually every traditional characteristic of science has been challenged by one of the major schools in the philosophy of science. The two broad schools of thought in the philosophy of natural science, as noted already, are scientific realism and empiricist antirealism. Scientific realism can take forms that include, among others, verisimilitude realism, advanced by Popper (1959, 1965), according to which scientists seek truth-likeness; cognitive realism, exemplified by Rohrlich (2001), which endorses coherence and cumulativeness despite acknowledging ontological pluralism; and entity realism, defended by Hacking (1983), which holds that postulated entities that serve to aid scientific discovery may be real even if the theories in which they were first formulated turn out to be flawed. Empiricist views of science include, among others, the logical empiricism of Hempel (1965), the conventionalism of Duhem (1904–1905), the constructive empiricism of Van Fraassen (1980, 2008), and the evolutionary epistemology of Toulmin (1977). Few philosophers from any school mentioned have been willing to consider discarding the claim that science is characterized by progress. Some sociologists, pursuing what they call the "strong programme" (e.g., Bloor 1976), minimize "progress" as they try to show that debates in the natural sciences are primarily influenced by sociological factors rather than the theories' exhibiting "truth" or "nearness to the truth."

Kuhn (1970) argued that the things that are compared in the natural sciences are "paradigms"—or what he later called "disciplinary matrices." A paradigm includes key methodological principles and examples of good science. Because these broader frameworks or paradigms contain terms and concepts that are incommensurable, there can be no "theory-neutral" language available to express the results of experiments that are meaningful in more than one paradigm. Thus, there is no way to express observations that might adjudicate competing paradigms. Because of this incommensurability, the new paradigm is accepted on grounds other than the rational application of logical principles. Kuhn thus argued that there is no purely rational grounding for regarding new theories or paradigms as superior to their predecessors. Those who see scientific progress as the increasing extent of what is covered can view progress either as empirical progress, in which there is a greater accumulation of facts over time, or as theoretical progress, in which newer theories encompass the earlier theories and add to them. Kuhn's denial of progress through paradigm change rejects both sorts.

Kuhn argues that progress in the natural sciences is not what it is commonly understood to be because scientists operating within different paradigms do not genuinely engage one another on the same terms. Suganami (1996) claims that IR theorists often fail to engage one another because their causal explanations for the major phenomena they study—notably interstate war and conflict—that appear to conflict are often designed to explain different specific events. For example, two authors may claim to be explaining World War II, but upon a careful reading, it may become evident that one is trying to explain why there was a global war starting in the late 1930s while the other is trying to explain specifically why Germany invaded Poland (see Suganami 1996). In Suganami's view, many disputes in political science may turn on an ambiguity over which particular question is under discussion. The roles of pragmatic and contextual aspects of explanation are considered more fully in Chapter 6. But for the present, it is important to note that this book adds another possible explanation for the lack of progress in security studies, namely that scholars in the field may be doing somewhat different things from one another when they claim to be explaining security issues, especially entertaining different ideas of which criteria must be met for an explanation to count as a good one.

The notion of progress in science was vigorously debated in the 1960s, with Popper's (1959) view being challenged by Kuhn (1970) and Lakatos (1978). Popper advocated a rational account of the demarcation between what does and what does not count as good science, which emphasized ***falsifiability,*** or the idea that a good scientific theory could, at least in principle, be shown to be false if certain specifiable phenomena were to be observed. When a theory is falsified, a new, unfalsified theory will supplant it. According to Popper, good science offers bold conjectures, which are then subjected to rigorous scrutiny; the conjectural theory is retained so long as it continues to pass rigorous tests. In this way, over time, science progresses by achieving greater and greater verisimilitude.

Imre Lakatos (1978) developed an alternative account of scientific knowledge that sought to resolve the conflicts between Popper's and Kuhn's accounts by agreeing with some points of each account and disagreeing with other points. Lakatos disagreed with Popper's view of how scientists treat theories when anomalies rise. He claimed that when a theory's implications are contradicted by experimental results, scientists do not typically reject the accepted theory. Rather, scientists look for ways to reconcile the anomalies with the entrenched theory, which sometimes results in scientists' rejection of the anomaly. But when reconciliation requires theoretical emendation, usually only minor changes are needed. New theories thus produced are typically quite similar to the ones they replace. The history of science shows, then, that the accepted body of knowledge in the subject area can produce a pattern in which scientists accept a sequence of related theories. Lakatos agreed with Kuhn that whatever sorts of things scientists compare at moments of revolutionary advances (e.g., a series of related theories and various methodological rules), they are broader than individual theories. Lakatos referred to the broader frameworks, with their successive theories, as research programs (RPs). He argued that, when faced with anomalous observations, scientists do not try to retain all statements in a research program with equal tenacity. The statements that are essential to the RP, which scientists will fight hard to keep, constitute its "hard core." The statements that scientists are willing to modify or abandon constitute the RP's "protective belt of auxiliary hypotheses." Methodological guidelines include the rules of retaining the hard core (the so-called negative heuristic) and, when changes are necessary, modifying the appropriate statements in the protective belt (the "positive heuristic").

There are many points at which Lakatos's position is closer to Popper's, including the important tenet that advancements in science proceed rationally. When faced with anomalies, the scientist always has a number of different ways to resolve the inconsistencies. Lakatos argued that some of the options available constitute good scientific practice, whereas others do not. And he presented an account of the relevant differences between the two types of procedures. This contrasts sharply with Kuhn's position that when paradigms change, the process is not guided by rational procedures.

Consider some of the anomalies that scientists discovered leading to questions about Ptolemaic cosmology and celestial mechanics. There are different ways of dealing with such anomalies, including the addition of extremely ad hoc hypotheses that postulate new "forces," which does nothing but eliminate the anomalies. If this is done, then the theory has been made more complex, even though it has added no new content to the theory and there are no other observable implications of the newly postulated force beyond what is needed to remove the contradictions of the anomaly. This type of theory modification is what Lakatos calls "degenerating." If the new, more complex theory not only takes care of the anomalies but also has new content and further observable consequences, then the shift is, according to Lakatos, a "progressive" one.

The notion of novel facts is perhaps one of the most important, and complex, in Lakatos's metatheory of science, and it is a mark of what shows one theory to be an improvement over others. Lakatos requires that the progressive theory or RP leads the researcher to look for novel facts. Hence the requirement of novel facts goes well beyond mere consistency with known but unexplained facts; it leads the researcher to develop certain sorts of new ideas. Lakatos's notion here is that if we accept the new theory, we will ask, if it is true, then what else might we expect from it that we have not previously thought to expect?

Those expected outcomes should then be investigated to see whether they obtain. In whatever fashion one settles the meaning of novel facts (and there are various interpretations), it is clear that the concept of progress not only is essential to Lakatos's notion of science but also plays a pivotal role in a technical capacity to distinguish proper from improper scientific procedures in actual scientific settings.[6] The disagreement of Popper, Kuhn and Lakatos constitutes a core part of the ways in which social scientists conceive of progress. The discussion that follows takes into account varying notions of scientific progress as it seeks to clarify what security studies authors mean by "better theory" in their application of criteria that are intended to show that their own explanations are better than those of their rivals.[7]

Progress in Security Studies

Early in the twentieth century John Hobson (1926) lamented the lack of progress in the social sciences. This lack still seems largely true in security studies. When we try to explain why this has been the case, several possible answers come to mind. One is that progress is inherently impossible, either because the subject matter is amorphous, unlike the determinate objects that the natural sciences study, or because the character of scientific theorizing is such that alternative answers to questions are inherently incommensurable. A second is that progress is possible, but proper methods have not been devised or implemented on a wide enough scale. And a third is that progress is possible but inhibited by scholars who, without recognizing this fact, talk past one another because they are attempting to accomplish different aims. The focus of this book is on one of the ways this might happen, the role of common or divergent uses of criteria, as expressed in H_1 and H_2.

As just discussed, Kuhnians hold that researchers in different paradigms do not truly engage one another's ideas and theories because of incommensurability; this has been used to explain the lack of progress in the social sciences. There are flaws with this explanation, one of which is that there are cases of progress; but a more extensive discussion of this is beyond the scope of this book.[8] The focus of this book is on a different explanatory factor, criterial divergence, which is like the incommensurability explanation, in that there is better evidence for it and in that, unlike in the case of incommensurability, there is a straightforward remedy.

The aim of this book is to probe what might improve the acquisition of knowledge in security studies and IR. The goal is not to identify which is the best theoretical explanation of nuclear proliferation, alliance formation, or democratic peace. The goals of the book are, rather, to investigate H_1 by determining whether scholars' uses of divergent explanatory criteria inhibit approach-to-consensus progress and to investigate H_2 by determining whether cases of such progress might be facilitated by scholars in fact largely agreeing on the appropriate set of criteria.

Finally, it is important to point out that H_1 and H_2 are falsifiable claims. To take the example of democratic peace, discussed in Chapter 5, suppose (as we will see) that there is a general consensus on the dyadic hypothesis—that is, the idea that liberal democracies avoid war with one another because they are liberal democracies. Then suppose that authors who debate the dyadic hypothesis show a high degree of overlap in the sets of criteria that they use. Suppose further that the next four wars are between liberal democracies. We would probably conclude after those wars that the evidence falsifies the dyadic hypothesis. However, our H_1 and H_2 would not thereby be falsified. They would be falsified, however, if the consensus that emerged around the negation of the dyadic hypothesis occurred if the scholars who came to agree that it is false did so on the basis of very different criteria. If the new consensus on the falsity of the dyadic hypothesis arose with the authors basing their conclusions on similar criteria, then H_1 and H_2 would remain unfalsified.

2 EXPLANATION IN THE NATURAL AND SOCIAL SCIENCES

WHEN AUTHORS ARGUE that one explanation is better than others, they necessarily make use of a set of criteria for what makes one explanation better than others and, of course, some sort of notion of explanation. To understand what they may be getting at, given that authors usually omit any statements about why they regard one explanation as best, it is necessary to survey the range of concepts of explanation and criteria that are found in the philosophical literature. This chapter begins by looking at the most influential notion of explanation in the natural sciences, the covering law model, which has been exported to the social sciences by many scholars. The chapter then takes up some of the key problems relating to explanation, including its relationship to causal claims, the ontological status of the things related in an explanation, and the idea that any attempt to explain will move knowledge forward. The overall aim of this chapter is to produce a list of ways that explanation has been conceptualized and criteria that have been offered for explanatory success, so that we will have a framework for categorizing the concepts and criteria used by the authors studied in Chapters 3–5. Once the list is completed and the authors categorized, it will then be possible to determine whether divergences in criteria may be hampering explanatory progress, that is, to assess whether we should accept H_1 and/or H_2.

1. CONTENDING VIEWS OF SCIENTIFIC EXPLANATION

What is regarded as constituting a good explanation depends upon which of the competing accounts of explanation is accepted. And these notions vary widely, from logical to linguistic to epistemological to psychological to historical-descriptive views. That is, some philosophers of science hold that proper scientific explanations are purely formal arguments and that the key aspect is the relationship of premises to conclusion. Some philosophers hold the view that explanations perform a linguistic function, parallel to what speakers do then they warn an audience of impending danger. For other philosophers, explanations are probes into reality. Some regard explanations as rendering an unfamiliar event or process "familiar" or "intelligible," which produces a particular sort of change in people's psychological states. Some regard them as altering epistemological conditions by adding knowledge. And some regard them as providing historical antecedents that were significant in leading up to the event to be explained. The criteria for a well-formed explanation differ from one conception to another. What different political scientists think they are doing when they offer explanations depends on what sort of a thing they believe they are expected to produce.

Empiricism and Scientific Realism

Empiricist and positivist philosophies dominated discussions of science throughout the first half of the twentieth century, but they were challenged from the 1950s onward. This approach included the powerful schools of logical positivism and logical empiricism, which advanced the widely accepted deductive-nomological (D-N) model of scientific explanation. Like other doctrines that gained acceptance, empiricism in the early and mid-twentieth century was carefully scrutinized and subjected to an array of criticism, which focused notably on problems with the verification criterion of meaning (e.g., Hempel 1950), the stark observation-theory distinction (Putnam 1962; Maxwell 1962), and the analytic-synthetic distinction (Quine 1951, 1969).

In the 1950s and 1960s many philosophers came to view the problems with empiricism as damaging enough that a new doctrine of scientific realism began to gain adherents. Three major points that scientific realism addresses are how we can know, what science can tell us about the natural world, and what the aim of science is. Among the most influential recent scientific realists are Hilary Putnam (1982), Jerrett Leplin (1997), and Richard Boyd (1973). In the late 1970s empiricism made a comeback in the form of constructive empiricism, which came to hold a major position in the philosophy of science. Bas Van Fraassen (1980, 2002) has been the most influential empiricist in the past thirty years.

Empiricists and scientific realists differ on issues of truth, existence, reference, and belief. With respect to truth, scientific realists regard the best current scientific theories as true, or at least as approximately true; for empiricists, theories help scientists and others draw correct inferences about things we can observe, and they help people do things; empiricists do not agree that the theoretical claims of scientific theories are to be read literally and should be regarded as true or false. Empiricists point out that physics is taken as the most methodologically developed and epistemically credible science, and modern physicists accept both quantum theory and relativity theory, even though the two doctrines disagree on the fundamental point that all theories must be covariant. Both theories are fully accepted today. Empiricists argue that because the two are mutually exclusive—and thus it is impossible to maintain that both are fully and literally true—it follows that literal truth cannot be required of good explanatory theories. This would seem to be a problem for scientific realists' understanding of both truth and scientific theories, but it presents no problem for empiricists and, especially, instrumentalists. Scientific realists' view of truth leads them to accept both the fact that if a theory generates predictions, then it is true, and the fact that a scientific theory may be approximately true, even if some of its predictions turn out to be false. In contrast, for empiricists the core of good science is its ability to help draw successful (true) predictive inferences about the observable world.

With regard to existence and reference, scientific realists maintain that theories make genuine claims about real-world existence. According to their view, whenever a scientifically accepted theory invokes terms that appear to refer to things in the world, even if those things are only postulates of the theory, the scientific realist is committed to the claim that those things are real. Antirealist empiricists treat theoretical terms only "as if" they refer to things in the world, without accepting any ontological commitment.[1] As already noted, scientific realists believe that the best theories are true, whereas empiricists generally hold that good theories are used as if they were true, but they do not regard them as having the same status as sets of true statements about events or experiences that can be established or grounded in more secure epistemic forms. With regard to belief, the different views of reference have a connection to different views of what scientists should believe. Scientific realists regard belief as something that one has or does not have in a statement; by implication, one either believes or disbelieves a theory, since a theory comprises a set of statements. Scientific realists endorsed "abduction," a form of reasoning often referred to as "inference to the best explanation," which was articulated in the nineteenth century by Charles Sanders Peirce. According to this view, when a series of scientific explanations for a set of observations are compared, one of the competitors will emerge as the best. Scientists, then, are justified in inferring the truth of, and believing, the propositions that constitute that explanation. Empiricists, in contrast, generally hold that it is possible to have varying degrees of belief in scientific theories, depending on the strength of the scientific warrant for each one.

The History of Science as Philosophical Evidence

Scientific realists claim that the history of science supports their position; empiricists make precisely the same claim. Scientific realists argue that the history of the mature sciences shows progressive approximation to a true account of the physical world. In their view, the (approximate) truth of a scientific theory is the only possible explanation for the theory's predictive success over the long run. If we acknowledge that science progresses over the centuries, in that its predictions continually improve, then the theories must describe the real world, because if they did not, then the accuracy of their predictions could be accounted for only as a wild—indeed miraculous—coincidence. Thus, they argue, the history of science shows that scientific realism is correct.

Empiricists argue just the reverse, that the history of science shows the untenability of scientific realism. One way to see their claim is to note that scientific realists claim that science should accept as literally true the best theories; and given that, scientists should accept the existence of the entities postulated by the best theories. But the history of science is a series of theories that postulate various entities followed by new theories that often reject the earlier theory's entities. This would imply that the scientific realist view of science during earlier periods forces science to accept false claims about existence. And many widely and thoroughly accepted theories in the past have proved inferior to new theories. Thus, by inductive reasoning, it is highly likely that many or most current theories are false, at least when taken literally and in toto.

Empiricists argue that the scientific realist argument, based on history, commits a logical fallacy, that of affirming the consequent. They add that there is a second major logical mistake in arguing from history to scientific realism, namely, that the Duhem thesis, which if properly formulated is very difficult to deny, shows a severe flaw in scientific realism. One version of the thesis states that for any finite set of observations (the only sort of set that science ever achieves), there will always be many theories that are consistent with all observations.

Empiricists hold that the most important virtue a theory can have is to achieve ***empirical adequacy***, that is, to account for or remain consistent with all existing evidence. The propositions of the theory, together with conditions under which observations are made, must entail the existing set of observational statements. But this criterion cannot operate by itself; others are needed,[2] and in that role they emphasize ***explanatory unification*** and ***simplicity***.[3] Empiricists will claim that empirical adequacy is the most that science can ask of an explanatory theory, whereas others, especially scientific realists, will rank this highly but will accept trade-offs with other criteria. Empiricists also stress the importance of ***predictive accuracy***. For empiricists, an explanation's ability to satisfy these criteria renders it a better theory, but empiricists do not signify that the explanation is more likely to be "true" or to correspond to the real world. Rather, they have pragmatic virtues and render the theory preferable because the explanatory theory is more useful. They deal with the relations among the explanatory theory, reality, and the investigator or user of the theory.

Scientific realists regard the task of the natural sciences as discovering the true character of the physical and biological world around us. Social scientific realists have the same aim for the social sciences. One explanation will be better than its rivals because it does a better job of ***uncovering the true causes*** of the phenomena we observe, because it identifies causes that give us a view of the ***deeper causes*** that produce the phenomena by working from deeper levels of some sort, and because it ***identifies the causal mechanisms*** at work.

2. HEMPEL'S DEDUCTIVE AND INDUCTIVE MODELS OF EXPLANATION

The ancient Greeks differentiated between factual observations and explanations for those facts, including causal explanations. Aristotle held that good explanations consist of valid deductive arguments. He also believed that there are different meanings of the term *causation*. He distinguished four types of causation: formal, material, efficient, and final. He thus held that there were four corresponding sorts of explanation. In the history of modern philosophy, many important figures, particularly those in the British Isles, and later Kant, put a great deal of emphasis on developing a full account of explanation. In the middle of the twentieth century, as already noted, philosophers arrived at a near consensus on the deductive-nomological "covering law" model of explanation. Agreement among philosophers on such an important issue is rare.

After several decades, though, criticisms had amassed, many of which held that the covering law model did not do all that it was said to do.

The Deductive-Nomological Model

The original statement of the D-N model is found in Hempel and Paul Oppenheim's (1948) seminal paper, "The Logic of Scientific Explanation." Over the following decades, Hempel wrote extensively on the topic, rebutting objections and counterexamples to the original statement of the model and working on applications to the biological and social sciences.

The covering law account of explanation aims to illuminate individual events by showing that they fit into a larger pattern. When someone asks, "Why did x happen?" the answer, according to the covering law model of explanation, will have the following form: "Because there were conditions c, and it is a law of nature that under conditions c, things like x occur." Why did the pen fall from the table to the floor? Because under the conditions of Earth's gravitational field, objects that are not supported always fall until some obstruction stops them.

Hempel and Oppenheim's 1948 paper introducing the D-N model was one of the most influential publications in twentieth-century philosophy of science. According to their model, an explanation expresses a particular logical relationship between the elements of the explanation, which together form the *explanans*, and that which is explained, the *explanandum*. The explanandum might be a specific occurrence (the cracking of a car's radiator, to use Hempel's example) or a general statement (that water always flows downhill). According to the D-N model, a good explanation must be a deductively valid argument with premises that include both general laws and statements with empirical content, and furthermore, the premise statements of the argument must be true.[4] For a number of years after Hempel and Oppenheim published their paper, most philosophers, including prominent figures such as Ernest Nagel (1961), R. B. Braithwaite (1953), and Karl Popper (1959), regarded the nature of scientific explanation as having been definitively settled by Hempel and Oppenheim—perhaps pending some additional refinements.

In his early presentations of the D-N model, Hempel argued that the correct logical form required of an explanation was the same as the logical form required of a scientific prediction, a doctrine he called explanation-prediction symmetry.[5] The full explanation of an event involves (1) a statement of initial conditions, (2) a general statement that applies to those conditions, and (3) a deduction that makes use of the particular statement(s) in 1 and the general proposition in 2. An argument for a prediction has the same form. The difference between an explanation and a prediction is the temporal index, past versus future. But the logical forms of the two are identical.

The Inductive-Statistical Model

Hempel argued that his D-N account of explanation in the natural sciences does not directly apply to the social sciences. He proposed a variation on it, called the inductive-statistical (I-S) model, which adapts it to probabilistic rather than deterministic principles. On the I-S model of explanation, the explanans (i.e., the premise set) of the explanation is related to the explanandum (i.e., the conclusion) by means of a different inferential relationship, namely induction. For Hempel, the premises Pa_1, Pa_2, . . . Pa_n, Pb_1, Pb_2, . . . Pb_n, if true, show that the conclusion is probable. Hempel also identifies a third form of explanation, the deductive statistical (D-S) model, in which there are deductive arguments that hold between statistical laws; that is, some statistical laws logically entail other statistical laws (e.g., "most As are Bs" deductively implies that "most As are either Bs or Cs").[6]

All of these forms of explanations require the inclusion of laws. A law is a statement that both fits the definition of a "lawlike statement" and is true (Goodman 1947, 125). A lawlike statement must also be able to support counterfactual conditionals. That is, if the law of gravity is true, then, had MiaMaria dropped the pencil just now, it would have fallen to the ground. The latter counterfactual conditional statement is true because of the law of gravity.[7]

3. WHAT MAKES ONE EXPLANATION BEST?

As the various areas of security studies are surveyed here, we will ask what it is about each author's account that conveys understanding of the subject matter and how it does so better than rival accounts. Friedman (1974) points out that most of the philosophers who have developed precise accounts of explanation say little about scientific understanding (e.g., Hempel 1965; Nagel 1961), and most of those who have emphasized scientific understanding (e.g., Dray 1957; Scriven 1959; Toulmin 1963) are not very precise about what form an explanation should have.

Scriven (1959) sought to show that there are times when we "simply know" that we have an adequate explanation; in such cases, what is at issue is the search for real causes of the explanandum event. Scriven's argument, cogent as far as it goes, seems to fall short of showing that scientific explanation must seek causes. First, to illustrate he uses explanandum events from ordinary experience that provide ordinary explanations, like a person spilling ink from an ink bottle. But it is not obvious that what is required of a scientific explanation is precisely what is required of explanations of ordinary experience. Second, Scriven's argument shows only that sometimes (in situations of ordinary experience) a causal reply is adequate; it does not show that only the presentation of real causes is sufficient to constitute an adequate explanation.

As we have seen, Hempel and his many followers require that a good explanation be an example of the D-N, I-S, or D-S form. But does deductive or inductive character enable an explanation to explain? On the one hand, Hempel sometimes says that understanding and intelligibility are psychological concepts and belong to the psychology of science rather than the philosophy of science. A good explanation ***imparts understanding***. On the other hand, Hempel and other defenders of the D-N model have offered "expectation," ostensibly a psychological concept, as part of their account; the explanans gives rise to the expectation that the explanandum should occur. In any event, the deductive or inductive element does not qualify as "explaining" in the sense of imparting an understanding of why the explanandum event occurred. The (true) statement "Walruses have tusks or pigs cannot fly" entails (by the deductive rule of "addition") the statement "Pigs cannot fly." But the former does not in any sense explain why pigs cannot fly. So there is something else in the explanans that must do the explaining. Could it be the requirement that explanans lead to the expectation that the explanandum will occur? This is doubtful, since there are many things that we encounter that lead to expectations without explaining. Children in Scandinavia may have the expectation, upon seeing the trees shedding their foliage, that snow will fall within a few weeks, yet they may have this expectation without necessarily having any way of connecting the falling of the leaves to an explanation of the onset of the snow season.[8]

Bromberger (1966) developed a counterexample to the claim of the adequacy of the D-N model. First, people think of causation as asymmetric: if X explains Y in a particular instance, then Y cannot be properly be said to explain X. If the high measure of mean kinetic molecular energy in the room right now explains that Lydia feels warm, then Lydia's feeling warm cannot properly be said to explain the high measure of mean kinetic energy in the room right now. With that in mind, consider that a flagpole at the Hollywood Post Office has a height of X feet, so that at three o'clock in the afternoon on March 22 it casts a shadow of a particular length. The length of the shadow can be precisely calculated from the facts present and the knowledge that, over such distances, light travels in straight lines. According to Hempel's model, the height of the flagpole and the other facts explain the length of the shadow. This seems unproblematic. However, if we want to "explain" the height of the flagpole, according to Hempel's model we may equally do so by stating the length of the shadow and bringing into the "explanatory" argument the location of the flagpole and the time of day. Because this seems quite illegitimate, Bromberger (1966) regards it as a counterexample to the adequacy of the D-N model as an account of "explanation."

Van Fraassen, Pragmatics, and Constructive Empiricism

The constructive empiricism of Van Fraassen agrees with Hempel's logical empiricism in viewing the relationship between the explanans and the explanandum as a logical one. However, it is not the Hempelian relationship of premises to conclusion in a deductive syllogism; it is that of question to answer. For Van Fraassen, an explanation is acceptable because it provides an answer to a question about why a particular event, process, or so on, occurred rather than some alternative event occurring. Furthermore, an acceptable explanation is geared toward the specific question posed. If someone were to ask a question about why a traffic accident occurred, given the known level of competence or training of the driver, then an answer purely in terms of road conditions would not be adequate.

For Van Fraassen, science is not the practice of discovering eternal truths about an unobservable world of forces; rather, it is the creative practice of producing models. Van Fraassen emphasizes the epistemology of explanation, evidence updating, and the logic of why-questions. In this way Van Fraassen turns Bromberger's flagpole example on its head, so to speak. If we are asking the right sort of question, there is no problem that Hempel's D-N model allows the length of the shadow to explain the height of the flagpole. Consider a person whose spouse, a police officer, died heroically while defending the Hollywood Post Office, which is property of the US federal government, from a would-be attacker, and who now wishes to build a monument to the spouse. The surviving spouse wishes to erect a flagpole with height and location such that, at noon every year on the anniversary of the day of the attack, the shadow of the top of the flagpole will reach the spot where the officer died. If someone were then to ask the why-question about the height of the flagpole, the length of the shadow would indeed be a key explanatory factor. What appeared to be a counterexample under one why-question and context is not when considered in a different context. Clearly, context is critical.

Speech Acts

Some views of explanation build on J. L. Austin's (1962) account of language, one aspect of which was the distinction between ordinary description and "speech acts,"; the latter are utterances of sentences that "do things" that are much different from what utterances of declarative sentences do. The usual distinction between statements of fact and those of value was not exhaustive in Austin's view, because some utterances of some sentences constitute actions that go beyond merely the action of speaking. To say, "I promise I will repay the debt," is not merely to talk about the debt but to create an obligation. To say, "I now pronounce you husband and wife," in certain specific circumstances is not merely to describe what one is doing but to perform an action and to create a new state of affairs. Such statements are neither factual nor evaluative.

According to Austin, an utterance can have "locutionary force," which is its meaning and reference; it can have "perlocutionary force," which is the set of effects that it is intended to have on others; and it can have "illocutionary force," which is what one is doing with the specific utterance in a certain set of circumstances. Statements may not have all three sorts of force. When someone says, "The building is on fire," there is specific locutionary force relating to the building and its state of combustion. But it could be uttered with illocutionary force if it is intended to warn people in the building. In that case, it may have the perlocutionary force of inducing those people to flee. Austin (1962, 160–61) explicitly includes "explaining" along with "criticizing" on his list of illocutionary acts. So, according to this view, part of what qualifies a set of propositions as an explanation is the effect (illocutionary force) that the propositions have on the intended audience. Thus, the explanation comprises (a relationship between) a set of propositions and some aspect or state of the audience.

Achinstein on Explanations Having Causal Elements

Peter Achinstein is one of the most important philosophers to build an account of "scientific explanation" that draws on speech act theory. Achinstein finds persuasive Van Fraassen's argument that explanations are answers to why-questions only to the extent that the claim holds true for some but not all explanations. For Achinstein (1971, 1977), an explanation requires more than a logical relationship among the propositions, since some propositions must specifically be "content giving." An "explanation" includes the explainer's intention that the utterance make something understandable to the audience. The process of explaining is thus a speech act that involves a certain intention on the part of the explainer and is part of the explanation-product. Although Achinstein does not follow others in requiring that all explanations identify causal mechanisms, his descriptive account of what an explainer does includes a causal element. For Achinstein, rather than causation being a part of the notion of explanation, the explanation is part of a causal process according to which the utterance produces knowledge in the audience. The implications of the pragmatic and contextual accounts of "explanation" of Van Fraassen, Achinstein, and the application by Suganami, are revisited in Chapter 6.

Familiarity

Some scholars see explanations in a way different from that conceived by Hempel, Salmon (1971, 1984), and Van Fraassen (1980); specifically, they see them as serving an inherently psychological function. According to this view, the way an explanation explains (i.e., the way it renders the heretofore-mysterious explanandum less mysterious) is by connecting the operation of the explanandum event or process with something that one already understands.

An explanation must turn the unfamiliar into the familiar for the (social or natural) scientific community. One's ability to gain understanding is part and parcel of having one's curiosity assuaged; and while curiosity reduction is what accomplishes that goal, the goal itself is a change in the psychological state. The Nobel laureate P. W. Bridgman (1938, 37) said, "I believe that examination will show that the essence of explanation consists in reducing a situation to elements with which we are so familiar that we accept them as a matter of course, so our curiosity rests" (see also Dray 1957). In this case, what will count as a good explanation is again dependent upon the context of knowledge and the beliefs and assumptions held by the investigator or the audience. This is not the case for the standard D-N model. Still others, such as the early twentieth-century empiricists noted in Chapter 1, hold a more austere view of what actually constitutes the core content of scientific inquiry, or even of science properly conceived; for them, the function of "making the community more comfortable" is purely heuristic and not itself truly a part of science.

Intelligibility and Suganami's Account of the Causes of War

Suganami (1996) offers an analysis of causation that relies on a notion of explanation rather than on the more common view that causal analysis is one particular species of explanation. He argues that whether the focus is natural processes, events, or human behavior, a full causal explanation of the phenomenon involves determinative processes, conscious human actions, and chance occurrences. In his analysis of the causes of war, Suganami relies on the notion of rendering more intelligible as part of successful causal explanation. He sums up this element of the analysis by saying, "To explain the occurrence of an event is to render its occurrence more intelligible by solving specific puzzles we have about it" (Suganami 1996, 135). We might note here that Suganami's careful analysis of cause is aimed at the analysis of singular causal statements, in particular at statements about specific wars. The works surveyed in Chapters 3–5 seek explanations for all or many cases (of alliance formation, nuclear weapons decisions, and democratic behavior).

Coherence with Accepted Beliefs

J. J. C. Smart (1990) offers an account of the concept of explanation as it is used by scientists and historians and argues that, for both, coherence with accepted beliefs is a key concept. Smart focuses only on the "core" (as opposed to the "peripheral") uses of the term *explanation.* According to Smart, science seeks to explain events and laws, whereas history seeks to explain facts. Smart endorses a coherence account of knowledge but rejects coherence as the key to developing a sound theory of truth. In advocating a coherence theory of knowledge, he endorses the value of the web metaphor championed by Quine and Ullian (1978).

For Smart the notion of explanation in science and history is closely tied to that of fitting into accepted beliefs. Of course, if a fact or a law is to be explained, then it must fit into the existing body of accepted beliefs. If it does not fit in, then it is not an acceptable proposition and does not stand in need of explanation. But if it does need explanation, then, according to Smart, an explanation consists in showing how the explanandum fits in with the corpus.

Friedman and Kitcher on the Criterion of Explanatory Unification

Some authors argue that superior explanatory theories will succeed because of their ability to unify. Philip Kitcher (1981) and Michael Friedman (1974) both emphasize this aspect of superior science (see also Kinoshita 1990). The innovations of Newton and Darwin were widely accepted within the scientific disciplines of these men because their theories were so successful at unifying phenomena previously thought to be diverse (Friedman 1974, 13, 17; Kitcher 1981, 513–15). Friedman (1974, 14) draws this conclusion as a result of his effort to isolate "a property of the explanation-relation which is possessed by most of the clear, central cases of scientific explanation, which is common to the theories of scientists from various historical periods, and which has a demonstrable connection with understanding." There are several different ways in which explanatory unification may take place. We might learn that different arguments constitute good explanations because they all use the same pattern of argumentation or because they use the same types of premises (1974, 15). For Friedman, the number of independent phenomena is the key. After taking pains to define *independent phenomena* and defending it against various objections, he says, "A world with fewer independent phenomena is, other things equal, more comprehensible than one with many more" (1974, 15).

One consequence of the accounts emphasizing the concepts of comprehensibility, intelligibility, and familiarity is that what counts as an explanans is relative to time and place. And more seriously, any such "intellectual fashion" would remove what is often regarded as imbuing science with its special epistemic status, namely, that it is objective and rational (Friedman 1974, 13). The "familiarity" view could regard these as "prejudices" that would affect a scientist or a scientific community. Friedman says, "I cannot see any reason but prejudice for regarding some phenomena as somehow more natural, intelligible or self explanatory than others" (1974, 13). Because Friedman accepts that science is generally regarded as objective and rational, he holds that the rules that guide good science should, if at all possible, be objective and rational.

For Friedman it is the global rather than the local nature of scientific explanation that allows for a rational and objective account of explanation: "our over-all understanding of the world is increased; our total picture of the world is simplified via a reduction in the number of independent phenomena that we have to accept as ultimate" (1974, 18). He concludes, "We thus genuinely increase our understanding of the world" (1974, 19). Friedman invokes the development of the Newtonian program and the advent of Darwinian theory to support his claim. What made both of those things work for as long as they were regarded as "working" was their ability to unify knowledge. One of the impressive aspects of Friedman's analysis is that the analysis itself functions to unify. It brings together what philosophers and others have found appealing about various different attempts to explain scientific explanation. Furthermore, Friedman lists some of the widely discussed counterexamples to the covering law model of scientific explanation and shows that the reasons we regard them as counterexamples—that is, what it is about the examples that impels us to treat them as nonexplanatory—is that they fail to perform a unifying function.

Kitcher (1981) expands on the unification approach. Referring back to the debate about the nature of light, he says, "Dynamic corpuscularianism remained popular so long as there was promise of significant unification" (1981, 513). And with regard to evolution, Kitcher quotes Darwin, too, as saying that his theory will succeed or fail only insofar as it groups and explains diverse phenomena (1981, 514). Darwin claimed that "the eventual unification would consist in derivations of descriptions of these phenomena which would instantiate a common pattern" (1981, 514–15).

Toulmin and Hanson on Predictive Powers and the "Natural Order"

Toulmin (1963, 45) argues that the ability of the explanans to explain or impart understanding to the scientific community is a result of its representing what the scientist accepts as "the regular order of Nature." The scientist regards such processes as "unmysterious," and scientists are thus, in a sense, primitives in the process of understanding. When processes that do not conform to this "regular" pattern are encountered, the ideas of the regular order must be extended or modified so as to encompass the explanandum. Again, for a "natural order" account, what counts as a good explanation is relative to the time and place in which it is proffered.

N. R. Hanson (1961) focuses on the importance of predictive power. He argues that theories gain scientific legitimacy through stages. A theory begins as a set of formulae stating relationships among the elements in its domain and that stands in need of testing; however, the internal workings are essentially opaque. As the predictions of the theory are increasingly corroborated though experiment, the theory comes to be more fully accepted. The theory gains further acceptance as it goes beyond an accuracy-of-prediction stage by connecting phenomena that had not previously been considered connected. This is a form of explanatory unification. At this point, scientists come to regard the theory as exhibiting the natural order and as qualified for use in an explanans to explain new mysteries.

Explanatory Ontological Commitments

Hempel's D-N model requires that the premises of the syllogism must be true, as noted earlier. For Hempel, the premises and conclusion of the D-N explanation are propositions. For the many scientific realists who accepted the D-N model during its period of dominance, the propositions of that (or any) sort of explanation must be true. For these philosophers, this also means that reference to any putative entities entails the existence of those entities. Thus, in the context of metaphysics and the philosophy of science, scientific realists require that the things referred to in explanations exist.

Empiricists and other nonrealists are able to avoid these ontological commitments, as Salmon showed in his 1971 book *Statistical Explanation and Statistical Relevance.* In that work, Salmon treats explanations as consisting of sets of sentences that contain probability laws, which can be reformulated so as to avoid ontological commitments. In an important paper, Achinstein (1977) showed that both the D-N and the I-S models can be interpreted in such a way as to limit these ontological commitments. Achinstein (1977, 14) concludes, "Thus the D-N theory, which as ordinarily expressed does have ontological commitments, can be reformulated so as to be neutral between product and no-product views."

One criterion that authors invoke is explanatory depth. This leads one to ask what exactly qualifies one explanation as deeper than another. Presumably, if "depth" is a desideratum, then one explanation is better than another because, among other things, it draws upon deeper aspects of reality (see Strevens 2009). This, of course, relies on an ontology according to which various aspects of the real world have different levels of depth. One answer to what makes one explanation deeper than another is that the former refers to things that explain the latter. On a causal view, this could mean that the former gets at the component parts of things referred to in the later explanation. Or it could mean that the deeper explanation goes back earlier in time (since earlier events may explain later ones). We should also add that some authors believe that the best theory will be demonstrable over and against its rivals and thus its acceptances will entail elimination of alternative theories. This is argued on the grounds that the evidence leading to the acceptance of the superior theory should be consistent with the new theory and should be complete enough to show that all existing rival theories are incorrect.[9]

To summarize, those who support scientific realism on ontological questions have generally held that real causal mechanisms must be found if an explanation is to succeed. Any entities the explanation makes use of must be real. The earlier and more extreme empiricists held that explanation is simply not a part of good scientific practice; Duhem (1954, originally published 1904–1905) rejected the need for explanation, and a decade or so later, Russell (1918) rejected the need for the concept of causality. Some of the ontological concerns bear directly on the debates over methodological individualism described in this chapter. The most thoroughgoing empiricists eschewed unobservable entities, instead adhering closely to terms that refer only to real, observable things. However, as noted already, because advances in the predictive and unifying power of modern science often arise from theories that postulate unobservable entities, empiricists have come to acknowledge a role for unobservables.

One of Hempel's contemporaries among empiricist philosophers of science in Berlin was Hans Reichenbach, who was mentioned earlier in connection with Salmon. Reichenbach (1971) emphasizes the importance of the robustness of an explanation. Robustness may be viewed as a criterion of a good explanation or as a criterion of an argument for a good explanation. The basic idea is that the explanans should draw on evidence in such a way that it is not dependent on the particularities of the underlying assumptions or narrowly specified rules for coding the cases. For example, we will see that different political theorists have varying definitions of what makes a state a democracy. Some of the definitions are quite similar to one another. Suppose that an author explains the enduring peace between two states by invoking the "joint democracy" factor. However, if the author were to have adopted one of the similar alternative definitions and the result were a dramatic decrease in the ability of the explanans to explain, then the explanation would not be robust. Philosophers of science who emphasize the importance of robust explanations do not necessarily claim that robustness guarantees the adequacy of an explanation. First, it is possible that two competing explanations are robust. Second, Simpson's (1961) paradox shows that robust associations may not be able to support a causal claim. Reichenbach argues that a good causal explanation must be robust, but he also notes that there are robust statistical associations that cannot support any causal or other explanation. The oft-used example of the reading of a barometer is useful here. The falling of the indicator on a barometer and the occurrence of rain may be connected by robust statistical association, and thus a robust explanation may be offered for either on the basis of the other.[10]

Other Criteria of Explanatory Superiority

Empiricists and scientific realists agree that, other things being equal, if two sets of propositions explain phenomena equally well, but one can extend the explanatory schema to a ***greater domain of cases***, then most people would regard it as superior. Some would especially note whether the cases were previously viewed as cases of different types. Pragmatists and others argue that a good scientific theory is able to aid people in doing new things that they wish to do. Hence, some have held that ***the ability to control the environment*** is the principal advantage that science confers on human society.[11] For these thinkers, the ability of a field of science or a theory to aid people in doing things is central. Hempel (1965, 333), too, connects the human desire to control the world with the scientifically enabled ability to predict.[12] Finally, we should add that most naturalists will endorse the goal of ***value neutrality***, whereas interpretivists, especially followers of the Frankfurt School, will deny that any human activity can be value neutral and will instead acknowledge the superiority of explanations that self-consciously promote certain goals, especially human emancipation and the expansion of the freedom of individuals.

To finish the listing of criteria of explanatory superiority, recall from Chapter 1 that Popper emphasized the importance of falsifiability, and the account of the growth of knowledge developed by Lakatos emphasized the importance of a progressive research program's ability to explain by generating ***novel facts***. The Lakatosian approach has support from many of the major figures in international relations (IR) and the study of war. Vasquez (1998, 28), for example, endorses the Lakatosian view, according to which the superior theory (1) has excess empirical content (i.e., can predict novel facts); (2) explains unrefuted content of the older theory; and (3) includes excess content, some of which is corroborated.[13] Some philosophers of science (e.g., Resnik 1994) add the criterion of methodological conservatism, according to which a theory is to be preferred over rival theories if, other things being equal, it shares the most content with the previously accepted theory that the various rivals are all proposed to supplant. This is related to coherence with background knowledge as a criterion of acceptance and to consistency with knowledge in other fields, noted by Vasquez (1998).

4. EXPLANATION AND CAUSATION

The search for a way to conceptualize the notion of explanation has long been connected to the notion of causation. For Aristotle, knowledge requires explanation, and explanation, in turn, requires a search for causes. We believe ourselves to have knowledge of a thing when we grasp its causes (*Posterior Analytics* 71b). The knowledge of a thing is the explanation of that thing. Aristotle distinguishes the four senses of "cause" identifiable in Greek usages: material, efficient, formal, and final. Aristotle made the case for the unique significance of final causes, since such causes have explanatory priority over efficient causes (see Aristotle, *Parts of Animals*, bk. 1, 639b). Many modern authors, including Hempel, agree with Aristotle that the search for causes is the core of knowledge, especially scientific knowledge.[14]

Causation was traditionally viewed as relating one event to another event; the cause event brings about the effect event. The event of the moving cue ball colliding with the stationary eight ball causes the event of the eight ball moving. Today it is more common to think of classes of events or types of events as standing in causal relationships to one another; the class of events "moving cue balls colliding," under specifiable conditions, causes the category of events "stationary eight balls move."

One of the difficult aspects of naturalism is that generalizations are typically probabilistic, whereas explanations, in the natural science model, need to be deterministically causal. Can statistical phenomena be causal? This depends in part on what a statistical causal claim, or any statistical claim, is held to convey. There are several ways authors have handled this. For Von Mises (1964), the key to understanding statistical claims is "relative frequency." According to this view, the statement "E is 80 percent likely, given C," means that if an unlimited set of Cs was examined, the frequency with which we would find E would approach eight out of ten as a limit (see also Keynes 1929). This solves many well-known problems but is not ultimately satisfactory for philosophers and scientists, who want to know what it means to say something about *individual* probabilities—perhaps about events that could never be conceived of as having an unlimited number of instances, such as, "There is a 50-50 chance of all-out nuclear war between India and Pakistan." There simply is no long-run frequency of nuclear war between India and Pakistan.

Kyburg (1990, chap. 12) argues that statistical causality is, at bottom, the same sort of thing as deterministic causality. The difference is that, in the statistical case, the causal force is less pronounced and amounts to a tendency rather than a guarantee. This account contrasts with those that invoke deterministic causality (e.g., E occurs whenever C occurs). According to this view, the statistical relationship between events C and E is one in which when C occurs, E will occur with frequency p (where $0 < p < 1$). This view states that the relationship is interpreted as meaning that circumstances C exhibit a causal tendency of degree p to produce E.

Rudolf Carnap (1950) developed a logical-linguistic interpretation according to which the relationship between two events is one of "partial entailment" of the propositions expressing their occurrence. In the familiar standard case, the statement "All men are mortal and Socrates is a man" entails the statement "Socrates is mortal." In contrast, assume it is true that there is a 90 percent chance that China will defeat Vietnam if the two were to go to war today. For Carnap, the statement "China and Vietnam commence war today" does not entail "China will win." Rather, the former partially entails the latter. Ronald Giere (1979, 180) explicates statistical causality as a sort of casual force that is such that, when C is present in all of the cases in one class and in no cases in the other class, then E will occur p of the time in the former and not at all in the latter. Finally, there is the subjective or Bayesian understanding of probability statements, according to which the probability of an event E, given the evidence set, is the degree to which those who have that evidence believe that the event E will occur (Bayes 1764). The exact degree can be shown by the individuals' behavior, in particular by what sorts of odds they would be willing to give in a bet on the occurrence of the event (see also Ramsey 1990; DiFinetti 1972).

To sum up, how one understands the meaning of statistical statements will affect the plausibility of different accounts of statistical causality. Some of the more intuitively appealing accounts of statistical statements, like the frequency theory, do not engender metaphysical difficulties but do not allow us to make sense of unique events. Anthropology, among the social sciences, would seem to have the most severe problem with this interpretation because, more so than other disciplines, it seeks to explain unique and individual cases. But security studies also has significant cases, like systemwide war or nuclear war, where invoking long-run frequencies to interpret statements about probabilities creates more problems than it solves. It is best to seek a balance between the philosophical merits of the account of such statements and the uses to which they may be put. One interpretation should be stressed over others only to the degree that it is necessary to solve a problem in that explanatory situation.

5. INDIVIDUALISM, ONTOLOGY, AND EXPLANATION

Because social behavior consists of actions by individuals and groups of individuals, some argue that explanations must appropriately focus on individuals. Thus, a key explanatory question is whether legitimate explanations must somehow boil down to statements about individuals or whether something larger or collective can be the focus of social science explanations. Several different claims have been made about individualism. The one most directly relevant for present purposes is that all individual and general social science statements must be formulable in terms of individual human beings and their properties, concepts, ideas, and behaviors. According to this view, any defensible social science claim about collectives or societies must be able to be restated in terms of individuals.

Individualism is seen as one answer to the traditional "levels-of-analysis" problem, well known to students of IR. In *Man, the State and War*, Waltz (1959) identifies the individual, the state, and the system of states as three possible levels of analytical focus. Hollis and Smith (1991, 9) distinguish four levels, including bureaucracy along with Waltz's three. Rosenau (1980) identifies six levels. All these typologies include the "individual level," which is the key level for methodological individualist accounts of social action. That is, the most important explanatory factors are traits, properties, or dispositions of individual human beings. We will see that this is important in the literature for the debate over the causes of proliferation.

Forms of Methodological Individualism

There are logically distinct forms of methodological individualism that involve some form of reductionism (from wholes to individuals). One principle is ontological, which states that all social entities ultimately are constituted of individual human beings and their dispositions and traits. According to this principle, no social entities are truly independent of individual humans. A second principle is conceptual, which states that the meaning of any social concept or term must be definable in terms of concepts that refer only to individuals and their properties. And a third principle—perhaps the most relevant for the chapters to follow—is explanatory, which states that any explanation of social entities must be formulated, or be able to be formulated, in terms of individuals and their properties.

There are several ways to formulate the microfoundations requirement, each with a different degree of strength. A strong view of methodological individualism states that any satisfactory explanation of macro-level phenomena must involve and focus on specific microprocesses (Watkins 1973). A slightly weaker form states that "we must have at least an approximate idea of the underlying mechanisms at the individual level if we are to have a credible hypothesis about explanatory social regularities at all" (Little 1991, 196). A still weaker version states that any explanation offered must be compatible with one or more possible (or plausible) micro-level processes; but no more is required, since it is difficult to be certain of the actual process involved (Chernoff 2005, 108–13). There are other views along the spectrum that rely even less on individualism, the extreme version of which states that microfoundations are in no way needed to explain higher-level phenomena.

With respect to the first principle, some philosophers of social science believe that if B is composed of As, then B may have properties of its own that none of the A constituents possesses. These properties are called emergent properties. Others have rejected this view. While Little (1991) accepts the ontological principle, he holds that it is rather trivial, in that truth does not tell us much about the status of the other two principles (see Kim 1993, 1999; for recent IR applications, see Leon 2010).

The conceptual thesis of methodological individualism states that social concepts have meanings that are reducible to concepts that refer only to individuals; the state, society, war, international law—these are social concepts that, according to the individualist conceptual-meaning principle, can be reduced to concepts about individuals. President Obama holds a pen, moves his hand, and produces marks on paper. This is the action of signing a treaty. Authors in the field of action theory, or the philosophy of action, have developed the notion of the basic action (Davidson 1980). Accordingly, the action of President Obama signing a treaty may appear to refer only to the action of that individual. However, treaties cannot be reduced to individuals and their properties, since they involve rules and institutions that arise only from the relationships and shared norms of individuals. The shared norms are not properties of any set of individuals or any particular individuals; rather, they are properties of the interactions among the individuals above and beyond the set of individuals and their properties.

The concepts used to describe observable behavior would have to refer only to individuals and their traits, beliefs, propensities, and the like. For any but the most trivial form of the concept-meaning principle of methodological individualism, some of the beliefs the individuals hold, especially beliefs about facts, would be out of bounds for concept reduction. If President Obama believes that the international system is increasingly governed by moral and legal norms, then on this account, we must recognize that his belief makes essential reference to things other than individuals and their properties. And his belief that the treaty on the table in front of him has popular support in the United States requires reference to the concept of the treaty, which cannot be defined or analyzed except by reference to social facts. For these reasons, many philosophers conclude that it is impossible to carry out meaning reduction, and thus that the concept-meaning principle of methodological individualism is false (see Little 1991). It seems clear, at the very least, that the ontological principle of individualism does not entail the concept-meaning principle, since the former may be true and the latter false.

Those who acknowledge that the ontological principle of methodological individualism does not entail the concept-meaning principle may still hold that the latter reduction is possible. Skeptics of the meaning principle may reply that, even if the reduction could be carried out, there would be no scientific necessity to do so, which undercuts the methodological individualist claim that all such meaning reductions are necessary. Whether or not the reduction can be carried out, good scientific theories do not always do so. Consider the well-corroborated and scientifically respectable theory of Newtonian mechanics, which can be applied to the behavior of ordinary (medium-size) objects. To refer back to an earlier example, together the scientific calculations, precise formulae of mechanics, and knowledge of the various forces provide adequate grounds to predict the trajectory of a medium-size object, like a baseball, as a given force is applied to it. There is no scientific requirement to define explanandum terms like "baseball" in terms of smaller objects or constituent molecules, even if we know the explanandum has such constituent parts.

A third version of methodological individualism is the explanatory principle, which states that explanations must make reference only to individuals and their properties, beliefs, dispositions, and so on. Supporters of methodological individualism regard an individual-level explanation as superior to those that focus on other sorts of entities and thus proceed at other levels of analysis.

Watkins on Methodological Individualism

One of the best-known defenses of methodological individualism is that offered by J. W. N. Watkins, who maintains that "social processes should be explained by being deduced from (a) principles governing the behaviour of participating individuals and (b) descriptions of their situations" (1973, 88). Watkins says that methodological individualism is supported by two principal claims. One is that social objects, unlike natural objects, are unobservable. Social objects, like treaties or legal systems, are created out of the beliefs or attitudes of individual humans. How they are formed must be derived from our knowledge of individuals. The social scientist cannot find out anything about social systems without knowledge of the behavior of the individuals. We may talk about the popularity of Queen Silvia of Sweden or the marriage rate in Peru, but knowledge of these subjects comes only from knowing at least something about the actions of individuals (e.g., what individual Swedish citizens say when asked about the queen, or what Peruvian couples choose to do to formalize their relationships). Watkins's second chief claim in support of methodological individualism is that social scientists do not have direct access to social structures, that is, to the interactions of individuals in the society. They know about them only from studying the individuals themselves. Watkins contrasts the natural and social sciences by noting that a chemist can derive knowledge of a system (the pressure of a gas in a container) without looking at the individuals (separate molecules) that interact to constitute the system, whereas a social scientist must look at individuals' thoughts and actions.

Individualism and Ideal Types

The various forms of methodological individualism have appeal, especially to those who accept the principle of reductionism, according to which inquiry gets to a deeper level of reality or truth when analysis is based on smaller and smaller units or subunits. This last claim needs a supporting argument. For example, methodological individualism draws on the idea that natural scientists often seek to explain the behavior of observable entities by reference to other entities that may be more fundamental, smaller, and/or unobservable. In such cases, scientific inquiry shifts to the study of the dispositions and properties of those more fundamental objects. In the social sciences many theorists turn to the behavior of individual humans to explain the behavior of bureaucracies, societies, and international systems. When the individual is the more fundamental entity, social scientists often follow Weber in making use of the ideal of "rationality." In general, individual ideals can be formulated on the basis of an ideal drawn empirically (1) from the way people ordinarily behave, (2) from the dispositions of specific individuals, or (3) from the ideally rational individual. On one interpretation of Weber, the ideal of rational behavior is used to identify those actions that deviate from the perfectly rational (Weber 1947, 110–11).

Social scientists are rarely satisfied merely to note that a particular behavior deviates from the ideally rational action. When these deviations occur, social scientists want to know why the actor behaved in a less-than-rational way. The political scientist or historian may seek more information about a particular leader to shed light on a specific action, for example, why a leader would continue to prosecute a stalemated war when a negotiated settlement would better serve the interests of the state. Given the information that the leader had at the time and knowledge of his or her objectives, the leader acted irrationally. The social scientist assumes that there is a reason for this departure from the rational course, and there are many conceivable reasons an observer might propose to explain it. Among the reasons cited for a political leader's deviation from the rational course, one might find claims like the leader's excessive focus on short-term consequences at the expense of the long-term consequences, or the leader's obsession to achieve some goal that eluded a specific predecessor in office. If the costs of prosecuting the war are hypothesized to outweigh the benefits of negotiation, then the social scientist looks for patterns in other decisions the leader has made and other experiences that could account for the deviation from ideally rational behavior.[15]

In summary, we observe that for most methodological individualists, any genuine explanation of social phenomena in IR must have microfoundations; they do not think it justifiable to end the inquiry at the structural level. In their view, as Little (1991, 196) puts it, "a putative explanation couched in terms of high level social factors whose underlying individual-level mechanisms are entirely unknown is *no explanation at all*" (emphasis added).[16]

6. FUNCTIONAL AND STRUCTURAL EXPLANATIONS

Those who reject the need to explain social phenomena by reducing them to individuals and their properties generally seek structural and functional explanations, which draw on an irreducible notion of system. Explanations of this sort make use of individual agents but cannot explain in terms of individuals alone. For example, some institutions and practices are said to exist because of the roles they play or the functions they fulfill in the larger society or system. Functional explanations assert that a social practice or institution has certain persistent effects and that the institution exists to promote those effects (Kincaid 1996, 105). In what is called purposive action theory, social scientists offer explanations that make use of beliefs, desires, and goals, and they do so without seeking to invoke certain other group-level entities, such as "group minds" or "group desires." Functional explanation is one of the most extensively utilized modes of social analysis. It is found in many social science disciplines, and it has been perhaps the dominant form of explanation in sociology and anthropology.[17]

There are various ways of locating what it means to say that an entity or trait serves a function in a system. One way of conceiving this is to regard the statement "X serves a function within system Y" as drawing on the idea of a homeostatic or cybernetic mechanism within system Y. On this relatively straightforward, causal conception, a thermostat serves the function of regulating a room's temperature by sensing when the thermometer drops below a certain point, at which time the thermostat switches on the heating mechanism; similarly, by sensing when the temperature exceeds a specified higher point, the thermostat shuts off the mechanism. This analogy serves as a simple causal explication and does not involve "reverse causation" or other philosophical problems sometimes alleged of functional explanations. Another way of understanding the explanation requires identifying systematic effects in an interconnected system, and perhaps claiming that the explanation of them has certain persistent capacities within the system. Another approach involves the use of so-called consequence laws. According to this view, the functional explanation proceeds by claiming that (1) A causes B, (2) that A persists because it causes B, and (3) that A is causally prior to B (see Wright 1973; Kincaid 1996). All three conditions invoke the notion of cause. We note that points 1 and 2 are straightforward causal claims and 3 refers to priority in causal relations; as such, 3 provides assurance that the analysis does not encounter problems of reverse causality.

Many authors argue that functional explanation is a form of causal explanation. Elster (1983) says that functional explanation is causal explanation with a feedback loop. Functional explanations provide an understanding of a social event, process, or institution by reference to the purpose the process serves in a domestic or international social system; a successful functional explanation will typically identify a feedback loop based on a selection mechanism, such as survival (Elster 1979, 28–35, 88–103). For example, the United States generally supports free trade because the United States is technologically advanced and industrially efficient, and because free trade confers more power and wealth on states with precisely those advantages.

Kincaid (1996, 114) agrees that all functional explanations are special cases of causal explanation. He argues that functional explanations can be evaluated empirically, much like other causal explanations, by utilizing both direct and indirect evidence. Direct evidence shows that each condition for the functional explanation obtains; and indirect evidence shows that functional explanations cohere with the corpus of one's accepted beliefs (Kincaid 1996, 115–16; see also Section 3). This is exemplified by biologists' support for functional analyses: many biologists accept design arguments that describe the sort of design that would best suit a certain system's purpose and then show that the explanandum under discussion matches the design specifications. A slightly weaker form of evidence appears in the form of stability arguments, which show certain traits that cannot be dislodged by new developments in the system once they have arisen.

Cummins (1975) draws on Braithwaite (1953), Hempel (1965), Nagel (1961), and others, to argue that functional explanations almost always proceed on the basis of two assumptions: that the goal of the functional explanation is to explain the presence of something (e.g., an organ, a process), and that performing its function consists of having certain effects on a larger system, where the effects contribute to the performance or maintenance of the system. Cummins, however, says that this limitation stems from philosophers' desire to emphasize the similarities between functional analysis and other, less controversial forms of scientific explanation. As a result, philosophers have both failed to offer rigorous defenses of the assumptions and have overlooked the truly distinctive nature of functional analysis of the natural sciences. Cummins argues that functionalists' universal acceptance of the two assumptions has stifled any critical examination of those assumptions; moreover, they would not survive scrutiny. Rejection of the assumptions makes it possible to develop a version of functionalism that circumvents the defects of the Hempelian version. Functional explanations ascribe a capacity to something, and that capacity is specified by the role the thing plays in a "containing system." Cummins (1975, 765) says, "When a capacity of a containing system is appropriately explained by analyzing it into a number of other capacities whose programmed exercise yields a manifestation of the analyzed capacity, the analyzing capacities emerge as function." He adds that this sort of explanation admits of degrees, so how appropriate the functional explanation will be is also a matter of degree.

In the physical sciences functional explanations have been abandoned. In the biological sciences there is still some appeal for explanations of this sort. Chameleons have the property of being able to change their color to match the environment, because the property of changing color to match the environment serves a beneficial (survival) function for chameleons. These explanations are acceptable in biology in part because they are proffered with a background theory of natural selection in the context of which there are abbreviated ways of explaining in terms of random mutations and survival. To draw upon the authority of the natural sciences, some social scientists make explicit use of the biological model and biological theorizing. Some political scientists such as Thayer (2000, 2004) have sought to draw upon the authority of natural science by arguing that the biological theory of natural selection supports political realist theories in IR.

Structural factors are often presented as explanatory by invoking the notion of permissive or passive causes. The description of the structure includes certain features that, under the circumstances of the event or class of events under discussion, lack any mechanism to prevent the explanandum event. The most familiar example in IR is war; the system of anarchy and self-help—such as described by Waltz (1979) and Mearsheimer (2001)—contains no mechanism to prevent naturally competitive states from going to war when competition is intense and the stakes of winning become sufficiently great.

7. CRITERIA USED IN THIS STUDY

This chapter has outlined forms of explanation and criteria that have been advanced to signify explanatory superiority. The latter include simplicity, empirical adequacy, uncovering true causes, finding deeper causes, identifying causal mechanisms, displaying greater range of explanatory domain, falsifiability, explanatory unification, imparting understanding, conferring predictive accuracy, providing new facts, value neutrality, and the ability to control the environment. Some of these will be hard to detect in any of the studies surveyed in the following three chapters, and others will show up in some of the debates and not others.

This study itself provides an explanation for explanatory stalemate and progress (namely H_1, that stalemate is worsened by divergence of criterial use, and H_2, that progress is aided by criterial overlap) that draws on the divergence and overlap of criteria. Thus, the explanation of this study itself relies on a set of criteria, which should be made explicit. The foremost criterion on which H_1 and H_2 will be evaluated is empirical fit. The argument also relies on true causes and mechanisms for the lack of progress, explanatory unification, falsifiability, and predictive accuracy. Precision and the elimination of alternatives are important but have lower priority-rankings when trade-offs with the five criteria just noted are at issue. And while simplicity is related to unification and is important, other things being equal, this study places a lower priority on it than on some other criteria, as it assumes that social phenomena are multifaceted and that it is reasonable to expect to find multiple explanatory factors, though not always having equal force. It is beyond the scope of this study to defend the causal-conventionalist metatheory that leads to an emphasis on these conclusions. They are defended elsewhere (Chernoff 2005; see also Chernoff 2002, 2007b, 2009, 2013).

This chapter has laid out the range of ways to understand *explanation* that security studies scholars have available to them. It is now possible both to examine security studies debates and to identify the ways particular authors interpret the notion of explanation, whether they invoke criteria explicitly or, more typically, implicitly. Because the thirty-three works considered in the following three chapters all made use of some form of naturalist explanation much more than interpretivist, this chapter has focused primarily on naturalist criteria of explanatory superiority—though there is a certain degree of overlap between the two. We thus will be able to see the (often unstated) criteria on which each author's arguments rest.

3 THE NUCLEAR PROLIFERATION DEBATE

Why Do States Build Nuclear Weapons?

IN THE FIELD of proliferation studies, two questions have dominated the debate: Why do states build nuclear weapons? What effects result from additional states acquiring nuclear weapons? Bernard Brodie answered the first question in the 1940s by arguing that nuclear weapons had only one purpose—to deter an attack on their possessor by any other state that acquires them. According to Brodie (1946), there is no need to match an adversary's nuclear arsenal in terms of number of weapons or specifications. Rather, it is important only to have enough weapons to do "unacceptable damage" to the adversary, and to have the weapons based in a way that they cannot be destroyed in a nuclear (or any other) strike that the adversary may be able to launch. Herman Kahn and others disagreed vigorously, contending that the sorts of weapons and the size of arsenals do matter. Kahn (1962) maintained that a nuclear war might well occur, and if it did, there would be a meaningful difference in the conditions of the "winners" and the "losers." Moreover, even if war does not occur, the size and quality of a state's arsenal can also increase the effectiveness of deterrence itself.

For forty years (from 1949 to 1989) both the United States and the Soviet Union possessed nuclear weapons. The two sides had conflicting interests, and they actively competed, as evidenced by their involvement in many "proxy wars" during the period. Nevertheless, in historical perspective, forty years is a long time for great powers to coexist without war. The historian John Lewis Gaddis (1987) attributes "the long peace" of the Cold War to the fact that both sides possessed nuclear weapons. Gaddis and others regard this as the classic example of the deterrent benefits of nuclear armed rivals, and they argue that it is unreasonable to ignore nuclear weapons as an explanatory factor for the long peace.

Some have used the Cold War superpower relations to argue optimistically that the possession of nuclear weapons by any pair of adversaries would deter both parties from initiating war. Supporters of this position maintain that as more states build nuclear weapons, peace will come to dominate previously violent regional rivalries. Waltz (1981), Bueno de Mesquita and Riker (1982), Brito and Intriligator (1996), and other scholars concurred that additional nuclear weapons states will behave as responsibly as the United States and Soviet Union did with respect to nuclear use. Most scholars, for a variety of reasons, disagree with this proliferation optimism. Payne (1997) and Hanson (2002) argue that nuclear weapons did not have a major effect on peace between the superpowers during the Cold War. And some have gone further, like Geller (1990) and MccGwire (1994), arguing that nuclear weapons not only fail to prevent war but also even lead to crisis escalation. Others have argued that the stability of the US-Soviet relation is not matched by other pairs of rival states that might acquire nuclear weapons.

Nuclear Proliferation and Nonstate Actors

While the causes and effects of horizontal proliferation—that is, more states acquiring nuclear weapons—have been at the center of proliferation studies, attention has also recently been trained on the danger of nonstate actors gaining access to nuclear weapons. Armitage and Nye (2004, 11) call the acquisition of nuclear weapons by nonstate terrorist actors "the nightmare scenario," and this has been widely discussed in the press and in academia. In terms of weapons acquisition, some people are concerned about a state transferring deployable nuclear weapons to terrorist groups. This prospect was one of the reasons the Bush administration offered for its 2003 invasion of Iraq. Other people are concerned that a terrorist group could acquire the components to build a nuclear weapon without a state transferring a completed weapon. Another danger is that a state might offer limited assistance to a nonstate actor in the form of financial or technical aid, or by transferring key weapons components.

There are many steps to building a nuclear weapon, and even some states with substantial resources have encountered major difficulties in bringing to fruition their nuclear weapons programs. Iraq and Libya are both oil-producing states with considerable financial resources and long-standing interest in developing nuclear weapons, yet neither was ever able to develop a nuclear weapon. Both had external setbacks. Iraq began each of the past three decades with damaging military clashes; it was bombed by Israel in 1981; it lost a war in Kuwait to a coalition under the auspices of the United Nations in 1991, which led to sanctions and intrusive inspections; and then it was invaded by the United States and its allies in 2003. Libya, like Iraq, was a client of the Pakistani metallurgist and nuclear arms merchant A. Q. Khan. Even more than Iraq, Libya experienced persistent problems with various aspects of its nuclear weapons program. Because of Libya's inability to make progress with its weapons program, and because it was caught in flagrante delicto importing illegal nuclear materials when the ship *BBC China* was interdicted in late 2003, Libya decided to terminate its nuclear weapons program in exchange for concessions it had long sought, including the easing of Western economic sanctions (Goldschmidt 2004).

The West has been worried about the possibility that Soviet-era nuclear weapons and stockpiles of fissile material might find their way into terrorists' hands. When the post-Soviet Russian economy began to crumble and the Kremlin made deep cuts in military spending, including operations and maintenance, such dangers were greatly increased. With the Russian economy collapsing in the 1990s, there were cuts in the troops who guarded sensitive stockpiles, and economic hardships raised worries that those who continued in those jobs could be bribed. The nuclear scientists who had occupied an honored place in Soviet society, which had translated into many privileges, were losing their Soviet-era status, economic benefits, and even their jobs. Many in the West feared that they could be hired away by terrorist groups to help build nuclear weapons. Serious concerns have been raised about violence, corruption, and organized crime in Russia. World leaders and institutions have addressed the problem of sealing Russia's borders as violence and instability have persisted in Chechnya, South Ossetia, and Dagestan.[1] The United States has worked with Russia and other states to set up nuclear detection sites at Russian border crossings. But the borders of Russia are not well guarded, and goods move across illegally with ease into, for example, Georgia.

There are two types of threats posed by terrorists who have nuclear materials. One is the detonation of a nuclear explosive in a Western city or so-called high-value target, such as a port, tourist destination, or military installation. The other is the detonation of a radiological weapon, a so-called dirty bomb. The former is a technically challenging task of the sort Iraq and Libya were unable to accomplish, whereas the latter is much less technologically complex, involving only a conventional weapons charge to explode radioactive material. The former destroys with blast, radiation, and the spread of nuclear fallout. The latter inflicts damage by spreading nuclear fallout thus contaminating a large area. The former, a nuclear weapon detonation, could kill tens of thousand or hundreds of thousands of people immediately and utterly destroy an entire city, whereas the blast from a radiological weapon might not lead to immediate death and destruction. Nevertheless, over a period of years the damage could be massive, with increases in lethal cancer rates. And there would be massive economic damage if large parts of central Paris, London, Tokyo, or Manhattan, for example, were to become uninhabitable. This would then affect each country's trading partners.

This chapter seeks to examine how various authors have tried to explain the acquisition of nuclear weapons by states that have pursued that course and the restraint by states that have not. We begin with several of the influential works published shortly after the entry into force of the Nuclear Nonproliferation Treaty (NPT) on March 5, 1970 (International Atomic Energy Agency 1970, 1).

1. GEORGE QUESTER'S *THE POLITICS OF NUCLEAR PROLIFERATION*

George Quester regarded nuclear proliferation as dangerous and argued for specific measures to prevent it. In his 1973 book *The Politics of Nuclear Proliferation* he discussed whether the best way to handle the danger and reduce unintended consequences would be via the NPT or through individual arrangements with potential proliferators. Quester examined not only political aspects of proliferation, as the title of his book suggests, but also military and economic aspects.

Quester takes seriously the national points of view of interested parties. His chapters are organized around the views of government actors in five nuclear weapons states and another dozen potential proliferators. However, Quester is very sensitive to the perspectives of different actors within each government, in part because his research is based on extensive interviews with government officials from various organizations, and in part because an awareness of bureaucratic politics was reaching a peak at that time in American scholarship in the fields of international relations and political science. There is variation in the degree to which Quester sees states' behavior as driven by divergent subnational actors, such as administrative bureaucracies or political parties. In some states there is much less disagreement among different internal actors.

Quester details the reasons for the Republican administration of President Eisenhower having reservations about nonproliferation initiatives, whereas the Democratic administrations of Presidents Kennedy and Johnson were more active on the matter. He outlines the different ways the political parties worked to secure an alliance commitment from West Germany (1973, 18), and the way the NPT could reverse some of the domestic political damage of the Vietnam War. Quester adds that the NPT was advantageous for the ruling Social Democratic Party in Sweden, despite limits that the treaty would impose on Sweden's nuclear options, because the Social Democrats had an image within Sweden of working for peace-enhancing projects. The NPT was more complex in Japan, since the right-of-center Liberal Democrats were inclined to oppose the treaty on nationalist grounds, yet they gained from cooperation with the United States.

At the time Quester was writing, it was still unknown whether India would sign the NPT; Quester rightly saw this prospect as unlikely. Quester assesses India's motivations very much from the points of view of national interest and security. For example, he argues that India is not swayed by economic considerations (1973, 80). He considers the negotiations with the United States and the Soviet Union that were aimed at enticing India to sign. He discusses India's 1962 war with China, its relations with Pakistan, and its coordination with Japan and the Federal Republic of Germany to ally in opposing the NPT. But the discussions are framed in terms of bilateral relationships.

A state's scientific community can become an internal political force. According to Quester, such groups often oppose internationalization and reliance on the International Atomic Energy Agency (IAEA) because of the risk of espionage, although Quester reported that scientists' attitudes were becoming "increasingly unpredictable," as they shift over time, as in West Germany, India, and Israel (1973, 85, 237–38). And military leaders always seem to find a military rationale for a nuclear weapon. Quester also makes frequent reference to possible political squabbles within the IAEA's inspection teams. Yet he holds that bureaucratic politics analyses of foreign policy have been taken too far. "If many of us had come to see international politics as a largely bureaucratic phenomenon . . . [,] the NPT has given a timely revival to the notion that it is nations that have conflicts, rather than bureaus" (1973, 233). He qualifies this comment by adding, "The crosscurrents that beset nations here must be discussed in terms of substantive issues, but they must also be discussed in terms of bureaucratic factions" (1973, 234). The dominant form of analysis in

Quester's book is, nevertheless, focused on the states' national security interests and their bilateral relationships with allies and adversaries.

Criteria of Explanatory Superiority

Because of the nature of Quester's argument strategy, he invokes relatively few criteria, either explicitly or even implicitly. But he makes use of only three other criteria of a good explanation. One is that a good explanation will identify *mechanisms*, in this case decision-making mechanisms. He implicitly holds that an explanation should *impart* understanding and that the key claims of the explanation should *support counterfactuals.*

2. KENNETH WALTZ

Kenneth Waltz is one of the best-known contributors to debates about nuclear proliferation. The bulk of his extensive writing on the subject deals with the effects of an increasing number of states acquiring the weapons, but he also says a good deal about why states build nuclear weapons. His analysis is very much entrenched in the security model, according to which states—whether small (1981) or great powers (1990)—desire to enhance military capabilities, one means to which is the acquisition of nuclear weapons.

Waltz's explanation of proliferation is connected to his view of deterrence. A state may attempt to dissuade others from attacking it either by means of a strategy of defense or deterrence. A strategy of defense seeks to erect physical barriers that will prevent any strike from succeeding in its objective (e.g., fortifications, weapons that attack incoming weapons). A strategy of deterrence offers no such physical barriers; rather, it requires the possession of weapons that would survive a strike and be available to inflict massive damage in response, as Brodie discussed; both sides would know that the attacking state would suffer retaliatory damage so great that it would greatly outweigh any possible gains of the initial strike. Waltz discusses deterrence as the goal of the United Kingdom, France, the Soviet Union, and many other states in developing nuclear arsenals.[2]

While some worried that further nuclear proliferation would upset the post–World War II system of stability and balanced alliances, Waltz was not among them. In fact, he holds that some alliance relationships can be strengthened by proliferation. For example, in his 1981 book *The Spread of Nuclear Weapons: More May Be Better*, he argues that the United Kingdom and France, both of which are members of the North Atlantic Treaty Organization (NATO), followed the United States down the nuclear path for security reasons, and they did so "at least in part as triggers for America's strategic deterrent. Given a sense of uncertainty combined with dependence, Europeans understandably strive to fashion their forces so as to ensure our commitment" (Waltz 1981, 9).

States outside of NATO also seek greater security through nuclear deterrence. For example, Pakistan could not possibly match the conventional forces of India, whose economy is seven times greater. Thus, Pakistan desired nuclear weapons to deter an attack by India. "For Pakistan . . . acquiring nuclear weapons is an alternative to running a ruinous conventional race with India. And deterrent strategies make nuclear arms races pointless" (1981, 23).

States that acquire nuclear weapons also limit certain freedoms of action, as they come under closer scrutiny. States that want to behave as freewheeling rogues have to stay out of the nuclear spotlight. A nuclear Libya during the Gaddafi years, for example, would have had to show caution, even in its rhetoric, lest Libya suffer retaliation in response to *any* untraceable attack on a third state. The argument here is that a nuclear-armed victim of an "anonymous" nuclear attack might quell public outrage by striking back against the most obviously obstreperous state with a small nuclear arsenal. A state like Gaddafi's Libya would have been a prime candidate. Thus, in Waltz's view, possession of nuclear weapons induces caution, especially in weak states (1981, 12).

Pakistan and North Korea have tested nuclear weapons, yet dozens of more advanced industrialized states have refrained, which poses a puzzle. Waltz explains the many cases of states that did not acquire nuclear weapons by means of the same rational security calculation he applies to acquisitions decisions: "Some countries . . . feeling threatened, have found security through their own strenuous efforts and through arrangements made with others" (1981, 30). Waltz does not appeal to any influences beyond strict security concerns. He continues, "South Korea is an outstanding example. Many South Korean officials believe that South Korea would lose more in terms of American support if she acquired nuclear weapons than she would gain by having them" (1981, 30). Waltz adhered to a strictly cost-benefit security explanation of acquisition and restraint.

Explanation, Theory, and Criteria

Waltz discussed proliferation issues in several publications, as already noted. It is in his 1979 book *Theory of International Politics* that he offers the fullest account of his view of a "good explanation" and of how a good theory can help us understand states' nuclear weapons decisions. Waltz begins by contrasting two characterizations of the notion of a theory. According to one, a theory must offer generalizations that connect two or more kinds of event or phenomenon. Waltz acknowledges that the study of international relations should include the formulation of general laws, which show not only a connection among events but also patterns in such connections. Theories are not sets of laws, nor do they apparently include laws. Waltz says, "Rather than being mere collections of laws, theories are statements that explain them . . . [and] are qualitatively different from laws" (1979, 5), which suggests that laws are not formally a part of theories. He adds that in international relations (IR) and political science the term *theory* is more often used to refer to interpretive accounts, although his use of the term is closer to that of scientists and economists.

In *Theory of International Politics* Waltz does not give much of an indication of what an explanation is until chapter 4, when he says, "What do I mean by *explain*? I mean explain in these senses: to say why the range of expected outcomes falls within certain limits; to say why patterns of behavior recur; to say why events repeat themselves, including events that none or few of the actors may like" (1979, 69). This still is a limited characterization or definition, as it indicates only that an explanation tells us "why" in connection with repeating patterns. Waltz specifies the why-questions. But we still do not know by virtue of what factors an answer to a why-question is a good answer.

For Waltz, "a theory depicts a domain and displays its organization and the connections among its parts" (1979, 123). In another passage of the book he says that a theory of international politics, like any theory, must be constructed in three steps: "first, one must conceive of international politics as a bounded realm or domain; second, one must discover some law-like regularities within it; and third, one must develop a way of explaining the observed regularities" (1979, 116). In a later paper, he says that a theory is "a picture, mentally formed, of a bounded realm or domain of activity. . . . Theory, rather than being a mirror in which reality is reflected, is an instrument to be used in attempting to explain a circumscribed part of a reality of whose true dimensions we can never be sure" (Waltz 1997, 913).

What a theory must do, as Waltz sees it, is tell us why the regularities hold. So while Waltz sees behavioral regularities as provably true by empirical observation, he sees the explanation for the regularities as changing from one theory to another. The quantified regularities are descriptions that lack any explanatory power or "theoretical meaning," he points out in the 1979 book *Theory of International Politics* (1979, 3). Descriptions may tell what we see, but they tell us nothing about what "it may mean" (1979, 65). Waltz does, however acknowledge an "interdependence of theory and fact" rather than strict observer neutrality (1979, 123; see also page 913 of his 1997 paper "Evaluating Theories"). Theories, or at least theory sketches, guide us in fruitful directions. As Waltz (1979, 17) says, "To proceed by looking for associations [without theories] is like shooting a gun in the general direction of an invisible target," which would be wasteful, and moreover, even if we hit the target, "no one would know it!"

Descriptions and observational regularities are framed in terms that deal with observation. But theoretical explanations are more than just straightforward inductions from the observations since they also contain "theoretical" terms, which are "invented, not discovered" (Waltz 1979, 5). Any theoretical notion familiar to us through physics is not directly observable; its meaningfulness is only inferred by application of the theory of which it forms a part. As physics progressed from Aristotle to Galileo to Newton, the theoretical concepts became "further removed from our sense experience" (Waltz 1979, 5).

Explanations are important because they give us at least a chance to exercise control over our environment. "Prediction follows from knowledge of the regularity of associations embodied in laws" (Waltz 1979, 6), but it does not allow humans any control, because prediction alone does not entail any ability to bring about desired changes. Only the explanations that come with theories allow the possibility of control. And the explanations can tell us counterfactually, "If we do X, then Y will result."

We might add that Waltz does not use his structural theory to deal with claims about foreign policy, because he argues that there is a sharp distinction between a theory of international relations, especially a structural theory like his, and a theory of foreign policy. Some prominent authors have questioned the legitimacy of this distinction (Fearon 1998, 289–313; see also Waltz 1996).

Waltz often says that a theory must simplify, but not necessarily by an analytical process of breaking the subject into small parts. Analytical reduction works in domains "where relations between several factors can be resolved into relations between pairs of variables while 'other things are held equal' and where the assumption can be made that perturbing influences not included in the variables are small" (Waltz 1979, 39). But in domains like IR, where one or both conditions fail, system effects will be substantial and a systems approach—not reductive analysis—is the most effective way to simplify. Either way, simplification is the goal for the explanation and it is what makes it superior to alternatives.

What makes one explanation better than another? We have just seen Waltz's paramount preference for simplicity. Waltz also believes that a good explanation should support counterfactuals. His acceptance of this criterion is implicit but clear as he argues that bipolarity has had the greatest effect on stability, especially in relation to nuclear weapons. Waltz here builds on the counterfactual claim that even if neither superpower possessed nuclear weapons, the forces the United States could and would deploy in Western Europe would be sufficient to prevent a Soviet invasion. He cites authors on both sides of the Atlantic who claim that, with or without nuclear weapons, the United States would not have permitted Soviet domination of Europe (Waltz 1964, 885).

In many places Waltz says that the best explanatory theory is the one that is most useful (e.g., Waltz 1997, 916). Neither assumptions nor explanations are true or false; the former produce theories that are useful to some degree or other, and theories are valuable insofar as they produce good explanations (Waltz 1979, 119). "Success in explaining . . . is the ultimate criterion of a good theory" (Waltz 1997, 916). And Waltz tells us explicitly that a good theory provides causal explanations that make use of the notion of rational behavior, and the criteria on which we judge one explanation superior to others are that it scores well on usefulness, simplicity, empirical fit, range of domain, and *support of counterfactuals.* A good theory will produce *accurate predictions,* which are necessary for *control over the environment.*

3. WILLIAM POTTER

William Potter, director of the Center for Nonproliferation Studies, has been one of the most influential and prolific contributors to discussions of nuclear proliferation over the past three decades. Potter's publications come in all forms, addressing both broad political problems and technical aspects of nuclear weapons and nuclear proliferation. His most comprehensive study is his 1982 book *Nuclear Power and Nonproliferation.* The book covers much ground, offering descriptions of the technology required for developing nuclear power and the connection to nuclear weapons, surveys of the published literature on related questions, inquiries into why states build nuclear weapons, and analyses of policy options.

The goal of Potter's study is to "explain" and "influence a nation's nuclear weapons posture." To do this, he must carefully describe the dependent variable, that of "being a nuclear weapons nation" (1982, 180), which many equate with conducting one or more weapons tests. However, Potter suggests that it may be more effective to think in terms of a "ladder" or set of stages of nuclear weapons proficiency, from having technical know-how and manufacturing capability to having a large, invulnerable arsenal of nuclear weapons and secure command and control systems.

Policy Focus

Potter begins by surveying main points in the debate of the early 1980s, such as whether nuclear-generated electricity would increase in the coming years and whether it would pose security dangers for the world. He notes that some authors claim that slower economic growth of the United States and other major industrial states might lead to a decrease in the rate of expansion of nuclear power plants; that newer plants are more expensive to build; and that the dangers, as illustrated by the 1979 Three Mile Island power plant accident in Pennsylvania, will reduce the political will to increase nuclear power plant expansion. Potter seeks to dispel some persistent misconceptions about nuclear power, for example, that "good atoms" are different from "bad atoms," and that plutonium can be reprocessed or denatured in a way that undermines its utility for weapons. Potter looks at concerns stemming from the easy availability of weapons-applicable waste from breeder reactors. He criticizes the claim that states in fact always pursue energy options that are the most economically rational, arguing that some states pursue economically suboptimal nuclear energy policies because of the potential military applications that might result. Such states are behaving rationally, but they consider factors other than strict economic efficiency.[3]

Because of his emphasis on policy relevance, Potter notes that the objective of nonproliferation must be put in perspective of the overall strategic goals of a state. Thus, while cost-free prevention of proliferation is surely desirable for the United States and weapons-possessing states (and those states that do not desire to acquire weapons), avoiding proliferation at all costs is not strategically or politically desirable for such states. For example, if the United States were assured that no new states would ever acquire nuclear weapons so long as the United States disarmed itself unilaterally, no American leader would find such a deal advantageous, since existing nuclear adversaries, and even allies, would gain a strategic advantage over the United States. This approach emphasizes the rational calculation of states.

The appropriate level of priority on the pursuit of nonproliferation must be calculated by considering both the costs of attaining the goal and the value of achieving it. The former requires different calculations for different target states, and the latter requires an assessment of the value of halting proliferation versus the dangers of more proliferation. These tasks are far from simple, and in 1982 there were already policy makers like Fred Iklé and scholars like Morton Kaplan (1957, 51), who argued that more proliferation might be stabilizing. Some scholars use the model of the US-Soviet relationship to infer that a nuclear balance between any pair of rivals can improve stability, and some have also cited Israel's nuclear arsenal as a source of Arab restraint. However, Potter points out numerous dissimilarities that would arise between the relationship of the United States and the Soviet Union and the likely relationships between various other rival states. He says that the Soviet-American nuclear balance is more accurately described as "delicate" than "stable." Further, the secure basing modes that provide the superpowers with retaliatory capabilities are unlikely to be present in any developing nuclear rivalries; and without secure basing modes, states will have increased incentives to strike in a crisis. Preventive strikes may occur as a rival is near to gaining operational weapons, as was the case in Israel's attacks on Iraqi and Syrian reactors. Potter says that the more states that get nuclear weapons, the greater is the chance of nuclear war by mechanical accident, unauthorized launch, or strategic miscalculation.

Many states view the US nonproliferation policy as intended to advance its own self-interest at the expense of others. An end to the spread of nuclear weapons would freeze the US nuclear advantage in place. Furthermore, limits on breeder reactor technology, which the United States advocated, would hurt European states since they lack natural energy resources, whereas the United States has abundant energy sources, including uranium. The policy question is complicated by the role of private industry. Potter cites one 1975 case in which a private US firm was trying to sell technology to Brazil while the US government was pressuring Germany to halt plans to supply Brazil with uranium enrichment technology (1982, 20).

The United States has long been the world's leader in exporting nuclear technology. From the 1950s onward, the United States regarded nuclear energy as beneficial for the world, and it regarded the export of US technology as good for the US economy. In 1978 the Nuclear Non-Proliferation Act placed much more stringent limitations on US exports. Critics argued that the limitations were counterproductive, since excessive restrictions on fuel exports would drive potential proliferators to find ways to produce their own fuel. At the time, the main source of concern was South Africa. Some held that the restrictions limited exports to Western Europe and Japan in a way that damaged US relations (1982, 23).

Case Studies

Potter summarizes factors that led to an outcome in which there are thirteen "nuclear capable" nations, defined as those that had by 1982 conducted nuclear tests or were then most able to do so. He begins with the US program, which he says was motivated primarily by security concerns, especially once the United States entered World War II. In the period before December 1941 the United States was largely interested in nuclear research for its potential in submarine propulsion, whereas Britain, already at war with Germany, was primarily interested in beating the Nazis to the bomb (1982, 145–46). As the incentives changed, so did the Americans' behavior.

The Soviet nuclear program had "different incentives and constraints" than the US program (1982, 147). Potter's analysis of decisions made in the early years of the program emphasizes the conflict within the Soviet scientific community. Established physicists regarded nuclear research as involving risks and thus resisted funding it, whereas younger physicists were excited by its potential for great long-term advancements. Because of the immediate danger that Nazi Germany posed during the early years of Soviet atomic science, the political and military leadership was focused on short-term outcomes, which, in their view, meant the need for conventional forces able to win on the battlefield, not a long-term scientific program with unknown payoffs. When the Soviets learned of German and American atomic research in 1942, they invested more heavily in the field, but according to Potter, Soviet leaders at that point were already thinking ahead to the postwar political order.

France's public justification for the decision to develop nuclear weapons was framed in terms of the military-security value of a nuclear arsenal, even though, according to Potter, the decision was equally the product of political circumstances and technological momentum. The key weapons decision was made before Charles de Gaulle's election. According to Potter, nuclear research proceeded without any major guidance—for or against military aims—from the French government (see also Scheinman 1965). However, Potter holds that considerations of prestige on the world stage, given France's embarrassing setbacks in Indochina (in 1954) and Suez (in 1956), were more significant than the military motivation (1982, 151). Potter points out that the theoretical justification was developed well after the key French nuclear decisions were made. Potter sees China's security position as offering much more reason to proceed than France's, because of China's conflict with the United States, a nuclear-armed superpower (1982, 154), but he nevertheless regards both China's and France's decisions as primarily motivated by prestige concerns and influence vis-à-vis their putative ally—the Soviet Union for China and the United States for France. The image Potter conveys includes a range of actors—states, political leaders, bureaucracies, private firms—and a range of internal and external military-security and economic incentives and disincentives.

India began nuclear power research during World War II, and its first experimental research reactor went critical in 1956. In India's 1972 decision to move forward with what became the 1974 nuclear test, "domestic politics, international prestige, and regional politics were all probably instrumental" (Potter 1982, 155), although Potter believes that it is hard to disentangle the distinct influences of each factor. Domestic political considerations were likely a major factor in India's decision because of the intense political and economic strife; the nuclear test was a way for the political leadership to divert the public's attention from labor strikes and a declining economy. This analysis is plausible, especially as it fits a pattern in which all major nuclear decisions were taken at times of internal political weakness (Potter, citing Sen Gupta 1978). The Nixon administration had recently begun its "opening to China" and had decided to "tilt toward Pakistan" in the 1971 war. In response, Potter argues, India may well have wanted to send a message to the United States and other leading powers that India was a major force in world politics whose interests could not be ignored. India's chief constraint on a full nuclear weapons program, as opposed to a single fission test, was the cost. And Potter suggests that the Indian military opposed nuclear weapons because of concerns about the need to maintain large and modern conventional armed forces.

Pakistan is generally seen as responding primarily to external security threats in its decision to move forward with nuclear research. Before becoming prime minister, Zulfikar Ali Bhutto said that if India were to go nuclear, then Pakistan would make any sacrifice to do likewise, "eating grass," if necessary. Both India and Pakistan made significant nuclear development decisions in the mid-1950s; both states (despite taking actions that suggested the opposite) joined virtually all non-weapons-possessing states in disavowing any interest in acquiring nuclear weapons. A decade later both states refused to sign the NPT.

Pakistan began operating its first uranium-fueled reactor in 1965, and a second in 1971. The Pakistani nuclear program was given a significant boost when the metallurgist A. Q. Khan began to send data stolen from Western nuclear facilities to Pakistan (though knowledge of his activities came about only after Potter's book was published). Khan volunteered his services in the aftermath of Pakistan's military defeat by India in 1971. Potter also deems "compelling" the claim that nuclear weapons development was good domestic politics in Pakistan (Potter 1982, 159, citing Kapur 1979, 205).

Israel, like India, gained independent statehood shortly after World War II, and like India, it evinced from the very start an interest in nuclear power research. Also, like India, Israel sought ambiguity with regard to its nuclear posture, although Israel pushed this farther. India publically tested a nuclear "device," claiming that it was for peaceful purposes only, whereas Israel has never admitted to possessing nuclear weapons and has promised only that it will not be the first state to "introduce" nuclear weapons into the region, where that key term was, and remains still, entirely mysterious. Israel was able to cooperate on its nuclear program with France and, to a lesser degree, the United States. In return for access to French research, Israel may have provided France with the results of its atomic science, especially "information on the production of heavy water and the extraction of uranium from low-grade ore" (Potter 1982, 165). France assisted Israel in the construction of the Dimona nuclear reactor, which became operational in 1964. According to Potter, "Many of Israel's proliferation incentives are reducible to international security considerations" (1982, 166).

For Canada, the incentive to build a nuclear weapon diminished as the strength of the US nuclear umbrella became clearer. With this level of security stemming from its location and relationship with the United States, Canada sought to present itself as a model of restraint. Because of the prominence of the security incentive for states' pro-nuclear decisions, one might even predict in 1982, says Potter, that the most threatened and vulnerable proliferation candidates (Pakistan, South Korea, and Taiwan) would move toward a nuclear weapon while the less threatened (Brazil, Argentina, and Canada) would not. However, the prediction is somewhat undercut by Potter's analysis of France and India, which built nuclear weapons despite facing lesser security threats. Still, "a small number of variables appear to be of primary importance in the nuclear weapons decisions for most of the thirteen states" (1982, 179).

In Potter's summary of cases, he says that the chief incentives remain international, not domestic. Security threats provided the main incentives for the United States, the Soviet Union, Britain (until 1945), China, and Israel. The disincentives appear to have changed over time; at the time Potter published the book, countries had to balance the advantages of nuclear weapons against the problem of angering or alienating the great powers by opposing the NPT, which the United States, France, the United Kingdom, and the Soviet Union all supported. But Potter points out that it may have been less a change in the times than a change in the types of states contemplating nuclear acquisition. Because the early proliferators were major powers, they did not have to worry excessively about angering higher-level powers. Since the mid-1960s, the states moving toward acquiring nuclear weapons have been smaller or regional powers and have thus had to consider the possible reactions of those at a level well above them—both allies and adversaries.

Causal Explanation

Potter's book contrasts alternative explanations of many sorts, involving different causes, reasons, and motivations for states' pursuit of nuclear arsenals. He discusses both subnational and transnational terrorist groups and other nonstate actors.

Potter also believes that the analysis of necessary and (especially) sufficient conditions can illuminate states' actions on nuclear weapons. Potter identifies two sets of sufficient conditions for a state to go nuclear, namely, "The balance between underlying proliferation incentives and disincentives, and the presence of one of several situational factors that might precipitate a decision to go nuclear whenever incentives outweigh constraints" (1982, 143). The focus on incentives and disincentives reinforces the emphasis on state-level rational security calculations. The situational factors involve reference to structural influences on the state's decision.

Potter is interested in policies that will slow, as much as possible, the horizontal spread of nuclear weapons. He believes that the debate about policy options has focused too little on seeking an understanding of the causes of proliferation: "surprisingly little is known about the conditions affecting national decisions to 'go nuclear' or decisions to acquire the capabilities to do so," as many of the claims are "speculative and contradictory" (1982, 131). Potter's method is to list possible factors that could affect decisions and then to develop, in his terms, a "focused comparison," in which the goal is to find general "incentives and disincentives," "country-specific" factors, and necessary and sufficient conditions.

Once he examines the debate of the previous twenty years, Potter proceeds to abstract twenty-four different factors that affect nuclear weapons decisions. He identifies two "national prerequisites," namely economic wealth and scientific and technological expertise; nine "underlying pressures," which can be either external (e.g., military advantage) or internal (e.g., economic spillover); another nine "underlying constraints" inhibiting a nuclear acquisition decision, which may be external (e.g., absence of a perceived threat) or internal (e.g., economic costs); and four "situational variables," which are mainly external (e.g., weakening of security guarantees and vertical proliferation). Potter discusses international prestige as a factor, along with bureaucratic and domestic politics, which include incentives that push a state toward nuclear acquisition and disincentives that push a state away from going nuclear.

Criteria

For Potter, what emerges is a successful explanation that identifies the rational move among the various options, which is based on the incentives and disincentives operating at the time, and that is consistent with all available cases and observations. Still, Potter holds that states do not act exclusively on grounds of narrow or short-term economic incentives. They may also act on the basis of long-term economic payoffs, as with Pakistan, and/or international prestige, as with France, India, and others. The responses to the incentive structures are nondeterministic but comprehensible. Rather than speaking of "deterministic causes," Potter's analysis mixes incentives, pressures, and constraints, which are understood as propensities. His analysis is based on four categories of such factors that arise from two binary distinctions: military versus politico-economic, and domestic versus external. Potter distinguishes high versus low levels of threat on the military-politico dimension and presence versus absence of a security guarantee from a nuclear-armed ally on the internal-external dimension.

Potter consistently treats decision makers as responding to incentives. He frames his case studies almost entirely in terms of incentives and disincentives of states and leaders, and in some cases other actors. But the level of analysis, or key actors, shifts from a focus on states to one on national political leaders, to subnational units (the military services and nuclear industry), to factions within subnational units (the established versus younger physicists in the 1940s Soviet scientific community). In this way Potter sees his explanation as *uncovering true causes.* Potter regards his explanation as more satisfactory also because it displays *simplicity*, is *empirically adequate* in dealing with the record of past cases, and accounts for a *greater range* of cases.

4. STEPHEN MEYER ON DYNAMICS

Stephen Meyer's 1984 book *The Dynamics of Nuclear Proliferation* is an important contribution to the literature on why states build nuclear weapons. Meyer contends that the various anti-proliferation policy positions conflict with one another in part because they adopt different proliferation hypotheses, which the various authors accept largely on faith and without careful scrutiny.

Meyer argues that an accurate understanding of nuclear proliferation requires a focus on the "pivotal point," which is the "proliferation decision," rather than the decision to construct or to test nuclear weapon. He contends that a decision to develop nuclear technology need not lead to proliferation of nuclear weapons. Meyer distinguishes "a capability decision, acquiring or possessing a latent capacity, a proliferation decision, and ultimately possessing functional nuclear weapons" (1984, 5). A capability decision, for example, may be directed specifically at developing the means to generate electricity with no aim, at that time, of developing weapons. Sweden made the decision to develop nuclear technology but has never gone forward with weapons acquisition. In contrast, when the United States and the Soviet Union decided in the 1940s to pursue a nuclear capability, they made the weapons acquisition decision at the same time. Even weapons acquisition decisions do not automatically lead inevitably to the production of a functional nuclear arsenal because some states have trouble overcoming technological problems, as has happened with Libya; some states are struck by preemptive military action, as Iraq and Syria were by Israel; and some states reverse their proliferation decisions before testing a weapon, as India did in 1966 because of domestic politics, and as South Korea did in 1975 because of intense external pressure from the United States (1984, 127).[4]

Research Design

Meyer considers the countries that have acquired basic nuclear capabilities and examines what differentiates the thirteen decisions to go forward with weapons programs from the various restraint decisions (1984, 7). He observes that the first five proliferation decisions were taken during World War II (Germany, Japan, United States, and the Soviet Union, and the United Kingdom's initial decision to work in partnership with the United States). As noted earlier, in all five cases the decision to develop a basic nuclear capability was also a weapons acquisition decision. The following three decisions occurred during the early Cold War (the United Kingdom's second decision, France, and China) and were simultaneously nuclear program and weapons decisions. However, many states since then have decided to pursue nuclear research to develop power generation only, which creates a "latent" weapons capability. Some, such as Sweden, have not subsequently decided to apply that capability to a weapons program, whereas others have later decided to weaponize (e.g., India's first decision in 1965, reversed in 1966, and its second decision in 1974, as well as Israel, South Africa, and North Korea). Future proliferation decisions are most likely to resemble the calculations of these non-European and non-major-power states, as future proliferators are likely to come from those two categories.

Meyer's study aims to produce the best explanations by surveying the literature and identifying key variables. He develops appropriate indicators and tests the hypotheses. Meyer follows a multimethod approach, using both "subjective" scholarly analyses and opinions as a source of evidence, and "objective" empirical indicators (1984, 45). He uses each to check the other, leading to a number of cases in which codings are revised. Meyer employs the hypothetico-deductive method, examining each of the explanations, drawing observable consequences from them, then marshaling data and empirical tests that reveal whether the expected outcomes match the results of the tests. Meyer is very straightforward—and appropriately modest—in assessing the strength of the evidence available to test the competing proliferation hypotheses. He acknowledges subjective limitations and potential pitfalls in the data that he and other scholars rely on, including "informed opinion and speculation" (1984, 44).

The terminology can be confusing, since Meyer does not draw clear distinctions between the terms *account*, *hypothesis*, *explanation*, and even *assumption*. There are passages in the book in which each is used interchangeably with at least one of the others. The "motivational hypothesis," according to Meyer, "explains" most cases, and it is the "best account" (1984, 18).

Core Debate and Competing Explanations

Meyer's study seeks to find the best explanation for the pattern of proliferation and restraint observed at the time of writing. Meyer considers two popular types of explanations found in the literature, which he refers to as the "technological imperative" and the "motivational hypothesis." Each type includes a number of specific variations. Meyer says, "The motivational hypothesis offers a relatively *simple* explanation for proliferation decisions" (1984, 91, emphasis added) and is thus superior.[5]

The technological imperative claims that the proliferation process is essentially automatic. Once a state attains a nuclear capability, it is only a matter of time until the state exploits that capability for military purposes. Meyer identifies three versions of the technological imperative. One is very deterministic: it states that claiming that once a state has a nuclear capability it will quickly make the decision to weaponize. The second is fully deterministic with regard to the final outcome but less so regarding the timing, asserting only that the state will eventually make a proliferation decision. The third is probabilistic, claiming that the higher the level of nuclear technology of a state, the greater is the probability that it will make the decision to weaponize.

On the motivational view, decision makers conduct a rational cost-benefit analysis. All versions of the motivational view hold that nuclear proliferation occurs because states seek to advance foreign defense and domestic policy goals. There are three general types of rational incentives to build nuclear weapons: international political power and prestige incentives, military or security incentives, and domestic political incentives (1984, 46). However, Meyer says that all of the incentives of the first two sorts are "filtered through" domestic political considerations (1984, 47). As Meyer uses the terms, *aids* and *restraints* render the process of developing nuclear weapons easier and harder, respectively, but they are distinct from incentives and disincentives (1984, 15). Both the motivational and the technological hypotheses make use of political and technological factors. The differences in the two types of explanation are not in the sorts of factors they consider, but rather in the different primary roles they assign and the different emphases they place on each sort of factor.

Meyer lists twenty incentives (1984, 48–49, table 3), which he ties to "motive conditions" that various authors claim to be possible influences on proliferation. Examples include the "presence of a security threat from a nuclear-armed adversary" and "asserting political-military independence." However, some cannot be directly connected, and Meyer treats them implicitly (1984, 65). Meyer also lists nine "dissuasive conditions" that, when present, reduce the impulse to build nuclear weapons (1984, 68, table 7), such as "an alliance with a great power" and "international legal obligations." He contrasts the motivational and technological hypotheses to the null hypothesis; that is, there is no general explanation for proliferation decisions, and each case must be examined to find the unique features that produced the outcome. In other words, "the pattern is that there is no pattern" (1984, 17).

Findings

Meyer argues that the technological imperative does not adequately explain nuclear weapons acquisition decisions. Those who accept it draw erroneous conclusions about which states are in fact proliferating. Meyer says, "One cannot distinguish between countries that go nuclear and those that do not merely by examining relative capabilities" (1984, 165). He adds, "Empirically . . . we are on fairly secure ground in rejecting the technological imperative as a single explanation for decisions to initiate nuclear weapons programs" (1984, 88).[6] Meyer argues that, when sufficient capabilities are present, many different types of state can make the decision to proliferate. In terms of policy approaches, Meyer concludes that, because different states make proliferation decisions based on different factors, the best strategy to combat nuclear proliferation is to focus on their diverse motivations and to design policies to fit the unique features of each potential proliferator's motivations. The "cure" for the disease of nuclear proliferation is to reduce states' motivations to possess nuclear arsenals.

Causation and Explanation

Meyer seeks explanations for proliferation decisions, as noted earlier, and causal accounts are required for good explanations. The superior explanation will involve a rationally grounded process of decision making. But it is not clear that the explanations he regards as inferior fail simply because they do not involve rational processes; the way he phrases it, the technological imperative appears to fail primarily because the empirical evidence shows that the rationally oriented hypotheses provide a superior explanation.

Meyer offers some clues to his view of the elements of causation and explanation. He distinguishes the concepts of necessary conditions from triggers, catalysts, and precipitating events. While all are relevant for explanations of events, none can ever be regarded as "the cause" of an outcome. Meyer says, for example, "While the assassination of Archduke Francis Ferdinand was a trigger of the First World War, it was hardly the cause" (1984, 17); existing nuclear infrastructure can aid proliferation decisions, but it is not a "cause" (1984, 150). In the following paragraph Meyer equates such an aid to a "catalyst," which he also distinguishes from a cause.

Causal claims are sometimes analyzed in terms of *support of counterfactuals.* And counterfactual claims are often taken as presupposing certain causal assertions. The former is evident, for example, when Meyer compares the history of nuclear weapons programs to a hypothetical case in which many countries had insecticide-manufacturing plants that could be converted to produce chemical weapons. This counterfactual analysis highlights one aspect of the causal role of nuclear weapons in international security, which is that states do indeed make decisions to convert civilian plants to make weapons.

Both the technological and motivational explanations require individuals to make choices, which constitute *mechanisms* of a psychological nature (1984, 18). Meyer says, "Capabilities are often seen as affecting psychology and decision-making" (1984, 12). The technological explanation involves "momentum," and motivational explanations involve "specific politico-military conditions that stimulate—that is, cause—national decision-makers to initiate a nuclear weapons program" (1984, 13). This appears to mean that stimuli are causes.

Meyer requires that a good explanatory hypothesis pass tests of statistical association given all relevant data (compare his rejection of the first technological imperative model, at page 77), and if a hypothesis is to be accepted, it must go beyond consistency with available aggregate data. It must also be able to explain why the particular states that made proliferation decisions did so. In his critique of the second version of the technological imperative, Meyer says that the data "do not allow us to accept model II as an explanation for proliferation decisions . . . [because] model II does not help us determine which countries will make proliferation decisions. . . . In other words, model II fails to link latent capacities to subsequent proliferation decisions other than to state that the former is *necessary* for the latter" (1984, 83). Thus, if the explanatory hypothesis is not able to identify particular states, then it has not explained the outcomes.[7] To succeed here the explanation must have the sort of mechanism, or connection from cause to effect, that will specify outcomes in more than a statistical fashion.

One of the more striking statements about causation is the claim that both technological and motivational conditions are necessary for a nuclear decision, but only the latter is a cause. With respect to the roles of technology and political motivation, "It should be obvious that each is necessary but that only both together are sufficient for proliferation decisions. The *actual cause* of proliferation decisions is politico-military motivation" (1984, 142, emphasis added). With a sufficient motivation, a state will develop the technology. He adds, moreover, that "technology is not a cause, it is an aid . . . [that] provides the opportunity to implement proliferation decisions" (1984, 142). But in a slightly puzzling comment, he goes further by saying that technological progress on nuclear capability can affect a state's view of the balance of incentives and disincentives (1984, 143; see also his chapter 7), as occurred in the cases of South Africa and Israel; in those cases "the technological imperative hypothesis was stood on its head" (1984, 117). Perhaps an even stronger reason that Meyer views politico-military motivation more than technology as causal is that the former varies more, both increasing and decreasing over time, whereas the latter moves slowly and mostly in a single direction (1984, 119). If so, then variation is essential to our assigning causal and explanatory status.

In terms of the criteria that Meyer makes use of, we have seen that he regards his explanation as *simple* (1984, 91) and holds that it is the stronger explanation for that reason. Like other authors, Meyer argues that his explanation benefits from its *empirical adequacy*. The argument from the hypothetical insecticide production case shows his endorsement of the idea that causal explanations *support counterfactual* claims and survive counterfactual analysis. And he endorses the idea that good explanations identify *mechanisms* (1984, 12, 18).

5. ETEL SOLINGEN AND ECONOMIC ORIENTATION

Etel Solingen has argued that the best way to explain states' decisions to acquire or to resist acquiring nuclear weapons is to examine the survival strategies of states' leadership regimes. In a series of publications over the past twenty years she has emphasized that a focus on the state and its interests, which is typical of the realist security model, cannot produce satisfactory explanations. Whether a regime is "outward directed" or "inward directed" affects the sort of survival strategy that the regime will pursue. This directedness factor interacts with some systemic factors.

Outward-looking leaders seek to advance their own interests by pursuing integration in the world economy, which requires that they maintain cordial relations with the major industrial powers; their goals cannot be met if they become the targets of major powers' anger and punishment. In contrast, inward-looking leaders enhance chances of advance by avoiding integration and, to various degrees, insulating themselves from the rest of the world, such as by autarky and import-substitution development policies. These regimes are less vulnerable to the anger and economic retribution of outside powers. According to Solingen, the effects of the external factors vary, depending on how they are mediated by domestic political calculations.

Outward-looking leadership regimes see the reputational costs and possible economic sanctions arising from nuclear weapons acquisition as likely to retard integration into the world economy. Those regimes have thus been willing to pay costs to participate in many international institutions, including refraining from nuclear acquisition, because they then gain the greater good of economic integration. The different regimes' "domestic filters" affect their behavior because, as states compare their rivals' power resources to their own, they process the comparisons through a series of "domestic filters" (Solingen 2007, 4–5; compare the discussion of Meyer's view of domestic filters in the previous section).

Solingen argues that, in the years since the NPT came into force, different geographical regions have seen different patterns of proliferation, and the latter fit with different types of leadership regimes. Most states in East Asia have chosen the path of economic integration and renounced nuclear weapons acquisition. In contrast, Middle East states have shown great interest in acquiring nuclear weapons. Iran, Iraq, Israel, Libya, Syria, and possibly Saudi Arabia have made moves toward nuclear weapons acquisition. There are notable exceptions in both regions, China and North Korea in East Asia, and Egypt in the Middle East. China and North Korea both vigorously opposed economic integration and most other forms of internationalization at the times that they made their nuclear weapons decisions. All of the Middle Eastern states just listed that have pursued nuclear weapons, at various points, had adopted import substitution and closed economies. Moreover, many of the inward-looking regimes in the Middle East are in states with vital resources, notably oil, which renders them far less vulnerable to economic retaliation. In any case, Solingen argues that, for both types of cases, the concept of regime security provides better explanations of behavior than does a focus on state security.

Methodology

Solingen's 2007 book offers a focused comparison of two regions, the Middle East and East Asia. The comparison is appropriate in her view because the two regions also differ in both explanatory factors (independent variables) connected with their political systems and in the proliferation outcomes (dependent variables). Moreover, the two regions are especially important in policy terms because, as she points out, nine of the fourteen states that have been regarded as most interested in pursuing a nuclear weapons program post-NPT are in these two regions.

In considering Solingen's methodology and her results, we should recall that various authors hold that the sorts of methods a scholar adopts will have an effect on the results. George and Bennett (2005, 25) observe that case studies are much better at determining whether and by what process a factor mattered to an outcome. Quantitative studies, in contrast, are much better at assessing how much a factor mattered to the outcome. Solingen's publications are thus much better designed to discover which factors are important and how they operate to bring about the effects.

Explanation

Solingen asks what causes some states to seek nuclear weapons and others not to seek them. In offering an answer, she discusses the way in which a particular factor can add an "explanatory layer" to the overall picture (2007, 13). The metaphor of explanatory layers may shape how she sees the functioning of explanations. She also invokes what is presumably (though not obviously) a different dimension of explanatory prowess with the metaphor of "deeper" explanations that provide an account of what happened at an early point, especially the origin of the process under discussion (2007, 13). Her example of a deepening factor is domestic political action, which can help explain why an alliance was forged in the first place. She seems to contrast two dimensions of a state's alliance with a great power. One dimension is the "inner" versus "outer" explanatory layers, where alliances are external and domestic politics are internal, and the other dimension is the "shallower" versus "deeper" explanations, where the shallower are chronologically closer to the explanandum event and the deeper go farther back.

Solingen's criticisms of realism and neorealism include the charge that the theories have multiple possible outcomes: states might address their security needs by acquiring nuclear weapons, by seeking great power guarantees within the NPT, or by pursuing an ambiguous nuclear posture (e.g., India from 1974 to 1998; Israel post-1968). She raises the concern that, for this reason, the theory may not be *falsifiable* (2007, 26; compare Vasquez [1997], who makes a similar argument). Solingen prefers theories "that are posed with sufficient clarity and linked to appropriate observable implications" (2007, 304n8).

In the course of her discussion of the effects of systemic norms, Solingen argues that structural and constructivist explanations will be inadequate without a "lower level" explanation. Here the "level," whether high or low, constitutes a different dimension from the "depth" dimension just cited. She says that unless there is an account of how the domestic actors interpreted the norms, the explanation will be underspecified and incomplete. In her view, the structural level "must be complimented by" a domestic level explanation (2007, 16).[8] Constructivist accounts, in Solingen's view, also need a "complimentary" theory of domestic factors that lead some states to take systemic norms to justify nuclearization and others to justify avoiding nuclearization (2007, 16). For Solingen, analyses of domestic politics help to explain several phenomena that otherwise remain mysterious; for example, domestic factors are sought to help explain behavior such as the different priorities that different states place on alliances, the occasional pursuit of nuclear weapons when there is no clear security need for them, and restraint when it appears that there are threats to the state (2007, 18). Thus, the spatial metaphors include those of outer and inner layers, deeper and shallower depths, and lower and higher levels.

Solingen contends that the failure to examine one variable will lead to an overestimation of the effects of the other variables. Thus, she holds that the failure to study inward versus outward economic orientation has led to an overemphasis on the efficacy of other factors. Her key independent variable, inward versus outward economic directedness, is "probabilistic, bounded, and refutable" (2007, 18). It is probabilistic in that it does not suggest any causal determinism. The empirical association between "inward-lookingness" and nuclearization, Solingen says, is more than happenstance; there is some sort of causal connection. The former may be a necessary condition. To be precise, she refers to it as a "near-necessary" condition (2007, 18). But she notes that an inward-looking orientation is not a sufficient condition of nuclearization, since some Middle Eastern states (e.g., Sudan, Syria) did not pursue nuclear weapons.[9] Japan, Taiwan, and South Korea all had the capability to build nuclear weapons and had serious existential security concerns, yet they had leadership regimes with outward-looking economic policies; consequently, they did not build nuclear weapons.

Solingen regards her central claim as bounded in several ways, including by structural constraints. In particular, the state's leadership regime itself is not the only political-economic orientation relevant. If there is a widely adopted approach within the region, that approach will reinforce one's own political-economic orientation or cause resistance against it. Thus, the presence of many domestic leadership regimes in a state's region that are similarly inward or outward directed will reinforce the orientation of the state's leadership. The incentives for proceeding with a nuclear weapons program will also vary depending upon what stage the program has already reached. Leaders are less prone to give up what they have than to forgo future gains.

Explanatory Criteria

Solingen's text contains a number of criteria for evaluating explanations and thus for choosing the best among those available. Some of the criteria are implicit, especially those covered in her main discussion, but others are stated explicitly, especially in her summaries and critiques of the competing theoretical explanations. In her main analysis of the theoretical explanations, Solingen implicitly sees as superior those whose key claims are *supported by counterfactuals.* This emerges in her critique of neoliberal institutionalist explanations of the restraint in nuclear weapons acquisition exercised by so many states since 1968. According to Solingen, "Asserting that the NPR [nuclear nonproliferation regime] accounts for progressive denuclearization is inherently difficult, because its effects must be weighed relative to hypothetical histories (counterfactuals) without the NPT" (2007, 31). She also discusses the limitations of counterfactual analysis, including that such analysis "cannot prove or disprove a proposition" (2007, 305n14).

In her critique of realist explanations, Solingen cites Schweller's (2006) analysis of realism and the criteria he invokes to assess the merits and limitations of realist explanations. She criticizes neorealism for citing hegemonic protection and says that it is neither necessary nor sufficient for any particular nuclear weapons decision (2007, 27). Solingen seems to accept these criteria and she repeats them in her summary, especially: *precise specification, falsifiability, simplicity, predictive accuracy,* and *empirical fit* (2007, 27). She adds that explanations in the realist tradition fail because "of underdetermination, incompleteness, lack of parsimony," and an inability to eliminate competing hypotheses (2007, 252).

In her discussion of constructivists' uses of norms to explain international cooperation and conflict, she says, "The theory must explain extensive departures from the norm in the Middle East but not in East Asia . . . [and] must be able to explain regional anomalies such as North Korea" (2007, 36). This appears to commit her to a *range/corroboration* criterion, at least implicitly, since she says that an adequate explanation must be able to account for national and regional variations in behavior. Solingen is clear that, in her view, a theorist is not permitted, on the basis of likely fit, to pick and choose the set of cases to which a theory will be said to apply. There must be a clear and theoretically driven statement of the domain that defines the extent and limit of the theory's application (as Waltz [1979] insists). If an explanatory account is applied to one region but there is an exception, and the exceptions are said to be outside the range of the theory, then there should be a sound theoretical or methodological reason why the theory is limited in that way. And if the theory is said to apply to one region but not to others, then there must also be a rationale for the limited applicability. Solingen also requires that explanations be judged in a *comparative* context; if one explanation appears adequate, it cannot be accepted until it has been compared to the competing existing explanations. She says, "Normative explanations have been used to explain Japan's 'nuclear allergy' but they compete with other accounts of the rationale for Japan's abstention," such as Japan's political motives (2007, 36).

Solingen's methodology involves restricting the cases so that she considers only those occurring after 1968, when the NPT had come into force. The NPT was not there to provide incentives for restraint for states going nuclear prior to 1968. The NPT certainly changed the way researchers might try to explain contemporary proliferation decisions, which is why this chapter looks at the post-1970 debate; this book's goal of identifying patterns of agreement would be undermined by treating as a single debate a period which had subperiods (e.g., pre- and post-NPT) in which the possible explanations were so clearly different. But Solingen's restriction to post-NPT cases is somewhat different and could beg a central question, namely, did the NPT have any influence on states' decisions? For her purposes the exclusion of the pre-NPT cases removes cases that could shed light on the process of going nuclear.[10] This is especially important given that Solingen endorses support for counterfactuals as a criterion because the overall number of cases of states going nuclear is quite small, and if there is some mixture of motives and forces operating, and if the earlier cases that were probably more clearly security driven are excluded, then there could be a problem of selection bias.

6. SCOTT SAGAN

Scott Sagan has written extensively on issues of nuclear proliferation. In addition to the widely read debate with Waltz on the benefits of nuclear proliferation (Sagan and Waltz 2003), Sagan has written influential papers seeking to explain horizontal proliferation, principally "Why Do States Build Nuclear Weapons?" (1996–97). That study considers the various works on proliferation "to assess whether they provide more or less compelling explanations for proliferation decisions" (1996–97, 63). But what does he mean by "compelling explanation"?

Sagan's paper "Why Do States Build Nuclear Weapons?" offers one of the most influential critiques of the realist, security-based explanation. He does not dismiss realism, but rather argues that it must be supplemented, because there are many cases it cannot explain. Sagan argues that, for both theoretical and policy purposes, it is just as important to examine restraint decisions, since a focus on acquisition decisions biases case selection and thus produces misleading conclusions. Sagan examines the security "model" to explain nuclear proliferation and restraint. But because of gaps in its explanatory range, he considers also two alternatives, which he calls the domestic politics and norms models.

The Security Explanation

The first of the three explanations Sagan considers, what he calls "the security model," had been the most widely accepted account of states' motivation to acquire nuclear weapons. During World War II all states pursuing nuclear weapons did so knowing that their enemies were doing likewise and that whoever succeeded first might well win the war because of that success. They hoped that nuclear weapons could compel an enemy to cease military operations and surrender. Thereafter, as long as the nuclear weapons were maintained in a secure basing mode, the arsenal would be able to deter attacks on the state's territory by nuclear and conventional forces. Under the security model, states' nuclear arsenals deter other states from attacking by virtue of the threat of nuclear retaliation.

Another purpose for acquiring nuclear weapons might be to compel an adversary to stop doing something it is already doing. This goes well beyond simply deterring the adversary from doing something it has not yet done. According to this analysis, states are seen as acting rationally and calculating what is in their best interest (see Schelling 1963, 1966). The personal traits of the leaders, the strength or weakness of the governing parties, and the economic costs or incentives are deemed to be of less importance. States seek to gain as much as they can, especially when measured against the gains and losses of rival states.

The standard security explanation runs into problems with certain cases. South Africa sought nuclear weapons as it faced hostile neighbors, some of whom, in the 1970s, gained increased backing from the Soviet Union. Because South Africa saw the forces arrayed against it as overwhelming, one could argue that developing nuclear weapons to support a policy of deterrence-aided self-defense was very rational. By the end of the 1980s South Africa possessed an arsenal of several nuclear weapons. Just a few years later, by which time the Soviet Union no longer existed (and thus could not aid South Africa's rivals), South Africa publically declared that it would dismantle its arsenal. The security model, which treats the state as a rational unitary actor making decisions based on security factors, has been used to explain both the nuclear arming and disarming of South Africa. But, as outlined in this section, Sagan argues that it is inconsistent with the security explanation.

After the political and economic costs paid for nuclear acquisition, what incentives could a realist cite to explain South Africa's decision to decommission the arsenal? Superpowers had made negative security guarantees, that is, promises not to use nuclear weapons against nonnuclear states. But such guarantees are connected to the notion of a security regime, and thus do not fit well into the realist framework. Any attempt to create a regime explanation within a realist framework requires theoretical concessions to liberalism or constructivism so great that realist theory abandons its central principles.

According to Sagan, the NPT-based nonproliferation regime is seen as an institution "permitting non-nuclear states to overcome a collective action problem. Each state would prefer to become the only nuclear weapons power in its region, but since that is unlikely if it develops a nuclear arsenal, it is willing to refrain from proliferation if, and only if, its neighbors remain non-nuclear" (1996–97, 62). But the key condition is not met here, since it was quite plausible for South Africa to believe that it might succeed in remaining the only nuclear state in the region after the collapse of the Soviet Union, when no major power was willing to provide nuclear aid to its regional rivals.

Bureaucratic Politics and Domestic Politics

Sagan regards decision-making studies, rather than structural or functional analyses, as most effective in explaining why states build nuclear weapons. The emphasis shifts away from system-level explanations or functional explanations. He believes that progress is possible because of the extensive information available from within weapons-possessing states (1996–97, 54). The bureaucratic politics model treats bureaucracies as the relevant actors. But when the detailed studies are offered in the bureaucratic politics literature, as in Sagan's paper, the focus often moves to individuals whose interests are partly formed by the bureaucracies they inhabit (1996–97, 62–63).

The bureaucratic politics explanation envisions that because of the importance of such decisions, in actual cases the state's top political leader, rather than a cabinet or parliament, makes the final decision regarding if and when to acquire a nuclear weapons capability. This creates a somewhat different picture of the causal interactions of the process from what political scientists envision for military, economic, education, or other types of decisions.

Various individuals have the chance to shape the top leader's decision by making some options appear to have greater or lesser appeal (1996–97, 64). These individuals will have had their own views shaped by their education, career advancement aspirations, and backgrounds in a particular government bureau or industry. These beliefs are different from the sincere beliefs of others whose perceptions have been shaped by service in different bureaucracies. These individuals—in industry, the military, science, and political staffs—may work together to see a nuclear weapons agenda built or blocked. But the theory, as Sagan spells it out, holds that the individuals work as individuals and does not address how any specific bureaucracy or industry behaves in a particular way. Thus, ultimately, Sagan's bureaucratic model appears to be a first image, or methodologically individualist explanation.

Sagan comments that, on the bureaucratic politics account of proliferation, unlike the realist account, nuclear weapons are not solutions to some sort of objectively present external threat but are solutions looking for a problem (1996–97, 65). The idea that the reality of threats is subject to considerable interpretation is a significant departure from realism, so much so that some might support building nuclear weapons to deal with their image of the threat, whereas others oppose them as effective ways to deal with their alternative views of the threat.

Sagan argues that the bureaucratic and domestic politics model applies to South Africa, because the expectations that arise from that model are met, while those from the realist model are not. He says, "From the domestic model's perspective, one would expect that reversals of weapons decisions occur not when external threats are diminished, but rather when there are major internal changes" (1996–97, 69). While South African leaders cited the Cuban and Soviet involvement in Africa, especially in Angola, as justification for their nuclear program, the key decisions were made in 1971, four years before Cuba's involvement in Africa. The conditions holding at the time the decisions were made—both to go forward with the nuclear program and to terminate it—were tied to internal, not external, changes. Similarly, Sagan points out that Argentina and Brazil ceased their pursuit of nuclear weapons at points when there was no evident reduction in external threats—rather, they did so in the wake of Argentina *losing* a war to the nuclear-armed United Kingdom. Realists would not expect a retreat from nuclear weapons programs to be the likely reaction to such a loss. Pakistan went in the opposite direction after its 1971 defeat. There were, however, domestic political changes in both countries at that time (on this point, see also Solingen 1994, 2007).

Sagan argues that realist-grounded expectations do not fit with the timing of various key Indian decisions, especially the 1974 nuclear test, which occurred twelve years after losing a war with China and a decade after China's test. The Indian test came only three years after defeating and dismembering its second major rival, Pakistan, at which point India would seem to be more secure than ever before. Sagan notes the varied views of nuclear acquisition held by certain key figures in the nuclear establishment, especially leaders in India's Atomic Energy Commission. Moreover, a number of details surrounding the reaction to the test indicate that the decision was made in haste. Sagan shows that selected historical facts do not fit empirically with realist, security-driven expectations, but they do fit with the expectations derived from the bureaucratic and domestic politics models.

Symbols and Norms as Explanations

Sagan challenges the realist security explanation by offering not only the bureaucratic and domestic politics account but also the norms account. This explanation places much more emphasis on the power of norms, symbols, and ideas in influencing states' decisions about nuclear weapons, though it does not exclude a role for great power military pressure. The norms explanation emphasizes the positive or negative connotations that states throughout the international system associate with the acquisition of nuclear weapons.

According to the norms explanation, states make decisions based on leaders' beliefs about what is most appropriate to do, given their view of the identity of the state. Certain norms take hold in one or a few societies and then spread to many other societies. While sociologists find sociological mechanisms for the spread of these norms beyond individual states, political scientists stress the role of power in internationalizing the norms, via individuals or groups. If, by whichever process, a new norm takes hold in a great-power society, and if that norm, on an international level, would work to the material advantage of the great power(s), then the great power(s) may well use military means to enforce the norm throughout the system. For example, the United States and United Kingdom, which were highly industrialized and vigorous international traders, benefited materially from an absence of slavery. As a result, they used military force to help eradicate slavery globally. Norms that are advanced by the United States "can have a strong influence" on many states and "push others toward policies" that serve US interests (Sagan 1996–97, 82).

States sometimes make symbolic gestures. Symbols as well as norms have an effect on states' behavior. Leaders accept certain norms and value the symbolic effect of certain actions. The source of the leaders' beliefs about symbols is the education they receive about their world, though the content of those beliefs can change over time. The beliefs lead to actions that are not necessarily calculated to produce or maximize material gain. Leaders of very small states have sometimes supported forming national airlines or national science boards, even though, in such states, they may not be economically rational or efficient; however, they add prestige that states regard as important for their identity.

The independent state of Ukraine was formed in the wake of the Soviet Union's huge losses of territory, resources, and population. In that context Ukraine was concerned about the threat posed by the nervous and unhappy leaders of Russia, the successor state to the Soviet Union. Most neighboring states worried that Russia might try to regain some of what it had just lost. The strategic calculations of the security model are inconsistent with the heightened threat that Russia posed to Ukraine, and the operation of the bureaucratic model's key factors are inconsistent with the facts that Ukraine's then president Leonid Kuchma had risen through a career in the Soviet rocket industry and opinion polls in Ukraine showed rapidly growing public support for maintaining nuclear weapons. Ukraine's foremost goal at the time was to be recognized as a sovereign state, which required that the world see it as clearly distinct from the status it had as a republic ruled by Moscow. Since Russia was taking over many of the Soviet Union's obligations and responsibilities, including its membership in the NPT as a nuclear state, Ukraine saw that if it were to become a signatory to the NPT as a nonnuclear state, there would be an unmistakable legal divide between itself and Russia. This overriding desire led to decisions that were not optimal from a strict military power standpoint, such as denuclearization.

The role of norms has been highlighted by "new institutionalist" sociologists (Suchman and Eyre 1992; Finnemore 1993; Ramirez and Boli 1982), who "emphasize the importance of roles, routines and rituals: individuals and organizations may well have 'interests,' but such interests are shaped by the social roles actors are asked to play" (Sagan 1996–97, 74). Ukraine's decision to give up the nuclear arsenal it inherited when it separated from the Soviet Union is best explained by norms and symbols. The decision was driven by symbolism and international norms rather than by security or internal politics. In the first two decades after World War II nuclear weapons acquisition was a symbol of great power status and military power. New nuclear states would join the elite great-power "nuclear club." However, over the quarter century after its inception, the NPT exerted an influence that gradually reversed the character of the nuclear norms; the NPT "created a history in which the most recent examples of new or potential nuclear states were so-called 'rogue states' such as North Korea, Iran and Iraq" (Sagan 1996–97, 81). By the 1990s the pursuit of nuclear weapons took on a different symbolic character, connoting international "roguery" rather than scientific accomplishment. States that sought nuclear status in the 1990s joined the club of new aspirants whose membership included Iraq, Libya, and North Korea.

Criteria for Explanatory Adequacy

The criteria Sagan cites for evaluating an explanation are conformity with past cases and consistency with principles of the theory. He regards an explanation as doubtful if it fails to "stand up . . . against either existing evidence or logic" (1996–97, 77). In the case of the French decision to go nuclear, both the security explanation and the bureaucratic politics explanation fail to satisfy these criteria. The timing of the key decisions preceded the events that are typically used to explain France's growing insecurity, especially the post-Suez fear of the United States as an unreliable ally. Further doubt is shed on the security explanation by observing that many other technologically capable industrial states in Western Europe did not build nuclear weapons, even though, unlike France, they had greater geographic vulnerabilities and lacked a superpower ally.

Sagan sees a "stronger explanation" in the norms account (1996–97, 77). Based on evidence from the public pronouncements of political leaders, including President de Gaulle, the proper conclusion is that the driving force was the goal of regaining French *grandeur*. Again, anomalies in the other explanations are solved by invoking the norms explanation, since "a number of puzzling aspects of the history of French atomic policy become more understandable" (1996–97, 77). This invokes the criterion of *imparting understanding*. Sagan, like other political scientists, regards the French policy of "proportional deterrence" not as strategically sound, but rather as a justification for nuclear acquisition that was driven by symbolic concerns. Sagan's abbreviated analysis of Ukraine's decision favors the norms explanation because it is the only one of the three models that does not produce anomalies. It is thus superior based on the criterion of empirical adequacy.

Since the dominant explanation for proliferation in political science literature and in popular discussion is security, Sagan's strategy is to show that the approach does not explain all recent cases of proliferation and restraint. Realists say that each country that has developed nuclear weapons since World War II has had a nuclear-armed rival. But Sagan tries to discredit realism on grounds of empirical adequacy by looking not only at the fact that a particular country made the decision to go nuclear but also at the timing of the decision, and then contrasting it with changes in the level of threat and the nuclear infrastructure capability. He argues that, if security had really been the overriding factor, some of the states would have built nuclear weapons much earlier, notably India—or later, notably France. The argument invokes not only *empirical adequacy* but also the criteria of *mechanisms, simplicity,* and *support of counterfactuals.* He accepts the criterion of falsifiability, evident in his criticisms of several explanations. Ultimately, Sagan's resort to multiple models relies heavily on fit with historical cases as a criterion of explanatory success. Sagan's more complex set of models also seeks depth of causes.

7. T. V. PAUL

T. V. Paul is an important contributor to debates on nuclear proliferation, IR, and Indian foreign policy. His book *Power Versus Prudence* (2000) deals directly with the question of nuclear proliferation—both acquisition and especially restraint. It focuses on state decisions to resist nuclear weapons acquisition, to halt nuclear programs once begun, and to dismantle existing arsenals. Paul contrasts the restraint and denuclearization cases to three recent acquisition decisions. In a subsequent paper, Paul (2003) examines states' restraint and the survival and expansion of the nonproliferation regime amid major structural change in the international system.

Paul's book is aimed at explaining the nuclear decisions of states that have the scientific and technological capability of developing nuclear weapons but which are mid-level regional, not global, powers. Mid-level regional powers of this sort are the most likely near-term proliferation candidates. His strategy is to compare four pairs of restraint states, in which members of each pair are similar to one another in significant ways. He examines two "aligned" major economic powers, Germany and Japan; two aligned middle powers, Canada and Australia; two neutrals, Sweden and Switzerland; and two nonaligned states, Argentina and Brazil. Paul offers neither a distinction between *neutral* and *nonaligned* nor guidelines for the other classification decisions.

Paul's "Prudential Realist" Theory

In the 2000 book *Power Versus Prudence* Paul aims to explain the nuclear patterns by means of his theory of prudential realism. Standard realist theory does not work well with states that could build nuclear weapons but have not, and especially for the scores of states that have signed and abided by the NPT. Similarly, certain liberal theories work well for cases where realism fails, but fail for states that have developed nuclear programs and have chosen to ignore international norms and to avoid institutions. Paul explicitly rejects accounts that invoke bureaucratic and organizational politics, symbols, norms, culture, and traits of individual decision makers (2000, 26); such factors can accelerate or decelerate a nuclear program but cannot lead to a decision to go nuclear in the absence of the principal variables.

Paul uses variables drawn from both liberalism and "hard realism," and the additional variable of level of regional conflict. This variable tells us when to expect military security considerations to drive states' behavior and when to expect regime norms and reciprocal cooperative advantages to drive behavior. He argues that patterns of proliferation and restraint depend upon whether a state is in a region of high, medium, or low conflict. The dynamics of geographical regions involve regularized interactions in which states' security concerns are mutually linked; national security decisions require that one state take into account the concerns of neighboring states. Measurement of the conflict level in a region will involve various indicators, such as "severity, intensity, duration, and scope of conflicts involving key states" (2000, 19). Western Europe is a region of low conflict, whereas the Middle East and East Asia are regions of high conflict. Weapons "choices are largely a function of a state's security environment" (2000, 33). In regions of low conflict there are typically lower-level security threats and more economic interdependence. As a result, the gains from acquiring nuclear weapons are small and the costs of violating norms, like that of nonproliferation, are high because of greater economic vulnerabilities. States in regions of low or medium conflict usually recognize that neighboring states will view nuclear acquisition as threatening. This can stimulate arms escalation, possibly including other states' acquisition of nuclear weapons, which thus unintentionally undercuts the state's security.

Paul considers two other factors that may explain states' nuclear forbearance or acquisition decisions: enduring rivalry (Goertz and Diehl 1993) and alliance with a great power. The former can spur a nuclear acquisition decision that would not otherwise be expected, and the latter might spur restraint in a zone of medium or high conflict, where "worst-case planning" usually predominates. For example, during the Cold War, neither North Korea nor South Korea developed its own national nuclear force because an attack on either by the other would very likely bring about a powerful retaliatory response by the victim's superpower ally. Thus, according to Paul, even a state in a region of high conflict with an enduring rival might not need nuclear weapons to be secure.

Domestic Politics

Paul's book appeared in the wake of the widely influential papers by Solingen and Sagan that explain proliferation on nonsecurity grounds, especially bureaucratic politics, symbols and norms, and economic growth strategies. Paul acknowledges in his chapter "Non-Aligned States" that domestic politics played a larger role in the cases of Argentina and Brazil than in other states. He says that these two cases "present significant theoretical and policy puzzles" (2000, 99). However, even a careful examination of Paul's discussion of Argentina yields a less clear-cut conclusion; the events Paul cites suggest a major role for domestic politics. In the 1970s both Argentina and Brazil were moving forward with nuclear programs that were seen by one another, and by much of the rest of the world, as having military aims. And Paul makes a strong case both for the low conflict level in South America and for the interactions between the two rivals and the effects each had on the other. Both eventually halted weapons-related work and renounced the goal of acquiring nuclear weapons. Perhaps the most important change in Argentina that led to the policy reversal was the transition from the military to civilian government. The domestic political "regime-type" appeared to be central to the nuclear reorientation. There were many steps in the process of change, including many bilateral summits, which began under Argentina's military junta but accelerated after the civilian government began to reorient its economic and security priorities.

Paul occasionally falls back on exogenous factors that might drive nuclear arms decisions. He talks of the sort of foreign policy orientation that leaders choose. This does not fit consistently with his otherwise parsimonious theory. For example, Paul mentions several developments that could lead Japan to acquire nuclear weapons, some of which follow from his model (e.g., intensified rivalries with China or other regional states). But he then adds that Japan might become a nuclear weapons state "if Japan decides to become a great military power concomitant with its economic clout" (2000, 145). Thus, the process that would lead to the acquisition of nuclear weapons has nothing to do with the explanation developed throughout the monograph. Similarly, in the difficult cases of Argentina and Brazil, Paul says, "Brazil's ending of its historic ambition to become a great military power . . . also seems to have influenced its decision to forgo nuclear weapons" (2000, 146). Again, if an internal decision of this sort is a major factor in whether states acquire nuclear weapons, his framework would appear to be unnecessary, or at best only a part of the appropriate framework.

Causation

In Paul's theory the causal relationships hold between states, as opposed to between individuals or subnational groups. States calculate what is and what is not in their best interest. There are passages in which Paul regards domestic politics as having had an effect, as just noted, for example, in the case of Brazil (2000, 107–9). But overwhelmingly Paul sees states as acting *rationally* and leaders as looking at what is best for the state by balancing security needs against the desire for economic growth: "Decision-makers in the states that forgo nuclear arms calculate that they can achieve security by eschewing the same weapons that otherwise could provide defense or deterrence" (2000, 15). After describing the decision-making processes in the three newest nuclear-armed states, Paul supports the rational-calculation explanation by stressing that both left-wing and right-wing governments proceeded in the same ways. Sweden and Switzerland made decisions that resulted from "a conscious cost-benefit analysis and the belief that nuclearization might upset their neutrality," as well as their "benign strategic environment" (2000, 97). The unit of analysis is the state; states act rationally to maximize their interests.

Paul's central use of the notion of regional dynamics also commits him to a structural framework, which would presumably include the NPT regime after 1970. In Paul's framework, structural factors have causal influence. It "was American power and diplomacy [rather than the NPT] that put a temporary lid on the nuclear activities" of the most determined NPT violators (2000, 29). While Paul attributes some legitimacy to liberal IR theories, as noted earlier, he sees the NPT only as a "facilitator" (2000, 163n35), not as a determinant or cause (2000, 28) of the outcomes. The distinction is never explained beyond the statement that the NPT "becomes more important once a state chooses a non-nuclear policy, as it provides assurances of similar behaviour by other states" (2000, 28).

Regimes

In his paper "Systemic Conditions and Security Cooperation: Explaining the Persistence of the Nuclear Non-Proliferation Regime," published three years after *Power Versus Prudence*, Paul (2003) attempts to explain the longevity of the NPT regime with a third-image approach that builds upon Jervis's (1982) structural theory presented in his paper "Security Regimes." For Jervis, security regimes arise when major powers desire them, when states believe that others seek mutual security, or when all states agree that expansion does not produce security and agree that war is costly. Paul finds that the NPT regime, unlike most other international regimes, deals with security. The survival and expansion of the regime, despite serious inequalities, pose a challenge to existing theories of international security. It is interesting to note that Paul (2003, 138) says, "I develop an argument, based on classical realist conceptions of systems, national roles and interests, that posits that security regimes and their norms do matter to varying degrees." He attempts to explain where "the initial impetus for a sovereignty-sacrificing and unequal security regime come[s] from" and why it has been able to endure (2003, 137). Since Paul sees liberal and realist explanations as each accounting for only parts of the proliferation puzzle, he believes that his alternative *unifies* the field.

At times *Power Versus Prudence* presents a necessary condition analysis. For example, the book considers hard realist objections to any theory purporting to explain nuclear restraint—objections according to which the predicted acquisition of nuclear weapons by certain states may simply have not yet occurred (see Tetlock 2005, 9). Paul (2000, 154) replies that the cases of restraint may turn into cases of acquisition "only when a zone of low or medium conflict becomes one of high conflict and when states in such a region lose the protection of their allies." But the understanding of causality in the book goes beyond necessary conditions in that Paul wants to show that his analysis fits with the record of states that do not acquire nuclear weapons, as well as with those that do. Explaining India's or Israel's decision to acquire nuclear weapons requires more than showing that the necessary conditions were present; all technologically advanced states that lack the protection of a great-power alliance in high-conflict regions satisfy the necessary conditions—yet only these two built nuclear weapons.

There is also a question of whether the case studies offer varying degrees of support for Paul's theory, or if all consistent cases add equal weight. At times Paul lauds his theory because cases are consistent with it, but at times he seems to have a form of support that goes beyond mere consistency. For example, he says that South Africa, Ukraine, and South Korea are "consistent with" his model, but later on the same page he says that the three recent acquisition decisions (India, Israel and Pakistan) "strongly uphold" the model (Paul 2000, 146). It is not clear from the context whether these are different ways in which cases relate to and provide evidence for a theory.

Explanatory Criteria

Paul's research design is aimed at examining different types of states, such as aligned and nonaligned, neutral and nonneutral, developed and less developed, and great and smaller powers. As is the case with most other security studies authors, the arguments Paul offers implicitly endorse his criteria. The most important criterion appears to be a theory's *empirical fit* with the greatest number of cases. Paul regards the goal of *unifying* the heretofore-diverse observations as a major achievement of his theory, and as a principal reason his theory is superior to its chief rivals, hard realism and liberal institutionalism. Paul uses the "level of regional conflict" to unify both of the chief theoretical approaches. He argues that each theory works well with a part of the empirical record. Paul establishes causation at a number of points by implicitly invoking the criterion of *support of counterfactuals* (2000, 16, 90, 145). Paul believes his theory is superior because it fits with both the empirical record and a *greater range* of cases.

8. SONALI SINGH AND CHRISTOPHER WAY, AND QUANTITATIVE TESTS

Many security studies debates are heavily infused with statistical arguments, as evidenced by the debates over alliance formation (Chapter 4), democratic peace (Chapter 5), polarity and system stability, extended deterrence, and many others. The debate over nuclear proliferation has not followed that pattern, primarily because the small number of states that have acquired nuclear weapons is not enough to support statistical tests. Sonali Singh and Christopher Way (2004) are among the few to offer a research design that allows a quantitative approach. They cite only Kegley, Raymond, and Skinner (1980) and Meyer (1984) as predecessors.

Singh and Way (2004, 881) note that there is no consensus among the "abundance of explanations for proliferation decisions." One reason for the lack of consensus is, in their view, the mismatch between the use of "probabilistic claims and . . . multiple causal variables" (2004, 881) and the case-study methodology that dominates, since case studies "implicitly apply deterministic standards based on an (often implicit) univariate logic of inference and samples on the dependent variable" (2004, 881).

Research Design

Singh and Way believe that policy makers and scholars who desire to explain nuclear proliferation should pay attention to various earlier points in the weapons development process and not just the nuclear detonation stage. Their research design considers the condition of "no noticeable interest in nuclear weapons," and three stages of pursuit: "serious exploration of the weapons option, launch of a weapons program, and acquisition of nuclear weapons" (2004, 861). They also contrast "non-pursuit." Beyond complete nuclear restraint, there are thus three values for the dependent variable.

The authors test the models for each of the values for the dependent variable just noted. The database for the models includes 154 countries; each is examined for crossing the threshold from one stage of proliferation to the next. However, a country is placed back into the pool if it reverses course and moves to a lower level, such as by ceasing to consider a nuclear weapons program (e.g., Sweden), by abandoning an active nuclear weapons program (e.g., Libya, Iraq), or by dismantling its weapons (e.g., South Africa, Ukraine).

All possessors of nuclear weapons have in fact acquired the weapons by means of their own programs; none purchased weapons outright, which would have entailed skipping stages. This contingent fact eliminates one possible research design problem of using "stages." However, Singh and Way recognize that a state may reach full weapons possession stage without a nuclear test detonation, which is the traditional indicator of nuclear status. Israel, Pakistan, and South Africa presumably had usable nuclear arsenals before they conducted any tests. In coding country-year cases, the authors used the dates of acquisition rather than testing for those three states. Furthermore, by considering cases of states that increase proliferation efforts and those that do not, Singh and Way avoid the common error of case selection bias. Their research design allows them to see what is different between states that do and do not proliferate.

Because most of the time no states are crossing any proliferation thresholds, any research design must take account of the fact that rare events are the subject. They must also note not only that thresholds are crossed but also just at the point when they are, which requires examining chronologies of internal and external developments. And the values of the variables may change over time. The authors prefer a "survival" model, which indicates for each year the "risk" that a country will move to a new level of proliferation. However, they also assess the reliability of the event-history results by running multinomial logistic regression models, which are more appropriate when there is an outcome that has several possible values and when one wishes "to assess the contingent nature of successive steps along the proliferation path" (2004, 877). The results are generally consistent with the initial survival or hazard models.

Independent Variables

The authors test variables associated with three kinds of explanation of nuclear weapons decisions: technological, external threat, and internal dynamics. Each explanation type includes several particular explanatory variables. The technological argument holds that once a state reaches a stage of development of economic prosperity, literacy levels, and scientific development, it will possess the latent capacity to go nuclear. As the state continues to advance in these areas and as the costs of nuclear programs proportionally decline, the temptation to go nuclear will become too great to resist. Singh and Way say that the latent capacity at least serves as a necessary, though not sufficient, condition for weapons acquisition (2004, 862–63). The variables included in this explanation are per capita gross domestic product (GDP); industrial capacity index; and energy, electricity, and steel production and consumption.

External factors have been emphasized by many scholars, particularly realists in IR. But, as noted, Singh and Way point out that previous studies frequently focus only on states that possess nuclear weapons and examine threat and other factors that led to proliferation decisions. States have different levels of intensity of rivalry with others and different frequency of involvement in militarized disputes. Nevertheless, it may be that some states with high threat levels go nuclear while others with similar threat levels do not. The presence of a clear external threat could be offset by an alliance with a major power, especially with nuclear weapons. Moreover, such an ally may be more significant in a bipolar system, as some have argued, and lessened in a multipolar system. The variables included in external explanations are enduring rivalry, frequency of dispute involvement, and security guarantee.

Domestic-level political and economic factors have more recently become popular in explanations of nuclear proliferation, mainly because of the work of

Solingen and Sagan. Furthermore, various scholars have argued that proliferation patterns are affected by whether a regime is democratic (see Chapter 5); is inward or outward directed (Solingen 2007); is in transition to democracy (Mansfield and Snyder, 1995a, 1995b, 2005); and has elite groups able, for parochial reasons, to push for nuclear weapons development. To investigate these various domestic-level explanations, Singh and Way look at democracy and democratization, economic interdependence and liberalization, and status inconsistency and symbolic motivations.

Results

Singh and Way ran tests for all three values of the dependent variable, fully aware that there might well be different factors that explain each of the three stages through which nuclear proliferators pass, described earlier. According to their interpretation of the hazard model analysis, explanations of stage escalation based on (external) security and (internal) technology are successful, and others are not. On the domestic side, the economic factors played a greater role than the political factors. The independent effect of participation in a rivalry produced a nearly fourfold increase in the probability that a state would explore the nuclear option, and more than a sevenfold increase in the likelihood that a state would acquire nuclear weapons (eight of the ten states that acquired nuclear weapons were involved in enduring rivalries at the time of acquisition). An increase of two in the number of militarized interstate disputes (in a five-year moving average) increased the chances by nearly 40 percent that a state would explore the nuclear option and by more than 50 percent that it would acquire nuclear weapons. And the presence of a great-power ally would decrease the chance of exploring the nuclear option by nearly 50 percent and decrease the chance of acquiring nuclear weapons by more than 60 percent.

For the technological explanation, the results showed that a basic threshold of technology was important for a state to consider the nuclear option and develop a nuclear weapons program. But further advancement of the technological development *decreases* the likelihood of a state actually acquiring nuclear weapons. For weapons acquisition, industrial capacity is an important factor, while other economic factors, especially per capita GDP, are not important; the Soviet Union, China, India, and Pakistan had low per capita wealth when they became nuclear weapons states. A poor country that increases its per capita GDP by US$500 increases the chance of exploring a nuclear weapons program by 26 percent and the chance of acquiring nuclear weapons by 12 percent. An equivalent increase in per capita GDP in a wealthy country moves in the opposite direction; it decreases the chance of exploring nuclear weapons and of acquiring them by between 17 percent and 20 percent. An increase in trade openness substantially decreases the chance of exploring the nuclear option but has only a small negative effect on a state acquiring nuclear weapons. On Singh and Way's scale, a 20 percent increase in trade openness decreases the chance of exploring by 72 percent and decreases the chance of acquiring by 2 percent. The level of satisfaction with the leading regional or global state does not have a significant effect.

The results of the multinomial logistic regressions, as indicated already, are similar to the results of the hazard models. They show that the security and technology explanations have a good deal of value. The economic development variables continue to have effects on consideration, program institution, and acquisition, and the results have both substantive and statistical significance. The major difference between the results of the hazard models and those of the multinomial logistic regression models is that the latter indicate a greater effect of the domestic-level factors (2004, 878–79).

Singh and Way's analysis shows that security threats drive states to develop nuclear arsenals. So, the main policy conclusion they draw is that leaders should refrain from threats to potential proliferators, since hostile behavior toward potential proliferators greatly increases the chances of their proceeding to higher stages of nuclear development.

Causation

Singh and Way often use explanatory language that conveys a causal sense, such as the statement, "Enduring rivalries are powerful spurs" (2004, 875). Clearly, a "spur" is a factor that is not merely associated with an outcome but also has the power to help bring it about. Singh and Way frequently use the term *determinants* of nuclear proliferation, which carries a connotation of determinism. They use phrases like "much of a state's behavior is determined by shared beliefs and norms" (2004, 865). However, they specifically reject deterministic accounts; the arguments in the existing literature, which they interpret in ways that they can test, provide *probabilistic* hypotheses (2004, 860–61). Singh and Way, either implicitly or explicitly, treat explanations of proliferation as probabilistic, as they identify incentives and tendencies rather than deterministic forces. They argue that quantitative models give a more appropriate probabilistic perspective of the explanatory factors and offer a more transparent view of the multiple causes that may be at work in proliferation decisions.

Explanation and Criteria

Singh and Way note that the economic explanations of Solingen (1994, 2007) and Paul (2000) seem to be supported by the results of their tests. Yet they distinguish *correlation* and *causation*, stating, "The causal linkage remains somewhat opaque and unpersuasive" (2004, 882). Hence the statistical finding is not enough to show causation; *mechanisms* are also required. They seem to accept that even when the values for some of the variables are low, a high enough value for others can produce a proliferation outcome. (This is a bit puzzling because earlier they seemed to conclude that a threshold of economic development was a necessary condition for proliferation.) On this basis, they project into the future when they argue that Syria is a "strong candidate" for proliferation despite its low level of economic development. They conclude that one explanation is better if the methodology fits the nature of the claims made; and to the extent that criteria of good explanations are evident, they are tied closely to higher measures and significance on the statistical tests one may perform.[11] And Singh and Way are interested in finding the "best guide to understanding decisions to go nuclear" (2004, 860). The sort of empirically supported, probabalistic, explanatory causal model that Singh and Way defend is quite clear. Thus, an explanation should *impart understanding*. In terms of the other criteria discussed by philosophers of science, they appear to rely on statistically grounded *empirical fit*, and the identification of *mechanisms*.

9. JACQUES HYMANS'S INDIVIDUALIST MODEL

Jacques Hymans has written several works drawing on individual psychological variables to explain states' nuclear weapons decisions. In his book *The Psychology of Nuclear Proliferation*, Hymans offers a theory of what he calls "revolutionary" foreign policy decisions (2006, 13–14), decisions in which the ramifications and consequences are substantial but very unpredictable. These decisions are rare and based on little or no solid information about consequences, for which reason leaders fall back on deep-seated, and essentially unfalsifiable, beliefs about world politics (2006, 14).

Hymans is interested in explaining both acquisition and restraint decisions. This requires attention to the huge gap between the many states technologically capable of pursuing nuclear weapons programs and the few that have done so. While only nine states have tested and currently possess nuclear weapons, and only two or three others have active weapons programs, more than a quarter of all the states in the world today have the scientific-technological base to begin a weapons program. Hymans agrees with Sagan that the security model is inadequate, and with Solingen that constructivist and liberal regime explanations do not suffice, but he disagrees with both Sagan's and Solingen's alternatives.

Hymans disputes claims that the NPT regime has led various states to refrain from going nuclear. He says that the NPT explanation holds only if it can be shown that many states capable but currently without nuclear weapons today would have pursued such programs in the absence of the NPT. Here he relies on *counterfactual reasoning*. But Hymans points out that even when the NPT was signed, the gap between those that could initiate programs and those that had done so was nearly as great as it is today, since there were in 1970 already more than forty states that had the technological base to begin a weapons program. Furthermore, the states that have pursued nuclear weapons are not restricted to irresponsible international rogues: two of the last three states to conduct their first nuclear test were India and Pakistan, both of which are active international citizens, participate in many international institutions, and contribute quite significantly to many UN peacekeeping forces.

Hymans says that a good answer to the proliferation question requires an "explicit, theoretical account of the *demand* for nuclear weapons" (2006, 8). He says that Sagan's "brilliant theoretical synthesis" nevertheless fails to answer questions about why so many states that have the physical and scientific means to build nuclear weapons do not do so because he focuses on the three "utterly quotidian motivations . . . [and thereby] deepens the puzzle" (2006, 8–9). Hymans argues that because the decision to acquire nuclear weapons is so consequential "on every level of politics," and because the effects are so hard to predict, the choice, unlike most other foreign policy decisions, is a very difficult one for states to make (2006, 11). For this reason, "the standard menu of motivations for foreign policy choice is insufficient" (2006, 10). Hymans thus argues (1) that his answers will apparently continue to be "motivations" rather than structural causes, such as at the state or system levels, and (2) that the puzzle of why some of the capable states choose to build nuclear weapons must be intimately connected to the question of why so many more capable states refrain from doing so. In this way, the questions of nuclear acquisition and restraint are not separate.

Hymans follows Alexander George, Robert Jervis, Philip Tetlock, and others in using individual psychological factors to explain important aspects of world politics. Hymans's account is unique in making use of leaders' general views of their states' statuses in the world, which is the "national identity conception" (NIC). The NIC comprises how much confidence leaders have in their nations (i.e., pride) and their sense of the magnitude of the threats their states face (i.e., fear). The emphasis on pride and fear entails a focus on leaders' *emotional* compositions rather than purely *rational* bases for their decisions, thereby rejecting rational choice analyses.

The NIC definition draws on two distinctions. The first separates "oppositionalist" leaders, who see their own state and its rivals as interacting through pure competition, from "sportsmanlike" leaders, who view the relationship as moderated by a context of norms and rules of behavior. The second distinction separates "nationalist" leaders, who regard the state as equal or superior to the chief rival(s), from "subalterns," who regard the state as inferior to its chief rival(s).[12] The nationalist dimension has to do with "how high 'we' stand relative to 'them' in the international pecking order: are we naturally their equal, or even their superior, or will we never measure up?" (2006, 24). Nationalists are those who have high self-esteem, whereas subalterns may enjoy "the trappings of independent statehood, [but] typically still express a negative national self-image" (2006, 25).

The two distinctions yield a two-by-two matrix of leaders' conceptions of their nations, which frames the central conclusion of the book: of the four possible types of leader, only "opposition nationalists" take the state across the nuclear weapons threshold. Subaltern leaders, whether oppositionalist or sportsmanlike, would not regard their states as having the ability or right to develop advanced nuclear technology. And sportsmanlike nationalists may believe that their states have the capability and right to develop nuclear technology but would not likely be inclined to go ahead with weaponization.

The NIC conceptions can vary from one leader to another in the same country—for example, in 1981 the conception of the president of the United States changed with the transition from Jimmy Carter to Ronald Reagan, and a leader may see the rivalry with one state differently than he or she sees it with another. An Indian leader may feel that India is superior to Pakistan but inferior to China. This would put the same leader in different cells at the same time.

Although Hymans says that these psychological conditions drive nuclear decisions, he nevertheless also makes use of another factor: politically weak governments in democratic states. His analysis of France includes the claim that leaders in weak coalitions could not make long-term decisions, since they had to focus on short-term goals and projects. This constitutes an additional independent factor. Hymans himself raises this as a possible objection to the monocausal approach he takes. But since he does so only in the final three paragraphs of the book, there is no chance to deal with it in any substantive way. Indeed, earlier passages suggest that he is using political structure and domestic political power configurations as another variable. Australia is another example in which Hymans invokes an additional variable. Prime Minister John Gorton, whom Hymans analyzes as oppositional nationalist (2006, 57–63), did not decide to develop nuclear weapons because of the political weakness of his position during the time he held office. At one point, Hymans recognizes this, calling it a "surprise" for his theory and a "partial success for the theory" (2006, 133). But it is hard to see how it is a success. He recognizes that further theoretical refinement is needed.

Defining the Outcome to Be Explained

What is the precise type of event that Hymans wants to explain? He says that it is the crucial decision to become a nuclear weapons possessor, which is taken well before any test is authorized or conducted. He says, "The top-down political decision to go nuclear is the most significant, and indeed unavoidable, step along the way to the acquisition of nuclear weapons" (2006, 44). Even if factors later intervene to prevent a test, the top-level decision to order a full nuclear weapons program is the fateful event. Hymans's subject is the order from the top leader.[13]

Hymans thus treats the definition of a "case" as relatively unproblematic, which is somewhat surprising, since many authors recognize the difficulty of identifying what should be regarded as the proper moment when the key decision is made to acquire nuclear weapons. At least into the 1960s it was easy to assume that until a state tested a weapon, it was not truly a nuclear-weapons-possessing state. Any state that had not conducted tests would not have enough confidence that the weapon would function in combat and that rivals would not reliably be deterred. No leader could assume that tests were the hallmark of access to a nuclear arsenal once it became clear that Israel and later Pakistan had a stockpile of weapons or ready-to-assemble components available, even though they had not conducted tests (though Pakistan did eventually test in 1998). So the simple demarcation criterion of testing was no longer applicable. Then it seemed to many experts that some states had developed technologies that, even though they might not have had nuclear weapons components ready to assemble, they could, with relatively little notice, take the last step in development of nuclear weapons. In some contexts, in international crises, states like Pakistan (in the years before it tested) and Israel would have the same advantages of threat and deterrence as states that had nuclear arsenals that had been tested.[14]

Explanation and Causation

Hymans believes that there is a single correct explanation of the proliferation decisions of states. He says that the right research design will help "to sort out the *real explanation* for the ultimate outcome from the pretenders" (2006, 12, emphasis added). That explanation will tell us about multiple aspects of the outcome, since a good explanation will answer questions not only of why but also of when and how (2006, 12). Hymans does see his own account as *causal.* Some argue that motivations and reasons do not qualify as causes in the proper sense. This issue does not arise with Hymans, who clearly refers to his own "causal argument about decisions to go nuclear" (2006, 18). Hymans describes his preferred factor, leaders' NIC, as a "driving" force and not merely as reducing other options. Hymans clearly distinguishes his theory from those that focus on leaders' frameworks by producing a logic of appropriateness; the explanatory variables of the latter eliminate various theoretically possible options as inappropriate for a particular situation but are not causally efficacious enough to drive a leader to a particular decision (2006, 18–19).

Criteria of Choice

Hymans's goal is to provide an explanation of past cases that is superior to the most widely discussed existing accounts. He offers an alternative whose principles provide an understanding of why a state would act in the way that it does and whose implications accord with past observations better than others, and thus is superior on grounds of *empirical adequacy.* In comparing his explanation to Sagan's, Hymans argues that the reader would not be able to tell when each of Sagan's three models would be expected to apply to a case of proliferation or restraint, which undercuts the *falsifiability* of Sagan's account.

The claim that there is one trait of a leader that explains proliferation and restraint decisions shows that Hymans regards the *simplicity* of his explanation as one of its strengths. For Hymans, leaders' beliefs are causes and the deeper beliefs are causal in a *deeper* way. And we noted that Hymans believes uses *counterfactual support* as a reason why his explanation of restraint is superior to those based on the NPT regime. Hymans also holds that the NIC constitutes a genuine causal *mechanism* for states moving toward, or resisting the move toward, possessing nuclear weapons.

10. DONG-JOON JO AND ERIK GARTZKE ON STATISTICAL ANALYSIS

Another of the relatively rare quantitative studies of nuclear weapons proliferation is the paper "Determinants of Nuclear Weapons Proliferation" by Dong-Joon Jo and Erik Gartzke (2007). Jo and Gartzke claim to offer more than prior studies in that they seek to "evaluate a variety of explanations in two stages of nuclear proliferation, the presence of nuclear weapons production programs and the actual possession of nuclear weapons" (2007, 168). They use "data collected . . . on national latent nuclear weapons production capability and several other variables, while controlling for the conditionality of nuclear weapons possession based on the presence of a nuclear weapons program" (2007, 168). Their aim is to look at the differences in the factors that lead a state to develop a nuclear weapons program and to build nuclear weapons.[15]

Jo and Gartzke adopt an "opportunity" and "willingness" framework (Most and Starr 1989), which views actions as requiring both of those factors. Thus, any nuclear acquisition would require that a state be both materially capable of building such weapons and willing to shoulder international disapproval. A state's opportunity to build nuclear weapons involves at least three components: a technological base, access to fissile materials, and the basic economic capacity to afford the costs of a nuclear weapons program (Jo and Gartzke 2007, 170). Their willingness may be shaped by both domestic and international factors. To capture this notion, the authors consider various explanations that scholars have offered, including all three of Sagan's models.[16]

Variables Tested

Jo and Gartzke look at the period 1939–92 using a cross-section time-series analysis. Their cases are country-year, for example, Russia-1992. The authors test a wide array of independent variables corresponding to hypotheses in the literature. The opportunity-related variables are latent nuclear weapons production capability, economic capacity, and diffusion of nuclear weapons and technology.[17] The international variables relating to willingness are conventional nuclear vulnerability, nuclear threat faced, nuclear defense pact, and diplomatic isolation. The domestic willingness variables are domestic unrest and democracy. Variables related to norms are NPT membership and NPT system effects; and those related to status are major-power status and regional-power status.

For their dependent variables, Jo and Gartzke look at the existence of both a nuclear weapons program and a nuclear weapons arsenal. They employ the variables nuclear program years and nonnuclear years to help control for autocorrelation in the dependent variables. The former also helps to capture effects of bureaucratic politics and inertia (2007, 173). Their statistical test involves a probit analysis to predict the presence of a nuclear weapons production program, along with a "censored probit analysis" of the possession of nuclear weapons (2007, 175). Jo and Gartzke use two distinct variables, development of a nuclear weapons program and actual acquisition of weapons, because policies by major powers intended to dissuade proliferation might have turned out to be useful for one but not the other.

Jo and Gartzke argue that many authors' focus on domestic regime-type has led them to different explanations for proliferation (2007, 171). Some scholars have argued that autocratic rulers use proliferation to divert citizens from a focus on domestic problems, which implies that autocrats are more likely to develop nuclear weapons programs (Chubin 1994; Kincade 1995; Sheikh 1994). Others have claimed that democratic regimes are more likely to proliferate, because elected leaders need to have strong public support, and when support declines, they may calculate that a nuclear weapons project will excite the public (Snyder 2000; on India, Perkovich 1999, 404–24; on Pakistan, Nizamani 2000). Sagan and others have argued that a regime's effort to enhance its international status affects its desire for nuclear weapons, especially in the early post–World War II period. Katzenstein (1996) and Wendt (1999) have emphasized the antiproliferation effects of norms since the NPT entered into force.

Findings

Jo and Gartzke (2007) see considerable success with the opportunity independent variables in driving the creation of weapons programs. The power status variables are also important in connection with the acquisition of weapons. Security variables have an effect on weapons acquisition, given that there are weapons programs in place, but they prove much less effective in explaining the creation of nuclear programs. Norms have an important connection to the development of weapons programs but not for acquisition decisions. The variable of latent nuclear weapons production capability is associated only with developing a weapons program (and is significant), but it is not associated with acquisition of weapons. The variable of economic capacity does not seem to affect weapons programs but is associated with acquiring weapons and is significant (2007, 177).

The authors conclude that, unlike the opportunity variables, the willingness factors have similar effects on both nuclear programs and nuclear acquisition. The presence of a conventional threat increases both program initiation and weapons acquisition. The realist external-threat factors are significant, even if there is a nuclear-armed ally willing to defend the nonnuclear state. Nonnuclear states are not dissuaded, in a statistically significant and measurable way, from instituting nuclear weapons programs. In contrast, alliances with nuclear-weapons states do dissuade the nonnuclear states from moving ahead with acquisition of nuclear weapons. As Jo and Gartzke put it, "States that face rivals with nuclear weapons or nuclear programs tend to refrain from deepening nuclear proliferation. This finding supports the somewhat controversial arguments of proliferation 'optimists' that the fear of preventive war from nuclear rivals discourages the pursuit of proliferation" (Jo and Gartzke 2007, 176; see also Karl 1996; Sagan and Waltz 2003, 18–20).

The domestic politics variables produced some surprises. The domestic unrest variable did not affect either dependent variable; states apparently do not use nuclear programs to divert attention from domestic ills (Jo and Gartzke 2007, 179). And democracies are not more likely to institute weapons programs. Although, if a democracy has a weapons program, it is more likely than a nondemocracy to acquire weapons. Especially surprising is that diplomatic isolation does not have an effect on either instituting a nuclear weapons program or acquiring weapons (2007, 177).

Jo and Gartzke do not see the norms explanation as well supported by the models. While they find that NPT membership decreases the chance of a state instituting a nuclear weapons program, they do not attribute causality here, arguing that it may be that states lacking a preference for weapons are most likely to join the NPT (2007, 180). And the "system effect" of the creation of the NPT regime does not coincide with a decrease in weapons proliferation. Their result "indicates that the NPT has not curbed proliferation incentives since the 1970s" (2007, 180). Both variables of major-power status and regional-power status increase the chances of a state instituting a weapons program and of acquiring nuclear weapons. But the authors say that the explanation may be a result of either "realist or identity theories" (2007, 179). Thus, they make use of the *precision* criterion, in that they prefer an explanation that can be shown to eliminate alternative explanations.

Jo and Gartzke's research design, especially the inclusion of temporal variables, allows for the evaluation of bureaucratic politics theories. What they find is that "both temporal count variables are negative and statistically significant in their respective stage models" (2007, 179). The longer a state has had a program in place, the less likely it is to transform it into nuclear weapons acquisition. They conclude, "Although popular, bureaucratic politics and inertia explanations do not appear to be supported and are in fact contradicted by this evidence" (2007, 179). Among groups of variables associated with particular explanations, the opportunity and status variables are the most important. The former have more effect on instituting programs, and the latter have more effect on acquiring weapons (2007, 181). The security variables have an effect on acquisition of weapons but not on developing a nuclear program (2007, 181). The domestic variables have a minor effect. And norms have an effect on instituting nuclear programs but not at all on acquiring weapons (2007, 181).

Causation and Explanation

The authors regard their explanations as causal. They use the term *cause* (2007, 168) and often use the word *because* where they are clearly asserting that "Y is caused by X." For example, "States might simply join the NPT because they do not plan to acquire nuclear weapons" (2007, 179). In a number of other places, they identify the relationships between independent and dependent variables with this causal use of *because* (2007, 169, 171, 184, 186, 187). As with Singh and Way (2004), it seems that for Jo and Gartzke *explaining* is a synonym for *accounting for* (2007, 176). Moreover, some of the time they treat a statistical association, that is, an "increase in the predicted probability" of one factor on another, as equivalent to "explanation." Thus, it appears that the statistical association, if it is of the proper magnitude and significance level, is able to "explain" the outcome state.

But this interpretation seems to go against various passages in which they identify a statistical association but say that it stands in need of an explanation. Consider the passage just quoted, which states that "NPT membership decreases the likelihood of having nuclear weapons programs. These results do not necessarily imply that the NPT changes state preferences. States might simply join the NPT because they do not plan to acquire nuclear weapons" (2007, 179). Elsewhere, they say that power status variables "do prove consistent determinants of proliferation. *Major Power Status* and *Regional Power Status* increase the likelihood of having nuclear weapons programs and nuclear weapons" (2007, 179). Here the statistical association is evident, but there is still doubt about how to explain the association.[18]

Criteria of Explanation

Jo and Gartzke's argument relies heavily on the criterion of *empirical adequacy*. The authors deny that mere statistical association explains, as they require that other explanations must be precluded. We noted the authors' use of the *precision* criterion. The authors rely on the predictions of the models (2007, 175) throughout their paper. This would lead to the conclusion that *predictive accuracy* is an important criterion that can lead us to choose the best theoretical explanation. While the authors use this mostly in the context of retrodictions, they also conclude with a series of predictions. It is interesting that the two papers with the most similar methods and most similar criteria (and one specifically comments on the other) come to similar conclusions, at least in terms of realist variables versus nonrealist variables (Singh and Way 2004; Jo and Gartzke 2007). The main difference is that while both papers give much credence to classical realist rivalry variables, Jo and Gartzke's paper brings in systemic factors to a slightly greater degree, since there is an important impact on rivalries due to the decline of a bipolar structure, and the absence of "the nuclear umbrella of the Soviet Union" (2007, 187).

11. AGREEMENT AND DISAGREEMENT ON HOW TO EXPLAIN PROLIFERATION

For the first two decades after World War II only great powers acquired nuclear weapons. Debates about acquisition focused on how the weapons might be used, the probability of nuclear war, and what the consequences might be. Most theorists took for granted that great powers' nuclear decisions could be explained by security- and power-based realist theories. In the 1940s and 1950s there was comparatively little effort devoted to discussing the possibility of non–great powers acquiring nuclear weapons.

In the 1960s, when major powers began to push for a nuclear nonproliferation treaty, more work was put into explaining why non–great powers might seek nuclear status. Scholars began to question the realist-oriented security explanations that focused on the system of security dilemmas and on the nation-state as the proper levels of analysis. Consequently, a broader debate over the best explanation took shape. They considered variables beyond just national security and relative power, such as bureaucratic forces, domestic political factors, and the character and traits of the individual people who make decisions about nuclear weapons.

The Realist Versus Nonrealist Divide

A first step in summarizing the results of the nuclear proliferation debate may be taken by separating the authors who place the primary explanatory emphasis on realist factors like national security rivalry and international anarchy.[19] Table 3.1 lists the authors discussed in this chapter who focus primarily on realist security factors and those who focus to a significant degree on individual, bureaucratic, economic, and other nonrealist explanatory factors (as Table 3.1 shows, most authors defend more than one type of factor).

The next step is to find out whether authors' uses of various criteria affect where they stand on the adequacy of realist versus nonrealist explanations. Authors are regarded as realist if they keep realist power-based factors separate from other factors, like individual psychology, bureaucratic and domestic politics, and liberal-oriented systemic factors. The survey in this chapter shows that twelve of the criteria discussed in Chapter 2 were invoked at least once by authors in the debate over why states proliferate. (While Sagan also includes both realist and nonrealist variables, authors are coded as "realist" only when they rely primarily on realist power factors.)

Conclusion 1—There has been an absence of transparency about criteria chosen.

The discussion in this chapter leaves little doubt that authors, whether for or against realist security explanations, usually leave the reader in the dark about which criteria authors regard as the most important. Readers have to dig

Table 3.1 Theorists and realist versus nonrealist explanations

Nonrealist				*Realist*	
Individual factors	*Domestic and bureaucratic*	*Symbols and norms*	*Liberal economics*	*National security*	*International anarchy*
Meyer	Quester	Meyer	Solingen	Potter	Waltz
Hymans	Sagan	Sagan		Waltz	Paul
	Solingen			Paul	Jo & Gartzke
				Singh & Way	
				Jo & Gartzke	

through the publications to find them. Even when authors do state some of the criteria explicitly, their arguments generally make use of additional criteria that are left implicit. And interestingly, even when authors identify at least some of the criteria they are using and argue comparatively for the advantages of their explanations, they never identify the criteria on which their opponents have based their arguments. Thus, looking at any particular scholarly publication, it is not possible to tell whether an author's disagreements with his or her opponents are over research design and/or interpretations of the relevant historical events, or whether differences are in the realm of the philosophy of science, with respect to which of the (often-conflicting) criteria should be relied on and prioritized over others.

Conclusion 2—Consensus on the debate has moved from early realism to become more diffuse.

In the aftermath of World War II it was taken for granted that armament decisions resulted from realist-endorsed national security motivations. Once France and China acquired nuclear weapons, all major powers were nuclear weapons states. Therefore, after the 1960s and the signing of the NPT, horizontal proliferation would be by regional and small powers. And scholars cited a variety of factors to explain proliferation. That is, consensus moved away from this realist view but not toward a new consensus.

One way to see this is to divide the ten post-NPT explanations into two groups of five on the basis of their dates of publication. Each group of five explanations shows a three-to-two split between realism's supporters and its opponents. Solingen published the first version of her theory in 1994, which puts her in the first group. But her explanation had new impact a decade later in an elaborated form. So, in terms of the way the debate moved between the two theoretical-explanatory groups, one cannot overlook the impact of the appearance of the much-elaborated version of the theory in her book. The book was widely read and reviewed, and several years after it appeared in 2006, Solingen's profile in security studies increased even further, as she was elected president of the International Studies Association. One might suppose that after a period of debate, consensus has moved back toward realist explanatory factors. But this is inconsistent with the fact that two of the most influential works of the last five works surveyed, by Solingen and by Hymans, make the case for nonrealist factors. The movement of the debate between realist and nonrealists is shown in Table 3.2.

Table 3.2 Chronology of realist and nonrealist nuclear proliferation explanations

	Quester 1973	*Waltz 1981*	*Potter 1982*	*Meyer 1984*	*Solingen 1994*	*Sagan 1996*	*Paul 2000*	*Singh & Way 2004*	*Hymans 2006*	*Solingen 2007*	*Jo & Gartzke 2007*
Order	1	2	3	4	5	6	7	8	9	—	10
Realist		X	X				X	X			X
Nonrealist	X			X	X	X			X	X	

Three Possible Answers and Criteria of Explanatory Success

As discussed in Chapter 1, we want to investigate H_1 and see whether consensus and progress on security questions may be hampered by authors' use of different notions and measures of a "good explanation." We noted three possible answers to the question about the role of criteria choices. ANS-1 posits that, despite the authors' disagreement about whether power balancing is the key explanatory factor, they nevertheless make more or less the same choices about which criteria to rely on in their explanatory arguments. If that were the case, their understandings of "explanation" and "good explanation" could not be construed as an impediment to consensus and progress; any continuing controversy over why states build nuclear weapons would be a result of other sorts of differences. ANS-2 states that individual authors use different criteria but that the differences cannot be connected to their explanatory disagreements, because when the members of any explanatory group are aggregated, the uses of criteria turn out to be similar to the aggregate uses by other group(s). In that case, the different criteria employed would be equally distributed between the supporters and opponents of realist security explanations. If there are, for example, a dozen criteria used in the debate, and if each author uses several criteria (but fewer than all twelve), then the authors would, of course, be using different criteria; but the frequency of each criterion in the overall group of nuclear proliferation authors would be similar to the uses by those who advance the opposing explanations. Both ANS-1 and ANS-2 would allow us to reject H_1. ANS-3 says that groups of authors use different criteria and there is some association between the criteria they favor and the answers they give, which would support H_1. Table 3.3 displays which criteria were used by which authors in defending their claims of key factors and the factors operating on particular levels of analysis, as well as the levels of analysis of the key explanatory variables.

Table 3.3 Criteria and their uses by realist and nonrealist authors (in descending order of uses by the two approaches)

	Realists					*Nonrealists*					
Criteria of adequacy	*Potter*	*Waltz*	*Paul*	*Singh & Way*	*Jo & Gartzke*	*Quester*	*Meyer*	*Sagan*	*Solingen*	*Hymans*	*Total number of uses*
Empirical adequacy	X	X	X	X	X		X	X		X	**8**
Mechanisms			X	X		X	X	X		X	**6**
Simplicity	X	X					X	X	X	X	**6**
Supports counterfactuals		X	X			X	X		X		**5**
Falsifiability								X	X	X	**3**
Uncovers true causes	X		X	X							**3**
Depth of causes								X	X	X	**3**
Imparts understanding				X		X		X			**3**
Greater range of domain	X	X	X								**3**
Explanatory unification			X					X			**2**
Precision; eliminates alternatives					X				X		**2**
Predictive accuracy					X				X		**2**
Total number by each explanatory group			21					25			**46**

The small number of cases and data points, and the binary (nonscalar) nature of the variables, means that the conditions necessary to apply familiar statistical tests do not obtain. Still, several conclusions may be derived from the data in Table 3.3 and Figure 3.1. Instead of statistical tests, we begin with visual inspection of the data. We may compare which criteria each author uses to map the uses against the positions the authors take on the explanatory factors, in order to see whether there is evidence of a connection between the choices of criteria and the explanatory variables.

Conclusion 3—It is not the case that all authors use the same criteria of explanatory success.

The conclusion that all authors do not use the same criteria of explanatory success is evident from the fact that there are at least twelve different criteria used by the various authors, and none uses more than half of the criteria. This conclusion eliminates the possibility that ANS-1 is correct, and thus means that we cannot reject H_1 on the basis of the claim in ANS-1 that all of the authors more or less use the same criteria. There remains ANS-2, which makes a claim about the uses of criteria when the opposing groups are taken as wholes. The uses of criteria displayed in Table 3.4 are a rearrangement of the data from Table 3.2, to help evaluate ANS-2.

The relationship between realists' and others' uses of the criteria, with supporters and opponents of realist explanations aggregated into groups, can be seen clearly in Figure 3.1.

Of the twelve criteria used by one or another scholar, three (predictive accuracy, explanatory unification, and precision or elimination of alternative explanations) are used equally by those who support and oppose realist explanations; together they account for only six of the forty-six uses; forty are used unequally. Seven of the twelve criteria (listed at the top of Figure 3.1) are skewed (a difference of two or more uses) toward one group or the other, accounting for nearly three-fourths (thirty-two of forty-six) of the usages of criteria by the ten authors.

Conclusion 4—It is not the case that realist authors and their opponents employ specific criteria in similar proportions.

Conclusion 4 tells us that we may not reject H_1 on the basis of ANS-2—even though individual authors use criteria differently from one another, the two groups taken as wholes use them in similar ways. Table 3.4 and Figure 3.1 both

Table 3.4 Criteria, realist and other explanations, and authors' uses of criteria (in descending order of uses by explanations emphasizing realist factors)

Criteria of adequacy	*Realist and neorealist explanations*	*Nonrealist (individual bureaucratic symbolic) explanations*
Empirical adequacy	PT WZ PL SW JG	MY SG HY
Uncovers true causes	PT WZ PL	—
Greater range of domain	PT WZ PL	—
Simplicity	PT WZ	MY SG SL HY
Mechanisms	PL SW	QS HY MY SG
Supports counterfactuals	WZ PL	QS MY SL
Imparts understanding	SW	QS SG
Precision; eliminates alternatives	JG	SL
Explanatory unification	PL	SG
Predictive accuracy	JG	SL
Depth of causes	—	SG SL MY
Falsifiability	—	SG SL HY
Total uses by each group	**21**	**25**
Average use of each criterion	**21 / 5 = 4.20**	**25 / 5 = 5.00**

NOTE: Total number of uses = 46. Realist and neorealist: PT = Potter, WZ = Waltz, PL = Paul, SW = Singh & Way, JG = Jo & Gartzke. Nonrealist: SG = Sagan, SL = Solingen, MY = Meyer, HY = Hymans, QS = Quester.

show that the two groups diverge on the mix of criteria they use. It is therefore still possible that H_1 is correct in stating that one reason for the disagreement is the differences in the competing explanatory schools over the uses of criteria.

Conclusion 5—All the authors make use of generally naturalist explanations, and all use criteria based in natural science; both groups use two-thirds of the criteria that either side uses.

Conclusion 5 shows that there is broad agreement in approaching the problem of proliferation; the most widely cited works are not radical constructivist, primarily interpretivist, or poststructuralist accounts. Both groups use eight of the twelve criteria used by either group (the last eight in Figure 3.1).

Conclusion 6—Beyond a general naturalist approach to the question of why states proliferate, there is a low degree of overlap in authors' or groups of authors' uses of criteria of evaluation of explanations.

There is a great deal of disagreement among prominent scholars of nuclear proliferation, and that disagreement coincides with a great deal of difference in

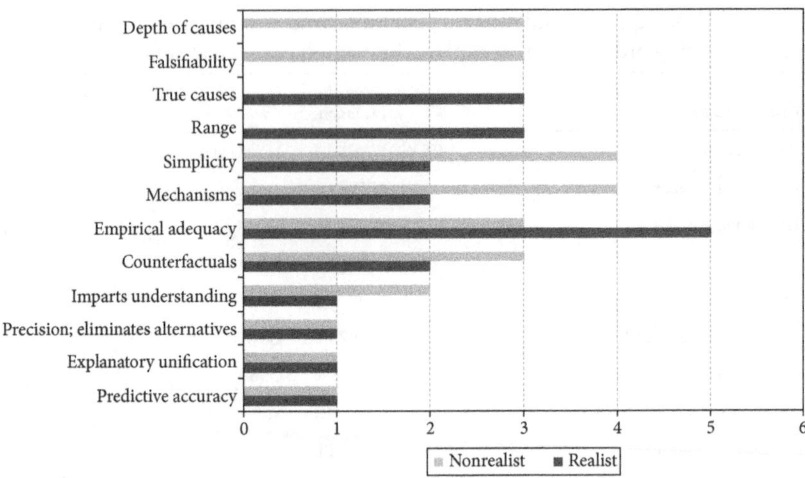

Figure 3.1 Realist versus nonrealist uses of criteria (in descending order of absolute differences between the two groups' uses of criteria)

their uses of criteria of evaluation. The analysis shows that ANS-1 and ANS-2 do not answer the question of alliance formation. This leaves ANS-3 as the only one of the three that is consistent with the evidence, which means that H_1 is a possible explanation for the pattern; differences in uses of criteria may be a key obstacle to greater agreement about why states build nuclear weapons. It will be possible to gain greater perspective on the degree of overlap in the uses of criteria by supporters and opponents of realist explanations after completion of the discussion of the alliance formation and democratic peace debates in the following two chapters.

4 THE BALANCE-OF-POWER DEBATE

Why Do States Form Alliances?

THE FORMATION OF ALLIANCES is regarded as one of the most important phenomena in world politics. Some see it as the core issue of the field (Liska 1962). The notion of balance of power has long been used to explain alliance patterns. Accordingly, this chapter examines answers to the question of why alliances form as they do and whether they result from balance-of-power calculations.

Theories of alliance formation are often tied to ideas about the onset of war. Some authors have argued that when power is balanced, systems are stable and wars are inhibited. The reasoning behind this centuries-old claim is that, if none of the powers in the system has enough of an advantage to be confident of victory, then none will be willing to initiate war. A second answer, advanced more recently, is that power imbalances lead to stability and inhibit war: when disputants' levels of power are heavily skewed toward one side, conflicts will be settled through negotiation because the weaker side will have no rational grounds to resist the terms offered by the superior power (see Organski 1958; Blainey 1973; Organski and Kugler 1980; Gilpin 1981). A third answer is that neither balances nor imbalances lead to stability in all circumstances; rather, whether balances or imbalances promote war depends also on the presence of or absence of other factors, such as how conflict-prone the region is (Paul 2004, 12).

Some theorists start with realist impulses but reject balancing, claiming that states pursue self-interest by following other patterns, such as bandwagoning (defined as joining up with rather than aligning against a rising hegemon), chain ganging (tying, or "chaining," one's security to another in hopes of enhancing prospects of successful defense in case of attack), and buck-passing (avoiding taking a stand against a threatening state in the hope that a party with more to lose or more prospect of success will do so instead). Liberals and constructivists reject both realist balancing explanations and argue that war and alliances result more from factors like shared liberal norms, identities and perceptions, economic structures, and free trade (Cobden 1836).

Standard Claims of Balance-of-Power Theorists

The term *balance-of-power theorist* is used in this study to refer to realist authors who see states exhibiting some form of balancing behavior driven by power calculations. While there is a wide range of theories that invoke balancing, according to Jack Levy (2004, 31), "All versions of balance-of-power theory begin with the hard-core assumptions of realist theory"; namely, the international system is anarchic, the important actors are territorial states, the goals of those actors are power or security, and states act rationally in pursuing those goals. Different theorists (e.g., those of the English School), add their own specific balancing principles to these four. Defenders of balancing theories claim that the position has a long history of support by distinguished authors, from Thucydides to Polybius in antiquity to modern thinkers like David Hume. During the Cold War many scholars and political figures viewed the rivalry between the Soviet Union and the United States (along with their respective alliances) as an example of balance-of-power politics.[1]

Balance-of-power theorists have typically argued that when the balance shifts away from a state, that state will seek to restore the balance either by internal balancing or external balancing. Internal balancing occurs when a state develops its own capabilities so that it becomes a more formidable military and/or economic force in the system, which will enable it to blunt its rivals' advantages. External balancing occurs when a state gains leverage from the outside by aligning with other states.

Most historians view America's founders as rejecting balancing as "amoral": a strategy of balancing requires a state to align solely on the basis of power considerations and requires that states overlook potential allies' track record in terms of respecting moral values. Isolation from European great-power intrigues was possible for the United States because of its abundant natural resources and geographical isolation. Most historians see the United States as abandoning isolation from alliances and engaging in power calculations, at least briefly during World War I, and then permanently after the bombing of Pearl Harbor (Claude 1962; Little 2007, 6).

In the 1960s, as the US-Soviet rivalry stabilized, international relations (IR) scholars began to puzzle over the stable coexistence of the two superpowers. In the decade after the Cuban missile crisis, the chance of war between the superpowers seemed to decline. By the time the Cold War came to an end it had become the longest period of great power peace since the modern international system began in 1648 with the Treaty of Westphalia (surpassing the period from 1871 to 1914). As noted in Chapter 3, the so-called Long Peace was unique and in need of explanation (Gaddis 1987). Balancing was a popular explanation: the efforts of the United States and the Soviet Union to balance each other led to international systemic stability. In the 1980s a group of scholars came to question traditional realist balancing explanations, arguing that states may engage in balancing, but they balance threats rather than power capabilities.

Multiple Meanings and Competing Conceptualizations

Authors have long commented on the many meanings theorists have attached to the term *balance of power*. The term can be used descriptively, as a theory about how states in fact behave, and prescriptively, as a theory about how states can attain various sorts of objectives. Some realists make the descriptive claim that balancing is an "automatic process" that occurs as states seek power. The balances develop even if no state desires "balances" as a goal. Claude (1962) and Waltz (1979, 128) hold this view. Similar views are advanced by Kaplan (1957) and Wolfers (1952).

Levy (2004, 32) says that "the single most important theme in the balance of power literature" is the prevention of a system hegemon. Levy (2004, 32) quotes Polybius's *The Histories*: "We should never contribute to the attainment by one state of a power so preponderant, that none dare dispute with it even for their acknowledged rights" (bk. I, 83.6–8). According to Levy, two propositions thus follow: "sustained hegemonies rarely if ever arise in multistate systems and a balancing coalition will form against any state that threatens to gain a position of hegemony that would enable it to impose its will on others" (2004, 35).

Post–Cold War Puzzles—Hard Versus Soft Balancing

Thus far in the post–Cold War period, US hegemony has not been opposed by any formal, counterbalancing alliance. This leads to the question, can balancing theories continue to prove acceptable in the post–Cold War power configuration? Many of the works considered in this chapter were written during the Cold War, but they make claims about the "inevitability" of balancing that are intended to hold under any systemic configuration. These claims are regarded as dubious, since the demise of the Soviet Union left the world with a single great power for a quarter century, yet there has been little genuine balancing against the United States in that time. Some have responded that there will be balancing, but it simply has not yet begun, while others have revised or expanded the concept of balancing. Paul (2004, 2) notes, with regard to this controversy, "The crucial question for social scientists is who is likely to be more accurate in this debate?" The last three works considered in this chapter incorporate the further question of why, even twenty years after the end of the Cold War, no formal alliance has developed to counter US hegemony through "soft balancing."

1. HANS MORGENTHAU: *POLITICS AMONG NATIONS*

Hans Morgenthau's *Politics Among Nations* (1954), first published in 1948, is one of the most influential works in the study of IR in the twentieth century. It was a comprehensive theoretical statement of a major school of thought as well as a widely used textbook in colleges and universities. The book advanced what is today referred to as classical realism. Morgenthau focused his theory on the nation-state, which he regarded as "power seeking" by nature. Political power is a psychological relationship between two or more agents, consisting of the "mutual relations of control among the holders of public authority and between the latter and the people at large" (1954, 26). As Morgenthau saw it, "When we speak of power, we mean control over the minds and actions of other men" (1954, 13).

The international system is one in which those states engaged in international politics continually compete with one another for power. The "iron law" of international politics is that "politics is governed by objective laws that have their roots in human nature" (1954, 4). Moreover, "statesmen think and act in terms of interest defined as power" (1954, 4). Consequently, state action should be evaluated in the framework of political benefits for the state, rather than by moral, legal, or economic consequences. In this way Morgenthau sought to make IR more scientific without attempting to fit it to the behavioralist model of science. We might note that, while *Politics Among Nations* is heavily descriptive and explanatory, for Morgenthau it is important to identify leaders' moral obligations, which require prudent behavior, regardless of how non–decision makers might evaluate the actions.

Morgenthau treated the process of "explaining" a phenomenon or process as tantamount to "gaining understanding" of it. He says, "Geopolitics is the attempt to understand the problem of national power exclusively in terms of geography. . . . Nationalism tries to explain exclusively . . . in terms of national character" (1954, 148). Thus, to the extent that Morgenthau holds that explanations *impart understanding*, his study seeks explanations for the behavior of states. Morgenthau says, "The natural aim of all scientific undertakings," including those in the social sciences, "is to discover the forces underlying social phenomena and how they operate," and the first goal in the book is to "detect and understand the forces that determine political relations among nations" (1954, 14). He holds that the purpose of a theory is "to bring order and meaning to a mass of phenomena, which without it would remain disconnected and unintelligible" (1954, 3).

Morgenthau relates the notions of prediction and complexity to each other. He says that the world is complex and that theories cannot do all that we might wish. "The first lesson the student of international politics must learn and never forget is that the complexities of international affairs make simple solutions and trustworthy prophecies impossible" (Morgenthau 1954, 18). The world of international affairs has "powerful and contradictory tendencies" operating, and while there are bound to be surprises, leaders have to "assess the probabilities for the different conditions and tendencies to prevail in each set of conditions. *Facts* are more malleable than other social scientists would hold; they are subject to interpretation and "are essentially ambiguous and subject to continuous change" (1954, 18).

Morgenthau expresses skepticism about prediction in IR, in part because so many authoritative predictions turn out to be wrong; he cites George Washington's expectations regarding the length of the Revolutionary War. However, in chapter 11 of *Politics Among Nations*, Morgenthau seems to backtrack, in that he says, apparently predictively, that states struggle against one another for power, which "leads of necessity to a configuration that is called the balance of power" (1954, 155), though he remains cautious about saying that any outcome is "necessary."

The Cold War context of Morgenthau's ideas led him to emphasize caution. At the time he was writing, Morgenthau noted that the world had become even more challenging for American foreign policy, because there had recently been a "threefold revolution" in international affairs: a shift from multipolarity to bipolarity, a loss of "moral unity" among great powers, and technological changes that made "possible total war" (1954, 20; see also Mearsheimer 1990). For Morgenthau two possible paths to peace remained: the "self-regulatory mechanism of social forces which appears in the form of 'balance of power' policies and the normative constraints of law, morality and public opinion" (1954, 20).

The Balance of Power

Morgenthau identifies four meanings of the term *balance of power*: a policy that is intended to bring about a balanced result, the actual outcome of states' behavior, a distribution of power among major states that is roughly equal, and any distribution of power whatsoever. He adds that the "default" meaning is the last (1954, 155n1). Whether balances must form, or whether they do so necessarily and inevitably, is hard to determine. Although Morgenthau argues that roughly equal balances are stabilizing and, indeed, "inevitable," he adds later that the term *necessity* must be used carefully.

For Morgenthau, balancing occurs within an "international society" (1954, 160). Morgenthau says that "the balance of power operates and fulfills its typical *functions*" of creating stability, however precarious that stability may be, and of preventing hegemonic domination, thereby ensuring states' "freedom" (1954, 161, emphasis added). Thus, the function is to prevent hegemonic domination by any state. Morgenthau also considers a range of behaviors that are typically found in interstate relations, such as divide and rule, compensation to rivals, arm races, arms limitation treaties among rivals, alliances, and imperialistic domination of outside territories. Yet according to Morgenthau, all these sorts of behavior are examples of different forms of balancing. Morgenthau thus encompasses a wide variety of actions all under the single rubric of "balancing." The book makes concerted attempts at both *simplification* and *explanatory unification.*

Explanation and Criteria

Morgenthau sees the explanatory force of the concept of balance as deriving from an early modern metaphor, when the entire universe was understood as a cosmic mechanism with a complex system of balancing forces (1954, 185). This reveals another form of explanatory unification as well as an instance of *methodological conservatism*, since a much older form of explanation is the basis for people coming to see "balancing" as explanatory in the case of world politics.

According to Morgenthau, an explanation must provide a set of general principles from which the specific events can be derived. A good explanation must fit with "the evidence of history"; that is, it must be empirically adequate (1954, 47). In looking for "motives" for wars over long periods, Morgenthau finds that very few wars were ever were fought primarily for economic gain, even in periods of imperialist foreign policy (1954, 47). A good general explanation must be in conformity with historical evidence. Marxist theories of imperialism and war thus fail to prove empirically adequate, but they appealed to many as an explanation largely because of their simplicity (1954, 46–47).[2]

In his later *Purpose of American Politics*, Morgenthau (1961, 25n1) says, "The value of any concept used in political science is determined by its ability to explain a maximum of the phenomena that are conventionally considered to belong to a certain sphere of political activity. Thus the coverage of a concept of political power, to be useful for the understanding of international politics, must be broader than the coverage of one adopted to operate in the field of municipal politics" (see also Morgenthau 1954, 96; 1972, 106). This is an example of *greater range of domain*. Morgenthau says that some causes of decline are outside of human control, but some are within human control. Also, theoretical knowledge of world politics is important, because one reason for decline is the lack of correct evaluation of the power of one's own nation against the power of other nations (Crabb and Savoy 1975, 226).

The foregoing summary of Morgenthau's views shows that in some cases he explicitly argues for the advantages of his theory, and in some cases implicitly, on the basis of *simplicity*, *explanatory unification*, *range of domain*, *causal depth*, *causal mechanisms*, *imparting understanding*, *predictive accuracy*, and the ability to provide *control over the environment*.

2. A. K. F. ORGANSKI'S *WORLD POLITICS*

A. K. F. Organski's 1958 study *World Politics* focuses squarely on the theory of balance of power, but it turns the theory on its head, arguing that, in the modern world, great-power war is most likely in situations in which systems are coming into balance.

Organski divides history into three epochs: preindustrialization, the post-1750 period of industrialization, and the world after all states have become industrialized. Organski holds that the best theory will be state-centric because, since industrialization, states have become internally strong today and function as unified actors. This was not true before industrialization; and little is knowable about what the world will be like after full industrialization, including whether there will even be states.

Power Balances and Stability

Organski defines *power* as "the ability to influence the behavior of others in accordance with one's own ends." Power may be exercised by means of persuasion, rewards, nonviolent punishments, or the use of force. Because the three most important determinants of national power are wealth, population, and government efficiency, the best single power index is national income, since it reflects population, economic development, and various lesser factors.

Organski says that power "is surely one of the most important goals that nations pursue" (1958, 53), but he departs sharply from realists, holding that power "is not the only goal, and it is not always the principal goal" (1958, 53). States' primary goals may vary over time: Sweden and Germany have replaced relative gain goals with absolute gain goals, and the United States has done the reverse. These are influenced by the state's relative power standing, the current "climate" of the system, the domestic regime-type, and the cohesion of the ruling elite.

Organski says that, generally, wealthy nations tend to pursue wealth more than power, whereas powerful nations pursue power more than wealth; powerful nations tend to pursue both nationalistic and humanitarian goals, whereas weaker states focus on the former; nations at the peak of their power and those in decline value peace more than rising nations do. Autocratic states tend to have more unified goals and more long-range goals, whereas democratic states have more pluralistic and short-term goals. In general, industrialization has led states to place more emphasis on productivity, increasing standards of living, and developing more destructive weapons, the latter of which has created the possibility of even more horrific wars (1958, 91–92). Organski says that, speaking precisely, we must admit that only individuals and not states possess goals. So what appear to be goals of a state are a function of the goals of the most influential individuals and groups of individuals within the state.

Criticisms of the Balance-of-Power Explanation. Balance-of-power theories fail, according to Organski, for a variety of reasons, including their vagueness-induced unfalsifiability and the fact that they treat all states as having the same goals. They treat states as easily able to change alliances and as lacking permanent ties to one another. While this may have been true in the preindustrial world, in the modern world commercial ties create an interdependence of raw materials, markets, and capital flows that makes it extremely difficult for states to break off relations with existing partners.

Organski attacks the central claim of balance-of-power theory, namely, that alliances form to balance against the potential hegemon, because a state that gains preponderant power may act aggressively against weaker states. Both World War I and World War II were started by the weaker powers, and the theory offers no possible explanation for the actions of Germany and Japan. If balance-of-power theory "cannot explain the two great wars of recent history" (1958, 293), then it has left a great deal unexplained. The failure to meet the criterion of greater range is invoked here.

Organski offers two other counterexamples. Britain in the nineteenth century is often said to be the balancer par excellence. But what Britain was doing cannot properly be said to have been balancing, since it was, in fact, clearly the most powerful state in Europe. And in the late 1950s, when *World Politics* was first published, the system was seen as led by two roughly equivalent great powers, with alliances forming around them. However, Organski points out that the power of the United States was not only greater than that of the Soviet Union; it was vastly greater. The United States had the world's highest gross domestic product (GDP), nearly three times that of the Soviet Union, and the United States also ranked first in per capita GDP, whereas the Soviet Union ranked fourteenth (1958, 205). If balance-of-power theory is correct, there should have been a large coalition forming around the goal of blunting the advance of American power. But there was not.

Balance-of-power theory endured for so long despite the flaws identified, according to Organski, because of theoretical inertia and the fact that in the preindustrial world it may well have provided a good explanation of events. But the theory "became truly obsolete after the industrial revolution" (1958, 293; see also page 307). He adds, it would be "strange, indeed, if explanations offered by practicing politicians in that pre-industrial age turned out to coincide exactly with the best explanations that can be devised to explain the world today" (1958, 282).

The Power Transition Alternative. Each state goes through three periods: preindustrial, industrializing, and fully industrialized. The second period is when a state may overtake other states. Because industrialization typically leads to increases in every component of power, states will surpass one another more during this period than in the other two periods. If all states industrialized simultaneously, there would be internal transition from preindustrial to industrial society, but there would be no "power transition" in world politics. In his survey of great-power relations since industrialization, Organski finds that the most powerful state leads an international order (1958, 322). At some point that state is challenged by a rising industrializing state, which usually results in war. But how do we explain cases when war does not result, as with the United States surpassing Great Britain in the twentieth century? First, the United States became the leading power "reluctantly," primarily because of internal developments in North America. For this reason Great Britain was not threatened by the rise of United States, and even benefited from its capital investments in the United States. Furthermore, the United States did not challenge the prevailing "Anglo-French international order," "working rules," "economic or political institutions . . . or ideology" (1958, 323). And third, the power potential of the United States was so great relative to Britain that war would have delayed only slightly the inevitable leadership of the United States. Because of the weakening of its power through the twentieth century, Britain achieved greater power by partnering with the United States than would have been possible without the rise of the United States.

The Current System

The international system in the modern world has two distinctive features, major power shifts occur mainly because of internal economic and demographic transformations. Realignments are more difficult than they were five centuries ago for reasons noted earlier (Organski 1958, 316–17). States are also connected in an "international order" of rules, which by design benefit the powerful states that instituted them.

Organski considers two distinctions: whether or not states are either satisfied with the status quo, and whether or not they are rising in power. This creates four possible types of state. Rapid industrialization can create dissatisfaction both externally and internally, and both can, in a powerful state, push it toward war. External dissatisfaction results when the state regards the existing international order as contrary to its interests, which may tempt it to try forcibly to overturn the rules. Internal dissatisfaction results because industrialization transforms society, leaving some groups in worsened conditions. The government can deflect anger away from itself by inciting external conflict. The most dangerous states are those rising in power to the point that they approach the leading state. "Peace is threatened whenever a powerful nation is dissatisfied with the *status quo* and is powerful enough to attempt to change things in the face of opposition from those who control the existing international order" (1958, 325).

Organski claims to have "established that world peace is guaranteed when the nations satisfied with the existing international order enjoy an unchallenged supremacy of power and that major wars are most likely when a dissatisfied challenger achieves an approximate balance of power with the dominant nation" (1958, 371). However, we have observed that challengers have attacked before reaching balances, and there are transitions, like the United States surpassing the United Kingdom, in which war does not result; for Organski, "Clearly, there are other factors at work" (1958, 333). For example, war is irrational and thus unlikely to occur if a rising state is so small that it could never approach the leader or if it is so large that, when fully industrialized, it would be unstoppable as a dominant power. "Surrender to the inevitable makes sense, but surrender to what is perhaps possible is cowardice" (Organski 1958, 334).[3]

Explanation and Criteria

Organski explicitly supports a scientific approach to IR (1958, 5); scholarly works must follow the canons of logical reasoning, deal with empirical facts, be testable by experience, be objective, and provide explanations (1958, 5–6). Organski says from the outset that his primary effort is to provide causal explanations. He says, "Science must . . . explain [facts]. This is done through the construction of theories, which are extremely general, abstract statements or 'laws' according to which empirical phenomena behave. If the theory is good, it should be stated in such a manner that it can be tested with empirical evidence. A good theory should be empirically testable" (1958, 6). He adds, "The emphasis [of the book] is on a search for general principles, for regularities, for patterns that recur in case after case, and at a deeper level, the search is for the causal explanations that underlie these regularities" (1958, 6). Organski seeks *true underlying causes.*

Organski says, "A good theory must be clearly formulated and logically sound, and it must be consistent with the data. Furthermore, it must explain something about the data that one would not otherwise know, and it must provide a more satisfactory explanation than any rival theory can offer" (1958, 283). This makes it appear that he views explanations as arguments that must be valid, as Hempel requires in his D-N model (since to be "logically sound" is by definition to be a valid deductive argument with true premises). Thus, Organski endorses several criteria of theory acceptability and choice. He appears to separate the explanatory component of a theory from its internal logic and its correspondence with events, as he says that the theory of the balance of power must be rejected because "its concepts are fuzzy, it is logically unsound and contradicts itself, it is not consistent with events that have occurred, and it does not explain them" (1958, 298).

Organski often invokes *counterfactual conditionals* to support causal explanatory statements. He tells the reader what would happen in world power relations if one particular state were to undergo industrializing while " the rest of the world were standing still" (305). An explanation that proceeds by the use of *simpler* concepts is preferable to others. Organski seeks the simplest index that can do the needed work, for example, in developing the economic components of his explanation (1958, 157).

Theories rely on assumptions. The projections into the future hold true consistently only if the assumptions hold true. This account of the role of assumptions and their connections to predictive theories strongly supports identifying true causes as a criterion. If the theory's assumptions fail, the theory will not accurately predict. In the fully industrialized epoch, when states' relative status is highly stable and transitions are slow and rare, current theorists' assumptions drawn from the "industrializing" period will be unlikely to hold true.

Organski argues that some theories repeatedly shift the meaning of *balancing* and are thus unacceptable because in doing so they lose their ability to satisfy the Popperian criterion of *falsifiability.* Organski anticipates Lakatos's major point about "degenerating" research programs when he criticizes balance-of-power theorists' treatment of anomalies by continually offering qualifications and addenda to explain away recurring anomalies (1958, 283). Organski also invokes the criteria of *empirical adequacy, greater range, simplicity,* and *the identification of deep and true causes.*

3. INIS CLAUDE: *POWER AND INTERNATIONAL RELATIONS*

Inis Claude's 1962 book *Power and International Relations* focuses on the danger of war arising from uncontrolled great-power competition. Claude seeks to find a set of policies or arrangements of states that, if followed, would promote peace and stability. Conscious adoption of such policies would lead causally, through stages, to a political stability and peace. He identifies three, each of which occupies a different point along the world politics continuum of decentralization-centralization: balance of power, collective security, and world government.

The world has had little experience with collective security (perhaps the League of Nations) and world government (a few empires acquired through conquest). But there is a fairly extensive record of examples of balance-of-power arrangements, especially those that arise from power-driven state decisions that produce systems of competing alliances (1962, 90). Some have produced stability, but others have failed disastrously, like that which led to the Napoleonic Wars and World War I (1962, 90). Because balance-of-power systems have not consistently been stable and peaceful, Claude rejects power balancing as a prescription for peace.

Claude's book, like Waltz's (1959) *Man, the State and War*, reviews a wide array of international relations literature to evaluate various prescriptions for enhancing the prospects of great-power peace. Which options garner serious consideration at any given moment depends on several factors, including the prevailing intensity of the fear of major war. In centuries past the anarchical and unregulated competition was sometimes praised by scholars and national leaders (at least those not in states that disappeared in the competition) for allowing states to express full autonomy and range of action while also permitting only tolerable, small-scale wars. At other times, especially when memories of the horrors are fresh in peoples' minds (e.g., after World Wars I and II), leaders are willing to look carefully at more radical proposals. Thus, discussions of "general disarmament" were taken somewhat seriously after World War II. But in Claude's view, general disarmament will not occur; people, whether organized into nation-states or other groupings, will not give up the ability to kill one another. In the post–World War II period, fear resulted not only from devastation in Europe but also from the awareness that future conflicts could bring nuclear war.

In a collective security system, "threats to the common peace may arise within the community, and . . . they must be dealt with by the combined power resources of members of the community, cooperating under the auspices of its central institutions" (Claude 1962, 114–15). Claude describes this system as relying on the theory of deterrence, since any potential aggressor has to heed the other states' pledges to stand against it should it act aggressively. A question that often arises concerns how a collective force is developed. One possibility is that states identify a fraction of their military that would be available to the collective security organization when needed, as with the League of Nations. Another possibility is that an international armed force be created under the command of the collective security organization. But both arrangements have drawbacks.

Collective security is a way of using power to maintain stability; it is not a way of turning a blind eye to the reality of power, as some critics of Wilsonianism have charged. Claude notes that the use of force involved in the collective security system led to criticisms of Wilson as a "militarist."[4] In Claude's view, the balance-of-power system is the default when there is no system of control like collective security or world government (1962, 93). The default international system of the Cold War also showed that balancing can be stable when certain conditions obtain.

World government is a more extreme departure from the prevailing anarchy of the international system. The idea of creating a world government with the goal of eradicating war is more recent than balance of power or collective security. World government would follow a "federalist" model and would permit the existence of independent states with sovereignty over internal matters. They would be limited in conducting foreign relations, especially because states would have to surrender their right to resort to arms. But there would be a centralized institution with the legitimate authority and power to prevent violence between states and to enforce war-prevention rules. The national military establishments would be limited so as not to be able to counter the force possessed by the world government.

World government is at one end of the centralization-decentralization spectrum. As Claude puts it, "Rule of law and disarmament are key themes in world government thought—the former standing for the development of central authority in the system of international relations, and the latter for the elimination of the capacity of states to challenge that authority" (Claude 1962, 207). He adds that the only attempts at world government have come from instances in which states have sought conquest. There have been no cooperative efforts to institute such an arrangement. Because history has provided no models of a cooperative world government, evaluation of its ideas "is almost exclusively a matter of examining theory, rather than practice" (1962, 207). Claude proceeds to analyze the idea but begins his lengthy discussion of world government with the qualification that it is a proposal that has no prospect of being implemented "in the foreseeable future" (1962, 208).

Balance of Power

Claude uses the term *balance of power* to refer to a system in which there is a conscious attempt to maintain independence of action by preventing the rise of a hegemonic state or coalition. Balance-of-power systems may or may not yield an equilibrium of power (1962, 88). For this reason, nothing follows "of necessity" from balance-of-power systems. Contingent events shape outcomes. Claude says that there may be inherent traits, but there are no inherent results.[5]

With regard to mechanisms, collective security and world government can arise only by design, whereas a balance-of-power system can arise (and in most cases has arisen by default) without any conscious direction (1962, 93). For a balancing system to produce stability, a number of specific conditions must obtain. There must be an absence of ideology, a fear of war on all sides but not so much that states are afraid to issue threats, agreement by all sides that only wars with limited objectives are available options, some limits on hegemonic ambitions of states, and skilled diplomacy in which each side grasps the relative capabilities of all major players—it is also especially helpful if one player sees itself as the "balancer" (1962, 90–91). In any event, a successful balance system produces not "perfect peace" but rather "rough stability"—some wars will still occur. A system of this sort requires active management at all times; it is not an automatic mechanism akin to the "invisible hand."

Most balance-of-power theorists argue that a balancing system comprises a collection of autonomous units of power and policy; the states are related so as to make reciprocal action necessary; the system lacks an organ of overall control; states that have power over others are not to be trusted and are a threat to others; the only way to counter power is with one's own power; an equilibrium of power inhibits aggression and produces stability; and the fear of potential hegemons leads others to counterbalance. But authors differ on the sorts of mechanisms that produce balances, whether lawlike "automatic" ones akin to an "invisible hand," "semi-automatic" ones that operate when a state like Britain operates to balance others, or ones that are "manually operated" by skilled statespersons "who manage the affairs" of the states. The objective working of the system is the same in all three cases; the difference is the level of conscious motivation by national policy makers (Claude 1962, 50–51).

Explanation and Criteria

The goal of a balancing system is to prevent violence. To see what factors might be most effective in enhancing the prospects for a violence-inhibiting world government, Claude considers the analogy of war between states under a hypothetical world government and civil war within a nation-state. In this context, Claude reconstructs Dean Acheson's (1955) explanation of the American Civil War. Civil war was obviously an option for Americans in the mid-nineteenth century, but one hundred years later it is not. There is a difference, which does not stem from any greater confidence in the rule of law. It results, rather, from Americans' belief that all parties will rely on the nonviolent formal and informal means of satisfying their needs and demands. The American political system has evolved to encompass "a high adjustment potential" (Claude 1962, 266).

Claude explains the war by contrasting the strength of two causal forces, the resources available to bring about peaceful adjustment, and stakes of the political conflicts between sectional groupings (1962, 265, citing Acheson 1955, 35). Claude sees explanations in primarily causal terms, proceeding both by identifying stages and by citing *mechanisms*, and he explains by means of rational and individual analyses. And a good explanation should exhibit *empirical adequacy* in fitting the historical record.

4. KENNETH WALTZ: BALANCING AND POLITICAL STRUCTURES

Kenneth Waltz has written extensively on the balance of power and polarity in world politics. In his book *Theory of International Politics* (1979) and in both earlier and later writings (e.g., Waltz, 1964, 1997), Waltz advances the claim that balancing is central to IR theory. As he puts it, "If there is any distinctively political theory of international politics, balance-of-power theory is it" (Waltz 1979, 117). Waltz's writings offer a detailed picture of his theory of balancing. And the discussion of Waltz in Chapter 3 summarized his understanding of the notion of explanation in *Theory of International Politics* (see also Waltz 1997, 916).

System Structure

Waltz acknowledges that many types of factors affect international outcomes, but he argues that the most important is the structure of the international system. He compares international political structures to domestic political structures to make a number of points, and he argues that like systems will behave in like ways. But of course, since systems can be compared to one another in so many different ways, the question arises, alike in what respects? Waltz answers that there are, in particular, three most important aspects of political systems: their ordering principle, the functions of their units, and the distribution of capabilities among their units. The first refers to whether the units in the system are ordered hierarchically or anarchically; the second refers to whether the units serve similar or diverse functions within the system; and the third refers to how many major powers or poles of power there are in the system.

According to Waltz, all modern international systems are classifiable as "anarchic." Waltz cites empirical evidence to defend the claim that the key difference between international and domestic politics is the anarchic and self-help nature of the former and the hierarchic nature of the latter, not the level of violence. He says that, even though the twentieth century was the most violent ever in terms of interstate war, domestic political violence took as many—in fact, more—lives. Violence is not the difference. It is rather the ordering principle, that is, whether the system does or does not have a legitimate hierarchy of authority. His inclusion of ordering principle as one of the three defining features of political structures comes not from any direct perception of systems but rather because, when we assume that international systems are anarchic, we can explain the behavior of systems better than if we assume they are hierarchic. This is one of many clear illustrations of Waltz's embrace of empiricism as a doctrine in the philosophy of social science; he does not seek "true" assumptions and theoretical posits; he judges only on the basis of whether certain assumptions and posits do their jobs, most important of which is providing explanations of observable phenomena.

With regard to function of units, all states in modern international systems have the same functions, namely, to survive and to flourish. Domestic political structures have different sorts of units, both within a single political structure (the unit of "president" is different from "legislature") and when different political structures are compared to one another ("presidential" versus "parliamentary"). But in international systems, realists see the important units as states, and all have the same functions. The differences we find between one international system and another are found in the third defining factor, distribution of capabilities. Multipolar systems behave differently than bipolar systems; the latter are generally more stable and less war-prone.

Moreover, key features of the international system cannot be discovered by studying domestic political structures; the system-level analysis does more than aggregate state-level features; it provides new understandings. No matter how carefully one looks at individual states, the structure of alliances or anarchy itself cannot be detected. We are able to see properties of this sort only when we look at systems as wholes, and at the interactions among units. Philosophers call these "emergent properties" (see Kim 1993, 1999). Many authors have applied these insights to the social sciences and IR (e.g., Leon 2010).

The difficulties of engendering cooperative behavior result from the so-called collective action problem. War will continue under anarchy, and other problems will persist, such as arms races and environmental degradation. However, these problems do not provide reasons to seek a hierarchical system, because, as noted, more violence results from internal conflicts under hierarchical governing systems. The violence and inefficiencies that would occur under a so-called world-governing body would be worse than the problems of the existing system (Waltz 1979, 110).

Balancing and Causation

For Waltz (1979, 20), the characteristic pattern in the system will be balancing, no matter how many or how few states balance, as long as two conditions are met: that the system is anarchic and that the units within that system wish to survive. Most realists say that states generally seek survival and power, and some states seek to dominate the system. They add that states address security challenges by means of internal strategies in which they develop their economic and military capabilities and/or external strategies of alignment with other states (Waltz 1979, 117). States seek to avoid being dominated by rivals and even by alliance partners, and some states seek to dominate others and generally do not seek to produce balances. However, because all states work in ways to avoid being dominated whenever it becomes a danger to them, the outcome is a series of balances. But when a disruption occurs by a state attempting domination, a new balance will soon follow.

Waltz explains how new balances arise and continue by means of a carefully formulated account that distinguishes two types of causes: active (or precipitating) causes and passive (or permissive) causes. So, on Waltz's account, when people talk about the assassination of Archduke Franz Ferdinand as the cause of World War I, they invoke the notion of an active or precipitating cause. But that action, had it taken place in another sort of system structure, possibly one of two great powers in which the allies were of very minimal significance, would not have led to systemwide war. So the assassination as "cause" only had the effect that it did because the international system was structured the way it was, namely, anarchical, with multiple great powers that were interconnected, thus creating two powerful and tightly bound alliances. The system structure was therefore as much a "cause" of the war as was the assassination. In this way, Waltz bolsters the claim that a theory of IR should focus on the causal efficacy of passive or permissive factors like properties of an international system; the structure of an international system is itself a cause.

Waltz raises the problem of theory testing in the context of balancing theories. He says that theories of IR are difficult to test because they are seldom stated in precise enough ways that allow them to be subjected to rigorous testing (1979, 124). Some balancing theories, when applied to the case of the alliance between Germany and Austria-Hungary in 1874, would predict that France and Russia, as great powers, would be likely to form a counteralliance. But 1875 came and went without an alliance, as did 1876 and 1877, and so on. Does that falsify the theory? Or does the fact that France and Russia did ally in 1894 corroborate it? How long a lag is consistent with the (indeterminate) nature of the theory? Waltz lays out a set of procedures for such testing, which involve drawing consequences and comparing them to observed outcomes. He argues that theories can be both falsified and corroborated. But he thinks that theories are in fact rarely precise enough to allow the application of such procedures.

Explanation and Criteria

In his balancing discussion in his 1979 work *Theory of International Politics*, Waltz says, "For those who believe that if a result is to be produced, someone, or everyone, must want it and must work for it, it follows that explanation turns ultimately on what the separate states are like" (1979, 121). According to Waltz, if the foregoing were true, then it would follow that theories "at the national level, or lower[,] will sufficiently explain international politics [and if] the equilibrium of a balance is maintained through states abiding by rules, then one needs an explanation of how agreement on the rules is achieved and maintained" (1979, 121). Here Waltz is moving back chronologically: if X explains Y, then we still need to move back in time to event W, before X occurred, to find out how X came about. Waltz continues, "One does not need a balance-of-power theory, for balances would result from a certain kind of behavior explained perhaps by a theory about national psychology or bureaucratic politics. A balance-of-power theory could not be constructed because it would have nothing to explain" (1979, 121). Here Waltz posits levels of explanations; one action causes an outcome, but the action was caused—not only by something that "happened" previously but also by a set of conditions, like the presence of psychological states or bureaucratic systems. The rules about balancing explain the resultant balance, but the rules themselves need to be explained.

Most of Waltz's attention to the meaning of "explanation" and the criteria he uses to advance his explanation are found in *Theory of International Politics*, as discussed in Chapter 3. They are consistent with, but go into more detail than, his comments in his many other publications. In Chapter 3 we saw that Waltz supports the criteria of simplicity, range of domain, empirical adequacy, control of the environment, and support of counterfactuals. The last can be seen in his citations of authors on both sides of the Atlantic who claim that, with or without nuclear weapons, the United States would take almost any steps to prevent Soviet domination of Europe (Waltz 1964, 885).

5. HEDLEY BULL'S *THE ANARCHICAL SOCIETY*

Hedley Bull's (1977) major work, *The Anarchical Society*, offers an account of how an international system under anarchy can become an international society. The book focuses on the notions of order and disorder in international politics and how order, and ultimately societies, can arise even though there is no legitimate hierarchy of authority. When states interact with one another in such a way that one state's decisions affect others, there is an "international system." But an "international society" of states exists only when the system exhibits rules, institutions, and order. To say that there is order in the system, there must be more than just patterns and regularities. The Hobbesian state of nature exhibits regularities and patterns, but those produce disorder. Social order specifically requires patterns that promote the features that make *society* possible, principally security, enforcement of promises and contracts, and stability of possessions. An international society requires that states be conscious of common interests and that its members "conceive themselves to be bound by a common set of rules" (Bull 1977, 13).

Bull acknowledges that the social aspect is only one among several important features of international systems. Justice is often regarded as a vitally important feature of any international system. Bull's focus on "international society" is an analytical choice rather than a statement that it is the preeminent feature; the notion of justice in international systems is no less deserving of study. Despite the fact that he invokes sociological dimensions of international relations, Bull does not follow the constructive path of emphasizing constitutive relations over causal explanations.

Society, Rules, and Institutions

Bull holds that although the international system is anarchical, there are distinct types of anarchy based on sociological relationships. In a Hobbesian form of anarchy all of the units seek to add to their power by taking what others possess. And in a Kantian system each unit (moral agent) is enlightened and rational enough to understand moral imperatives. The imperatives lead to actions that may benefit others and that do not derive their force from the existence of juridical states. The Grotian and Lockean order falls between the Hobbesian and Kantian ones and offers the possibility of a functioning society that operates within an hypothesized state of nature (see Grotius's 1690 *Mare liberum*; Locke's 1690 *An Essay Considering the True Original Extent, and End, of Civil Government: The Second Treatise of Government*).

For Bull, institutions—such as diplomacy, conventions, and even war—are crucial to the analysis. International organizations that promote order, like the League of Nations and the United Nations, are not fundamental causes of order; they are manifestations of the underlying factors, which are institutions, that truly create order. Because the United Nations generates so much observable and quantifiable output in the form of resolutions, votes, and reports, it is convenient for social scientists to focus on those things, which leads them to overestimate the causal force of the organizations. It is important to examine the rules and institutions that existed in the system before the founding of the League of Nations or United Nations and that may continue after the demise of the organizations; these are more fundamental. As Bull puts it, these "basic causes" (1977, xiv) of conflict and cooperation are found at a deeper level: "economic and social injustice in human society have deeper causes than the existence of the states system" (1977, 291). Bull can thus be seen as interested in *uncovering true causes* and as ranking causes on *levels of depth.*

Balancing

Bull draws on Emmerich de Vattel for his understanding of the international balance of power. The balance is "'a state of affairs such that no one is in a position where it is preponderant and can lay down the law to others'" (1977, 101, citing Vattel's *Law of Nations*). A "simple balance" consists of two great powers, whereas a "complex balance" involves three or more. Both notions are idealizations in that, according to Bull, there have never been actual balances that are perfectly simple or complex. There are always some states beyond the recognized "great powers" that have been able to influence the course of events. Bull says that most scholars hold that in complex balances it is possible to "exploit" the existence of other powers. Consequently, on this view, complex balances are more stable than simple balances (Bull 1977, citing Wright 1964). Bull notes also that there may be regional or global balances as well as different local balances.

Bull believes that a society that is orderly will conform to laws that can be derived by systematic observation. But he does not define social order in terms of conformity to scientific laws and predictability, and he adds that the predictability of behavior in such societies is one of the things that gives them value to human beings (1977, 7–8). Certain forms of disorderly behavior, such as social revolutions, may also conform to observed regularities and scientific laws. Again, one sees Bull viewing good explanations as uncovering true causes.

Goals. Order occurs when the basic goals of the system are fulfilled, namely, preservation of the system and the society of states, maintenance of continued sovereignty of individual states, and maintenance of peace as the normal state of affairs. With regard to the first, there have been challenges, but the general consensus on the value of this goal has stimulated many states to work to defeat these challenges. With regard to the second, each state recognizes the sovereignty of other states in exchange for their recognition of its own sovereignty; although states have permitted occasional annexations, they have justified such changes by regarding them as compensating certain states or enhancing the balance of power and thereby helping to preserve the system. And with regard to the third, the goal is to prevent violence from becoming the normal condition among states (1977, 16–18). Balancing is a means of achieving both the second and the third goals. In fact, Bull says that systemwide balances have prevented any world empire from developing, and local balances have helped to preserve the independence of many states. When balances exist, either locally or globally, they enhance the effectiveness of the other order-promoting institutions of international politics, such as diplomacy, organizations, law, great-power negotiations, and war (1977, 106–7).

Causation. Central to good causal explanations, according to Bull, is the identification of causal relationships. Rules and institutions are important both because of their ability to promote order and because of their "causal" effects on the actors in a system. The rules and institutions are part of the "efficient causation of international order" and "are among the necessary and sufficient conditions" of international order" (1977, 74–75). Bull doubts the legitimacy of structural-functional explanations in domestic societies, and even more so in international relations, because they are predicated on the assumption of the "wholeness" of the system or society they purport to explain. The assumption does not hold in the context of international relations because in structural-functional explanations, parts are explained in terms of their fit into the whole, which confers a form of primacy on the whole that is not applicable in the case of states or the international system.

Bull concludes that the balance of power is the most significant of the various causal mechanisms that promote stability in international systems. He says that "the actual institution of the balance of power," as a conscious mechanism to thwart hegemonic ambitions, arose with "the coalition against Philip II and its preservation was an implicit objective of the Peace of Westphalia" (1977, 32). In the fight against Louis XIV, the balance of power became an institution in international society. The balances of the early Westphalian system were different from ancient balances because the modern process required continuous diplomatic interaction and a focus on the system as a whole. A simpler form of balancing occurred in antiquity, when balancing operated on a micro level rather than a system level. Bull cites Hume's discussion of Polybius's account in *The Histories* of Syracuse's decision to side with Carthage in the hope of limiting Roman expansion (1977, 105).

To produce stability and order, a balance must be both objective in its material configuration and subjective in that states believe there is a balance. International order also requires "reciprocity," which erodes under hegemony. When balances erode, hegemons may "lay down the law" to others as they choose. Thus, "it is a paradox that . . . the steps necessary to maintain the balance often involve the violation of the injunctions of international law" (1977, 108). The requirements of order take precedence over those of international law or the rights of small states (1977, 109). Bull believes that a theoretical explanation should *impart an understanding* of international systems. Any such theoretical enterprise "is an intellectual and not a practical" one (1977, 308).

The Cold War Balance. At the time Bull published *The Anarchical Society*, the major actors in the system (the United States, the Soviet Union, China, and Japan) shared a "common stock of ideas," but did not share a common culture, did not operate on the basis of an agreed set of rules, and did not seek balance as a goal of the system in the way that eighteenth-century Europeans did (as codified in the Treaty of Utrecht in 1713, at the end of the War of Spanish Succession). For three hundred years after the Treaty of Utrecht, the great powers had rough equality in terms of power, similar kinds of power, diplomatic "mobility" in terms of ability to change alliances, and generally accepted "rules of the game." And, unlike the United States and the Soviet Union during the Cold War, the European monarchs shared a common culture (1977, 115–16). Bull holds that balances were to be expected under the conditions of early modern Europe. But he argues further that balances can operate even in the absence of those conditions. Bull agrees with Keohane and Nye (1975, 1977) that the major players in one issue area (e.g., military power, monetary policy, trade, investment) are not necessarily the major players in other, different issue areas. Nevertheless, "we cannot do without" an overall assessment or scale of power (Bull 1977, 114).

Mechanisms and Criteria

Bull does not require an automatic mechanism for balances. He does not think that we may assert universally that powerful states emphasize above all the search for hegemony, or that smaller states always balance against the potential hegemon. These happen only when leaders decide they will. If leaders choose otherwise, equilibrium may be absent and order may not emerge. There is no "inevitable tendency" to act in any of these ways (1977, 112).

Bull contends that any successful explanation must include both agents' intentions and causal *mechanisms* that connect the intentions to outcomes. He clearly endorses intentional choices that constitute mechanisms (1977, 71, 126, 160). Bull uses counterfactuals to draw various alternative theories and compares them to observed outcomes, especially in his chapter 10, where he considers which of the four alternative conditions would lead to international order: complete disarmament, Grotian "solidarity" among states, ubiquitous nuclear proliferation, and ideological homogeneity. Bull discusses the value of rules and institutions to control and contain military power (1977, 229), which shows the value of aiding in the control of the international environment. As noted, Bull believes that an explanation should *impart understanding* and identify *true* and *deep* causes. In the hypothetico-deductive manner, Bull draws consequences from some of the conditions required by each prescription and argues that those consequences do not accord with historical processes. The arguments draw on the criteria of *empirical adequacy* and *environmental control.*

6. STEPHEN WALT—BALANCING THREATS

In his 1987 book *The Origins of Alliances* and various papers on alliances Stephen Walt develops an explanation of alliance formation that he calls balance-of-threat theory. He describes this as a structural theory that is in many ways similar to, and a variant of, Waltz's balance-of-power theory. But there are important differences. According to Walt, states' decisions to align are driven not by the distribution of power or capabilities but by calculations about the distribution of threats. The states with the greatest capabilities are often also the most threatening, but when they are not, alliances will form to counteract the most threatening state rather than the strongest one (Walt 1987, 265). According to Walt, the threat a state poses results from its power capabilities, geographic proximity, offensive arsenal, and perceived aggressiveness. Walt tests the explanations by examining thirty-six alliances in the Middle East involving eighty-five separate state decisions over a period of twenty years.

Walt advances the case for his balance-of-threat explanatory theory by comparing it to other prominent alliance-formation explanations, such as balance of power, bandwagoning, ideological affinity, and foreign aid and/or transnational penetration. Bandwagoning, as noted earlier, occurs when states choose to work with rather than against a hegemon because they are attracted to its strength. This results in the creation of alliances that support the preponderant power in the system. The hypothesis of ideological affinity holds that two or more states are more likely to align with one another if they share an ideology, such as socialism, liberalism, monarchy, and the like. Another explanation is that providing foreign aid and "penetrating" another state's government could induce states to align with one of the great powers. On this view, state A gains influence over state B by creating loyalties among B's public officials, by lobbying to change perceptions of B's leaders, or by propaganda campaigns to change mass opinion in state B. In hypothetico-deductive fashion, Walt draws a set of hypotheses from each explanation that can be subject to empirical tests.

In Walt's view, states balance either because, by curbing the power of a rising hegemon, they protect themselves and enhance prospects for survival, or because, by joining the weaker alliance, the state gains a greater relative share of power than it would have were it to align with the rising hegemon (1987, 18–19).

Results

Walt summarizes his four main findings as follows: "First, most obviously, external threats are the most frequent cause of international alliances. Second, balancing is far more common than bandwagoning. Third, states do not balance solely against power; as predicted, they balance against threats" (1987, 148). Fourth, offensive capabilities and intentions increase the likelihood of others joining forces in opposition, although the precise impact of these factors is difficult to measure" (1987, 148). Walt elaborates on the third point: "Although the superpowers choose alliance partners primarily to balance against each other, regional powers are largely indifferent to the global balance of power. Instead, states in the Middle East most often form alliances in response to threats from other regional actors" (1987, 148).

Walt concludes his analysis by arguing that balance of threat has the greatest explanatory power of any of the explanatory hypotheses about alliance formation. Ideological affinity has some explanatory value, but its impact declines rapidly as threats increase. That is, when threat levels are low, ideology has an effect, but when they rise, it becomes much less relevant. All of the others provide little explanatory power except for ideological affinity, which has at least some. Explanatory power is measured by how well the expectations that are generated from the explanatory hypotheses—for the specific circumstances of each state in the Middle East at each particular time—match up with or contradict both the alignments that are formed and the reasons provided by the states' leaders.

Walt argues that his explanation is not dependent on evidence taken from a particular region or time period. He observes that most studies of alliance formation, and most studies of the behavior of states generally, draw their hypotheses from, and base their conclusions on, European history—especially behavior of the great powers. Walt believes that his study is more satisfactory because he takes hypotheses drawn from one data set, European history, and tests them against another data set, Middle Eastern states' behavior and decision making.

Policy Implications

Walt agrees with others that the formulation of effective policies requires a correct understanding of alliance formation. If we live in a world in which states bandwagon more often than balance, then different policies will be effective. The hope of creating an imperial realm, for example, looks very different if states are in fact more likely to balance against the aggressor or are more likely to bandwagon with it. As Walt puts it with regard to balancing and bandwagoning, "The two hypotheses depict very different worlds" (1987, 17). The particular implications Walt draws for the United States were very comforting for the United States in the world of 1987. He argues that the United States should drop its hostility to left-leaning governments and relax its concerns about the spread of communism because states align on the basis of regional threats, not global superpower competition. The Soviet Union is much more threatening, which gives the United States a major advantage. The less interventionist the United States is, the more it will look like the safer superpower with which to ally.

The Role of Assumptions

Walt treats assumptions differently than does Waltz (e.g., 1979, 122), who accepts assumption as justifiable if they enable a theory to explain and predict. For Waltz, the utility of the explanations and the accuracy of the predictions justify the theory, and when the theory is justified, there is justification for the theory's assumptions. In contrast, Walt treats assumptions as premises that require empirical support. Walt offers support for his assumptions by examining the internal debates about alignment in his case studies. Once support is presented, as Walt sees it, the reader must then accept the assumption as true in their own right.

Criteria of Evaluation

Walt relies on both implicit and explicit criteria. One of the latter is the range of phenomena the explanation covers. He says that the balance-of-threat explanation he offers has greater range since it is supported by evidence "from several different contexts," both Europe and the thirty-six Middle East alliances he surveys (1987, 15). Walt holds that his theory compares favorably to Waltz's and to other theories of balance of power because "balance of threat is more general and abstract" than balance-of-power theory (1987, 263n3) and thus has a *larger domain* than Waltz's. Walt dismisses foreign aid and penetration in part because the content of those explanations is "subsumed within the more general" elements of balance of threat (1987, 268). Hence, an explanatory theory is superior to a rival if it is more general and able to subsume the rival.

Since his theory is not reliant on a single European dataset for the results, Walt sees his theory as more *robust* than others. The coalitions that defeated Germany in World Wars I and II were far more powerful than balance-of-power theory would predict, and Walt says he can explain it, as Germany not only was powerful but also combined "proximity, offensive capabilities, and extremely aggressive intention" (1987, 264). And to explain the changes in Egypt's alliance relationships, balance-of-threat theory can draw on Nasser's apparent intentions as an explanatory factor, which balance of power cannot (1987, 264). He also endorses the criterion of *simplicity* at various places, such as when he says, "Balance of threat theory improves on balance-of-power theory by providing greater explanatory power with equal or greater parsimony" (1987, 263; see also page 239).

Walt believes that a good explanation will be acceptable if it produces more *accurate predictions* than its rivals, and he says that his theory does better than the other theories he examines, including balance of power. To support his claim of predictive prowess, Walt adds a set of cases that occurred after he completed his main analysis of cases from 1959 to 1977. He applied his explanatory hypotheses to a subsequent period and concluded that the predictions were accurate (1987, 269–73).

Waltz's balance-of-power theory makes use of microeconomic principles and Riker's theory of minimum-winning coalitions. The latter scores very well on the criterion of *explanatory unification*, since it is alleged to apply to business relationships, domestic politics, international politics, and so on. But the expectations of minimum-winning coalitions do not match actual behavior, as coalitions against Germany and its allies in World Wars I and II were much larger than "minimum." Balance of power fails on the criterion of empirical adequacy. And balance-of-power theory cannot explain why no Arab state, in their many alignments and realignments, ever aligned with Israel, a significant regional power. The reason Walt gives is that power is only one aspect of the calculation that states make, according to his balance-of-threat theory. Walt's theory explains the formation of very powerful winning coalitions in World Wars I and II, and in general how states form alliances "when a state's potential allies are roughly equal in power. In such circumstances, a state will ally with the side it believes is least dangerous" (1987, 264).

Walt prefers theories that provide *true causes* and *deep causes* of behavior. In considering methodological obstacles (1987, 14, 49), Walt discusses the importance of the foundations of the intentional action of participants. He claims that his elite interviews provide the true causes of state action and separate the superficial causes from the deeper causal forces. Walt rejects the "transnational penetration" theory for several reasons, one of which is that, even when it accords with outcomes, threat is a more important factor because it is a prior causal factor (1987, 48). This reveals another implicit criterion of deep causes. Walt conceives of causal forces and their relationship to explanation in such a way that if an A-type event causes a B-type event, which in turn pushes forward a resulting C-type event, then the explanatory value is to be found in A rather than in B. Thus, the temporal precedence of A renders its causal role somehow deeper than B's.

Walt seeks explanatory power, consistency with observed behavior, and parsimony. His theory, which incorporates proximity, offensive potential, and states' intentions, appears to be less parsimonious than balance of power. However, he argues that it is equally parsimonious, because "balance of threat theory . . . is more general and abstract. Whenever one moves to a more general or abstract level of analysis, one inevitably includes more variables. More general theories by definition incorporate a broader range of phenomena. But a more general theory is not less parsimonious as long as the principal ideas that organize its relevant variables are as few in number as . . . [those of] the less general theory it replaces" (1987, 263n). Ultimately, Walt says that his theory "improves on traditional balance-of-power theory by providing greater explanatory power with equal parsimony" (1987, 263). He is clearly endorsing the superiority of explanations that excel in explanatory power and simplicity.

Another criterion he relies on to mark a good explanation is its ability to *support counterfactuals.* Walt dislikes a strictly case-study-based method of supplying evidence, because theories that are defended with cases alone "may not tell us much about how different states would behave in different circumstances" (1987, 8). States may balance more often, but they may bandwagon under certain conditions. But he does believe that it is important to know which is generally more prevalent. In summary, Walt relies on the criteria of *simplicity, range of domain, predictive accuracy, robustness, explanatory unification, true causes, deep causes, mechanisms, imparts understanding, empirical adequacy,* and *support of counterfactuals.*

7. JOHN MEARSHEIMER'S "BACK TO THE FUTURE"

John Mearsheimer is one of the best-known structural-realist theorists. He has authored several very influential and provocative works, such as "Back to the Future: Instability in Europe After the Cold War" (1990), "The False Promise of International Institutions" (1994–95), and *The Tragedy of Great Power Politics* (2001), as well as several controversial works with Stephen Walt on US Middle East policy (Mearsheimer and Walt 2007, 2012).

Mearsheimer's famous post–Cold War article, "Back to the Future" (1990), appeared less than a year after the fall of the Berlin Wall. In 1985 Mikhail Gorbachev rose to the leadership position in the Soviet Union, and from the start he proposed a series of sweeping changes in Soviet domestic and foreign policy. Some people in the West, most notably leaders in the Reagan administration, dismissed these as insincere ploys intended to weaken Western resolve and lull the more gullible Europeans and Americans to trust him so that Moscow could take advantage of them. However, some scholars took the gestures as genuine and argued that, if Gorbachev were to continue the policies, the proper US response could bring the Cold War to an end (Mueller 1986, 1).

In "Back to the Future" Mearsheimer argued that if the Cold War were to come to a complete halt, Europe would return to its old, familiar ways of instability and violence. That article was among the first to make a compelling case for pessimism about Europe after the Cold War. Mearsheimer argued that, because the balance of power is fundamental to war and peace, any change therein resulting from the decline of the Soviet Union would have far reaching and destabilizing effects. Because "Back to the Future" was so widely read and discussed, it is the most appropriate focus among Mearsheimer's writings for this chapter; it had considerable impact in IR and influenced other realists. (The influence of the paper is clear also from its influence on authors discussed in Chapter 5). Moreover, while a few differences are noted here, Mearsheimer's conception of explanation in "Back to the Future" is generally in line with his ideas in subsequent works.

Mearsheimer's Offensive Realism

Mearsheimer contrasts his offensive variant of structural realism to Waltz's defensive version. While both authors treat survival as the state's chief priority, Mearsheimer, in comparison to Waltz, believes that states place a higher priority on the expansion of power. In "Back to the Future" and *The Tragedy of Great Power Politics* (2001, 30–32), Mearsheimer identifies five assumptions that offensive realism makes: the international system is anarchic, the great powers possess offensive capabilities, certainty about others' intentions is impossible, survival is the primary goal, and great powers behave rationally (see also Mearsheimer 1994–95, 10).

The strategy of the argument of "Back to the Future" is to offer an explanation for "the Long Peace" between the superpowers during the Cold War, to argue that the theory from which that explanation is derived leads to a prediction of less stability in the post–Cold War period, to identify the leading theories that offer different predictions (i.e., equal or greater stability), and to show ways in which offensive realism is superior. Mearsheimer sees the principle explanatory rivals as liberal independence, democratic peace, and a constructivist-like social learning theory, according to which Europeans have come to understand that there are no benefits that can outweigh the massive costs wrought by the death and destruction inherent in modern warfare. Mearsheimer then derives both predictions and policy prescriptions from his theory.

Europe's stability during the Cold War was, according to Mearsheimer's argument, a result of three fundamental forces: the system of two great powers, the rough military equivalence of those two great powers, and the presence of nuclear weapons. Each of these is a general causal element that led to greater stability than would otherwise have occurred. Mearsheimer regards the structure of the international system as the most important of the three factors. During the first half of the twentieth century, with multipolarity in place and nationalism raging, Europe was war-prone and violent. But even nationalism, ostensibly a domestic factor, was shaped by the systemic multipolarity in which leaders used hypernationalist rhetoric to justify the costs of military competition (1990, 12, 20–21).

Mearsheimer says that wars occur when the benefits of military aggression outweigh the costs. Thus, the expected favorable outcome is a crucial explanatory factor in understanding the onset of war. He stays firmly within the framework of rational calculation, according to which some factors (active causes) impel actors to act and some factors (passive or permissive causes) create conditions in which it is easier for the active causal factors to produce their effects. An example of the latter is offered when Mearsheimer presents comments such as, "Multipolarity also created conditions that permitted" (1990, 24). Polarity is crucial to Mearsheimer's theory, because the balance of power is central to leaders' calculations of expected costs and benefits. Under anarchy each state's survival results only from its caution and vigilance. This fact often leads states to try to build up capabilities of their own and reduce those of their rivals.

Mearsheimer defends all three elements of his explanation—bipolarity, military parity, and nuclear arms, first by proposing theoretical rationales showing the plausibility of the proposed causal connections, and then by providing empirical evidence. One rationale for believing that bipolar systems are more stable is that in such systems the number of major-power conflict dyads is smaller. Another rationale is that deterrence works better with two great powers because there are fewer power imbalances and fewer possible miscalculations of rivals' capabilities and intentions: "Simplicity breeds certainty; certainty bolsters peace" (1990, 17). If states perceive a power inequality, the most powerful state has an incentive to go on the offensive (1990, 18). Deterrence is most effective when states see very high costs of going to war, and nuclear weapons add greatly to the prospect of high costs (1990, 19–20).

Mearsheimer criticizes both of the principal rival theories, economic liberalism and democratic peace, on grounds that they have flawed general principles and are unable to account for the historical record. He says, "The main flaw in . . . [economic liberalism] is that the principal assumption underpinning it . . . is wrong" (1990, 44). Economic liberalism fails to conform to the historical record because a century ago Europe was economically very interdependent, yet war erupted in 1914. He notes parallel failures for the "peaceful democracies" theory, which are discussed in Chapter 5. Mearsheimer thus uses the criterion of *empirical adequacy*.

Methodology

There are three ways that Mearsheimer says his explanation of the Cold War peace can be proved correct: by showing that the general theory from which it is derived is "valid," by showing that the theory can explain both the first forty-five violent years of the twentieth century and the peaceful forty-five years that follow, and by showing that the rival theories "cannot account for" the long peace, where the term *account for* seems to function in a way entirely parallel to *explain* as employed earlier in this sentence. While all three steps seem to be required to establish Mearsheimer's explanation, his phrasing here indicates that any one of the three would suffice: "one can establish . . . in three ways: first . . ." (1990, 13). Thus providing two or three of the foregoing would support the explanation all the more persuasively.

Mearsheimer accepts the realist rationality assumption. Furthermore, many natural and social scientists (e.g., Waltz) hold that a theoretical assumption need not be literally true. The assumption has value if it helps to produce a theory that yields retrodictions that are consistent with past behavior and yields predictions that subsequently prove accurate. Mearsheimer disagrees with Waltz and others on this point. As just noted, he said that the "main flaw" in one rival explanation is that its "principle assumption . . . is wrong" (1990, 44). Like Walt and unlike Waltz, Mearsheimer believes that the central theoretical assumptions scholars use to produce theoretical structures and social science explanations are either true or false, and that good theories are based on true assumptions. He says in *The Tragedy of Great Power Politics*, "Although I agree explanatory power is the ultimate criterion for assessing theories, I also believe that a theory based on unrealistic or false assumptions will not explain much about how the world works. Accordingly, each of these five assumptions is a reasonably accurate representation of an important aspect of life in the international system" (Mearsheimer 2001, 30). And the causes Mearsheimer seeks are *true causes*. Thus, while Mearsheimer's substantive theory is quite closely related to Waltz's, his metatheory is very different.

Mearsheimer's chief method of analysis is "process tracing," which he uses to recount stages of decision making and to discover patterns. However, in so doing, he assumes that states and leaders rationally maximize security and power, even when this is not explicit in documents. Moreover, in "Back to the Future" Mearsheimer acknowledges that he has "focused on aspects of the international system surrounding Germany. This focus reflects my view that systemic factors were more important" (1990, 25). For most theorists there is some interplay between theory and evidence. But Mearsheimer is here acknowledging that his commitment to structural realism leads him to emphasize system structure. Mearsheimer treats Nazi Germany's violent foreign policy and genocidal domestic priorities as two distinct phenomena. Many others see them as two manifestations of a single sociopolitical force, which adds to the ranking on the criterion of *simplicity*. Mearsheimer's realist belief in the priority of the international does not fit easily with this view and leads him to embrace a less simple explanation postulating two separate forces that led to these two manifestations of Nazi violence.

Explanation and Criteria

Mearsheimer's theory includes a search for causes. He clearly treats explanatory factors as regarded as causal. War can be caused by both international factors, especially the distribution of military power and the character of military forces (1990, 6), and domestic factors, like hypernationalism in the early twentieth century. But the international structural factors can themselves be causes of the domestic conditions. "Back to the Future" includes explicit endorsements for the role of IR theory to guide policy because IR theory contains causal generalizations that allow us, albeit very imperfectly, to *predict*. Mearsheimer correctly states that in every policy prescription decision makers invoke causal generalizations, which—whether they acknowledge it or not—can be justified only by theories. Mearsheimer thus freely offers singular and general causal claims.

In the search for patterns and associations, Mearsheimer notes that there is "a perfect correlation between bipolarity, equality of military power, and nuclear weapons, on the one hand, and the long peace on the other hand" (1990, 21). Since Mearsheimer is looking for patterns and associations for nearly half a century of peace in Europe, he fails to note that a similar period of peace among the great powers ran from 1871 to 1914 without the presence of these three conditions.

Another criterion Mearsheimer relies on is *support of counterfactuals*. He says, "German power could have been countered before both world wars had the other European powers balanced efficiently against Germany" (1990, 22). The type of explanation Mearsheimer offers is of the causal, stage variety. The structural condition of anarchy leads to a determinate sequence of stages, in which multipolarity and other conditions produce instability, while bipolarity produces a different sequence of stages. Mearsheimer uses memoirs and internal communications to show intentions and individuals' calculations at various stages of crisis or negotiation. He sees explanations as rational and intentional, and as proceeding in stages. He relies on criteria of *true causes, mechanisms, support of counterfactuals, imparts understanding, empirical adequacy,* and *predictive accuracy.*

8. RANDALL SCHWELLER—BALANCING AND BANDWAGONING

Randall Schweller's 1994 paper "Bandwagoning for Profit" has helped to shift the terms of the balance-of-power debate, particularly since he rejects the usual dichotomy between balancing and bandwagoning and draws new distinctions (see also Schweller 2006). Schweller sees the two not as aiming at different goals but as being alternate ways of reaching the same goal under different conditions. Balancing aims to avoid losses when threats are high, and bandwagoning aims to produce a new distribution of goods in the system, regardless of the level of threat. Bandwagoning, when undertaken for gain rather than security, is more akin to "passing the buck" to an aggressive major power and amounts to "riding free on the offensive efforts of others" (Schweller 1994, 74n11). Consequently, this sort of bandwagoning is more directly opposite to defensive buck-passing than it is to balancing.

The strategies of balancing and bandwagoning are generally adopted in different sorts of systemic environments: bandwagoning is more likely in systems that are in flux, whereas balancing is more common when systems are stable. Schweller agrees that states use balancing strategies, but he says that they balance neither power capabilities, as Waltz holds, nor threats, as Walt holds; rather, they balance "interests." Moreover, states' calculations are fundamentally different from what other balancing theorists say, in that they do not involve a single, unified notion of power. Schweller's new distinctions produce a novel typology that, in his view, more accurately captures states' behavior.

Offensive Versus Defensive Realism

Contemporary realists generally follow Waltz in holding that states' primary goal is to achieve security and maintain what they have. They see all states' behavior as essentially the same, regardless of their political system or ideology. But Schweller cites cases in which states were willing to take substantial risks and pay heavy costs to achieve gains. Classical realists like Carr (1939) and Morgenthau (1954) acknowledge this; indeed, Schweller cites a long list of early postwar realists who distinguish status quo from revisionist states. But contemporary authors generally deny that there are different "types" of states seeking different sorts of goals (Schweller 1994, 85n59). Schweller notes that Mearsheimer is one of the few contemporary authors who recognizes states as risk-prone.

Schweller disagrees with Waltz's statement, "If states wished to maximize power, they would join the stronger side. . . . [T]his does not happen because balancing, not bandwagoning, is the behavior induced by the system," because Waltz does not distinguish different types of state (Waltz 1979, 126, cited by Schweller 1994, 86). Schweller adds, "Staying in place is not the primary goal of revisionist states. They want to increase, not just preserve, their core values and to improve their position in the system" (1994, 87). Weaker states often join the side they believe will win, in order to gain a share of the spoils of victory: Austria-Hungary and Turkey were revisionist states during World War I that made their alliance choices in hopes of gain, and Mussolini joined Hitler in World War II to share in conquest (1994, 86). In these instances states did not appease out of coercion, rather they sought to add to their power and prestige in the system. In Schweller's view there is no single political goal or concept of interest that all states pursue. Two states, under the same set of regional conditions, possessing the same strengths and vulnerabilities, might well choose different alignment paths, depending on their political goals. For Schweller, "the most important determinant of alignment decisions is the compatibility of political goals, not imbalances of power or threat" (1994, 88). Schweller sees his theory as better because Waltz's fails on grounds of *empirical fit*; it "is simply not true that the first concern of states is security" in all cases (1994, 86).

Typology of States and Motivations for Alliance

Schweller departs from other balancing theorists in viewing the notion of interests as varying from state to state. The "balancing" of interests he discusses operates at the system level, where it refers to the alignments between status quo states versus those of revisionist states, and at the state level, where it refers to balancing the costs the state is willing to pay for the expected gain when measured against the value of the gain. The state-level decisions result in states balancing their own revisionist impulses to seek gain against their conservative impulse to hold onto what they have under the status quo (1994, 99).

Schweller develops two binary distinctions, which yield a fourfold typology of states. One distinction is between great and small powers, and the other is between states that value the status quo and those that value the advancement of their relative position—by gaining territory or promoting favorable changes in institutional norms. Some great powers desire to maintain the status quo. Schweller uses the metaphor of a *lion* to describe those states. They are sometimes opposed by revisionist great powers with unlimited aims, whom Schweller likens to, predatory *wolves.* Schweller says that the wolves are "the prime movers of alliance behavior; status quo powers are the 'reactors'" (1994, 105). The obvious examples of unlimited-aim revisionist wolves are Napoleonic France and Nazi Germany. Lions have to be able to frighten wolves to maintain the status quo, otherwise they will have to fight to defend it (1994, 101).

The lesser powers will behave differently from one another on the basis of their political values. Some weaker states—the *jackals*—seek to align with the lions to gain a share of the spoils as the powerful revisionist state expands its power, and sometimes to protect themselves against the wolves. Some weaker powers are willing to align with a powerful revisionist, even if there is risk involved, as long as the smaller state prizes political gain. The small power may also choose to align with the revisionist state simply because it is safer; the revisionist power is willing to make concessions to the weaker state in exchange for the latter agreeing not to join the other side, which could turn the balance of capabilities against the revisionist, as happened when Hungary, Bulgaria, and the Soviet Union aligned with Hitler (1994, 94). When they align with a major-power wolf just before it is about to win a war, there is little risk to them; they are merely "piling on." Some small powers—*lambs*—are more timid and have no interest in paying high costs to expand, or even to defend what they have. These are weak states that lack material resources or have internal sociopolitical divisions—or both—and they are prey for the wolves of the system. Some choose to bandwagon out of fear of the stronger states, while others seek neutrality in the hope that the wolves will "eat them last"; as long as they continue to survive, they may entertain hopes of the tide turning away from the predator (Rothstein 1968).

The usual form of bandwagoning occurs because leaders of powerful states believe that they have to continue to fight and win wars; if they do not, others will begin to work against them. Thus, they expect that as long as they continue to move forward, they will be seen as successful, and other states will not form balancing alliances against them but will join their bandwagon. Another form of bandwagoning occurs outside of wartime or high-threat conditions when states come to believe that one or more states have been successful and represent the "wave of the future." This positive view, not based on fear, can lead smaller states to bandwagon with, rather than counterbalancing against, a revisionist state. During the Cold War many states aligned with China and/or the Soviet Union, believing that socialism was proving to be the best system; others after the Cold War aligned with the West, believing that liberal democracy was the wave of the future. This causal process is akin to Nye's (2004) theory of soft power, according to which a state with certain sorts of positive traits can gain influence and attract others to its side without coercive tactics (2004). For Schweller (1994, 96), "the Soviet success of sputnik caused more dominoes to fall than Soviet military pressure ever could." Thus, states may have "rational reasons" for following revisionist major powers (Schweller 1994, 96). This form of bandwagoning is often spurred by charismatic leaders, ideology, and military victories. We see that states may bandwagon for a variety of reasons—both jackals and lambs may choose to bandwagon rather than to pass the buck (as noted in the discussion on Waltz) or to balance by joining the weaker coalition.

Explanation and Criteria

Schweller's new distinctions produce an explanation that has greater empirical fit with key historical decisions. The theory yields expectations about behavior, given that one knows which conditions obtain (whether peacetime, crisis, war prosecution, or war termination) and which "species" of states are involved (whether lions, wolves, jackals, or lambs). The nature of the states and the conditions that obtain provide a mechanism for generating the outcome. But the additional factors *decrease* the theory's level of simplicity.

Schweller appeals also to *explanatory unification.* He discusses the process of choosing major-party nominees in US presidential contests. "States, like delegates at party conventions, are lured to the winning side by the promise of future rewards" (1994, 88–89). Schweller quotes a work on nominating processes: "Delegates wish to be on bandwagons because support of the nominee at the convention will be a basic criterion for the later distribution of Presidential favors and patronage" (Pomper 1963, 144).[6] Schweller thus cites another set of political processes that operate with the same incentives and produces the same outcomes as alliance choices. Two different political processes, one domestic and one international, are brought together as conforming to the same dynamics and patterns. There is no reason to inject the domestic discussion of American presidential politics except to add persuasive force to his theory. Schweller is implicitly drawing on the criterion of explanatory unification to display the superiority of his version of bandwagoning.

Schweller's extensive use of the animal species metaphor to get at the power and motivations of states strongly suggests that he believes he has discovered the real causes of states' alignment behavior. We might note that there is, presumably, some explanatory value from the zoological metaphor. Also, likening states to animals in the wild has specific connotations (e.g., predator and prey) and conveys a specific, certain image of states and their interactions.[7]

Schweller offers *counterfactuals* to support causal explanations. For example, he argues that states often bandwagon in situations when balance-of-power theories would predict balancing. He points out that states bandwagoned with Napoleon and made the decision to balance only when they became the targets of his aggression. Support comes in the form of counterfactual reasoning: "The Allied coalition . . . would never have come together in the first place, much less held together, had Napoleon not attacked his own allies and neutrals" (1994, 92).

Schweller draws on the criterion of predictive accuracy. He believes that his theory has predictive ability, at least over the near term, when he says that the change in the international system at the end of the Cold War will lead to concerts. He says that the post–Cold War system is likely to move away from balance toward a concert because major states agree on an acceptable status quo. Schweller adds, "Balance-of-interest theory, by focusing on variations in actors' preferences, can account for this change; structural balance-of-power theory and balance-of-threat theory cannot" (1994, 106). His theory takes into account finer-grained differences in what states desire and prefer, and it shows that states bandwagon and buck-pass rather than simply balance power, threaten, and the like (see also Nexon 2009). The theory is intentional and causal, and the set of criteria he relies on to defend it includes, as noted, *empirical adequacy, depth of causes, mechanisms, explanatory unification, predictive accuracy*, and *support of counterfactual* conditional statements.

9. JACK LEVY ON BALANCE OF POWER

When the Soviet Union collapsed, Waltz and other structural realists predicted that second-level powers would coalesce to form a new coalition to counter American power. A decade later, with evident failure of that prediction, those authors were forced to confront the question of why no such alliance had formed. A number of major IR scholars addressed this question, and three of the most important accounts are considered in this section and the following sections—those by Levy, Pape, and Brooks and Wohlforth. Also, note that

Mearsheimer's 1990 paper "Back to the Future" argued that the comfortable stability of the late Cold War would end.

Some authors in the 1990s began to argue that a new form of balancing was occurring, which was harder to detect. This "soft balancing" was contrasted to traditional military-economic "hard balancing" alliances. The new term drew on Nye's notion of soft power, according to which influence can be exercised beyond the traditional military-economic hard power. Nye had long argued that, while the United States has had preponderant hard power, much of its influence resulted from its soft power, which is evident because even America's hegemonic hard power is not sufficient to explain its much greater level of global influence. Moreover, states like Denmark and Sweden enjoy an image that has enabled them to affect other states' decisions to a degree that does not fit with their limited hard power. As Nye (2004, ii) puts it, soft power "is the ability to get what you want through attraction rather than coercion or payments. It arises from the attractiveness of a country's culture, political ideals, and policies."

Jack Levy, who has published many influential works on IR questions related to the onset of war and aspects of balance-of-power theory, added a new distinction to the debate over whether states were engaged in hard balancing, soft balancing, or no balancing.[8] His most thorough statement appeared in his 2003 paper "Balances and Balancing: Concepts, Propositions, and Research Design," which was part of the widely read collection *Realism and the Balancing of Power: A New Debate*, edited Vasquez and Elman.

Terminology

Levy, like other authors discussed here, laments that theorists often fail to define the key terms of *power*, *balance*, and *hegemony* (2003, 129). He notes the range of theorists who modify traditional balancing, like Walt's (1985) balance of threat, and who offer alternatives, like Schweller's (1996) analysis of bandwagoning and Barnett's (1996) constructivist-oriented national identity–based alternative. Levy also notes the high stakes of the debate for theory and policy, offering an argument similar to Walt's (1987, 17; see also the discussion of Walt in this chapter). In general, two great powers acting rationally would make different choices if they held different beliefs about the accuracy of balancing theory.

In the vast IR literature on balancing, most supporters, according to Levy, converge on two related hypotheses: whenever a state approaches hegemonic status, a balancing coalition will form against it, and hegemons rarely arise in multistate systems (2003, 133, 139; see also Levy 2004, 35). Critics of balancing contend that the historical record does not back up balancing claims. The debate thus continues. Levy attempts to settle it by adding a new distinction, between rising regional hegemons whose power is primarily *land based* and those whose power is primarily *sea based.* The central thesis of Levy's 2003 paper is that counterbalancing coalitions have historically formed to stop the former but not the latter (2003, 145).

Balance-of-power theorists' claim that the goal of a balance-of-power system is stability, defined as "great power peace." Levy disputes this claim because it implies that states prize peace above all else, which is inconsistent with the historical record, as states often resort to war when peace is possible. It thus lacks *empirical adequacy.* Moreover, Levy rejects the core realist tenet that it is rational for states to fight for national survival, security, autonomy, and territorial integrity. Levy also argues that it is always a mistake to speak of the "goals" of a system. States are guided by individuals, and only individuals may properly be said to have goals. A system makes no conscious decisions and cannot be said to have traits that require decisions. Since balance-of-power theorists are generally realists, they view state strategies as promoting national interest and agree that institutions have little effect on world politics. However, some, like Morgenthau and Bull, see norms and institutions as relevant to systems. The latter are designed by state governments to promote systemic goals. Levy clearly endorses methodological individualism and denies the value of social science functional explanations of the sort discussed in Chapter 2. But recall that many biologists, without presuming a "Designer," speak of the goals or purposes of biological systems, with statements like "The purpose of the spots on a leopard is to conceal the predator as it approaches its prey."

Methodological Obstacles

Levy argues that many scholars continue to disagree about balancing, in part because there have been so few proper empirical tests. He proposes settling the matter by testing the core balancing principles, which requires that he find a way to overcome the methodological obstacles and confusions. One obstacle has been the level of abstraction in the debate and the vague use of terms. To enable empirical debate to move forward, Levy proposes to add precision, which will allow variables to be operationalized and coded with unambiguous rules.

Levy offers various instances of the vagueness. Scholars say that if a state announces its opposition to a rising hegemon, or joins a counterbalancing peacetime coalition, it is "balancing." But at what point in the hegemon's rise must the state take this action for it to qualify as "balancing"? If weaker states form an antihegemonic coalition only after the hegemon has launched a war, have they balanced? There is no clear set of timing constraints as to when alliance formation should count as balancing for coding purposes. (In Levy's view a coalition formed after war begins should not count as balancing.) Furthermore, the mere formation of an alliance may not be enough to code a case as "balancing" if there is minimal commitment of resources (2003, 136). But again, there is no agreement about how much investment is needed to count a state as part of a coalition. Iraq was denounced by the United States and the United Kingdom as a rising hegemon because of its pursuit of nuclear weapons; Costa Rica announced support for the US- and UK-led war in Iraq but committed no resources. Was Costa Rica balancing? There is also no clear answer to the question of which measures of power should be used in balancing theories. Furthermore, there is no agreement on how powerful a rising state must be, on the basis of those measures, to qualify as a "rising hegemon." There is thus a clear lack of conceptual precision in defining and operationalizing the key terms.

In this context we note that hegemonic stability theory states that systems are more stable when there is a single hegemonic leader (2003, 145). This conflicts with the stability claims of balance-of-power theorists, who hold that states fear and avoid the dangers of hegemony. Levy's answer is that balance-of-power theories define power and hegemony on the basis of different measures, specifically, military capabilities for power, and financial and trade measures for hegemony.[9]

Levy says that correctly coding instances of balancing sometimes requires a judgment about motivations for the use of force—and these tie into the idea of unobservable balancing. Because Frederick I knew in advance that Austria was planning to form a balancing coalition against Prussia in the spring of 1757, he launched an attack on Austria in 1756. Accordingly, Prussia's attack was a reaction to the balancing already under way; had there been no balancing, there would have been no war. This example also shows Levy's acceptance of *counterfactual* tests of causation. Similarly, if Hitler saw conditions as more favorable for an attack on the Soviet Union in 1941 than they would be later, and if he also believed that the Soviet Union would eventually join the Allies and push Germany into a two-front war, then Hitler's attack on the Soviet Union should be regarded as a response to the prospect of Soviet balancing (Levy 2003, 137; see also Copeland 2000). On this interpretation of the Prussian and Nazi cases, there may have been no "observable" balancing, even though the tendency to balance was present and the unobservable motivation had a causal impact on the resulting wars. Levy agrees with many historians' understanding that Hitler's invasion of the Soviet Union was not a preventive war in anticipation of balancing, but resulted from a number of different German policies. Cases that involve assessing intentions (and use of counterfactuals) add to the difficulty of statistical analysis.

Levy contends that balancing studies encounter case selection problems and endogeneity. The balancing literature typically examines how various states behaved prior to and during interstate wars. Yet because states (correctly) expected that target states would balance against them, much of the behavior that is relevant to assessing the relationship between balancing and resulting stability concerns wars that did not take place. Similarly, because wars occur when states expect others not to balance, some beliefs about nonbalancing behavior are relevant to the assessment of balance-of-power theory. Levy concludes that scholars underestimate the causal impact of balancing because of unobserved balancing behavior, though the degree of underestimation is, in his view, difficult to gauge.

Scope Conditions—Biases of Existing Theories

Waltz, as noted, has said that all theories must specify the scope of their domains, stating which phenomena they do and do not claim to cover. Levy (2004, 37) faults balance-of-power theorists for failing to identify the pertinent scope conditions and for presenting the theories as if they were "universals, applicable in principle to any international system." Two limitations are especially important. One is that balance-of-power theories are almost always focused on the behavior of great powers.[10] A second limitation is that balancing theories, even the most influential theories of Morgenthau, Claude, and Waltz, typically draw all of their evidence from the history of European politics. The East Asian pattern was quite different; a great empire was built out of a set of distinct states. Moreover, since theorists now generalize globally, it is not obvious or knowable a priori which sort of pattern is more generalizable when taken beyond its own regional context.

Levy identifies several possible mechanisms that could explain how systems of states come into balance. One is that the rising state will stop short of such hegemonic expansion if it knows that continued expansion will lead other states to balance against it. Another is that the hegemon may be prevented from domination by being defeated in war against a newly formed counterbalancing coalition (Levy 2003, 130–31). In the 2004 paper Levy adds another mechanism, according to which the rising hegemon expands power when resistance is light but ceases doing so when it faces a counterbalancing coalition or an undesirable arms race (Levy 2004, 36).[11]

Levy provides a mechanism in offering his explanation for balancing by means of the distinction between land-based and sea-based hegemons. He can thus show how smaller states' motivations differ in their dealings with the two types of rising hegemons. Levy explains why balancing coalitions form against land-based but not maritime hegemons, namely, that the former but not the latter, by their very presence, threaten the territorial integrity of other states.[12] As noted, Levy also explains why many balancing theorists have missed this solution, which is that they rely on data from the European continent and thus observe a great deal of countercoalition formation.

Criteria

Levy endorses the importance of *greater content* and *predictive accuracy* to evaluate explanations. Levy argues that the more content a theory has, the better it is; and he argues that predictive implications add empirical content. For Levy (2003, 133), "a theory that predicts only that balances will form, or that multistate systems will not be transformed into universal empires, has far less *empirical content* and can explain far less variation in the empirical world than a theory that *predicts* state strategies as well as international outcomes." Theories that predict both outcomes and state strategies have more empirical content. Levy says that most balance-of-power theories do both; that is, they "predict strategies of balancing as well as the absence of hegemony," which confers on them greater "analytic power" because they are superior "in terms of empirical content and degree of falsifiability" (2003, 133). He acknowledges the tradeoff that added specificity can diminish their empirical adequacy (2003, 133).[13] These passages make it clear that Levy relies on content, which is connected to *greater range*, *predictability*, and *falsifiability* as important criteria.

We see Levy's expectation of mechanisms in his discussion of levels of analysis. There is a sharp contrast between system- and state-level approaches to balancing. Classical realists like Morgenthau refer to state strategies, while structuralists like Waltz emphasize the systemic outcomes. Levy notes that Waltz separates his theory from state strategies: "Waltz is free to argue that balancing is not a necessary condition for balanced outcomes, but it is incumbent on him to specify the alternative causal mechanisms through which nonhegemonic outcomes repeatedly (or always) arise, and to do so in a way that is consistent with the basic assumptions of neorealist theory" (2003, 133). Thus, we see again that for Levy a good explanation must include *causal mechanisms.* We noted already that Levy (2004, 32) invokes the criterion of *empirical fit* and the need to approach problems at a level of analysis that allows for a methodological individualist explanation. And in the discussion of methodological obstacles and the Prussian attack on Austria, we noted his reliance on support of *counterfactuals* as a form of support for causal explanatory claims.

10. ROBERT PAPE ON SOFT BALANCING

With the Cold War over for fifteen years and the US invasion of Iraq a recent event, in 2005 the journal *International Security* published a set of papers on soft balancing. Robert Pape's best-known work on the subject, "Soft Balancing Against the United States," is part of that issue. Pape sees the context of the debate as Levy does, as prompted by the mysterious absence of a new alliance to counter the hegemony of the United States.[14]

The difference between hard and soft balancing is that "soft-balancing measures do not directly challenge a unipolar leader's military preponderance, but they can delay, complicate, or increase the costs of using that extraordinary power" (2005, 17). And this process can create a cooperative framework and systemic effects to pave the way for future hard balancing. He agrees with Levy that soft balancing can be understood as a way that states can slow the increase of American influence without requiring the use of force or the creation of any formal alliance. The precipitating cause of the extensive soft balancing, in Pape's view, was the "unilateralist" approach of the George W. Bush administration. Without those policies, the other major powers would likely have continued their cooperative relationship with the United States. Pape relies on "reputation" as an important causal factor. He says that states did not traditionally balance against US power, even though the United States had often intervened with military force, because they viewed the United States as desiring to strengthen international stability.

The US decision to invade Iraq changed perceptions of the United States because it was strongly opposed by most other states, including three of the five permanent members of the UN Security Council. The invasion would be seen as part of a drive for relative gain because the financial benefits would be small compared to the overall US GDP, whereas the relative gain, in terms of control of Middle East oil, would be great. As Pape puts it, "Conquering Iraq puts the United States in a strategic position to control virtually all of the Persian Gulf's vast oil reserves, potentially increasing its power to manipulate supply for political and even military advantage against Europe and Asia" (Pape 2005, 30).[15] When the hegemon is a revisionist state, "second-ranked states that cannot solve their coordination problem by traditional means may turn to soft-balancing measures to achieve this aim" (Pape 2005, 17). This is at least in part because "nonmilitary tools . . . can have a real, if indirect, effect on the military prospects of a unipolar leader" (Pape 2005, 17). Other states would respond differently to the leader when they saw it shift from a status quo, absolute-gain maximizer to a revisionist, relative-gain maximizer.

One of the interesting puzzles about a system in which there is one dominant power (whether hegemony or unipolarity) is that such a state has presumably benefited mightily from the existing order. Thus, it would be in the leader's interest to preserve the existing order as much as possible. For that reason the leader would be regarded as a status quo power. However, many authors note that when a state achieves a certain margin of superiority over the next most powerful states, it will come to see itself as having greater security needs than ever and will then move to change the system to accommodate those intensified needs. It will then transform from a status quo to a revisionist state.

Explanation

Pape observes that three prominent balance theorists, Waltz, Walt, and Mearsheimer, gave slightly different answers to the question of why there has been no balancing against the United States. Waltz (1997, 915) argued that the balancing simply has not happened yet but will. Walt (1987) and balance-of-threat theorists claim that because the United States is much less threatening than most great powers, and because balances form against threats, not simply material capabilities, no balance will arise as long as the United States remains nonthreatening. Mearsheimer (1990, 2001) believes that the grand strategy of the United States over the past hundred years has been as an "offshore balancer," placing a higher priority on preventing the rise of hegemons in any region than on seeking hegemony for itself. For this reason, other states have a much lower need to oppose US power that they would if the United States had primarily sought hegemony for itself.

Pape believes that all three balancing explanations have an "element of truth" to them. But he thinks that one of them focuses on a more significant explanatory variable, namely the "degree of perceived threat" (2005, 20). The truth of the causes is important, and it is better to have more truth. He refers as well to true motivations as causal (2005, 24). Pape adds that the crucial systemic factor is the distinction between two types of distributions of capabilities, namely, a "balance of power system and a hegemonic one" (2005, 13), and his explanations focus on the difference between direct threats and indirect threats. He thus makes extensive use of the concept of threat in explaining alliance formations in what he calls balance-of-power systems (2005, 13), and so, in effect, uses a balance-of-threat factor in his explanations of specific alliances. A proper comparative evaluation of existing accounts will lead to discovery of the best single explanation (2005, 20), though it is possible for others to identify important explanatory factors. The different levels of causal efficacy are clear when Pape says, "The *root cause* of widespread opposition to U.S. military policies" is neither the other states' values nor increased US power (2005, 24–25), and "the *key reason* [for soft balancing] is that the Bush strategy is changing" the reputation of the United States (2005, 25). Other states agree with the goals of nonproliferation and counterterrorism but fear the unilateral methods that the United States is willing to use. Pape seeks an explanation that uncovers *true causes.*

The contrast between balancing in multipolar systems and unipolar systems is somewhat surprising. One would expect that balancing in the former is more likely to succeed, and so would be more common than balancing in the latter type of system. However, Pape notes that in multipolar systems any particular second-level power would prefer that some other second-tier power take the lead in balancing, since there are various ways to thwart the ambitions of an aggressor in multipolarity. It is then more rational for each state to pass the buck and seek to ride free in the hope that another will take the antihegemon lead, even though it may turn out that no counterbalancing alliance forms until the rising hegemon acts aggressively. However, in a unipolar system all second-tier states know that coordination among them is the only hope to impede the aims of the leader, and they are less likely to buck-pass. This type of mechanism changes the hegemon from stability seeker to power seeker, because its political leaders are seen as choosing to alter their calculations, but it does not portray the decision as fully determined by objective circumstances. The Bush administration made the decision to pursue unilateralism and proceed as a revisionist state, but another US leader at that time might have made the decision to remain a status quo power. And a successor US president may decide to return to a status quo foreign policy (2005, 34).

Throughout the article, Pape analyzes states as unitary actors and treats them as rationally responding to incentives, though their choices of a rational path are probable and not deterministic. Pape discusses the "logic of balancing" and of "passing the buck" (2005, 15–16), portraying states as choosing to balance when the incentives render balancing the rational move (2005, 15). Actors also have imperfect information because they have to rely on beliefs about other actors' motivations. And they can err regarding other states' intentions, as those in the Bush administration did with regard to other states' inclinations to balance against the United States.

Much of the phrasing of Pape's argument appears in conditional form of this sort: "if one sort of event occurs, another event of a particular sort will follow." But he often makes it clear that causal force is probabilistic, such as the *likely* counterbalancing against an aggressive hegemon (2005, 35). In general, outcomes are "likely" and "not destiny" (2005, 8, 10), and the logic he uncovers "would suggest" various outcomes. Pape does not endorse a mechanistic determinism about soft balancing (2005, 40).

Causation

Pape offers a set of causes of states' alignment and balancing decisions. He regards the perceptions of states as the precipitating cause in most cases; that is, he relies on the subjective concept of threat to do the causal work in his explanations. He says that what is even more important to a state is how others states in the system perceive the motives of the leading state and how aggressive it is regarded (2005, 14). Even small changes in that perception "can significantly increase the fear that it would make a bid for global hegemony" (2005, 14–15). Ultimately, other "major powers . . . [react] to concerns over U.S. intentions, not U.S. capabilities" (2005, 45).

Because Pape does not regard any form of balancing against the United States as mechanically predictable or inevitable (2005, 10), it is only because the perception of the United States changed with the Iraq War that soft balancing really began in earnest; the war is the "principle cause" of balancing against the United States (2005, 10). Pape argues that the consequences of the Bush administration's policies will be "momentous" (2005, 8); that even in 2005, reaction to the 2003 invasion of Iraq is evident in the form of "early states of balancing." He predicts that soft balancing against the United States will intensify if the United States does not change its unilateralist foreign policy.

Criteria

Pape makes extensive use of the criterion of *empirical adequacy.* He criticizes one account as claiming that its flaw is that evidence does not support the analysis (Pape 2005, 24–25n31). He expects that a good theory will generate *accurate predictions.* He is critical of the theory that Bush administration decision makers relied on, which erroneously predicted how second-tier powers would react to the US decision to go to war. Administration leaders' understanding of world politics did not factor in the precise ways reputations change, which then affects how major states will respond. Those inside the Bush administration expected the invasion to change the reputation of the United States in a way that would enhance other states' willingness to work with the United States. But people outside the administration, well before the war, said that if the United States were to invade, others' views of it would hurt US leadership and interests. Indeed, one of the major premises of Pape's argument is a prediction: that "soft balancing is likely to become more intense" if the United States continues Bush's unilateralism (2005, 10). We have seen also that Pape relies on criteria of *counterfactual support, mechanisms, true causes,* and *depth of causes.*

11. STEPHEN BROOKS AND WILLIAM WOHLFORTH

Stephen Brooks and William Wohlforth's 2005 paper "Hard Times for Soft Balancing" was published in the same issue of *International Security* that included Pape's and other articles. They have written other works on balancing (e.g., Brooks and Wohlforth 2008); Wohlforth also authored (1999) an important earlier paper on the balancing debate. Brooks and Wohlforth argue that it is important to assess the soft-balancing explanation because if it is correct, it is said to be precede serious hard balancing, which would portend future limitations on US power. However, they argue that the case for soft balancing has been seriously overstated—mainly because of the strong prima facie appeal of the familiar balancing metaphor and because of the absence of rigorous comparisons of soft balancing with alternative explanations.

Brooks and Wohlforth propose four alternative explanatory factors: national economic interests, regional security concerns, policy disputes with the United States, and second-tier states' domestic political incentives. They consider the strength of each explanation in the four cases that soft-balancing supporters most often invoke: Russia's coordination with China and India, Russia's aid to the Iranian nuclear program, European Union–guided military coordination, and major second-tier states' opposition to the invasion of Iraq. This comparative assessment shows, in their view, that "there is no empirical basis" for supporting the soft-balancing explanation . . . Put simply, soft balancing is not a compelling argument for U.S. restraint" (2005, 75). They conclude that "the soft balancing argument has no traction" (2005, 106).

Brooks and Wohlforth adopt the strategy of drawing a comparison of US allies' actions during and after the Cold War with their actions surrounding the Iraq War. When France opposed the US invasion of Iraq, IR analysts jumped to the conclusion that France was turning against the United States and was seeking to balance, that is, seeking to restrain the use or growth of American power. However, during the Cold War, America's NATO allies, to say nothing of other Western democracies, often took stances that sharply opposed US policies, interests, and preferences. Brooks and Wohlforth cite a list of such actions.

At first glance these actions look every bit as opposed to US interests as the way France and Russia behaved in the period leading up to the invasion of Iraq. There were various reasons, such as those just cited, that led allies to act contrary to US preferences. But during the Cold War when France withdrew from NATO's military command and opposed the Vietnam War, or when Japan and Germany refused to devalue their currencies, or when France acted to undermine the Bretton Woods system, analysts were not claiming that those states were engaged in balancing US hegemony. One major reason no one described these actions as "balancing" the United States is that the Soviet Union was engaging in *genuine* balancing—forming a European military alliance, arming anti-Western insurgencies, supporting anti-US client regimes, and building massive conventional and nuclear arsenals. In contrast, the actions of France, Germany, Japan, and others were mild. The problem today is that when France, Germany, Japan, or other states do things similar to what they did in previous decades (e.g., in the UN Security Council), there is no real, Soviet-style balancing going on with which to compare it. Consequently, French, Japanese, or Chinese actions may more easily be misinterpreted as a form of balancing. Brooks and Wohlforth conclude that these other explanations appear to be powerful, but a precise comparison remains very difficult (2005, 81).

Explanation

The soft-balancing explanation posits real and tangible balancing according to which states behave with the intention of limiting US freedom of action; it is not a claim solely about "signaling" or symbolic actions. Thus, to defend soft balancing, proponents must show that balancing behavior has genuine costs to the balancers and observable effects on the United States. Brooks and Wohlforth look at the principal cases and show that these conditions of proof are not met.

With respect to the Iraq invasion, Brooks and Wohlforth argue, as already noted, that soft-balancing theorists do not consider alternative explanations. It is possible that France, China, Germany, and others simply thought that going to war in Iraq would produce the opposite result from what the Bush administration claimed to seek—putting a brake on nuclear proliferation and striking a blow in the war on terrorism. At the United Nations and elsewhere, many states contended, correctly, that the invasion policy was mistaken because US analysis of its intelligence was flawed. With regard to the "policy dispute" explanation, one might add that even George W. Bush's father said that war in Iraq was a mistake because it could unleash severe civil unrest, there was no clear exit strategy, and the financial costs would be exorbitant—all of which turned out to be correct (Bush and Scowcroft 1998). Thus differences over which policy would be the most effective would seem to be a simpler, and certainly empirically adequate, explanation of the actions of France, Germany, and others.

Brooks and Wohlforth emphasize that the plan for war was very unpopular in Europe, and Chancellor Gerhard Schröder, "facing near-certain defeat," saw a chance to recapture "two key left-wing constituencies, both of which had long-standing antiwar preferences" (2005, 95). Schröder initially only expressed reservations about the war, but his later vigorous campaigning against it increased his popular support sufficiently to enable him to win reelection. Domestic political wrangling led Turkey to create obstacles for the Bush administration's plans. The United States requested but did not receive permission to use its military bases in Turkey to launch a second-front ground assault in northern Iraq. Domestic political factors influenced leaders in France and Russia to oppose the war as well, according to Brooks and Wohlforth.

When Russia, China, and four former Soviet Central Asian states formed the Shanghai Cooperation Organization (SCO), some argued that this showed significant soft balancing against the United States. But Brooks and Wohlforth argue that the SCO involves coordination of only minimal significance on problems like drug trafficking, Islamic extremism, and separatism, areas in which the SCO's members have obvious common interests. This sort of cooperation would likely occur with or without concerns about American hegemony. With regard to Iran's nuclear program, Russia's motivation is clearly economic. The demise of the Soviet Union and the Warsaw Pact left the Russian economy with little of value on international markets beyond natural resources, arms, and nuclear technology. Russia stood to earn up to US$8 billion in nuclear energy sales to Iran, which added very little to Iran's nuclear program compared, for example, to what Iran received from A. Q. Khan's network. Russian trade with Iran and China stems directly from Russia's economic self-interest, according to Brooks and Wohlforth (2005, 88).[16]

Finally, with regard to the European Union's plan for a rapid reaction force and combat battle groups, both public statements and planning patterns show that the motivation was not the fear that the United States would interfere excessively, but rather the contrary fear that after the Cold War, the United States would be much less willing to become involved in places where intervention would primarily benefit Europeans. Crises in Europe, especially in the Balkans, showed post–Cold War Europeans how little they could accomplish, even in Europe, without US assistance. EU force planning is clearly designed to complement rather than supplant or counter American military assets. Balancing explanations are even more dubious when one observes the declines in European military budgets, especially in research and development.

Brooks and Wohlforth's position can be seen by imagining that major states make decisions entirely without regard to their effects on the United States but rather on narrow economic needs, domestic politics, and local security concerns. Because the United States has interests around the globe, some of these decisions would fit with US preferences, some would have no effect, and some would work against US goals. Presumably, then, if soft-balancing theorists do not consider alternative explanations, they would notice only the actions that work against US preferences and would overlook those that accord with US preferences. But the actions that, by coincidence, work against US interests would be seen as consistent with the soft-balancing hypothesis. Thus, if no other explanations are held up for comparison, actions that were in no way motivated by states' desire to balance the United States would be interpreted as doing just that. Only a fair comparison of soft balancing with alternatives can show whether or not soft balancing is a significant part of states' foreign-policy strategies. By offering such a comparison, Brooks and Wohlforth say that they are able to show that the alternatives explain the key cases much better than soft balancing does.

Criteria

Brooks and Wohlforth are clearer than some authors about some of the important criteria of explanatory success that they endorse. They require specificity, which is clear in their criticisms of soft-balancing arguments on the grounds of vagueness and a failure to specify just what sorts of actions do and do not qualify as resulting from a strategy of soft balancing. They also require that a good explanation be able to eliminate alternative explanations; soft-balancing theorists fail to eliminate other explanations. As a result, any behavior observed that does not accord with US interests is presumed to be evidence of soft balancing. Brooks and Wohlforth quite clearly demand that the criterion of falsifiability be met by any acceptable theory, which is evident in their criticism of structural-realist theories as typically failing on this ground (2005, 77n12). And they require *empirical adequacy. Simplicity* in a theory is a good and ambiguity is a flaw. Brooks and Wohlforth favor explanations "with a parsimonious, generalizable theory [but] these advantages of the soft-balancing argument in no way make up for its lack of explanatory power" (2005, 107). Again it is clear that parsimony and generalizability are significant criteria.

Brooks and Wohlforth argue that soft-balancing supporters claim that the theory has "explanatory and predictive" advantages (2005, 78). Since they regard these claims, if correct, as conferring advantages on the theory, they appear to regard an explanatory theory as preferable if it is not only able to explain events but is also able to make *predictions.* And they hold that causal claims should support *counterfactuals* with comments such as, "Had the Bush administration's actions regarding Iraq caused France to perceive a direct security threat from U.S. power, as soft-balancing proponents maintain, this behavior would have been nonsensical" (2005, 105). The authors conclude, "Balance-of-power theory was developed to explain the behavior of states in systems with two or more poles in which war among the great powers was an ever-present danger. Neither of those conditions applies today. . . . Analysts [should not try] to stretch old analytical concepts that were created to deal with the bipolar and multipolar systems of the past" (2005, 107; cf. Organski 1958, 282).

12. CONCLUSION

This chapter has examined eleven of the most influential works both supporting and opposing balance-of-power explanations of alliances formation. The analysis seeks to identify the ways that authors conceive of a "successful explanation" and the criteria for explanatory superiority that they employ. Because the notion of power is so central to realism and realist balance-of-power theory, one important divide is between theorists who accept some form of balance-of-power explanation, where power is the focus, and those who do not.

As Legro and Moravscik (1999, 5) note in their widely read account of trends in IR, "Realists like E. H. Carr, Hans Morgenthau, and Kenneth Waltz sought to highlight the manipulation, accumulation, and balancing of power by sober unsentimental statesmen, focusing above all on the limits imposed on states by the international distribution of material resources. They viewed realism as the bulwark against claims about the autonomous influence of democracy, ideology, economic integration, law, and institutions of world politics." When subjective interpretations of *threat* are brought in as a key explanatory factor, "what it is" that the theory claims that states balance is fundamentally altered.

On the basis of this understanding of realist theory, we begin the analysis with a focus on the divide between the five authors who supported a balance-of-power explanation of alliances and the six who offered other sorts of explanations, including balance of threat.[17] As authors move away from power or capabilities specifically, they turn the discussion to factors like "friendships" or "affinities" between states. If states are "friendly" with one another, and that bond overrides the possibilities that a state has to wage war, the analysis moves to some form of nonrealist theory.

The first conclusion we may draw relates to the absence of explicit statements of criteria used by authors in proliferation studies:

Conclusion 1—There has been an absence of transparency about criteria chosen.

The evidence for conclusion 1 in the alliance formation debate is essentially the same as the evidence for the same conclusion in the nuclear proliferation debate. Other conclusions require further probing of the data and coding of the theoretical works. As with the survey of proliferation studies, there are not nearly enough data points to perform most of the standard statistical tests, both because the variables are all binary (yes-no) rather than quantitative, and because there are no degrees of freedom; the number of independent variables (criteria) exceed in number the eleven cases of theoretical explanations. Although we cannot perform the most familiar statistical tests, it is still possible to see various clusters or associations that might be present. Such clusters permit us to draw some suggestive, though not statistically supported, conclusions. We begin by a simple visual inspection to see if any patterns are evident. This takes us to conclusion 2.

Conclusion 2—Balance-of-power explanations were decreasingly dominant through the post-War period and were largely rejected a decade after the Cold War ended, but no consensus on an alternative emerged.

Although authors still disagree on the best explanation for alliance formation, there has been some discernible progress. The works are spread fairly evenly over time. In the 1940s Morgenthau first published *Politics Among Nations*, which for decades was read by a multitude of students and went through seven more editions. In the 1950s Organski published his first book and went on to elaborate the theory for another quarter century. In the 1960s Claude published *Power in International Relations*. In the 1970s Bull and Waltz published their major books on the balance of power. In the 1980s Walt published his book advancing balance-of-threat theory. In the 1990s Mearsheimer published his influential balance-of-power papers, followed by his book in 2001, and Schweller published his critique of balance-of-power explanations soon after Mearsheimer's paper. The three works dealing with soft balancing were published in the 2000s.

According to Table 4.1, there indeed appears to be some movement, though modest, toward agreement over the decades. When we consider the order in which the various explanations were developed, we see that, in the nearly seventy years since *Politics Among Nations* was published, there is a strong grouping of the balance-of-power theories in the first thirty-five years (four of the five of the works in that period). There was some interest in balancing approaches thereafter, but power played a decreasing role, with a shift to threat as an explanatory variable. And by 2000 it became clear that balance-of-power theorists were wrong in predicting that the demise of the Soviet Union would produce new alliances to counter US hegemony.[18] Once all three debates are discussed, a comparison between them will offer more perspective. But at this point we see more agreement than on the nuclear proliferation debate, yet considerable explanatory divergence.

Table 4.1 Chronology of alliance formation theories

Dependent variable	*Morgenthau 1948*	*Organski 1958*	*Claude 1962*	*Waltz 1964*	*Bull 1977*	*Walt 1985*	*Mearsheimer 1990*	*Schweller 1994*	*Levy 2003*	*Pape 2005*	*Brooks & Wohlforth 2005*
States balance power	X		X	X	X		X				
States bandwagon, buck-pass, or balance something other than power		X				X*		X	X*	X*	X

*Indicates balance of threat.

The goal of this study is to investigate H_1, which relates to criterial divergence and the slow progress in security studies. In the introduction we noted three possible answers to the question. ANS-1 says that authors all use more or less the same criteria, in which case H_1 is false, as the use of different criteria cannot account for continuing disagreement. ANS-2 says that, even though individual authors' criteria uses diverge, the overall aggregate of uses of criteria by each contending explanatory school (e.g., realist authors) is roughly similar to the uses of criteria by their opponents, in which case, again, criterial differences cannot account for slow progress. And ANS-3 says that H_1 is consistent with the evidence because the groups of authors use different criteria and there is some association between the degree of divergence of their use of criteria and the degree of stalemate, understood as lack of approach-to-consensus.

Divergent Uses of Criteria

Conclusion 3—Authors do not all agree on which criteria are most appropriate.

It is not difficult to see that ANS-1 does not fit with the pattern uncovered in the preceding survey of influential security studies works. Table 4.2 below displays each author's use of the criteria of explanatory adequacy and provides support for conclusion 3.

Table 4.2 shows quite clearly that the authors do not all make use of exactly, or even nearly, the same criteria. Since it is not the case that all the authors use the same criteria, we may eliminate ANS-1 and thus not use it as a basis to reject H_1. We next investigate ANS-2 by asking whether the uses of criteria in the two groups, when the authors are aggregated, use the criteria in approximate conformity with one another.

Conclusion 4—Realists and nonrealist authors do not use criteria in similar proportions.

Table 4.3 illustrates the proportional uses of the criteria by the two groups. The center and right columns of Table 4.3 can be read as a histogram contrasting balance-of-power authors with authors of alternatives explanations. It is clear that, even taken as groups, balance-of-power theorists and their opponents do not rely on the individual criteria in similar proportions. If we use a difference of two as the threshold to say that a criterion is skewed (i.e., used differently by the groups), then seven of the fourteen criteria are skewed to one group or the other.[19] Two criteria—*imparts understanding* and *control*—are used more by power-centric realists, whereas two are used equally, and the other ten are used more by non-balance-of-power theorists.[20]

Table 4.2 Uses crtieria by authors in the alliance formation debate (in descending order of uses)

Criteria of adequacy	*Morgenthau*	*Organski*	*Claude*	*Waltz*	*Bull*	*Walt*	*Mearsheimer*	*Schweller*	*Levy*	*Pape*	*Brooks & Wohlforth*	*Total number of uses*
Empirical adequacy	X	X	X	X	X	X	X	X	X	X	X	**11**
Mechanisms	X		X		X	X	X	X	X	X		**8**
Predictive accuracy	X			X		X	X	X	X	X	X	**8**
Supports counterfactuals		X		X		X	X	X	X	X	X	**8**
Uncovers true causes		X			X	X	X	X		X		**6**
Depth of causes	X	X			X	X				X		**5**
Imparts understanding	X			X	X	X	X					**5**
Greater range of domain	X	X		X		X			X			**5**
Simplicity	X	X		X		X					X	**5**
Explanatory unification	X			X		X		X				**4**
Control over environment	X			X	X		X					**4**
Falsifiability		X							X		X	**3**
Precision; eliminates alternatives											X	**1**
Robustness						X						**1**
Total uses												**74**

Table 4.3 Explanatory criteria used by balance-of-power explanations versus other explanations (in descending order of total uses)

Criteria of adequacy	*Balance of power (5 explanations)*	*Other explanations (6 explanations)*
Empirical adequacy	MG CL WZ MS BL	WT LV PA SC BW OG
Mechanisms	MG CL BL MS	WT PA SC LV
Predictive accuracy	MG WZ MS	WT SC LV PA BW
Supports counterfactuals	WZ MS	WT LV PA SC BW OG
Uncovers true causes	BL MS	SC OG WT PA
Depth of causes	MG BL	OG WT PA
Imparts understanding	MG WZ MS BL	WT
Greater range of domain	MG WZ	WT LV OG
Simplicity	MG WZ	OG WT BW
Explanatory unification	MG WZ	WT SC
Control over environment	MG BL WZ MS	—
Falsifiability	—	OG LV BW
Precision; eliminates alternatives	—	BW
Robustness	—	WT
Total uses by each group	**32**	**42**
Average use of each criterion	**32 / 5 = 6.40**	**42 / 6 = 7.00**

NOTE: Total uses of criteria = 74. Realists: MG = Morgenthau, BL = Bull, WZ = Waltz, MS = Mearsheimer, CL = Claude. Nonrealists: WT = Walt, OG = Organski, PA = Pape, SC = Schweller, LV = Levy, BW = Brooks & Wohlforth.

Table 4.3 shows clearly that ANS-2 does not apply to the alliance formation debate. The two groups of authors' uses of criteria diverge in fully a third of the "citation instances." As far as we know at this point, the two main groups of authors' divergent explanations (pro and con balance of power) might be divergent because the authors base their arguments on that substantial proportion of different criteria citations. This will be clearer when we can draw on the analyses of all three debates to gain comparative perspective.[21] But at this point conclusion 4 is substantiated.

Conclusion 5—All the authors make use of generally naturalist explanations, and all use natural science-based criteria.

Conclusion 5 shows that there is a broad agreement in the approach to the problem of proliferation; among the most widely cited works are not radical constructivist, primarily interpretivist, or poststructuralist accounts. Eight of the twelve criteria, or three-fourths, used by either group are used by both groups, a slightly higher proportion than in the proliferation debate.

Conclusion 6—Beyond a general naturalist approach to the question of why states proliferate, there is a moderate degree of overlap in authors' or groups of authors' uses of criteria of evaluation of explanations, slightly more than in the proliferation debate.

As in the proliferation debate both sides use roughly the same naturalist criteria. And there is a bit more overlap in the alliance formation debate; three-fourths of the criteria that either side uses are used by both groups.

Overall, the analysis of this chapter shows several important results in our inquiry into H_1. The debate has failed to move toward a consensus explanation because, perhaps among other reasons, there are differences in how different individual theorists and groups of theorists evaluate a good explanation. The uses of criteria are rarely made explicit (conclusion 1). In comparison with the nuclear proliferation debate, there has been somewhat more approach-to-consensus—at least theorists now agree that balance-of-power predictions were wrong and a strict balance-of-power explanation is not an option (conclusion 2). And there is still divergence in uses of criteria. Among the non-power-based theorists, the differences between balance-of-threat and other explanations of alliance formation do seem to be a result of those different uses of criteria, though the small number of cases makes confidence in this conclusion more tenuous at this point. In Chapter 6, with all three debates analyzed, it will be possible to offer a fuller comparison of both criterial overlap and degree of approach-to-consensus, which will indicate whether there are more far-reaching conclusions that follow from the patterns observed in the three debates.

5 THE DEMOCRATIC PEACE DEBATE

Why Do Democracies Act the Way They Do?

OVER THE PAST QUARTER CENTURY the most extensively debated set of questions in security studies, and perhaps in all of international relations (IR), are those connected with "the democratic peace." This chapter examines in particular the "democratic dyad" debate over whether—and if so, why—democratic dyads (i.e., pairs of democracies) behave differently toward one another than any other sort of dyad. The claim that democracies are generally less violent and war-prone than other sorts of states is known as the monadic hypothesis. And the claim that pairs of democracies consist of members that fight each other less often than members of other sorts of dyads is known as the dyadic hypothesis. The latter is the core of democratic peace theory, since the claim would have to be true if the prescription for the Kantian notion of a peaceful system of democracies were to have merit. The term *democratic peace debate* in this chapter refers primarily to the debate over the claim that democratic states, by virtue of their liberal democratic nature, deal peacefully with other democracies.

The idea that nondemocracies would behave less violently than traditional monarchies and autocracies goes back many centuries. Thucydides in *History of the Peloponnesian War* describes the democratic Athenians behaving as much different from Spartans, but Athenians were different because of their exceptional energy and aggressiveness, not their pacific nature. Machiavelli commented that democracies may be less violent. And as Chapter 1 noted, the fountainhead of contemporary democratic peace studies is Kant's 1795 *Perpetual Peace*, in which he argued that a system of states, having a separation of the executive and legislative powers (i.e., republics), would be a much more peaceful system.

In the twentieth century a number of authors examined this claim, often commenting in favor of the peacefulness of democratic states but without being able to muster strong empirical support for it. Quincy Wright, in his monumental 1942 book *A Study of War*, did not find a statistical basis for the claim. Lewis F. Richardson, in his pathbreaking 1960 work *The Statistics of Deadly Quarrels*, came to a similar conclusion. The volumes by Wright and Richardson are broad inquiries into international conflict that looked at regime-type as one among many other factors. However, in the late 1960s several papers focused specifically on the question of democratic peace. East and Gregg (1967) compared regimes with freedom of the press to those lacking such freedom and concluded that the latter group was more violent, but Wilkenfeld (1968) argued that those same data produced less clear-cut results.

In two brief papers Dean Babst (1964, 1972) advanced a pair of dramatic claims: no two democratic states had ever gone to war against each other, and the current global trend was an accelerating increase of democratic states. Small and Singer (1976) published an influential paper in which they criticized Babst, principally for not explaining his method and coding rules. Using an improved research design, Small and Singer tested claims of democratic peace (DP). They concluded that democracies are roughly as war-prone as nondemocracies are, but not toward one another. However, they argue that the peaceful behavior of democracies toward one another stems from democracies' geographical separation from one another, not from their nature or structure. Rummel challenged this skepticism about the dyadic peace in a 1983 paper in *Journal of Conflict Resolution*, which was in turn challenged by Weede (1984) and Chan (1984) in a later issue of the same journal.

Michael Doyle and Bruce Russett were at the center of the democratic peace debate as it developed over the past thirty years. Doyle published several widely read works (1983a, 1983b, 1986) that led to an extensive debate. And Russett (1990, 1993, 1995), often with collaborators, especially Zeev Maoz (Maoz and Russett 1993) and John Oneal (Russett and Oneal 2001; Oneal and Russett 1997, 1999, 2001), offered a series of quantitative analyses of key democratic peace claims. This chapter looks at a dozen widely read works, some supporting and some opposing DP claims, with the aim of getting the best picture of how authors have understood the concept of a "good" explanation. The publications considered here are generally the most cited by the authors, some of whom have written multiple works on the subject. Bruce Russett has, for example, authored or coauthored twenty works that deal with DP questions. However, when there are differences between the most cited and other works, those differences are noted.

There was a great deal at stake in the DP debate, in terms of both theory and policy. The theory implications were significant, since corroboration of any DP claim would appear to undercut realism's core principle that all states behave alike. The policy significance was even greater because in the 1990s many new regimes and constitutions were being formed, either because states were breaking apart (like the Soviet Union, Yugoslavia, Czechoslovakia), or because most states that had been dominated by the Soviet Union (including all Warsaw Pact members) were undergoing fundamental regime change as they shed their communist structures. Western states had to decide what level of resources they should commit to promoting democracy in those countries. If scholars found solid evidence that an increase in democracies in the system would enhance peace and stability—which benefits Western states—it would justify a much greater commitment of resources for democracy promotion.

Because of the policy significance, many people were interested in whether the emerging scholarly consensus on democratic peace claims would become rooted in the minds of political leaders and the public, thus affecting foreign policy. As a result, there was heightened attention to DP studies from both supporters and opponents of the chief claims. The scholarship by opponents came primarily from political realists; there have also been constructivist critiques, though they have not played as prominent a role in the debate.

1. MELVIN SMALL AND J. DAVID SINGER, "THE WAR-PRONENESS OF DEMOCRATIC REGIMES, 1860–1965"

One of the first quantitative tests of the democratic peace claim was conducted by Melvin Small and J. David Singer, founders of the Correlates of War project. In their 1976 paper, Small and Singer explicitly built upon the empirical work of Wright (1942) and Richardson (1960), yet regarded their work as a tentative first step in the more general investigation of regime-type and war-proneness (1976, 56).

Any rigorous test of the relationship between democracy and peace requires a commensurately rigorous definition of those two terms. For a conflict to constitute a war, Small and Singer required a minimum of one thousand military battle deaths. To test the DP claims, they had to ascertain which states fought against which, the duration of each war, who initiated each war (crossed a frontier or fired the first shot), and how many battle deaths resulted. They found fifty interstate wars in the ninety-five years they studied, and another forty-three that they classified as colonial or "extrasystemic" wars.

The problem of defining democracy and identifying appropriate indicators was much more complex, since there is no widely accepted definition of democracy or classificatory scheme for regime-types, and there were no established databases coding democratic regime-type at that time. Small and Singer pointed out that even if there had been such a typology, there would still be much dispute over how to classify particular states within it. They settled on a four-part definition, which requires that a democratic state have (1) a legislature that is representative of most classes, (2) authority at least equal to the executive, (3) two or more political parties and freedom of expression, and (4) franchise extended to "at least ten percent of the adult population" (1976, 54–55). They use the term *bourgeois democracy* to denote the regime-type in which they are primarily interested: "it was the bourgeois who were most successful in overturning the more autocratic regimes in Europe, the Far East and the Western Hemisphere during the nineteenth and early twentieth centuries" (1976, 54).

Small and Singer note that there are prima facie reasons to think that democracies might fight shorter wars (Mueller 1973), but also reasons to think that democracies might fight longer wars (Lippmann 1955). When they compare the data on duration of wars, they find that wars involving democracies last about sixteen months, compared to twelve months for other wars. This result, however, depends on the inclusion of the severest wars; when those are eliminated, the average for wars involving democratic states is slightly less than the average for other wars. In terms of battle deaths, the average per nation was about 92,000 for wars involving democracies and 167,000 for all other wars. Small and Singer point out that, even though the differentials are large, they might be a result of chance, as the significance tests prevent them from concluding that democratic regime-type is what makes the difference. Finally, Small and Singer, in their comparison of wars initiated by democracies to those initiated by nondemocracies, found no appreciable difference. They add, however, that this observation is not included as an attempt to label the "aggressor" or to assign blame.

In contrast to their generally negative findings about the salience of democratic regime-type, Small and Singer do finally accept the dyadic hypothesis as an accurate description of behavior. The only exceptions they find are the

French attack on Rome in 1849 and the Finnish association with the Axis powers in 1941, which, for various reasons they refer to as "marginal exceptions" (1976, 67). However, they reject their democratic nature as the *explanation* for the peaceful pattern among democratic dyads, conjecturing, as noted, that geographical separation is the reason for the observed behavior.

Explanation and Criteria

Small and Singer certainly present themselves as empiricists; and as one proceeds through the first 90 percent of text and tables, the word *explain* does not appear. Small and Singer's paper is heavily descriptive in the sense that they seek to answer various questions about what has in fact happened and which patterns can be discerned: whether democracies fought more wars than nondemocracies, whether the wars are longer, and so on. They "ascertain," "compare," and "determine" many things throughout the paper but use the term *explanation* only in the last two pages. Nevertheless, they clearly claim to be considering how best to explain, given that they reject the statistical support for the dyadic hypothesis as an explanation. Small and Singer offer, at least tentatively, an explanation based on the importance of geographical proximity and shared borders in understanding interstate war. They note that 85 percent of all wars have been fought between states that either bordered each other or bordered the other's colonial possessions, and since 1816, there have been relatively few democratic dyads that have had a common a border. For Small and Singer, "If war is most likely between neighbors, and if bourgeois democracies have rarely been neighbors, this may well explain why they have rarely fought against one another" (1976, 67). Their explanation conforms to the realist view of material forces and power considerations as driving war.

Small and Singer seek accurate generalizations about the behavior of democratic polities, and in particular generalizations concerning aspects of war-proneness. Since the term *war-proneness* appears to be a propensity or disposition, Small and Singer are apparently inquiring into dispositions. The statistical tests tell us which generalizations are true and which generalizations, for that reason, stand in need of explanation. The explanation draws in part on the propensities of various types of states. But one might argue that those propensities themselves require explanation.

Small and Singer do not explicitly state their criteria of explanatory merit. Why, then, do they prefer the geographical explanation to the DP explanation? The main reasons seem to be *empirical fit* in the use of data and *methodological conservatism,* in that their preferred explanation is superior because it fits with an already-known pattern. Moreover, they contest Babst's conclusion that democracy is the reason on grounds that better coding is needed, which implies that Babst's (1972) analysis is not *robust* enough to withstand changes in such procedures (Small and Singer 1976, 52). Overall, Small and Singer clearly conclude with clear skepticism about the dyadic hypothesis.

2. R. J. RUMMEL ON LIBERTARIANISM AND WAR

One of the most important figures in the democratic peace debate is R. J. Rummel, who has published many works bearing on the central questions of DP studies, including the five-volume study *Understanding Conflict and War* (1975–81). One of his most frequently cited works is his 1983 paper "Libertarianism and International Violence." Rummel has consistently argued that both the monadic and the dyadic hypotheses are true.[1] Rummel's advocacy of DP principles follows Kant's lead. Rummel holds that "free states" engage in less international violence than do nonfree states and entirely avoid violence with one another. As the title of his paper indicates, Rummel uses the term *libertarian* to refer to what, roughly speaking, Kant called "free states," and what others call "democratic" or "liberal democratic." At times, Rummel appears to equate libertarianism with classical liberalism (1983, 67; see also Rummel 1968).

Rummel's description of the causal mechanism of peaceful behavior arises from the fact that states that enjoy various "individual freedoms and civil liberties and . . . competitive and open elections" (1983, 27–28) also have multiple elites with divergent interests, checks, and balances among them, and require the support of the public for decisions that incur substantial costs to the taxpayers. Public opinion in a free society can sometimes incline toward war. But war will occur only when there are fundamental motivating reasons that can unify the usually divergent interests of various elites and the general public. Rummel's description of the mechanism that inhibits "libertarian" dyads from going to war includes an element of perception, namely, whether or not the public recognizes a foreign state as a "sister free state." If it does, then pressure is greater for political elites to avoid war.

Rummel tests three hypotheses: (1) libertarian states have no violence between themselves; (2) the more libertarian two states are, the less their mutual violence; and (3) the more libertarian a state is, the less its foreign violence. The first, which Rummel calls the "joint-freedom proposition," is a deterministic version of the dyadic hypothesis. The proposition is deterministic because it does not speak of probabilities or likelihoods; it says that war is "precluded." As Rummel points out, a single counterinstance would falsify it. The second, which Rummel calls the "freedom proposition," is a version of the monadic hypothesis. Rummel formulates it as follows: "Freedom inhibits violence (the more libertarian a state, the less it tends to be involved in violence)" (1983, 29). Rummel formulates two "general research hypotheses," subject to empirical testing, that are implied by the second hypothesis listed earlier. In the section "Freedom Proposition," Rummel proceeds to test the just-noted H_2 and H_3 (1983, 52).

One of Rummel's aims in the paper is to carry out further tests of propositions he defended in *Understanding Conflict and War*. Rummel begins the process by summarizing the DP literature and offering a tally of studies that support and oppose DP claims. But his aim is to conduct his own tests. One set of tests uses the Correlates of War post-1816 database, and another uses a database he constructed for the five years spanning 1976 to 1980, which includes all levels of conflict and violence between states. The paper uses standard statistical methods, where appropriate, such as regression analysis, binomial, and chi-square tests. Rummel's coding of variables is validated by independent individuals coding the same cases.

One of Rummel's hypotheses deterministically predicts zero wars between libertarian states. But because wars are rare events generally, one might reject Rummel's result as simply due to chance. Rummel circumvents this criticism by hypothesizing that if the causal mechanism that precludes libertarian war is correct, then there should be a reduced level of conflict of all sorts, including nonviolent conflict, among liberal dyads. Rummel must devise quantitative rather than binary coding and must consider many levels of "freedom" and of "conflict intensity." The database requires a multistep construction process involving seventeen different forms of conflict and the coding of dyadic events of various levels, from low-level accusations and protests all the way to large-scale military action. In this way dyads that are in frequent low-level conflict will be represented as conflictual, though quantitatively they will remain below dyads that engage in violent conflict.

For his libertarian independent variables, Rummel develops two related notions: one, political freedom, consists of civil liberties and political rights, and the other, freedom, consists of the first conjoined with economic freedom. To develop his own measures of freedom, Rummel draws on Freedom House's coding. He says, "Political rights are defined [by Freedom House] by an open, competitive electoral process through which leaders are clearly elected. States rated 1 have these characteristics; those rated 7 have none—those at the top believe they have the right to govern without challenge and are not constrained by public opinion or tradition" (1983, 31). Rummel regards states with central controls on the economy as less free than states that do not have such controls. Sweden and Denmark enjoy political freedoms, but because of their "semi-socialist" systems, they lack economic freedom (1983, 30), and states of that type (more frequently the United Kingdom and Israel than Scandinavian countries) engage in more conflict.

Explanation

Rummel, like Small and Singer, investigates questions that are largely descriptive. Indeed, that is the main purpose of his paper. But he clearly argues for an explanation for the patterns. He rejects "the possibility that chance explains the zero violence" between members of politically free dyads (1983, 41). Rummel argues that his explanation is better than Small and Singer's. Rummel discusses other objections, the last of which holds that the statistical results lack "practical significance" because "the variance in violence that libertarianism explains is low" (1983, 70). Rummel's reply is twofold. First, he notes that the variance is high "for the functions fitting the highest magnitudes of violence" (1983, 70). It appears, then, that he believes he has explained at least one part of the observed variance. While he says that "explaining the variance is not the essence of this study" (1983, 70), explanation is at least one of the goals. He says that the essence of his paper is to assess the accuracy of "the prediction of no violence, or of decreasing violence as libertarianism increases," and, if true, whether it would be a result of chance (1983, 70). From his rejection of the null hypothesis that chance can explain peace, it is clear that Rummel regards the explanation of the result to be found in libertarian regime-type. If his finding is not "due to chance," then it is "due to," or "explainable" in terms of, libertarian regime-type (1983, 70).

Norms and Criteria

Rummel pursues a notion of explanation that is naturalist, treating the social world as if it were subject to "forces" and regularities the way the natural world is. However, Rummel does acknowledge, "All studies of conflict have some explicit or implicit normative premises or point of view" (1983, 67). In his view, scholars should not try to eliminate the normative element but should try to make their normative commitments as explicit as possible (1983, 67–68).

Presumably Rummel believes that it is not possible to eliminate the normative entirely, although he does not say precisely this. In terms of his own ideological orientation, Rummel says, "Obviously I favor freedom, especially when defined in classical liberal terms" (1983, 67). It is not clear in what way Rummel's "favoring" liberal rights changes the design or results of his analysis, other than in the obvious way of guiding him to study the subject. In any case, Rummel sees political inquiry as always involving normative assumptions.

Rummel does, however, seem to argue that the normative assumptions, once made explicit, can be tested, at least most of the time. "The best check against normative bias involves two stages. One is presenting clear and precise data and methods, using systematic and objective techniques, and making tests and conclusions intersubjectively verifiable. The second is even more important. It is the actual attempt to refute through reanalysis or new data what one believes to be biased or wrong" (1983, 68). This is a form of *falsificationism.* Rummel continues, "It is, in short, through the dialectical process of presenting controversial results and the attempts at their public refutation that we check bias" (1983, 68).

Rummel strongly supports the democratic regime-type explanation for the pattern of war and peace, arguing that Small and Singer are right that democracies have not fought one another but wrong when they say that this is best explained by democratic states' lack of shared borders. Rummel ties explanatory success to predictive success. Rummel believes that prediction is intimately tied to explanation. He says, for example, "Nonetheless, as theory predicts . . ." (1983, 66). Rummel sees accuracy of prediction as a criterion of a good explanatory theory (see also his discussion of chi-square tests of explanations, at page 41). Rummel supports the criterion of *robustness*, which is evident when he says that his approach to testing and his use of two samples (the "full" and "max") will "make any positive results for Hypothesis 3 more robust" (1983, 37). He uses statistical tests and predictions as criteria for advocating the strength of that explanation. He relies on criteria of *falsifiability, empirical adequacy, predictive accuracy*, and *robustness.*

3. MICHAEL DOYLE'S "KANT, LIBERAL LEGACIES, AND FOREIGN AFFAIRS"

Michael Doyle's two-part article, "Kant, Liberal Legacies, and Foreign Affairs," which appeared in *Philosophy and Public Affairs* in 1983 had considerable impact when it was published; it helped prompt the subsequent flood of scholarship on DP studies that followed in the 1980s and 1990s. In the two papers, Doyle defines "liberalism," endorses the claim that liberal states have been peaceful toward one another, considers a range of alternative explanations offered by those who deny the role of liberalism, and then turns to Kant's view of peace. According to Kant, peace arises from states that have the sort of structure that allows them to resolve internal conflicts by means of mutual concessions. Although Doyle holds that liberal states are peaceful toward one another, he acknowledges a seeming paradox: liberal states are peaceful toward one another, not toward other sorts of states. Liberal states' "wars with nonliberals have not been uniformly defensive" (1983a, 221). The first part of the paradox is the subject of part 1 (1983a) "Kant, Liberal Legacies" and the second is the subject of part 2 (1983b).

In part 1, Doyle offers a detailed characterization of liberalism, observing its "positive and negative freedoms" (1983a, 206–7). Liberalism as a domestic structure has proved highly successful, with liberal states proliferating, thus leading to existence of scores of liberal states today, in contrast to the mere trio that existed during Kant's time: France, the Swiss cantons, and the United States (1983a, 209). However, in foreign affairs liberal states' considerable successes are less noted (1983a, 213). Liberalism's central focus is freedom of the individual. The process of ensuring this freedom generates various "rights and institutions" (1983a, 206). The positive freedoms include equal opportunity in education, employment, and health care, and democratic participation to ensure those benefits (1983a, 206–7). The negative freedoms include a prohibition on any state actions that infringe upon freedom of expression, equality under the law, and private property rights.

The type of legitimacy that is almost exclusive to liberal states arises from their recognizing the rationally grounded rights of individual citizens. The type of relationships liberal states have with one another stems from this legitimacy, including mutual respect, noninterference in the affairs of other liberal states, and the possibility of unfettered private exchange. Two forms of post-Kantian liberalism, laissez-faire and social welfare, emanate from these basic ideas.

Counterexamples to the Liberal Peace

Doyle considers and rebuts two sets of counterexamples that have been proffered by critics of DP claims, one aiming to discredit the empirical claims of the dyadic hypothesis and the second aiming to discredit only the liberal-democratic explanation for it. The first set of counterexamples include mainly

World War I, the Ecuadorian-Peruvian War of 1941, and the 1967 Arab-Israeli War. World War I is an interesting case because of the unusual nature of imperial Germany. In a five-hundred-word footnote Doyle discusses the constitutional and customary powers, as well as the limitations of the German legislature; he concludes that in domestic affairs, Germany was a model of liberalism, but in foreign policy, the Kaiser had unrestrained, autocratic powers with no popular control or oversight. Whether one codes Wilhelmine Germany as a genuine counterexample depends on the precise DP hypothesis under consideration and the postulated explanatory mechanism. Doyle rejects the case of Wilhelmine Germany as a counterexample because the *mechanism* for liberal peace he postulates involves citizen control.

The 1967 Arab-Israeli War is complex because of the unusual pattern of behavior. Lebanon initially joined in the illiberal states' attack on Israel, but after Lebanon's aircraft were repulsed by the Israelis, "alone among Israel's Arab neighbors, Lebanon engaged in no further hostilities with Israel" (1983a, 213n7). War between Peru and Ecuador occurred when the states were only newly liberalized, and as such, the "pacifying effects" of liberalism had not had a chance to take root. This consideration is consistent with Doyle's postulated mechanism for liberal peace. The fact that less mature democracies are not peaceful has been investigated extensively by others, especially Mansfield and Snyder (1995a, 1995b, 2005).

Alternative Explanations

Doyle considers a second set of arguments against DP claims rejecting liberal democracy as the explanation for the dyadic peace. These arguments offer alternative, nonliberal explanations, such as prudent realist policy, offense-defense balance, shared ideology, absence of conflicts among liberal states, empire, balance of power, and hegemony. With respect to the first, Doyle says that realists describe the international environment as one of anarchy, self-help, and pure self-reliance. Force is a legitimate instrument of policy, and states are driven to act violently when their survival is in serious jeopardy. At any given time many states are vulnerable. This view of the international system is simply inconsistent with the record of peace among liberal states. Doyle makes use of the criterion of empirical adequacy when he says, "The Realists' prudence cannot account for more than a century of peace among independent liberal states, many of which have crowded one another in the center of Europe" (1983a, 220).

Next, Doyle notes that some realist-oriented political scientists have argued that peaceful behavior may be the result of differences between offensive and defensive environments (Jervis 1978). On this view, when offensive systems are more effective than defensive, or when there is no clear distinctions between offensive and defensive systems, there is a temptation to strike first because in a system of that type so much damage can be inflicted by the first to attack. However, when there is a clear defensive advantage, the disincentives of waiting and being struck first are lower, and are thus worth the risk, if the positive payoff is war-avoidance. Doyle makes use of *support of counterfactuals* here by arguing that offense-defense "cannot be the explanation for the liberal peace" (1983a, 222); if it were, with the defensive advantages of barbed wire, machine guns, and entrenchment, World War I would not have occurred.

Another criticism charges that, while liberal states have managed peace among themselves, any group of states that share a set of norms or a political ideology—whether feudal, fascist, or communist—would tend to see one another as friendly and avoid war. Doyle notes, however, that communist states have fought in Asia "recently" (presumably referring to China's 1979 invasion of Vietnam); moreover, the low numbers of socialist states prevent any rigorous test of a "mutual socialist peace" hypothesis. Doyle adds that feudal societies fought constantly, and fascist states, at least defined as "nationalist, capitalist, militarist" (1983a, 222), fought one another in the 1930s. Doyle here again rejects the explanation because it violates the implicit criterion of empirical adequacy.

The last set of counterarguments against the liberal position is drawn from Raymond Aron's (1968) claim that interstate peace can result from the presence of empires, power balances, and hegemony. With respect to empires, Doyle rejects Aron's claim by arguing that the peace is internal among the various regions within the empire, and not between independent states. For this reason empire cannot be the answer. Second, power balances are "regarded as a primary lesson in the Realist primer" (1983a, 221). Doyle next considers Aron's claim that states' aggressive search for hegemony impels other states to work together to oppose them, which in turn produces balances. But Doyle replies that this cannot explain peace among liberal states, because under bipolarity, there is only avoidance of great power wars, "not proxy or small power wars" (1983a, 224). And under multipolarity, balancing leads to states to go to war "to seize . . . territory for strategic depth against a rival expanding its power from internal growth" (1983a, 224). Doyle concludes that neither sort "accounts for general peace or for the liberal peace" (1983a, 224).

Doyle considers the claim that international hegemony, rather than domestic liberalism, explains the liberal peace. He argues that, while peace and stability benefit hegemons, we can see from examples like seventeenth-century France that hegemons do not always act as a "peace-enforcing police" working to prevent war (1983a, 223). Doyle argues also that the liberal peace can persist even when there is no hegemon, as it did with liberal states in the interwar period. Doyle notes that hegemons typically lack the power resources that would be necessary to prevent other states from going to war. For example, the interests of hegemonic Britain were damaged by challenges to its colonies in the nineteenth century. And even though it dominated the international system, the United States has been unable to prevent various destabilizing wars in the Middle East that harmed its interests in the past sixty years.

Doyle provides several reasons to think that these counterexamples do not undermine the dyadic hypothesis. Even a war between liberal democracies, should one occur, would not refute the general dyadic claim; Doyle says that "no one should argue that such wars [between two liberal democracies] are impossible," but the available evidence suggests there is a "significant predisposition" against their occurrence (1983a, 213). Doyle thereby accepts the legitimacy of positing "dispositions." His position on this matter does not seem to fit with his discussion of alternative explanations in which he dismisses proposals on the basis of a minimal number of counterexamples.

Explanation and Description

Doyle separates analyses that provide descriptions from those that explain. Doyle (1983a, 224n22) cites Michael Haas's (1974, 453) discussion of characteristics of international systems and domestic structures "that are likely to avoid a high frequency in violent outputs." At the international level, the peace variables include collective security, stratification, and hegemony. On the domestic level, the war-related variables are bloc prominence, military mobilizations, public perceptions of hostility toward peoples of other countries, and high proportion of gross national product devoted to military expenditures (1983a, 224n22). Doyle then says, "These variables describe rather than explain war" (1983a, 224n22).

In a footnote Doyle adds that the Correlates of War scholars' "conclusions follow . . . from their homogenization of war and from their attempt to explain all wars, in which a myriad of states have engaged. I attempt to explain an interstate peace, which only liberal regimes, a particular type of state and society, have established" (1983a, 224n22). This comment shows that for Doyle, what counts as an acceptable explanation is dependent on the specific question in the context of which the explanation is sought (see Section 3 in Chapter 2, and Section 5 in Chapter 6). If one had a model of war in which Hass's variables played a part, and one asks why World War I occurred, an explanation may well invoke an answer like, "Great Britain and Germany were in an arms race, their peoples saw one another as hostile," and so on. So the factors function to describe conditions under which wars are frequent, but those factors have explanatory power in another context (or when the focus is on a different level of analysis).

"Explain," "Understand," "Guide," and "Account For"

The terms *account for* and *explain* may be intended by Doyle to function as synonyms. If so, we can make sense of his comment, "While these developments can help account for the liberal peace, they do not explain the fact that liberal states are peaceful only in relations with other liberal states" (1983a, 225). By substituting *explain* for *account for*, we can see Doyle saying that the developments can "help explain" the liberal peace. However, if they only "help," then they do not suffice by themselves and thus leave one aspect of liberal states' behavior unexplained.

Doyle also uses the term *guidance* in a way that appears to be a synonym for *explanation*. Doyle says that "Immanuel Kant offers the best guidance" (1983a, 225). What does he mean? In this context he has just discussed "explanations" that failed, and then offers Kant's theory in *Perpetual Peace* as somehow more successful in achieving what has just been shown to fail. Doyle seems to use *guidance* to mean *explanation* also where he says, "The Realist model of international relations, which provides a plausible explanation of the general insecurity of states, offers little guidance in explaining the pacification of the liberal world" (1983a, 218).

Can one theory explain events at one level while a different theory explains events at another level? It would appear not, but in the passage just cited (1983a, 218) Doyle says, "The realist model . . . provides a plausible explanation of the general insecurity of states, [but] offers little *guidance* in explaining the pacification of the liberal world" (1983a, 218, emphasis added). It seems possible that Doyle accepts that realism is able to explain some aspects of international affairs, but he rejects it as able to explain the liberal peace. Is Doyle saying that realism explains the general presence of war while liberalism explains the specific pacification among liberal states? Or is he saying that realism looks good at one level, but probing farther one encounters its weaknesses, which entail that one must reject it? In any event, he certainly does not accept liberalism as a complete theory of international politics.

Explanatory Criteria

The explanation Doyle offers, drawn from Kant, includes a mechanism that proceeds in stages as states accept the three definitive articles of perpetual peace. Doyle holds that liberal regimes in early modern Europe slowly came to gain "deeper foundations" and more extensive "international experience" (1983a, 217, 225–32). Doyle sees Kant as presenting an explanatory mechanism that proceeds in stages. He says in his 1986 paper, "Perpetual peace, for Kant, is . . . most importantly, an explanation of how the 'mechanical process of nature visibly exhibits the purposive plan of producing concord among men, even against their will and indeed by means of their very discord'" (Doyle 1986, 1159, quoting Kant 1939, 108, and Kant 1963, 44–45).

Kant sees the "asocial sociability" of humans as leading both to security-driven life in groups and to interpersonal conflict. As a result, this "asocial sociability inevitably leads toward republican governments and republican governments are a source of the liberal peace" (Doyle 1983a, 228). Kant's "argument provides a plausible, logical connection between conflict, internal and external, and republicanism" (1983a, 228). Doyle thus endorses "coherence with background beliefs" as a criterion of explanation, since it is primarily in virtue of such coherence that an explanation can be judged "plausible." Also, somewhat like Small and Singer (1976), Doyle makes implicit use of "background beliefs." Having detailed the influential and well-known Kantian theoretical background to support his argument about democracies, Doyle knows that many scholars regarded empirical demonstration of the dyadic hypothesis as carrying with it a set of explanatory mechanisms for the observed pattern. As discussed earlier, it fits with many scholars' background beliefs held in connection to theories that they accept about the nature of democracies.

We have seen that Doyle requires a good explanation to be empirically adequate to account for descriptions and to provide a causal mechanism. The mechanism Doyle postulates for peace among liberal states is the development of liberal domestic norms, which gradually evolve after the establishment of a constitution. While various liberal theorists who cite economic and other factors are able to "help account" for peace between liberal states, "they do not explain the fact that liberal states are peaceful only in relations with other liberal states," since liberal regimes are "as war-prone and aggressive as any other" toward nonliberal states (1983a, 225). Doyle also draws on the established liberal theory accepted by many liberals to extend the argument to the democratic dyadic peace, making use of "methodological conservatism" or "coherence with background beliefs" (discussed further in Section 14 in this chapter). Liberal alternatives fail with regard to empirical adequacy. We should add that a good explanation identifies real or true causes. As Doyle says, "The liberals are fundamentally different [from realists]. It is not just, as the Realists might argue, that they [the liberal states] have more or less resources, better or worse morale. Their constitutional structure makes them—realistically—different" (1983a, 235).[2] Doyle relies on criteria of *empirical fit, imparting understanding, uncovering true causes, methodological conservatism* (i.e., fit with previous beliefs), and *support of counterfactuals.*

4. JOHN MEARSHEIMER: "BACK TO THE FUTURE"

As noted in Chapter 3, John Mearsheimer's (1990) controversial paper "Back to the Future" deals with several key security studies issues, including democratic peace theory. Mearsheimer derived his predictions from the theory of structural realism, which was supported in large part by how well it explains both pre–World War II instability in Europe and post–World War II stability. To provide a basis for his structural realist predictions, Mearsheimer offered critiques of the two alternative explanations for Cold War stability in Europe: economic liberalism and democratic peace theory.

Mearsheimer says that there are two explanations offered for why democracies have not fought one another. One is that democratic leaders are inhibited from acting aggressively because they are accountable to those who fight wars and pay for them, whereas autocratic leaders are neither accountable nor thereby inhibited. The second is that two democracies in a conflict will see each other as actors who place a high priority on protecting the rights of citizens and who see any attack on the other as a violation of their own values. Both explanations postulate rational behavior by individual leaders and causal sequences. Mearsheimer relies on *empirical adequacy*, since his principal counterarguments aim to show that these causal claims are not consistent with the historical record.

Mearsheimer adds two further counter arguments. One argument casts doubt on the claim that there have been no wars between democracies. He disagrees with Doyle's analysis of the role of the Kaiser in foreign-policy decision making, and thus argues that there is a strong case to code Wilhelmine Germany as a liberal state, which would make World War I a democratic war (1990, 51n77). Furthermore, democracies have come close to war on a number of occasions. The second argument is that the absence of democratic wars can be explained quite straightforwardly by realism, according to whose principles wars occur under anarchy in the struggle for survival and power—but only when there is something to fight over. Throughout history there have been very few democracies at any given time. Mearsheimer says that the democracies able to go to war with each other are minimal in number: Britain and the United States have both been democracies with the capacity to fight each other from 1832 until today, Britain and France from 1832 until 1849 and again from 1871 until 1940, and the Western democracies from the end of World War II until now. Mearsheimer contends that the absence of many democratic wars should not surprise us in view of the paucity of democratic dyads able to go to war. There have been a few democratic dyads able to go to war, but their peacefulness toward each other can be explained by noting that Britain and the United States, and later Britain and France, had common enemies. Realist theory, based on survival and power considerations, would predict that they would align together rather than fight one another.

Mearsheimer acknowledges that there may be a genuine reluctance of democracies to go to war against one another (1990, 49–50). But under anarchy the force of their mutual repulsion toward war is weaker than the forces that drive states toward war as they seek survival and security. Thus, Mearsheimer sees the world as including causal forces that have varying degrees of strength. As was seen in the discussion of his paper "Back to the Future" in Chapter 3, he sees explanations as rational and intentional, with causal processes proceeding in stages. He relies on criteria of *empirical fit, true causes, mechanisms, imparting understanding, support of counterfactuals,* and *predictive accuracy.*

5. STUART BREMER'S "DANGEROUS DYADS"

Stuart Bremer published a paper in 1992 comparing the results of studies of the war-proneness of different sorts of dyads. As noted earlier, Bremer's and Rummel's papers are the two most cited works in *Journal of Conflict Resolution* on democratic peace, and Bremer's is the most cited on any topic from that journal. Bremer proceeds by first surveying the literature on factors associated with war-proneness, in the course of which he identifies the most oft-discussed variables. He next conducts bivariate tests of efficacy for each against the dependent variable, onset of war. After this first cut, Bremer then runs multivariate tests, which he regards as providing a more accurate measure of the variables' effects; indeed, they yield some different results.

Existing Studies

Bremer's survey of the literature found seven factors most often seen as associated with war: geographical proximity, power parity, major-power status, alliance relationship, nondemocratic governance, economic development, and militarization. The most prominent is geographical proximity, which is widely accepted as a crucial variable. For example, Gochman (1990) found that two out of every three militarized interstate disputes occurred in dyads whose members either shared a border or were separated by no more than 150 miles of water. Many other studies cite geographical proximity as crucial. However, one of Gochman's findings was unexpected: despite centuries of improvements in the technology of weapons and delivery systems, the proportion of "disputing" dyads whose members were geographically proximate had increased in the period 1816–1976 (Gochman 1990, cited by Bremer 1992, 313). A second surprise Bremer (1992, 315) found in the published literature contradicts the expectation that allies tend to be friendly and cooperative; Bueno de Mesquita (1981, 159–64) and Ray (1990, 86) found that dyads of states that are allied with one another were more likely to go to war than nonallied dyads.

Methodological Concerns

In developing a research design for his study, Bremer investigated several problems that, in his view, undermine confidence in the conclusions of previous studies. One of the major problems is that wars commence between dyads, or small groups of states, and appropriately, the authors of some of the previous studies sought methods that would allow them to generate conclusions about dyads. However, Bremer notes that the studies are not relevant to dyadic questions because they are conducted at the national or system level and not the dyadic level. Bremer is especially concerned that bivariate analyses sometimes treat factors as independent when they are in fact associated with one another. Furthermore, studies vastly overemphasize evidence drawn from major powers in the post–World War II period and as such are not robust. And he says that cases are generally selected in which the outcome was interstate war, which fails to produce variation of the dependent variable.

Bremer is concerned as well that when different authors offer what appear to be multiple tests of an hypothesis, they fail to distinguish the "occurrence" of war from "the manner in which it evolves" (1992, 311). Existing DP and other studies of war do not adequately recognize that war can be treated either as an event or as a process. As an event it has a moment of onset with two or more initial belligerents. But wars are not static: they evolve as fighting continues, with belligerents sometimes changing sides and new states entering at various points along the way. Bremer also says there is something genuinely different about short wars with limited casualties, compared to long, bloody wars, and there are different motivations for states that initiate wars, compared to those who join later out of alliance commitment, solidarity, fear, and so on.

Bremer adds that studies that appear to be testing the same hypothesis are often, upon closer inspection, found to be testing different hypotheses. For example, some studies look at the onset of war and some at the evolution of events after the onset. Comparability problems are compounded by different authors' uses of varying methods and levels of analysis and different periods and regions. After making appropriate adjustments, Bremer runs tests of each of the seven variables against the onset of war as the dependent variable. He concludes that each is positively associated with war and that the most strongly associated is geographical proximity, followed by power status, alliance, militarization, democracy, development, and power difference. Bremer's replication of bivariate tests serves only as a starting point; he moves on to add other controls and to conduct multivariate tests, which he regards as more accurate, and which turn out to show some of the factors more strongly associated with war, and some less strongly associated, than the bivariate tests indicate.

Multivariate Tests

In the multivariate tests Bremer converts each of the seven variables into binary form: each is coded as 1 if a dyad has the trait associated with dyadic war, and as 0 if it does not. This method allows Bremer to create a set of ($2^7 = 128$) types of dyads. (Of course some types will be more common than others.[3]) The multivariate analysis showed (1) the correlations of militarization and alliance membership to be spurious, (2) no correlation between militarized allies and war, and (3) dyads of nonmilitarized allies were actually less likely to go to war than other dyads.

Bremer uses as a baseline the "least war-prone" type of dyad, that is, the dyad with 0 values for each of the seven variables (e.g., the two states are noncontiguous, both are democratic, both are economically less developed). Bremer's revised model calculates that the probability of this least-war-prone dyad of experiencing war in a hundred-year period is 0.003 (or 0.3 percent). From this baseline Bremer asks how much the probability of war increases when any one of the seven variables is switched from a 0 value to a 1 value. When the geographical contiguity value for the variable is switched from 0 to 1, the probability of war increases more than fivefold. When at least one state is economically developed, the probability increases by more than four times. The alliance factor has about the same effect. And with respect to DP claims, the subject of this chapter, when we switch from a dyad of two democracies to a dyad with at most one of the two members a democracy, the probability triples. The other three factors had smaller effects, less than doubling the probability.

Democracy

Since Bremer is critical of studies that failed to focus on dyadic independent or dependent factors, he begins by drawing on Chan's (1984) construction of a dichotomous measure of democracy. This variable is composed of two elements: (1) whether the state's chief executive is popularly elected, directly or indirectly, and (2) whether the state's legislature is elected, and authorized and able to constrain the executive. Bremer also uses the Polity II data set. The Polity project ranks states on 11-point scales (0–10) on both democracy and autocracy dimensions. Bremer creates a dichotomous democracy variable by classifying states with scores of 0–4 as "undemocratic" and those with scores of 5–10 as "democratic."[4] Chan's method codes one war as involving a democratic dyad, the Franco-Thai War in 1940. Polity II codes two wars as involving democratic dyads, Spain and the United States in 1898, and India and Pakistan (the Second Kashmir War) in 1965.

Bremer concludes that democratic dyads are more peaceful than nondemocratic dyads. However, as just noted, the influence of joint democracy is less than three other factors on the list: proximity, power status, and alliance. On both the Chan and the Polity II measures, dyads in which both members qualified as democracies were considerably less war-prone. On Chan's coding, dyads in which neither state was democratic were fourteen times as likely to experience war as democratic dyads. Thus, Bremer found support for the dyadic DP hypothesis on either system of coding. However, with regard to the monadic DP hypothesis, it made a difference which data set's coding was used. For Chan's data set, mixed dyads (i.e., those with one democratic and one nondemocratic member) were less war-prone than nondemocratic dyads, which is what the monadic hypothesis predicts; the probability of war was about four times greater in nondemocratic dyads than in mixed dyads. This contradicts the conclusion of the many authors who reject the monadic hypothesis. On the Polity II data set, mixed dyads were roughly as war-prone as nondemocratic dyads. He concludes, "Democracy has once again shown itself to be a *war-reducing* factor, and its effect is readily apparent even after the effects of many other factors have been removed. It would not appear that the bivariate relationship between democracy and war is spurious, as some have contended; on the contrary, democracy is once again shown to be a quite powerful inhibitor of war" (1992, 337). But the conclusion here is sensitive to the coding procedures and hence is not as robust as the explanation for the dyadic hypothesis.

Explanation

Bremer, like Rummel, sees his task as primarily descriptive but as including an explanatory element. He describes his "mission" as that of "fact-finding"; he says that he will not offer any "elaborate formal models" (1992, 312) and suggests that political scientists should be seeking necessary and sufficient conditions for the presence of dependent variables (1992, 310–11). While he chooses forms of analysis that have "explanatory power" (1992, 334), he also seems to use *predictor* as synonymous with *explanatory factor* (1992, 312–13), as well as *account for*, at least in some occurrences, as interchangeable with *explain* (1992, 333, 335).

Causation and Criteria

Bremer appears to be offering a causal analysis. First, there is one, but only one, occurrence of the term *cause*. Bremer says, "The militarization of a society may *cause* leaders and followers alike to conclude that war is inevitable rather than merely possible. Justifying the sacrifices that high degrees of military preparedness require may strengthen enemy images and even *lead to* collective paranoia" (1992, 318, emphasis added). Bremer draws no distinction between the way in which he characterizes the variable militarization from the others, which suggests that he could use explicitly causal language to refer to his understanding of the sort of force captured by those variables. Second, Bremer uses *because* in a parallel way, often describing the various arguments supporting the hypotheses by saying that a group of authors argues that A occurs "because" of B (1992, 312, 313, 330). Third, he has nearly a dozen references to the "effects" of the independent variables.[5] Fourth, Bremer takes patterns identified in the past and treats them not merely as statistically significant historical curiosities but as "predictors" of what is to come. This is not merely a loose use of *predict*. Bremer closes with a description of the factors that should be used as the bases for a "prescription for peace" (1992, 338). We see that Bremer's argument is naturalist and empiricist and employs criteria of *falsifiability, predictive accuracy, range of cases, robustness,* and *identification of true causes.* There is no emphasis on explanatory unification.

6. DAVID A. LAKE: "POWERFUL PACIFISTS"

In 1992 David A. Lake published a widely cited paper in *American Political Science Review,* "Powerful Pacifists." The paper not only supports the dyadic hypothesis, but goes farther in the assessment of the distinctive behavior of democratic states by claiming that democracies also are disproportionately successful in wars against autocracies.[6] Lake argues that the military success of democracies is especially puzzling on the surface, since it seems inconsistent with some of the structural analyses in IR according to which the war-initiating mechanisms in democracies are unwieldy and inefficient. Lake notes that studies have shown that authors in IR accept that democracies act one way with one another and a different way with nondemocracies; that is, they accept the dyadic hypothesis and reject the monadic hypothesis. He adds, "No theory presently exists that can account for this striking empirical regularity" (1992, 24). Lake thus acknowledges a class of purely empirical propositions and distinguishes them from "theoretical accounts" of those propositions. His comment also implies that the former demand that scholars supply the latter.

Lake claims to offer "one possible explanation" (1992, 24) drawn from his larger view of grand strategy. We note that his use of the expression in quotes leaves open the possibility that he views explanation either as the sort of thing of which there can be one best explanation, and his might be it, or as the sort of thing that will always admit of several adequate versions, and his might be one of the several.

Lake's analysis of state behavior draws on microeconomic theory and builds especially on the work of Frederic Lane (1979). For his analysis Lake defines the state "as a profit maximizing firm that trades services for revenues" (1992, 24; see also Lane 1979). The state is a service-producing firm with two functional attributes: it offers a protection service, which is characterized by "local monopoly" (i.e., there is only one state in any area at any given time), and it offers "coercive supply" (i.e., the state supplies the service only if it is able to obtain coercive power over society) (1992, 25). This definition of state appears to be more of a model or analogy. It would seem to qualify as what Kuhn describes a "relatively heuristic" model; it seems parallel to the example Kuhn's (1970,

184) provides of this type of model, namely, the electric circuit, which "may be regarded as steady-state hydrodynamic system; the molecules of a gas behave like tiny elastic billiard balls in random motion."[7]

Lake's explanation of puzzling differences in the behavior of democracies, as contrasted with autocracies, offers an analysis of the goals the idealized state seeks and offers differences in the ways that democracies and autocracies typically pursue those goals within an international system. Because of the differences in regime structures of democracies and autocracies, the differences in the way in which each rationally pursues state goals leads democracies to avoid armed conflict with one another, to direct more state resources to national security, and to direct those resources more efficiently. The explanation, then, is a structural-functional explanation, as it proceeds by providing a function that security serves within the domestic system of the state and a function that armed conflict serves in an international system.

The state has certain advantages over other monopolies, including that it can artificially increase the demand for its services, especially protection, "by extortion or racketeering" (1992, 25). The state can create an exaggerated perception of foreign threats from which it will then provide protection, which can create the temptation to use this and other means to charge "consumers the monopoly price for protection . . . [which is accomplished] by artificially inflating demand" (1992, 25). Consumers want protection at the lowest price; the state has an incentive to provide it at the highest price. The actual price will result from "how well individual citizens can control or regulate the rent-seeking behavior of the state" (1992, 26). And the latter is a function of citizens' ability to monitor state behavior, voice concerns through political participation, and exit (see Hirschman 1970). As compared with autocracies, in democratic polities, the costs to citizens, especially of the monitoring and voice options, is lower, sometimes drastically so. Monitoring is much easier in most democracies. And the rents extracted by the state thus tend to be much lower than in autocracies, since autocracies can more easily hide their actions from public awareness.

Lake offers to *unify* the answers to several distinct and seemingly unrelated puzzles under one analytic procedure. He maintains that his economic model of the state explains why democracies tend not to fight one another and why they tend to win wars against autocracies. He acknowledges that, as wars occur and democracies defeat autocracies, one should expect that democracies would have displaced autocracies. Thus, he puts his explanation to a test by drawing a consequence and checking for the truth of that consequence. He says that while democracy has not completely eradicated autocracy through war, there has been a strong trend of democracies replacing autocracies. In a long-term process of democratic advancement, there are some short-term reverses, since autocracies win some, about one-fifth, of the wars. Lake adds, "The relationship between democracy and victory is quite robust" (1992, 31; see also Reiter and Stam 2002, chaps. 2–3). We see that Lake defends his explanation by relying mainly on the criteria of *explanatory unification*, *empirical fit*, and *robustness*.

7. ZEEV MAOZ AND BRUCE RUSSETT—DEMOCRACY, STRUCTURE, AND NORMS

Bruce Russett has contributed more than any other author to the democratic peace debate. He has written three books on the subject, one coauthored with John Oneal (2001), and many important journal articles. His 1993 paper "Normative and Structural Causes of Democratic Peace, 1946–1986," coauthored with Zeev Maoz (Maoz and Russett 1993), is one of the most cited papers ever published in *American Political Science Review*, the flagship journal of the American Political Science Association.[8]

Maoz and Russett echo Lake and others in describing as a paradox the empirical support for the dyadic hypothesis but not the monadic hypothesis and in saying that any adequate explanation must deal with both findings (1993, 624). The many publications on the dyadic democratic peace are exceptionally consistent with one another, and there is "significant evidence that this finding is causally meaningful" (1993, 624). It follows, then, that there is something in the "internal makeup" of democracies that leads them to avoid war with one another (1993, 624), and Maoz and Russett ask what that something is. In surveying the literature on the subject, they find two popular answers, which they refer to as the normative and structural explanations. They set out to test both and compare the results. These two explanatory models constitute the two "most general and powerful explanations of the democratic-peace result" (1993, 624). The authors seem to equate *models* and *explanation*. It is clear from this locution that they see some models as more powerful than others, and thus they accept at least an ordinal scale of degrees of the "power" of explanations. The authors say, "A better understanding of democratic peace is required of the causal mechanism explaining" both the democratic peace and the lack of a difference in war-proneness between democracies and nondemocracies (1993, 624). They do not seek to separate *explanation* from *understanding* by using the terms in clearly divergent ways. They say that they can show that democracy, along with other factors, "accounts for the relative lack of conflict" (1993, 624).

The Normative and Structural Explanations

The normative explanation holds that democracies resolve internal conflicts by means of nonviolent compromise. The norms are expressed externally whenever it is possible to do so. In contrast, autocratic states' norms that permit the use of force to resolve internal disputes also guide external behavior. According to the normative model, "democracies do not fight each other because norms of compromise and cooperation prevent their conflicts of interest from escalating into violent clashes" (1993, 624). Those who have advocated this explanation include Kant, Woodrow Wilson, and Michael Doyle (discussed earlier). The explanation is defined by two assumptions. Maoz and Russett (1993, 625) state the first assumption as follows: "Assumption 1. *States, to the extent possible, externalize the norms of behavior that are developed within, and characterize their domestic political processes and institutions.*" As a result, when democratic states find themselves in conflicts with other democratic states, both sides expect peaceful compromise resolutions and war does not occur. The legitimacy of democratic leaders rests on their complying with the norms of a democratic society.

But when autocratic states are involved in conflicts, things work differently because of the second assumption, which they formulate as follows. "Assumption 2. *The anarchic nature of international politics implies that a clash between democratic and non-democratic norms is dominated by the latter, rather than by the former*" (1993, 625). When autocratic states have conflicts with other autocratic states, and when the stakes are high enough so that one side desires to prevail regardless of the other's concessions, the autocratic state may use force. When democratic states have conflicts with autocracies, in some instances the latter are willing to use force. As a result, democracies find themselves fighting wars. The norms explanation is therefore not inconsistent with the fact that democracies frequently fight wars with nondemocracies.

The structural explanation draws on the differences in the decision-making systems in democracies and autocracies and, like the normative, is characterized by Maoz and Russett by two assumptions (1993, 626). The first: "Assumption 1. *International challenges require political leaders to mobilize domestic support to their policies. Such support must be mobilized from those groups that provide the leadership the kind of legitimacy that is required for international action*" (1993,

626). Only in crises and emergency situations will democratic leaders use force in advance of the support of the population and or legislature. The second: "Assumption 2. *Shortcuts to political mobilization of relevant political support can be accomplished only in situations that can be appropriately described as emergencies*" (1993, 626). Maoz and Russett identify Lake (1992), just discussed, as a supporter of this view, along with Bueno de Mesquita and Lalman (1992), Rummel (1979), and others.

Research Design

Maoz and Russett wish to devise a way to test these two explanations independently of one another and at the same time control for other factors that the literature has identified as connected to war and peace: economic prosperity, economic growth, alliance relationships, geographical contiguity, and military-capability ratio. Maoz and Russet have to operationalize level of democracy, depth of democratic norms, and level of institutional constraints. They focus on the behavior over a forty-year period, 1946 to 1986. The study of just forty years imposes some limits on their research design.

For the first explanation, the authors use two scales from the Polity II data set that range from 0 to 10: one scale is for democracy and another for autocracy. They then produced an 11-point "power concentration" scale and use those three scales to make a regime index. For the dependent variable they focus on two main concepts, dispute involvement and dispute escalation. The authors use the Militarized Interstate Dispute (MID) data collection from the Correlates of War database (Gochman and Maoz 1984), and the International Crisis Behavior Project data (Brecher and Wilkenfeld 1989; Brecher, Wilkenfeld, and Moser 1988). The "two different data sets that were compiled for different analytical purposes and using different definitions" (1993, 628). This enables them to see how well the two explanations fare on the criterion of robustness.

With this preparation accomplished, Maoz and Russett test three hypotheses. The first is on level of democracy in a dyad of states: highly democratic dyads do not fight each other. The second, on depth of democratic norms in the two states: states with pervasive democratic norms do not fight each other. This outcome would be expected on the normative model. The third, on level of institutional constraints in the two states: highly constrained states do not fight each other. This outcome would be expected on the structural model.

The predictions based on the normative assumptions usually yield the same expectations as those based on the structural assumptions. So Maoz and

Russett must find situations in which the expectations would diverge; that is, they must distinguish a set of expectations that arise from the normative model from those that arise from the structural model. The solution they arrive at is to focus on two pairs of distinctions: older versus newer democracies, and presidential versus parliamentary democracies. Because the literature on the subject shows that all norms develop only gradually, states that have been democracies for long periods should have more causally efficacious norms than newer democracies. And to test the effects of structure, Maoz and Russett argue that the structural model should yield different predictions for presidential and parliamentary democracies.

By drawing on these two sets of distinctions, Maoz and Russett hypothesize that "the more deeply rooted are democratic norms in the political processes operating in two states, the lower the likelihood that disputes will break out or that disputes will escalate" (normative model), and that "the higher the political constraints on the executives of the two states, the lower the likelihood that disputes will break out or that disputes will escalate" (structural model) (1993, 627). The authors identify an appropriate set of cases. In one set the prediction of the normative model is high conflict and that of the structural model is low conflict; in the other set of cases the prediction of the normative model is low conflict and that of the structural model is high conflict.

Democratic norms are measured by the amount of political violence within a state. Two types of indicators are used for this purpose: deaths from political violence and extent of domestic conflict. Maoz and Russett's research design leaves open the possibility that democracy, if it is a cause of peace, might be one of several causes. Indeed, their analysis shows that wealth, economic growth, geography, and other factors are also relevant. Of course, they leave open the possibility that two or more aspects of democracies' "internal makeup," such as the normative and structural features, lead to peaceful dyadic behavior. It turns out that "both models received some empirical support" (1993, 631).

Criteria

Maoz and Russett offer implicit but clear criteria for a good explanation: *completeness*, *empirical fit* with statistical analysis, and *robustness*. For them, "Both the fact that the democratic-peace phenomenon is causally meaningful and the fact that we are beginning to move toward a substantive understanding of its causes carry important theoretical implications" (1993, 636). This implies that causal meaningfulness is connected to the statistical tests. It also implies that a "substantive understanding" of the statistical association is something that is subsequent to, and additional to, a determination of "causal meaningfulness." They attempt to distinguish the *true causal* nature of the impact of norms as compared with structure. The authors also seek correct *predictions* and note the importance of distinguishing the precise predictions from each model (1993, 626).

8. JOHN M. OWEN IV: LIBERALISM AND DEMOCRATIC PEACE

John M. Owen's 1994 *International Security* paper, "How Liberalism Produces Democratic Peace," is another very widely cited work from the early 1990s. Owen agrees with other DP supporters that the internal dynamics of liberal democracies lead them to avoid war with one another. But he defends the somewhat unusual claim that their democratic makeup also drives them to an increased frequency of war with nondemocracies. Owen pursues a two-pronged strategy. One involves deriving various consequences from the DP principles and providing support for them and the other involves defending DP claims from some of the criticisms. Owen identifies three main criticisms of DP arguments: that DP authors use ambiguous definitions of key terms, that wars are so rare that the lack of democratic wars is not significant, and that DP authors have no theoretical explanation for the DP phenomenon (1994, 87). Owen focuses primarily on the last. His research design utilizes a process-tracing analysis of a set of US foreign policy crises from 1790 through 1917.

Owen uses the term *liberalism* rather than *democracy* and says that a careful formulation of the definition provides the key to understanding dyadic peace. As he uses the term, liberal states have two essential features: competitive elections and free speech. Owen says, "Liberalism seeks to actualize the harmony of interests among individuals by insuring that the freedom of each is compatible with the freedom of all. Citizens [must have] leverage over governmental decision makers. Freedom of speech is necessary because it allows citizens to evaluate alternative foreign policies. Regular, competitive elections are necessary because they provide citizens with the possibility of punishing officials who violate their rights" (1994, 99). According to Owen, "Most explanations of democratic peace posit that democracies recognize one another and refuse to fight on that basis; but the researchers never test this assumption" (1994, 96). Owen cites Schweller (1992), Bueno de Mesquita and Lalman (1992, 156), along with authors discussed in this chapter: Doyle, Lake, Rummel, and Russett.

Mechanisms and the Acceptability of Empirical and Theoretical Claims

Owen attacks the realist argument that DP claims are unacceptable because they cannot be explained coherently. He focuses on the criticism that DP hypotheses cannot be accepted as true because "the democratic peace lacks a theoretical foundation. No one is sure why democracies do not fight one another and yet fight non-democracies. That we do not really know the causal mechanism behind the democratic peace means that we cannot be certain the peace is genuine" (1994, 88). Without an explanation, even the empirical observation must be held in doubt and may be spurious. He adds, "Some realists argue that there is no theoretically compelling causal mechanism that could explain the democratic peace" (1994, 118).[9]

Owen accepts that *causal mechanisms* are required for explanation and for the acceptability of claims of empirical regularities. He says that phenomena that occur require explanations, and various "considerations . . . suggest that democratic peace is a genuine phenomenon that simply needs a better explanation" (1994, 92). Owen argues that there is a causal mechanism, and his definition of *liberal* is what enables him to detail that mechanism. The mechanism Owen describes requires the joint operation of ideas and institutions. In his view ideas have causal force. And liberal ideas "give rise to two intervening variables, liberal ideology and domestic democratic institutions, which shape foreign policy" (1994, 93). Owen says that a proposed causal mechanism "may be logically coherent yet empirically false" when applied to specific cases (1994, 102).

Perceptions and the Liberal Mechanism

Owen includes perceptions as a key element in the mechanism that relates a state's liberal regime-type to its behavior. Perceptions change over time. The contemporary distinction between "democracy" and "nondemocracy" does not match up with the key distinction between "like us" and "unlike us" that American leaders and citizens have historically held. In particular, Americans often thought in terms of "republics" and "monarchies." Throughout the nineteenth century most Americans, including the presidents Jefferson and Madison, regarded Britain as different and France as similar because Britain was a monarchy and France was not (1994, 97, 110–11).

Europeans similarly saw "republicanism" as more significant than "democracy." For example, after World War I, despite its Weimar constitution, Germany was not regarded by France as having a kindred form of government.

The "Germanness" of the state overrode the constitutional structure. During the American Civil War, "British liberal affinity for the Union was rather weak. The resolution of the *Trent* crisis can be explained without reference to democratic peace theory: the administration of Abraham Lincoln backed down to a British ultimatum" on power politics calculations (1994, 111). At this point Owen allows that a factor like war avoidance among democratic dyads might offer a sufficient explanation of a phenomenon, but other sets of factors might equally do so without it. Here it is still left open as to which is the superior explanation. Owen seems to be saying that those who have reservations about the reality of DP forces and no such reservations about power politics forces may use the latter to explain and supplant the former.

The American public was reluctant to go to war against Spain in 1873 and Chile in 1892, according to Owen, because both were, like the United States, republics and not monarchies. Observations from historical cases like these two lead Owen to say "that democratic peace is a genuine phenomenon that simply needs a better explanation" (1994, 92). The liberal norms of a state have force because they are accepted by the society in general. Leaders who rise to power in that society are limited by the general acceptance of the norms, even if the leaders themselves do not personally accept them (1994, 99).

Owen thus holds the view that any genuine phenomenon must be explainable. This would seem consistent with, and indeed a consequence of, Owen's earlier-noted implicit principle that any hypothesized phenomenon must be explainable to be regarded as real. Again we see that, for Owen, the acceptability of theoretical claims, and even empirical regularities, requires causal explanations. Owen acknowledges that factors cited by opposing theories may be compatible and may work together because opposing theories may each mistakenly exclude factors that are included in alternative theories. In particular, Owen argues that both power politics and liberal democratic peace considerations may guide states' behavior (1994, 122–24). There are systems and agents that have properties that allow them to act in opposite ways. One sort of stimulus may propel them one way and a different stimulus may propel them in another way (see Elster 1993, 2–7).

"Explanation," "Account," and "Understanding"

Owen refers to various "accounts" of democratic peace (1994, 89), but the context does not tell the reader much about what he means by the term. It would seem to be intended to convey the broad range of possibilities of specific meanings that the term usually carries. What Owen does to improve on these accounts is to provide grounding for liberal ideology and to show by means of a stage process how states translate ideas into policy. Owen offers his own definition of liberal democracy and argues that norms and structure work to reinforce one another, or as he says, "Liberal ideology and institutions work in tandem to bring about democratic peace" (1994, 89).

Criteria

Owen relies on a number of criteria, most of which are evident in his attacks on the arguments of DP opponents. Owen invokes *falsifiability* as he defends DP claims from the charge that they fail to satisfy this criterion; for example, he denies the realist criticism that DP supporters continually redefine democracy to apply to dyads when the members are at peace and to exclude those same dyads if they commence violent action: "Realists claim that when power politics requires war with a democracy, liberals will redefine that state as despotic; when power politics requires peace with a non-democracy, they will redefine that state as a democracy" (1994, 120). Owen accepts that falsifiability is an important criterion and argues that DP scholars do not violate it.

Owen's theory of liberal peace can deal with ancient cases that critics argue are anomalies for DP defenders. Owen acknowledges that in the Hellenic world many democracies fought with one another. But Owen cites passages from Thucydides to argue that the various poleis in question do not satisfy the conditions of his definition of liberalism (1994, 98). Owen relies on the criterion of *greater range* of domain, in that he says an explanation that satisfies it will account for more cases, including anomalous cases that other explanations fail to handle successfully. Owen accepts the importance of *counterfactual reasoning* to causal claims in defending DP supporters from realists' charge that democracies would not even threaten one another, and that if DP principles were true, then the causal mechanisms, both structural and normative, would prevent democracies even from leveling threats against other democracies. His argument on this matter involves the use of counterfactuals. We have seen here that he also invokes criteria of *mechanisms, robustness*, and *empirical fit.*

9. CHRISTOPHER LAYNE'S "KANT OR CANT: THE MYTH OF THE DEMOCRATIC PEACE"

In the wake of several widely discussed works defending DP claims, especially those of Doyle, Rummel, Russett, and Maoz and Russett (discussed earlier),

DP opponents launched a number of attacks. In the fall of 1994 *International Security* published two papers critical of democratic peace, authored by Christopher Layne, "Kant or Cant," and the other by David Spiro (along with Owen's pro-DP article). The following year *International Security* published other papers on the topic (Mansfield and Snyder 1995a; Oren 1995).

Layne is interested in the DP controversy because of its connection to the important policy and theoretical questions discussed at the outset of this chapter. Layne's paper challenges the DP theorists by offering process-tracing analyses of four cases: the 1861 *Trent* affair, the 1895–96 Venezuela crisis, the 1898 Fashoda crisis, and the 1923 French invasion of the Ruhr. These particular cases, he says, should be "hard cases" for realism, because each one involved two democracies in a heated crisis, yet nonviolent resolutions were achieved. Also, they should be especially easy cases for DP theorists, since each had additional democratic peace factors that the theory says should produce cooperation, such as economic interdependence and special historical ties (1994, 7).

Realism and Liberalism

Layne presents a realist account of war in the international system that draws on Waltz (1979) and Mearsheimer (1990). According to realism, the best explanation for the unchanging character of international politics is the system of competition, self-help, and anarchy, not democratic norms. Layne follows other realists in holding that states' domestic behavior, contrary to DP claims, is different from their international behavior because, in domestic competition, losers typically live to engage in another round, whereas in international competition, losers confront "more extreme outcomes, ranging from constraints on autonomy to occupation to extinction" (1994, 11). Competition is a fight for survival in international affairs, which requires states to pursue balancing against rivals, both by developing their own defenses and by building alliances.

Layne lays out the democratic peace position primarily by citing Doyle (1983a, 1983b), Russett (1993), and Maoz and Russett (1993); he identifies versions of the norms and structural explanations that he regards as distinct but interrelated. Layne sees the two central claims of the norms explanation as: the internal norms of peaceful conflict resolution are manifest outwardly whenever possible, and democratic states assume that sister democracies will seek negotiation rather than violence to resolve conflicts. Layne derives propositions from three specific DP claims: (1) "public opinion should be strongly pacific," (2) "policymaking elites should refrain from making military threats" and preparations for war against other democracies, and (3) "democracies should bend over backwards to accommodate each other in a crisis" (1994, 13–14). He says there are two core principles of the structural DP explanation. First, because democratic governments must answer to the public and because citizens pay the taxes to support wars and serve as soldiers, we should expect that the public will oppose war in all but the most extreme cases. Second, war is inhibited by the system of checks and balances in democratic states, especially states that have "executives answerable to a selection party, institutionalized political competition, and . . . decision-making responsibility spread among multiple institutions or individuals" (1994, 9).

Democracies avoided war in each of the four cases, Layne argues, because at least one disputant saw its power interests best served by de-escalating the crisis, not because of any normative or structural factors that proponents of DP theory would invoke. He says, "In each of these four cases realism, not democratic peace theory, provides the more compelling explanation of why war was avoided. Indeed, the democratic peace theory indicators appear not to have played *any* discernible role in the outcome of these crises" (1994, 38). Layne goes on to argue, following Hintze (1975), that the realists' emphasis on the structure of the international system offers insight into why wars between democratic states are rare; namely, democracies rise in comparatively stable and peaceful areas. States that find themselves "in high-threat environments are less likely to be democracies because such states are more likely to be involved in wars, and states that are likely to be involved in wars tend to adopt autocratic governmental structures that enhance their strategic posture" (1994, 45).

Criteria

Given his method of identifying realist and DP principles, and of drawing expected consequences from them, Layne holds that any good explanation will fit the covering law model. Layne explicitly identifies three criteria by means of which theoretical explanations should be comparatively assessed, namely "the persuasiveness of a theory's causal logic," the theory's predictive ability, and "the robustness of the democratic peace theory's empirical evidence" (1994, 6). He says in this context, "I conclude that realism is superior to democratic peace theory as a predictor of international outcomes. Indeed, democratic peace theory appears to have extremely little explanatory power in the cases studied" (1994, 7; see also page 5). The implication here is that predictive capacity is the determinant, or at least a determinant, of explanatory power. In a later passage, Layne appears to separate prediction from explanation: "Democratic peace theory not only predicts a specific outcome—no war between democracies—but also purports to explain why that outcome will occur" (1994, 13).[10]

Layne goes on to make the significant claim, discussed also by Owen (1994, 88), that if the causal logic or explanation of a general observation does not hold up, then there should be doubts about the initial evidence that led to the empirical generalizations. In his subsequent investigation, Layne argues that the Confederate States of America was a democracy, and was so regarded by at least some European liberals, and that Wilhelmine Germany was as democratic as its Western rivals in 1914, and hence both the Civil War and World War I are counterexamples to DP generalizations (1994, 39–44). On several occasions Layne distinguishes the "correlation between domestic structure and the absence of war" and any "causal" principle (1994, 38). But if explanations cannot be developed for the observational generalizations, then the latter should be regarded as suspect. He is interested in the governmental *mechanisms* that lead to foreign policy decisions for war and peace (1994, 42). His arguments for causal influence draw heavily on what would have happened in other circumstances, and he thus believes an explanation should *support counterfactuals* (1994, 20, 21–22, 24).

Layne requires any good explanation to be causal: "Although democratic peace theory identifies a correlation between domestic structure and the absence of war between democracies, it fails to establish a causal link" (1994, 38). He continues, "Because democratic peace theory's deductive logic lacks explanatory power, a look at the theory's empirical support is warranted" (1994, 38). Layne here acknowledges, at least for the moment, the correlation between a dyad's democratic membership and absence of war, but he asserts that DP theory does not establish a causal link. He says, "When one actually looks beyond the result of these four cases . . . and attempts to understand why these crises turned out as they did, it becomes clear that democratic peace theory's causal logic has only minimal explanatory power" (1994, 38). The failure to show causality is apparently because the criterion of *empirical adequacy* is not satisfied; there is a lack of correspondence, at the various stages of the crises, of the deductively derived expectations from DP theory's general causal principles.

Layne questions the empirical adequacy of the DP claims based on the mismatch between outcomes expectations they generate, or in other words, their *predictive accuracy*. He sees *simpler* arguments as preferable, other things being equal. But the advantages of simplicity can be overcome by failure to meet other criteria (1994, 47). And Layne's desire to consider "hard cases" that would be likely to present difficulties for realism in order, ultimately, to lend weight to it (and undermine the credibility of DP hypotheses, the alternatives to his preferred realist explanation) is an example of Popperian *falsification*, which explicitly advocates the formulation of bold conjectures and rigorous tests of them.

10. DAVID E. SPIRO'S "THE INSIGNIFICANCE OF THE LIBERAL PEACE"

David E. Spiro argues against democratic peace theory by focusing, like Layne, on the publications of Rummel (1975–81, 1983), Lake (1992), Owen (1994), and Maoz and Russett (1993). Spiro (1994), like Layne, builds on Mearsheimer (1990) in formulating a realist alternative, but unlike Layne, he focuses his critiques primarily on DP theorists' statistical framework and research design. The main thrust of Spiro's critique is that liberal DP theory adds nothing to our knowledge because democratic dyads have historically, at least until 1945, been so scarce that no puzzle arises over the absence of wars between democracies. To cite an extreme example, over the first thirteen years of the period covered by the Correlates of War data set, the period 1816–29, there were only two liberal democracies, the United States and the Swiss Confederation (1994, 66). Moreover, both states were small, and they were geographically distant from one another. The absence of democratic wars in that period presents no puzzle that DP theory helps to explain. Over the following century more democracies arose, but both democratic dyads and democratic wars continued to be rare.

Democratic Peace Arguments

Spiro criticizes Rummel, alleging that his analysis is excessively sensitive to the use of a logarithmic scale (as opposed to using a direct dyad count to quantify war), and to the mere four-year time frame, 1976 to 1980. A number of dictatorships happened to be at war with one another in that period. Any generalization from this atypical sample risks committing a logical fallacy because "to show that underdeveloped dictatorships go to war is not to say that free nations do not go to war" (Spiro 1994, 77).[11] If Rummel were to adjust these two parameters, he would be unable to draw the same conclusion about the peacefulness of libertarian states.[12] With regard to Owen's (1994) paper, Spiro approves of its focus on the perceptions of each state's citizenry as the basis for coding democracy; this is an improvement on the use of static Polity or

Correlates of War definitions. But he says that Owen's solution to the problem is not applicable because there are as yet no databases with cases coded on that basis (1994, 58). Spiro disagrees with Lake's (1994, 26) claim that the Finnish alignment with the Axis powers is "an easily explained exception," since in whatever way it is explained, it remains "an exception" (Spiro 1994, 61).

Maoz and Russett's (1993) paper, according to Spiro, "provides the strongest empirical evidence that liberal democracy is an important factor in why nations do not fight" (1994, 77). Still, Spiro sees several flaws in their argument. One has to do with the way in which Maoz and Russett use pooled time-series analysis. They consider every dyad for every year and identify whether or not each was democratic, and whether it was involved in war. They then analyze the set of all dyads. But according to this procedure, in a forty-one-year period, the United States–Canada dyad constitutes forty-one separate observations, which Spiro says violates the assumption of observation independence; peace between two states in a given year is not independent of whether those states were at peace the previous year. Furthermore, Maoz and Russett's use of the indicator militarized interstate disputes rather than war inflates the number of dyadic disputes. When the variable war is used, the absence of war among democratic dyads is relatively well explained by chance. It is important to note, especially as the DP debate is compared to the others, that these charges do not go unanswered. As we will see, one of the distinctive features of the DP debate is that DP proponents respond to the specific charges of realist critics like Layne and Spiro.

Randomness and Explanation

Spiro argues that the predictions of DP theory do not justify its acceptance, particularly when the predictions are compared to those generated by assuming random processes. "If the absence of wars between democracies is predicted by random chance, this is not to say that chance is a good explanation for war. It does mean that an explanation we know to be untrue—random chance—predicts the absence of war between democracies better than liberal theories of international relations, and therefore the absence of wars should not be considered as confirming evidence of those theories. And if the absence of wars between democracies is not surprising, then there is no puzzle to explain" (1994, 51). What this passage states is that, if liberal theory does worse than randomness, and randomness is not acceptable, then liberal theory is not acceptable. According to Spiro, the outcomes in a series of coin tosses may be explainable by random processes, but wars are not because we know that wars do not arise from random processes.

The Alliances Constitute a Puzzle

Spiro holds that realism does a sufficient job of explaining war. Consequently, liberal DP theories should not be accepted because they do not add to realist explanations, the arguments on their behalf are flawed, and randomness predicts outcomes better than DP theory. The only apparent exception to the ability of randomness to explain dyadic peace as well as DP theory is the years 1914 to 1918, since many dyads were at war during those years and random chance would predict more than zero wars among democratic dyads. Spiro says, for that period, "we need to explain why no democracies fought one another" (1994, 69). The puzzle arises for Spiro because, unlike Layne, he views Wilhelmine Germany as nondemocratic. Spiro's solution to the alliance puzzle is that liberalism can help in the explanation of alignment patterns. In the early twentieth century democracies aligned with one another, and it was for that reason no democratic dyads fought when war began in 1914.

Spiro admits that the pattern of democratic alliances is irreconcilable with Waltzian realist theory, since that theory dismisses variations in behavior based on state-level factors. However, Spiro does not see this as a blow to realism generally but only as a blow to Waltz's particular structural version. Spiro says that classical realism includes elements of subjectivity that can account for different perception at the state level, and thus can account for the way that perceptions shape the national interest conceptions of states: "A more full-bodied realist theory that takes into account such subjectivity would have no problem in explaining how a liberal normative framework affects the choice of alliance partners" (1994, 80). Spiro believes that classical realism is capable of explaining democracies' alliance choices, and those choices, in turn, explain the absence of war in democratic dyads. But it is not at all clear that realism does a better job of explaining either of the two phenomena Spiro discusses, democratic-dyadic war and alliance choices.

Spiro's Argument and Assumptions

In his rejection of DP explanations, Spiro makes several moves that one might question. One is that Spiro's rejection of liberalism is based on an equivocation; a second is that he seems to conclude more than he has demonstrated; and a third regards his use of the assumption that realism is the reigning, accepted explanation of peace and war in the 1990s, which elevates the standards of proof for rival theories. With regard to the first, Spiro argues that random chance does as good a job of explaining the absence of war among democracies as does DP theory. He says, "If the distribution of wars among democracies *is not statistically different from* that which is generated by random chance, then the democratic peace is not confirming evidence for liberal theory" (1994, 63, emphasis added). This seems to be a plausible statement of the statistical state of affairs. But Spiro formulates his claim differently when he draws one of his key conclusions, quoted earlier: "random chance—predicts the absence of war between democracies *better than* liberal theories" (1994, 51, emphasis added). The claim that randomness explains the data better than DP theory is inconsistent with the claim that randomness and DP theory both predict a high probability of zero wars, in which case their predictions are *equally accurate*. This equivocation creates a serious problem for readers' acceptance of his conclusion. The most he has shown is that liberalism cannot be regarded proven at this stage.

Second, Spiro says that DP theory and random chance predict no war with high probability, and hence DP theory is unacceptable. It is not clear why accurate predictions should eliminate DP theory as an acceptable explanation. If we know that two explanations meet the criterion of empirical adequacy with respect to the known observations, and we know one of the explanations is incorrect, then, Spiro says, we must reject the other. But there are no reasonable grounds for doing so. Rather, if both explanations yield correct predictions, and if only one can be ruled out on theoretical grounds (since we know that war is not a result of random action), then it would seem the remaining explanation is all the more plausible. To put it another way, consider proposition 1 (P1): Theory A and Theory B both are consistent with all observations. Then consider P2: on grounds of explanatory mechanisms, we know that Theory B cannot be right. Then from statements P1 and P2, the logical conclusion would seem to be that we have good reason to accept Theory A.[13]

A third problematic inference stems from Spiro's assumption that realism is the accepted, standing theory in IR and thus it would have to be disproved by any "challenger" theory, like liberalism, to be supplanted. This assumption—along with his claim that liberalism, realism, and the null hypothesis all predict no war—leads Spiro to conclude that we should accept realism. Spiro implicitly draws on the criterion of *methodological conservatism* (see Chapter 2 section 3). But the criterion of methodological conservatism, if acceptable at all, is applicable only in cases in which a field of study (or at least the target audience of the publication) accepts the supposedly reigning theory. And on empirical grounds, we can easily see that it is not the case that the field of IR accepts realism over rivals (see Jordan et al. 2009, 31). If realism were accepted as explaining everything other than DP, then the picture would favor rejecting liberalism. But while realism fits with many background beliefs, so does liberalism. Spiro presumes that theorists accepted realism prior to the rise of liberal DP arguments; thus, he uses methodological conservatism as a criterion here (1994, 62).[14]

We have noted that Spiro denies any DP puzzle because democratic dyads have been so rare; as just noted, in the extreme case of the 1816–29 period there were only two liberal democracies. But one could argue that the small size of, and long distance between, those two democracies provides an explanation. And one need not be a realist to believe that two states that lack the capacity to fight each other will not fight. In other words, there is no puzzle because we already have an explanation. What we know about war provides us with an explanation of why there were no democratic wars. What does and does not constitute a puzzle is relative to background beliefs (see Section 5 in Chapter 6).

Explanation

Spiro regards *prediction* as important to a good explanation but perhaps not "essential" in the narrowest sense, and he does not endorse Hempelian explanation-prediction symmetry. There are cases of prediction when there is no explanation, since predictions may be useful even when there are no puzzles that require explanation. And there are cases of explanation when there is no prediction. This is clear for Spiro since explanations (e.g., of the last ten coin tosses) based on randomness do not provide a basis for an accurate prediction (e.g., of the next ten coin tosses). Hence there is a clear conceptual separation between explanation and prediction.

Spiro's analysis involves a somewhat unique distinction between "static" and "historical" explanations. He appears to regard them both as legitimate forms of explanation; but they cannot be compared with or tested against each other. Finally, we note that Spiro agrees with others who see consistency between explanation and understanding. He says, "Thus, while the nature of regimes does little to explain when and with whom they go to war, it is an important variable in understanding the composition of alliances" (1994, 79). So in some cases, for Spiro, an "account" may explain without being the basis of prediction. This may, however, only hold of randomness explanations, though Spiro does not address this.

Criteria

Spiro criticizes the DP theory's general principles by deriving consequences from them and then examining individual cases to assess whether they conform to those expectations. He is thus making use of the hypothetico-deductive method and drawing on a covering-law form of explanation (1994, 53). He also draws on the Hempelian use of *expectations* in describing explanation (1994, 60). His comment that political scientists "have done surprisingly little to show that elements of liberal democracy are causal influences on peace" implies that one goal of IR is to ascertain causal explanations (1994, 54).

One of the main points that Spiro seeks to establish is that the quantitative arguments for democratic peace are very sensitive to small changes in the ways in which the key terms democracy and war are defined. He notes that the highly quantitative work on the democratic peace requires coding decisions on every case in every data set, and codings vary; the Polity II data set used by Maoz differs from Doyle's data "for two thirds of the nations that either or both list as democratic" (Spiro 1994, 56). Spiro cites Mansfield (1988) to the effect that one's choice of "data sets on war determines the conclusions yielded by the data analysis" (1994, 59). Thus in Spiro's view, *robustness* is an important criterion, and DP studies do not satisfy it. Spiro is explicit about the advantages of theoretical debates in which the points of disagreement are clear, and the explanatory claims are *falsifiable.* He is critical of IR debates that are not of this nature (1994, 79). His rejection of randomness as an "untrue explanation" of war indicates that Spiro regards *true causes* as a criterion, along with *empirical adequacy* and *predictive accuracy.*

11. FARBER AND GOWA, "POLITICS AND PEACE"

Henry Farber and Joanne Gowa published a very influential paper in *International Security* in 1995 entitled "Polities and Peace," which questioned the dyadic DP explanation. This was the first of a number of papers on the topic over the following three years by Farber, Gowa, or both.[15] In "Politics and Peace," Farber and Gowa examine both the theoretical logic and the empirical analyses of DP supporters. Farber and Gowa note, as have Spiro and others, that most democratic dyads existed only after World War II, and thus data sets are heavily skewed. Since the 1945–90 period was also bipolar, they suspect that the system structure may be largely responsible for what is taken to be the relationship between democracy and peace. Their method is to disaggregate the historical data into distinct periods in order to compare the record of the period before

World War I to the period after World War II. They conclude that the alleged DP relationship is not genuinely causal.

The authors look at both the empirical analyses and the "logic" of DP claims, that is, the theoretical foundation and explanatory function of liberal principles that focus on the norms and the checks-and-balances structure of democracies. With respect to structure, they argue that "renegade leaders" (Farber and Gowa 1995, 127) of democracies have almost the same leeway to act aggressively as leaders of nondemocracies. Farber and Gowa analyze the period from 1816 to 1980 using the Correlates of War data for war and peace among states and the Polity II data to categorize states as "democracies," "autocracies," or "anocracies." A state is coded an "anocracy" if it has an intermediate score on the democracy and autocracy measure. Farber and Gowa group the cases into three periods: pre–World War I, World War I to World War II, and post–World War II. They observe that, while autocracies have remained in similar numbers, over time anocracies have diminished and democracies have increased.

Farber and Gowa criticize DP defenders' method of quantifying war. Since they are interested in the onset of war, each war should count only once. But while they treat a war that lasts one year as only one war in their analysis, they count a war that lasts three years three times; both wars should be counted the same (since there is only one onset). Another way in which they depart from most Correlates of War–based analyses is their distinction, following Levy (1985) and Vasquez (1993), between general war and other wars. Whether it is appropriate to use this distinction, they say, depends upon whether one believes that the dynamics of general wars are different from those of other wars, and on the specific question one seeks to answer.[16] They contend that dyadic behavior is important for most wars, but for general wars involving many states, dyadic relations are not relevant and do not shed light on dyadic behavior in other wars. States did not enter World War I or II as discreet pairs. "The dynamics of general wars, however, render a dyad a substantively meaningless unit of observation. For example, a dyad-based measure cannot capture the attempts to pass the buck that dominated the periods immediately before both World War I and World War II" (1995, 133). Since the differences cannot be tested statistically, because in the period they study there were only two general wars, World War I and World War II, they choose to remove all observations from the periods of the two wars (1914–18 and 1939–45). However, for comparability purposes, they also run tests using all of the years between 1816 and 1980, which enhances the robustness of their findings.

Depending how one conceptualizes peace between states, one must decide which indicators of peace are most appropriate. Is it appropriate to say that DP claims entail only that democracies do not go to war with one another, or is it more appropriate to require that such claims entail that democracies be free of all conflict, both violent and nonviolent conflict? If the answer to the first question is yes, then the appropriate indicator of peace is the absence of war. Scholars who argue that DP claims involve democracies' norms against violence toward sister democracies would presumably not accept that a democracy would even threaten force against other democracies. If peace among democracies is understood to mean the absence of both force and threats to use force, then tests of DP claims would have to use an indicator reflecting the absence of any militarized interstate disputes.[17] Farber and Gowa regard either factor as reasonable; the proper variable choice would depend on the specific formulation of the DP claim and mechanism proposed to explain the pacific effects. They therefore run the statistical tests using both wars and lower-level militarized interstate disputes as dependent variables.[18]

Farber and Gowa remind the reader that it is difficult to construct useful tests for very rare phenomena like interstate war. Some periods have no war among the specifiable groups, like democracies after World War II. While this is blessing for citizens, it is difficult to carry out statistical tests on events that do not occur. Farber and Gowa use a Pearson chi-square test, which they regard as both "straightforward and robust" with respect to certain assumptions (1995, 138). But they note that bivariate tests can be misleading because they may exclude other variables that have genuine effects, such as alliance status, wealth, major-power status, and geographic contiguity. The first two are difficult to test for, as they may create a biased parameter (1995, 138). And there is a lack of reliable data on wealth. But Farber and Gowa do control for major-power status and geographic contiguity. By means of linear probability models and logit tests, they estimate the probability of war against factors such as regime-type, geographical contiguity, and great-power status. The authors conclude that, because of the low percentage of democracies and infrequency of wars, the absence of war among democratic states is neither surprising nor different from what one finds among states in general (1995, 139). They therefore reject the monadic hypothesis: democracies are as war-prone as other states. Democracies have a probability of war of 0.0191, and nondemocracies have a probability of 0.0189.

Farber and Gowa, at this stage of their analysis, exhibit results that are consistent with the dyadic hypothesis; the probability of war is four and a half times greater for dyads that do not have two democracies (0.09) than for democratic dyads (0.02). But for reasons noted, they do not regard this as a sufficient level of investigation. Their next step is to break the cases into five time periods (pre–World War I, during World War I, the interwar years, during World War II, and post-1945). However, they are interested primarily in the first, third, and last periods. Because they believe that there is a fundamental difference between general wars and other wars, they test for the periods 1914–18 and 1939–45 but do not subject them to further analysis. The authors focus on the contrast between the pre–World War I period and the post–World War II period. In the former, "no statistically significant relationship exists" (1995, 141) between war and regime-type. The probability of war between democracies is 0.0007, and the probability of war between other states is 0.0010. However, after World War II, there were no wars among democracies, and the probability of war among all other dyads was 0.0004. They then present data on all conflicts—both violent and nonviolent—and find essentially the same pattern. That is, they find little difference between democratic dyads and other dyads before 1914, but they find a large difference after 1945. They conclude that the dyadic democratic peace after World War II was due to something in the bipolar international system structure, not to states' democratic regime-type.

Further Debate and Farber and Gowa's Follow-Up

Farber and Gowa's paper in *International Security* drew a good deal of attention. Their subsequent papers (see note 15) clarified their position and made adjustments based on criticisms by Oneal and Russett (1997), Thompson and Tucker (1997), and others. A very important point to note here is that the specific methods of argument of DP defenders are dissected by critics, like Layne, Spiro, and Farber and Gowa, and the supporters of the dyadic hypothesis respond in very specific ways, not simply by defending their methods and arguments, but often by *acknowledging* that their arguments *fail to satisfy* some of their critics' standards, making adjustments in the methods or data coding, running new tests, and publishing their conclusions.

Thompson and Tucker (1997) argue in *Journal of Conflict Resolution* that the statistical evidence does not support Farber and Gowa's claim that the democratic peace is a post–World War II phenomenon, at least when the structure of major rivalries is taken into account. Thompson and Tucker also take issue with

Mansfield and Snyder's (1995a) argument that newly democratized states are more war-prone. In their *Journal of Conflict Resolution* paper, Farber and Gowa (1997b) found that dispute rates between members of democratic dyads relative to other types of dyads vary across time. Thompson and Tucker argue that Farber and Gowa's analysis does not take into account "the structure of principal rivalries." These rivalries involved, among others, "two important democratic dyads"—that is, Great Britain and France, and Great Britain and the United States. The authors respond that if Thompson and Tucker applied their argument more broadly, the effect of democratic regime-type might disappear after 1945 as well. That is, if they were to control for all disputes related to the Soviet-American rivalry during the Cold War, they might find democratic dyads to be just as disputatious as other country pairs after 1945 (Thompson and Tucker 1997, 435).

Explanation and Criteria

Farber and Gowa say that they are going to investigate "both the logic and the empirical basis" (1995, 123) of the central DP claims, and it soon becomes clear that the former refers to explanatory mechanisms. They criticize the norms model charging, "Any explanation . . . based on the distinctiveness of the norms underlying them is not testable" (1995, 126), which shows that they believe that explanations should be falsifiable. Farber and Gowa also seem to regard an explanation with a larger domain as preferable; common interests explain both peacetime periods they consider, pre-1914 and post-1945. They see the key criteria as *falsifiability, extent of domain, empirical fit,* and *robustness.*

12. ERIK GARTZKE ON ECONOMIC LIBERALISM

Erik Gartzke has published a series of papers challenging some of the prominent works supporting DP claims. From 1998 to 2007 Gartzke published extensively on DP issues, including two papers in the *American Journal of Political Science* (1998, 2007), two in *International Studies Quarterly* (2000, 2001), and several coauthored articles and book chapters. This section focuses primarily on the most recent of the papers, "The Capitalist Peace" (2007), in which Gartzke argues that the widely accepted claims of peace between democracies are better explained by economic than by political aspects of liberal states.

Gartzke notes that many scholars accept that the dyadic hypothesis holds up to empirical scrutiny and that many have offered explanations for what it is about democratic polities that produce peaceful dyadic relations. But he argues that there is no single explanation that has generated consensus, or even widespread support. He regards the explanation of peace among democracies as remaining an open question. Gartzke seeks, by means of statistical tests, to establish that the fact of peace between democratic dyads is best explained not by liberal states' political character but by their economic features, especially, "economic development, capital markets integration, and the compatibility of foreign policy preferences" (2007, 166).

Two Traditions

Liberalism has both political and economic dimensions, but in recent decades political scientists trying to explain the dyadic peace have focused on the political. Gartzke cites a long tradition of liberals, including Cobden (1903), Mill (1998), and Angell (1933), who have argued that the changing character of manufacturing in developed economies and interstate trade render war obsolete; as states continue to pursue national interest, they gradually have come to see that their goals are more effectively realized through peaceful negotiations and trade. However, as Gartzke lays out his own position, he discounts the role of trade, emphasizing instead the roles of economic development, the integration of capital markets, and overlapping foreign policy goals (2007, 170).

Gartzke maintains that the occurrence of wars between developed capitalist states does not disprove the capitalist peace hypothesis, since capitalism inhibits war based on a range of policy goals that states have traditionally pursued; but the goals within this range do not exhaust the list of states' policy goals. Gartzke thus insulates his theory from falsification by individual counterinstances.

For a war to commence, states must be both willing and able to compete, and they must be unwilling or unable to manage the competition peacefully. When both members of the pair are weak, or both are unwilling to fight, war will not occur (2007, 171). Capitalism in the era of advanced industrial economies diminishes the chances of war between two states because, although the quest for resources has traditionally been a major cause of war, resources can be more effectively obtained through trade. Moreover, the development of advanced capitalist states creates enough wealth for them to break out of the historical patterns in which states, needing resources for their survival, would go to war to secure them.

The Development of Gartzke's Position

The argument that capitalist development is the key factor builds on Gartzke's 1998 paper by claiming, along with Layne and Spiro, that DP defenders have attempted to explain something that does not constitute a puzzle and thus requires no explanation. While it is true that democratic states have rarely if ever fought one another, Gartzke argues that there is no mystery to it, since liberal democracies have converging interests, for which reason conflicts are unlikely to arise. Thus, the absence of war between them need not be attributed to any special war-restraining features of democracies. "The Capitalist Peace" details the nonpolitical reasons that conflicts between developed liberal democracies are unlikely to arise; namely, they gain more by negotiating than by fighting.[19]

In his 1998 paper Gartzke developed an index of the similarity of states' preferences by drawing on UN General Assembly votes to show that the absence of wars and militarized disputes in general between democratic states can be accounted for by states' similar preferences. Since democracies have mutual affinities and similar preferences, there is no puzzle that requires a solution, and hence there is no need to invoke dubious claims about the structure of democratic polities. (However, we will see later that critics of Gartzke contend that this is simply another mechanism by which democratic structure induces peace among democratic dyads.)

Hypotheses and Evidence

Gartzke tests four hypotheses. The first is that dyads of developed, contiguous states are more powerful than either developing or noncontiguous dyads. Second, development leads noncontiguous dyads to be more likely to experience conflict. Third, similar state policy interests lead dyads to be less likely to experience conflict. And fourth, financial or monetary integration leads states to be less likely to experience conflict.

Gartzke argues that the hard case for the hypothesis that capitalist states do not fight one another is the situation in which there is the greatest number of capitalist states. That is, if capitalist states are sparse in the system, there will be a lower probability that in any pair one will have the ability and willingness to fight the other. Accordingly, Gartzke uses a sample containing all dyad-years 1950 to 1992. In most cases he uses indicators similar to those used by Oneal and Russett to facilitate the comparison of his results to theirs. This approach follows Popper's methodology of *falsification*; instead of looking for cases that confirm a theory, Gartzke is examining the cases that would seem most likely to falsify it.

For the democracy variable Gartzke uses a variation on the Polity IV database, adapted in a way similar to Oneal and Russett. For markets he uses

International Monetary Fund indicators for market size, robustness and liberalization. For the variable development, Gartzke uses two indicators; one uses gross domestic product (GDP) per capita for the less developed member of the dyad (with some adjustments to mitigate multicollinearity) and the product of GDP per capita and contiguity; this focuses attention on the level of development of the less developed member of the dyad. The second indicator is designed to highlight the effect of development on the states vulnerable to territorial aggression. Gartzke includes this measure because "it is most likely that a decline in the value of conquest will manifest itself in relations with neighbors, where territorial claims are most common and aggression most practical" (2007, 175).

The third of Gartzke's variables, interest similarity, is the most problematic; it was the subject of Gartzke's 1998 paper and the attacks by Oneal and Russett's (2001) study. For this variable Gartzke constructs an index called affinity, on a scale of 1 to –1 (from those with the greatest affinity to those with the least). The coding is based on the frequency with which the states voted together in the UN General Assembly during the period covered by Oneal and Russett (1999). Gartzke acknowledges the significant difficulties of measuring preference similarities, and even in identifying individual national preferences. He says, though, "Still, UN voting arguably distorts preferences less than available alternatives" (2007, 175). He points out that there is no agreement as to how to measure national preferences and that political scientists "must choose between measuring interests imperfectly, [and] not measuring them at all" (2007, 175). Beyond how to measure national interest, there is a long-standing debate over whether the concept is even meaningful (see Wolfers 1952). Many theories of foreign policy avoid a commitment to the problematic notion of national interest by focusing the analysis on bureaucracies, interest-group interactions, individual leaders, and the like.

Gartzke is primarily challenging the conclusions of Russett and Oneal regarding the statistical association between democracy and peace; thus, he makes use of the same control variables that Oneal and Russett use, such as geographic distance, major-power status, military alliances, capabilities, and regional location. He concludes that, on the dyadic level, any one of the economic variables in his theory "is sufficient to account for the effects previously attributed to regime-type" (2007, 166). The three factors he favors fit together theoretically and produce a greater *empirical fit* based on statistical association with peace than democracy does.[20]

Gartzke's Use of the Notion of Explanation

As is the case in almost all the studies surveyed in this book, and as is typical in academic political science, Gartzke does not lay out a philosophical theory of social science explanation, and he offers no explicit definitions of the key explanatory terms he uses. However, as is also typical, the context and structure of the substantive argument provide implicit definitions of those terms. First, we note that Gartzke seeks a causal account of the dyadic phenomenon. He understands "causes" in terms of mechanisms, which is evident from his attribution of causal force to the rise of global capital markets (2007, 166, 171).[21] Gartzke believes that a good explanation provides understanding, since scholars seek "an evolving understanding of the empirical relationship" of the dyadic hypothesis (2007, 176; see also 182).

As this book has noted, the term *account* is vague and often conveniently permits authors to escape any philosophical or metatheoretical label. In this passage, the term *account* seems to have the same meaning as *explain.* For example, Gartzke says, "Theories of democratic peace have also proliferated, in no small part because of the difficulty in accounting for the special dyadic nature of the observation" (2007, 168); it is hard to see what the term *accounting for* could mean here other than *explaining.* Given that he says, "One answer might be capitalism" (2007, 169), Gartzke is invoking his explanatory factor as that which accounts for the observation in question. There are other passages in which the term *account* would seem to function as a synonym for *explain*: "What else but democracy could account for liberal peace?" Gartzke uses the term *explanation* in a way similar to that of other naturalist political scientists (e.g., in terms of its relationship to laws and lawlike statements, theories, and the more general accounts). Additional evidence comes from Gartzke's quote of Waltz: "'theories explain laws'" (2007, 168n8). Gartzke cites Waltz without offering any qualification or dissent. In terms of what qualifies one set of explanatory factors as superior to another set, Gartzke relies on the results of controlled regression analyses.[22]

Replies, Responses, and Criteria

Gartzke, like Farber and Gowa, published several versions of the argument. At least one reason for the iterations of their arguments is that defenders of DP explanations published criticisms to which these authors responded. Gartzke, like Farber and Gowa, replied to those criticisms in quite specific ways and DP theorists, chiefly Russett, usually with coauthors, replied and retested their claims taking into account the critics' charges. For example, Oneal and Russett (1997, 1999, 2001) reject Gartzke's position by arguing that the similarity of preferences and interests that one finds among the UN states voting together is a result of their shared democratic structure. They run regression analyses that draw on the standard DP model to justify their conclusion. In his 2000 paper, Gartzke defends his position by replicating Oneal and Russett's tests and arguing that the residuals from regression tests of the mutual affinity that democracies exhibit, as seen in UN voting patterns, leave 93 percent of the variance unexplained. Gartzke also criticizes Oneal and Russett's conclusions, arguing that the strength of the results are "fragile" in that they fail if the model specification is altered or the variables are constructed differently. He is here criticizing their research design for its low score on the robustness criterion (2007, 167n3).

Gartzke relies primarily on criteria of *empirical adequacy, falsifiability, imparts understanding*, and *robustness*. He regards the dyadic hypothesis as a strictly empirical claim rather than an explanation. He connects joint democracy to various economic factors, including economic development, and regards them as jointly functioning as explanatory by means of the *mechanisms* they suggest.

13. RECENT WORK IN DEMOCRATIC PEACE

The natural sciences show a number of patterns, one of which is that scientists move toward consensus answers when accepted explanations are shown to have weaknesses. Even after a new explanation gains widespread acceptance, it will continue to be scrutinized by some researchers, and it will eventually be replaced by another when those who investigate it show serious flaws and when better explanations come along. Constant scrutiny is an important part of the natural sciences. At present, the DP debate has reached a consensus both that the dyadic hypothesis is true and that the best explanation is some form of liberalism. But this is not a permanent end of the story; the consensus may break down in the future.

At this time, while IR journals publish little to nothing on the dyadic hypothesis itself, they are still replete with papers asking questions about democracy and peace, often presupposing the truth of the dyadic hypothesis. The questions include: Do democracies win wars disproportionately? Do they fight harder once war begins? Over the past decade the five most pertinent journals (the three top-ranked journals and the two other most security oriented) have published thousands of articles, yet in contrast to the 1980s and 1990s, only a fraction of 1 percent raise questions about the truth or proper explanation of the dyadic hypothesis. Of the five, only one (*International Studies Quarterly*) has published any papers specifically on the dyadic hypothesis, and even then it has published very few.[23] The paper by Gibler (2007) questions the dyadic hypothesis, and the paper by Choi (2011) assesses what he regards as the two best and most influential explanations for the dyadic peace. Michael Mousseau published three papers in the last decade in that journal, and the last was published together with three alternative arguments: Dafoe, Oneal, and Russett (2013); Gartzke and Weisiger (2013); and Ray (2013).

Gibler's paper, "Bordering on Peace," which was followed by a book in 2012, is noteworthy because it is one of two main works of the past decade to deny the liberal explanation. In Gibler's view democratic regime-type is not a cause of peace. Stable borders are instead the key factor. He argues that states with borders along which there are no "issues" have a substantially reduced likelihood of war. Gibler identifies a mechanism to explain this outcome. Many contiguous states do not have border issues with one another; such states are then more likely to develop various violence-reducing traits, such as smaller armies, which can lead to less centralized forms of state administration, and more capital mobility, which can lead to lower taxation and greater economic growth; these factors in turn increase the likelihood that such states will develop democratic regimes. Gibler says, "A democracy is most likely to take root when the threat of fighting wars [at home] . . . is low" (2007, 513). Indeed, for Gibler, one of the best predictors of war is border instability (2007, 519–21). According to this mechanism, stable borders lead to peace, and democracy is merely a by-product.

Gibler draws on the steps-to-war theory developed by John Vasquez (especially Vasquez's 1993 book) and several coauthors, including Gibler (Vasquez and Gibler 2001). While Gibler's theory clearly opposes liberal explanations and his emphasis on territory is consistent with realism, his theory nevertheless deviates from pure realism. First, he draws on the steps-to-war theory, which regards stable borders as a form of international institution. Further, the steps-to-war theory holds that leaders learn to deal with border issues by means of realpolitik, but this is highly contingent; there is no implication that alternatives are impossible, for example, that new institutions might lead to an evolution of how leaders learn. In contrast, realists see realpolitik as a much more inherent feature of the international system.

Gibler's argument makes use of existing data sets, including Correlates of War, Polity IV, Minorities at Risk, MID, and Huth and Allee's (2002) study.

And to enhance robustness, he also runs tests of the models for three temporal periods (Gibler 2007, 509). Like most other DP critics, Gibler makes use of criteria of evaluation that are similar to those used by supporters of DP claims, specifically empirical adequacy, robustness, accurate prediction, causal mechanisms, and imparting understanding. These six are among the eight most heavily used criteria in the works surveyed in this chapter, and these six constitute two-thirds of all criteria used by the twelve authors.

Choi's (2011) paper reexamines what he regards as the two most widely accepted explanations in the DP debate, namely, the two liberal explanations discussed in this chapter, liberal democracy and capitalism. Choi's replication of Gartzke's analysis identifies several errors. One is that Gartzke omits a variable that reflects the number of years since the previous conflict, which, Choi says, is required by Gartzke's logit tests. Second, Choi says that Gartzke's inclusion of regional dummy variables causes "dropped observations," the implications of which Gartzke does not investigate (2011, 761–62). Third, Choi raises both theoretical and methodological questions about Gartzke's failure to focus on "politically relevant samples" (2011, 169). Choi is also critical of Russett and Oneal's statistical support for the liberal democratic explanation of dyadic peace. The main failure relates to the way they treat the measurement of how democratic each dyad is, since the two members of the dyad typically have different democracy scores. Choi argues that Russett and Oneal underemphasize the importance of the lower score in each dyad. Choi follows up by altering this coding of dyads and reruns the tests. His conclusion supports the liberal democratic political explanation: "democracy dies hard in the midst of the challenging forces" (2011, 767).

Choi evaluates the two studies largely on grounds of empirical adequacy, robustness, and predictive accuracy (2011, 766), which are among the most widely used by other DP authors. Aside from the fact that it is one of the few pieces published in *International Studies Quarterly* in the past decade on the dyadic hypothesis, Choi's paper is interesting for several reasons. First, Choi assesses the DP debate as having reached a point at which it has eliminated the realist position, and the remaining contending explanations utilize two aspects of liberalism—liberal democracy and liberal economics. This is especially significant for this study given that Choi's paper reaches essentially the same conclusions found in this chapter. (We might note also that Choi's paper appeared in print after the core claims of this chapter were developed and presented in lectures and conferences.) Second is the fact that Choi chooses an approach that involves replication of publications by Russett and Oneal (2001) and Gartzke (2007). Choi's method of replication of statistical tests strengthens the claim advanced in the next section that authors in the DP debate are directly addressing one another's arguments much more than in the other two debates, and that they have the greatest overlap of evaluative criteria.

Michael Mousseau is the other author published in any of the five above-mentioned major journals who denies the liberal explanation for the dyadic hypothesis. He has had three papers in *International Studies Quarterly* and others elsewhere. He does not deny that democracies have remained peaceful toward one another, but he argues that "contract flows" is a more powerful explanatory variable than "democracy" (2013: 186). A contract-intensive economy is one in which "most citizens in a nation regularly use the impersonal marketplace, rather than personal ties, for obtaining incomes, goods, and services" (2013: 196). He has said that contract-intensive economy is one of the most powerful explanatory variables in international conflict, as it causes "democracy within nations and peace among them."

The same issue of *International Studies Quarterly* in 2013 also published papers very critical of Mousseau's argument authored by Dafoe, Oneal, and Russett (2013); Ray (2013); and Gartzke and Weisiger (2013), who argue for a focus on regime-type difference-and-similarity to explain the behavior of democracies toward one another. The papers by Dafoe, Oneal, and Russett and by Ray probe errors they claim are committed by Mousseau in his approach to the data. Interestingly, the Dafoe, Oneal, and Russett paper (which appeared after the present volume was submitted for review) specifically mentions that scholarly controversies should be resolved in part by authors focusing on carefully outlining the criteria. Accordingly, they specify the criteria that should be used by all participants in a debate. These include consideration of the criteria that others use, simplicity, theoretical/causal plausibility, caution in the drawing of causal conclusions, use of best methods of analysis, and robustness.

As with the monadic hypothesis, after most IR scholars concluded that it had been falsified, Rummel continued to offer statistical evidence that it was supportable. For naturalists in the social science, there should be nothing surprising about Rummel's continued questioning of the near consensus on the rejection of the monadic hypothesis or Mousseau's continued questioning of the liberal explanation for the dyadic hypothesis. One can argue that a feature of scientific progress is approach-to-consensus rather than absolute consensus. Individual researchers typically continue to question accepted results, and this continued scrutiny keeps the scholarly community open to new ideas, evidence, and analysis. Indeed, as has been noted several times in this book, it is quite possible that at some point the dyadic hypothesis, or at least the liberal explanation, may come to be widely discredited. But this does not undermine in the least the claim that the DP debate has exhibited scientific progress with respect to the pattern of approach-to-consensus. Widespread rejection of either near consensus would constitute a new manifestation of near consensus, and it would represent a new state of knowledge (i.e., that one or both claims are false). Although it is true that even greater consensus was reached on Newtonian mechanics, still, others questioned it, initially on epistemological grounds (as Leibniz did) and later on empirical grounds (as the Rutherford experiment discussed in Chapter 6). But there is no doubt that on any account of scientific progress, Newton's system, although later rejected, was an enormous step forward in human knowledge.

14. CONCLUSION

The analysis of the DP debate shows some clear and significant contrasts with the alliance formation and nuclear proliferation debates.

Approach-to-Consensus

Unlike in the cases of alliance formation and nuclear proliferation studies, there is rough approach-to-consensus with regard to the power of the liberal explanation for the behavior of democratic dyads. While there is no single, precise accepted explanation, the disagreement between liberal and realist theorists has ended, and the debate today focuses on finding the most persuasive type of liberal explanatory factors.

Conclusion 1—There has been a significant degree of approach-to-consensus in the DP debate, with scholars accepting that the liberal explanations for dyadic behavior are superior to the realist explanations—both rejecting the negative arguments of realists attempting to discredit the dyadic hypothesis and providing positive supporting statistical and theoretical arguments.

As we have seen, the DP debate was ignited by a few people advancing the antirealist claim that regime-type makes a difference in the analysis of war. Scholars were well aware of the damage to realist theory that compelling substantiation of DP claims would inflict. Consequently, various realists attacked DP arguments and maintained that realism offers a superior explanation of the historical record. Similarly, many liberal scholars in IR joined the debate by defending DP claims, especially the dyadic hypothesis, which was the claim most closely tied to the Kantian notion of a pacific union. Both sides were familiar with a set of explanatory mechanisms, dating back to Kant and reinvigorated by Doyle (1983a, 1983b, 1986), that could plausibly link, in a step-by-step way, the various aspects of democratic polities that lead to war avoidance with other democracies.

Liberal theorists defended DP claims—both by showing errors in the realists' arguments and by acknowledging the flaws in the earlier DP arguments and, accordingly, reformulating them and/or presenting new and improved statistical tests. Each side was directly addressing the other's arguments. And a few major journals, notably *International Security* and the *Journal of Conflict Resolution*, published the works of prominent scholars on both sides and their replies to one another.

As noted earlier, the debate reached a peak in the early 1990s, which is reflected in the selection of books and articles considered in this chapter. Since then the role of regime-type has been widely accepted as an explanation for peaceful behavior between democracies. The best evidence that the debate over the dyadic DP hypothesis is now regarded as settled is that major journals slowed to a trickle the publication of papers on the acceptability of the dyadic hypothesis, as detailed in the previous section. There are many reasons a question can lose its prominence in a field, as conditions might change. But one would be hard pressed to find any explanation for the disappearance of vigorous debate on the dyadic hypothesis other than that scholars regard the liberal approach to explanation to have been shown superior. But to reiterate, the history of science shows that even more or less settled questions can be reopened on the basis of new insights, evidence, or methods of analysis.

One might object to conclusion 1 by arguing that there is no widely accepted causal mechanism, only a behavioral regularity about democratic dyads. There are two principal responses to this objection. First, the most intense period of debate was spurred by the Doyle papers (1983a, 1983b, 1986), which provided an extensive and careful, Kantian-inspired argument about how liberal democratic states differ from others. With this well-known theoretical background, many scholars regarded empirical demonstration of the dyadic hypothesis as carrying with it a set of explanatory mechanisms. The second observes that an acceptable causal-mechanistic explanation depends on the context: it must be more specific or finer-grained than causal claims accepted by the audience, and it must answer the particular causal question that interests the audience.

We have seen that some realists object that the DP debate does not really show more progress than the other two debates, because the most widely accepted liberal democracy explanation, stemming from Doyle's (1983a, 1983b, 1986) papers, is not specific enough to be adequate. The mechanisms proposed by DP defenders have certainly been, and properly should be, the subject of much scrutiny. Still, the behavioral claims were not presented in isolation from an extensive (Kantian-inspired) hypothesized causal mechanism. Second, we should recognize that an acceptable causal mechanism does not have some preassigned, context- and audience-independent level of specificity. How fine-grained and specific a mechanism must be to be deemed sufficient is relative to the particular question, and the aspects of that question, that an audience regards as of greatest interest.

Suppose, for example, that a parent informs his children that Cousin Monty crashed his car on the road. The children ask the parent to explain why the accident happened and are told that Monty was driving nonstop for fourteen hours, became drowsy, and ran the car into a guardrail on the right shoulder of the road. If the children specifically request that an explanatory mechanism be invoked, the parent might reply that Monty fell asleep and, being supported on his left by the car door, eventually leaned to the right, turning the steering wheel in that direction as he leaned. In some contexts that would be a satisfactory mechanism. For example, if the children thought that Monty had been driving his English-built right-hand-drive car, with the driver's-side door on his right, then the children's learning that it was a left-hand-drive car could explain why Monty fell to the right, and thus why the car swerved rightward. But in another context, say an automotive safety-engineering class in which the children are students and the parent is the instructor, the children might ask for a further explanation of the cause of Monty's turning the steering wheel to the right and the effect of the car moving to the right. The parent would offer a mechanism, possibly in terms of the workings of rack-and-pinion steering. What we see is that what counts as an acceptable causal mechanism to a particular audience depends on the setting, in particular interests of that audience. There is no absolute, context-independent answer to the question of which mechanism would explain the causal connection between the cause and the effect. One must know the particular context in which the question is asked in order to understand what sort of mechanism would count as an acceptable answer to the audience. The demand for a finer-grained analysis of causal chains does not undercut the statement that Monty's drowsiness caused the crash. Similarly, the request in security studies for more finely grained connections between joint democracy and peacefulness of democratic dyads does not degrade the causal status of democracy. Given the context in which the debate has taken place in security studies, democracy serves as a central part of the causal explanation of the observed pattern for anyone who accepts the dyadic hypothesis. That explanation should, of course, be subjected to new tests. And it is always possible to ask for finer-grained questions as new concerns arise. But in the context of IR scholarship, acceptance of the dyadic hypothesis is tantamount to acceptance of liberal democracy as a causal force until alternative mechanisms are proposed. Of course, at a later time the context might be different.[24]

The wide agreement on the dyadic hypothesis and on the liberal explanation for it has spurred other studies of regime-type and war. In any research program, when the central question is settled and most investigators accept an important causal claim, they will seek corollaries and other findings that draw on the newly established causal relationships. There has, accordingly, been a range of questions that make sense to pose only once the question of the basic liberal explanation for the behavior of democratic dyads has been settled. Bueno de Mesquita and colleagues (1999, 791) have identified "seven additional empirical regularities, all related to war-proneness and democracy, all based on empirical observation" that draw on democratic dyad studies.[25] And major IR journals continue to publish on DP studies, but only on questions that focus on corollaries of the DP dyadic claim, such as whether democracies are more effective in wars against nondemocracies, how democracies deal with terrorism, how democracies have acted in colonial wars, and so on.[26]

Conclusion 2—In recent years the DP debate has focused on questions that assume the superiority of liberal explanations for democracies' dyadic behavior and that seek the best explanation among various particular aspects of liberal states, such as liberal trade, structure, or norms, and as such shows more approach-to-consensus than the nuclear proliferation or alliance formation debates.

Someone might object to conclusion 2 that the alliance formation debate has progressed as much as the DP debate, in that there is little enthusiasm today for balance of power explanations in light of the absence of any anti-US counterbalancing coalition. This is progress, but it is negative progress, agreement that something is incorrect, as compared to the positive approach-to-consensus progress in the DP debate. In the alliance formation debate scholars have rejected strict balance-of-power explanations because a key predicted outcome has not materialized. But there is no movement toward any particular explanation. In contrast, in the DP debate the rejection of realist denials of the relevance of liberal democratic as an explanatory factor has led to a wide acceptance of liberal democracy as the major explanatory factor. There is still work under way trying to identify which aspect of liberal democracies lead to mutual peace and to find finer-grained explanations. But the general liberal explanatory approach has wide support.

Explanatory Criteria and Convergence

There has been progress in DP studies that exceeds anything detectable in the debates over balance of power or nuclear proliferation. Does the pattern of criteria invoked by DP authors help us understand the particular level of progress in the debate? H_1 states that different uses of criteria may be one reason that security studies authors continue to disagree in debates over the best explanation for security behavior. As conclusion 1 observes, in the DP debate there is substantial positive progress in terms of approach-to-consensus. Given the convergence, H_1 would be disconfirmed by the absence of significant overlap in the uses of criteria by liberals and their opponents as compared with the debates over nuclear proliferation or alliance formation.

As with the first two debates, there are not enough data points for statistical analysis. But an inspection of Table 5.1 shows the difference between this debate and the others.

Conclusion 3—There is significant overlap in the criteria of explanatory merit used by both sides in the debate.

There is more consensus and more criterial overlap than in either of the other two debates. Of the twelve works examined in this chapter, seven offer liberal support for DP explanations and five offer realist explanations. This division of the works is close to an even split of the twelve explanations studied. There are fifty-eight total instances in which one of the criteria is invoked to advance an argument. Nearly half of the uses (45 percent) are instances of one of the first three criteria listed in Table 5.1 (*empirical adequacy, robustness*, and *falsifiability*). And the overlap of criteria evident in Table 5.1 and more clearly in Table 5.2 indicate that the DP case is consistent with H_2.

Table 5.1 Authors' use of explanatory criteria in the democratic peace debate (in descending order of total uses)

Criteria of adequacy	*Small & Singer*	*Rummel*	*Doyle*	*Mearsheimer*	*Bremer*	*Lake*	*Maoz & Russett*	*Owen*	*Layne*	*Spiro*	*Farber & Gowa*	*Gartzke*	*Total number of uses*
Empirical adequacy	X	X	X	X		X	X	X	X	X	X	X	**11**
Robustness		X			X	X	X	X	X	X	X	X	**9**
Falsifiability		X			X				X	X	X	X	**6**
Predictive accuracy		X		X	X		X		X	X			**6**
Uncovers true causes			X	X	X		X			X			**5**
Mechanisms			X	X				X	X			X	**5**
Imparts understanding			X	X				X	X			X	**5**
Supports counterfactuals			X	X				X	X				**4**
Simplicity					X				X				**2**
Coheres with background beliefs			X							X			**2**
Greater range of domain					X						X		**2**
Explanatory unification						X							**1**
Total uses													**58**

Table 5.2 Uses of criteria by authors in the democratic peace debate (in descending order of total uses)

Criteria of adequacy	*Realism (5 explanations)*	*Liberalism (7 explanations)*
Empirical adequacy	SS MS LN SP FG	RM DL GR MR LK OW
Robustness	LN SP FG	RM BR LK MR OW GR
Falsifiability	LN SP FG	RM BR GR
Predictive accuracy	MS LN SP	RM BR MR
Uncovers true causes	MS SP	BR DL MR
Mechanisms	MS LN	DL OW GR
Imparts understanding	MS LN	DL OW GR
Supports counterfactuals	MS LN	DL OW
Simplicity	LN	BR
Coheres with background beliefs	SP	DL
Greater range of domain	FG	BR
Explanatory unification	—	LK
Total uses by each group	**25**	**33**
Average use of each criterion	**25 / 5 = 5.00**	**33 / 7 = 4.71**

NOTE: Total uses of criteria = 58. Realists: SS = Small & Singer, MS = Mearsheimer, LN = Layne, SP = Spiro, FG = Farber & Gowa. Liberals: RM = Rummel, DL = Doyle, GR = Gartzke, MR = Maoz & Russett, LK = Lake, OW = Owen, BR = Bremer.

We may see this by checking whether the two groups' uses of the criteria are roughly in line with the proportion of explanations studied by either of the two schools. Since the schools are represented in a 7:5 ratio—that is, 58 percent to 42 percent—the closer the actual uses of each criterion are to 58 percent by liberal scholars and to 42 percent by realists, then the clearer it is, at least by one measure, that the two sides are using the same criteria. In the next chapter we examine additional comparisons with the other two debates using a different ratio (see Section 1 of Chapter 6). We also note overlap as measured by the number of criteria used by authors on both sides of the debate. In the DP debate it is eleven, as opposed to eight and nine in the other two debates.

With regard to the first three criteria, two of them are as close as is numerically possible to split 55 percent to 45 percent in the case of empirical adequacy, and 50 percent to 50 percent among the six uses of falsifiability; and in the case of robustness, the split is within one usage the closest numerical split; it is 66 percent to 33 percent, and use by one other realist would have made it 60 percent to 40 percent. Also, there was an emphasis on empirical adequacy and *robustness*, as at least three-fourths of all the authors drew on each of them, and half of all the authors made use of *falsifiability* and of *predictive accuracy*. Of the twelve criteria from Chapter 2 that are used in this group of explanations, about half of all uses of criteria are of these four.

The DP debate has exhibited more progress than those over alliance formation and nuclear proliferation. And authors in the DP debate share more fully reliance on particular criteria of a good explanation. So, thus far it appears that one of the reasons that there has been progress in the DP debate may well be the closer agreement on what makes for a good explanation. The next chapter considers in more detail how reasonable this conclusion is. And as was observed in the discussions of Spiro and Gartzke, the similarity of criteria appears to have made possible the convergence described in conclusion 2, as H_2 states. When Layne, Spiro, Gartzke, and others published their criticisms of Russett and his coauthors, they were addressing clear and specific criteria of explanatory success, even if they did not always name them explicitly. The specificity of those criticisms led DP defenders to revise their research designs and run new tests that made it difficult for critics to continue to publish arguments aimed at discrediting the liberal democratic explanation for dyadic peace—even if there are still disagreements about whether the political or the economic features of democratic dyads play a greater explanatory role.

6 ANALYSIS, ALTERNATIVES, CONCLUSION

MANY INTERNATIONAL SECURITY QUESTIONS have been debated without significant progress toward agreement on the best explanation. In the natural sciences we see a historical pattern of approach-to-consensus. And the absence of clearly superior explanatory theories in international security affairs creates, in many cases, hindrances to effective policy making. In this study, we have examined one reason that there has been so little agreement as to the best explanatory answer, namely, opposing authors' uses of different criteria to defend their respective explanations. We have looked, in particular, at the hypotheses H_1, that progress in approach-to-consensus is slowed when authors use divergent criteria, and H_2, that approach-to-consensus is more likely when authors use similar criteria for "a good explanation."

The most important philosophers of natural science of the past two centuries, Peirce, Poincaré, Duhem, Hempel, Popper, Van Fraassen, and others, all have their own ways of characterizing key elements of scientific method and of defining scientific progress (see Chernoff 2004). Yet despite the differences in how they define "progress," they all concur that the natural sciences indeed exhibit progress, and they concur on almost all important cases of progress (e.g., the work of Einstein, Harvey, Boyle, and Darwin all constituted progress over previous theories). The various definitions of scientific progress build on some combination of the following: cumulation of knowledge across generations, accurate predictive implications of accepted theories, the enhanced ability to control one's environment, and patterns of approach-to-consensus when controversies arise. This study acknowledges that all are elements of progress, but it has focused on the last one.

This chapter aims to use the research approach of Chapter 1 and the criteria of evaluation described in Chapter 2 to answer the central question by comparing the patterns that emerged in the debates presented in Chapters 3–5. Section 1 shows that the patterns in the three debates conform to what one would expect on the basis of hypotheses H_1 and H_2. But just showing that the proposed explanation is consistent with the evidence is not enough to persuade most audiences of the adequacy of the criterial explanation, since other explanations may also be consistent with the evidence. This study makes use of the modified criterion of elimination of alternatives (modified in that we noted that complete elimination is not ever possible). To that end, Sections 2–5 offer arguments comparing H_1 and H_2 to possible objections and alternative explanations. The final section offers overall conclusions concerning how to account for the pattern of stalemate and approach-to-consensus, and suggests that the obstacles that many debates have encountered can be surmounted with additional—but not excessive—scholarly effort.

1. COMPARATIVE RESULTS OF THE SECURITY STUDIES DEBATES

Some striking results emerge from a comparison of the debates on balance of power, nuclear proliferation, and democratic peace.

Nuclear Proliferation

Chapter 3 examined ten leading studies seeking to explain why states build nuclear weapons. The analysis concluded with four principle observations about the patterns in the debate. One conclusion is that authors are not transparent about the criteria they use to advance their explanatory theories, which proved to be the case in all three debates. A second conclusion is that scholars largely agreed on proliferation-related explanations prior to the early 1970s, but that agreement soon decreased, especially when less-developed states began to approach nuclear weapons capability. In the past decade the highest-profile scholarly works supported very diverse primary explanatory factors—the trade orientation of leadership regimes (Solingen 2007), realist rivalry factors (Jo and Gartzke 2007), and individual psychology (Hymans 2006). With regard to the criteria the authors made use of in the nuclear proliferation publications, overlap was minimal, as conclusion 3 in that chapter stated. And as noted in conclusion 4, when we look at those who argued for realist explanations and those who argued for alternative explanations, even taken as groups, the authors

Table 6.1 Uses of criteria by realist and nonrealist authors in the nuclear proliferation debate

Criteria of adequacy	*Individual bureaucratic symbolic (5)*	*Realist and neorealist (5)*	*Total uses*	*Neorealist expected uses*	*Realist observed*	*Difference between expected and observed*
Predictive accuracy	1	1	2	0.46	1	0.54
Depth of causes	3	0	3	1.38	0	1.38
Supports counterfactuals	3	2	5	2.30	2	0.30
Imparts understanding	2	1	3	1.38	1	0.38
Precision; eliminates alternatives	1	1	2	0.92	1	0.08
Explanatory unification	1	1	2	0.92	1	0.08
Simplicity	4	2	6	2.76	2	0.76
Falsifiability	3	0	3	1.38	0	1.38
Mechanisms	4	2	6	2.76	2	0.76
Empirical adequacy	3	5	8	3.68	5	1.32
Uncovers true causes	0	3	3	1.38	3	1.62
Greater range of domain	0	3	3	1.38	3	1.62
Totals	**25**	**21**	**46**	**20.7**	**21**	**10.22**
Average difference for each criterion = 10.22 / 46 = 0.222						

on either side did not use the criteria in proportional ways. The summary in Table 6.1, which aggregates the data from Table 3.2, shows the differences between the two groups.

Table 6.1 shows the calculation of the expected number of uses of each criterion, on the assumption that the authors in the two explanatory groups—those supporting and those opposing realist-oriented explanations—use each criterion in proportion to the group's overall general tendency to use criteria. The expected-value calculation does not, of course, assume that all authors use the same number of criteria, and it does not assume that the average realist author uses the same number of criteria as the average nonrealist author. Our concern is in investigating the strength of hypothesis H_1, which deals with the proportional use of criteria by authors on opposite sides of debates.

The expected value for either of the two groups is based on the total number of times the criterion is cited by all authors, with the relative propensity of each group to cite criteria generally. For example, in the nuclear proliferation debate, there are forty-six total usages of all the criteria listed, of which twenty-one are by realists. Realists in that debate thus have a relative propensity to use criteria that is a bit lower than that of the nonrealist just group, namely, 21/46, (or .456), as compared to 25/46 (or .543) for the nonrealist group. If we take as an example the criterion of *uncovering causal mechanisms*, we see that six authors use it—two realists and four nonrealists. If the two groups had used that criterion proportionately (i.e., if it were not skewed to one group), the expected number of uses for realists would be $6 \times (21/46) = 2.73$, and for nonrealists it would be $6 \times (25/46) = 3.26$ (the sum of the expected uses of the two groups equals the observed uses by the two groups). The actual use of that criterion by realists is 2; so the difference is $(2.73 - 2) = 0.73$. When these differences are added for all criteria, we have the total disjuncture in the two groups' uses of criteria. And if we then divide by the total number of uses of all criteria for both groups, (= 46) the resulting quotient (= 0.222) is the average difference in the two groups' uses of the criteria.[1]

The goal here is to be able to compare the different propensities of each group to use each of the criteria of explanatory superiority. The key quantity is the average difference between the two groups in each of the debates. Thus, there is no need to repeat the calculation for nonrealists, since the expected value for that group will equal the observed total minus the expected value for realists. If in each debate we are looking for differences between a hypothesized evenly distributed set of uses and the distribution that in fact occurs in that debate, the difference will simply double in all cases if we look at both realists and nonrealists.

The criterial overlap in the nuclear proliferation debate is the lowest of any of the three debates. As noted in conclusions 2 and 6 of Chapter 3, in the nuclear proliferation debate there is a low level of consensus and little overlap between prominent authors' uses of criteria of a "good explanation." At this stage of the analysis, it is plausible to hold that H_1 is correct and that the lack of approach-to-consensus in the nuclear proliferation debate is due to the substantially different uses of criteria by realist and nonrealist authors. But the following comparisons will illuminate this further.

Balance of Power and Alliance Formation

As Chapter 4 discussed, realists and their opponents have long debated how best to explain the formation of alliances. Some of the alternatives are offered as mere emendations of realism, though they invoke significant "non-power-based" causes of alliance, and some are offered as clear alternatives to power-based realist explanations. Chapter 4 examined the modern debate and concluded with a summary of the differences in the criteria used by authors who rely principally on power as an explanation and those who rely on other factors, either in conjunction with or independent of power considerations.

Four points were emphasized in Chapter 4. First, as with the nuclear proliferation debate, criteria are usually implicit rather than explicit. Second, there has been some common ground found in the alliance formation debate, but no movement toward a commonly accepted explanation. The most influential works were fairly evenly spread out over the past seven decades. There was a good deal of agreement on the role of power balancing in the first half of the period covered by the publications. The clustering of views on the realist power-balancing explanation diminished in the last decade of the Cold War, and further diminished a decade after the Cold War ended, when it became evident that a counter-US balancing coalition, predicted by realist theorists, had not materialized (see Table 4.1). But no consensus on an alternative explanation emerged. Although there is no movement toward agreement as to which explanation is best, there it still more agreement in this area than in the nuclear proliferation debate. Third, as in the proliferation debate, there is no single set of criteria that all authors used.

The fourth conclusion was that there was somewhat more overlap in the set of criteria used by those supporting balance-of-power realist explanations and those who opposed them. This can be seen in Table 6.2, which shows that the average difference between realist expected and realist observed uses of criteria is 0.141. The average difference in the nuclear proliferation debate was 0.222, which is more than 50 percent greater. Overall, there was a modest level of approach-to-consensus in the decades of debate considered, especially after 2000: there was no positive convergence on the right answer, but there was general consensus that strict balance-of-power explanations should be rejected. And there was a moderate level of overlap of criteria that supporters and opponents of balance-of-power explanations used.

Democratic Peace

The analysis of the democratic-dyad debate showed several major patterns. One is that there has been a very high level of approach-to-consensus, which is evidenced by two main observations: after 2000 the highest-profile journals showed a precipitous decline in the number of articles published debating the dyadic hypothesis, and most of the prominent publications today that deal with DP issues focus on subsidiary questions that arise because of the widespread

Table 6.2 Explanatory criteria used by balance-of-power explanations and alternative explanations

Criteria of adequacy	*Balance-of-power explanations*	*Other explanations*	*Total uses*	*Realist expected uses*	*Difference between balance-of-power and expected*
Imparts understanding	4	1	5	2.15	1.85
Explanatory unification	2	2	4	1.72	0.28
Empirical adequacy	5	6	11	4.73	0.27
Control over environment	4	0	4	1.72	2.28
Mechanisms	4	4	8	3.15	0.15
Depth of causes	2	3	5	2.15	0.15
Predictive accuracy	3	5	8	3.44	0.44
Uncovers true causes	2	4	6	2.58	0.58
Simplicity	2	3	5	1.72	0.28
Supports counterfactuals	2	6	8	3.44	1.44
Greater range of domain	2	3	5	2.15	0.15
Precision; eliminates alternatives	0	1	1	0.86	0.86
Falsifiability	0	3	3	1.29	1.29
Robustness	0	1	1	0.43	0.43
Totals	**32**	**42**	**74**	**31.53**	**10.45**
Average difference for each criterion = 10.45 / 74 = 0.141					

acceptance that liberalism best explains the behavior of democracies toward one another. Some authors argue (following Maoz and Russett 1993) that dyadic peace is driven primary by normative factors; some, by structural factors; and others (e.g., Gartzke 2000, 2007) by economic aspects of liberalism. Thus, there has been a shift to a more focused sort of explanation for the behavior of democratic dyads, and there has been cumulation of knowledge, indicated by the fact that many high-profile journals now publish works that pose questions building on the view that the key realist-liberal question has been answered; scholars currently investigate other aspects of liberal democracies at war and peace (see Bueno de Mesquita et al. 1999, 791).

From Table 5.2 we can tally the number of realist and liberal explanations of dyadic behavior, and this tally is shown in Table 6.3.

When the differences between the two groups' uses of each criterion are summed together (= 3.56) and then divided by the total number of uses of

Table 6.3 Criteria used by realist and liberal authors in the democratic peace debate

Criteria of adequacy	*Liberalism (7 explanations)*	*Realism (5 explanations)*	*Total uses*	*Realist expected uses*	*Difference between realism and expected*
Empirical adequacy	6	5	11	4.73	0.27
Robustness	6	3	9	3.87	0.87
Falsifiability	3	3	6	2.58	0.42
Mechanisms	3	2	5	2.15	0.15
Imparts understanding	3	2	5	2.15	0.15
Simplicity	1	1	2	0.86	0.14
Supports counterfactuals	2	2	4	1.72	0.28
Explanatory unification	1	0	1	0.43	0.43
Greater range of domain	1	1	2	0.86	0.14
Uncovers true causes	3	2	5	2.15	0.15
Predictive accuracy	3	3	6	2.58	0.42
Coheres with background beliefs	1	1	2	0.86	0.14
Totals	**33**	**25**	**58**	**24.94**	**3.56**

Average difference for each criterion = 3.56 / 58 = 0.061

criteria (58), the quotient is 0.061. This is a much smaller realist-nonrealist difference than in either of the other two debates.

Comparison of the Analyses of the Three Debates

We see from the foregoing discussion and Table 6.3 that in the nuclear proliferation debate there have been low levels both of criterial overlap and approach-to-consensus; in the alliance formation debate there have been greater, but still moderate levels of criterial overlap and approach-to-consensus; and in the democratic peace debate there has been a much greater criterial overlap and approach-to-consensus.

We now have arithmetic estimates of the degrees of difference and overlap between realists' and nonrealists' uses of criteria. Since further statistical indices are not readily available because of limitations on the data, it may also be helpful to inspect the relationships visually. Figures 6.1–6.3 display the differences between expected and observed uses of each of the criteria in the three debates.

The relationships between the average differences between realists' and their opponents' uses of criteria in the three debates (evident in Tables 6.1–6.3) can be represented by Venn diagrams in Figure 6.4.

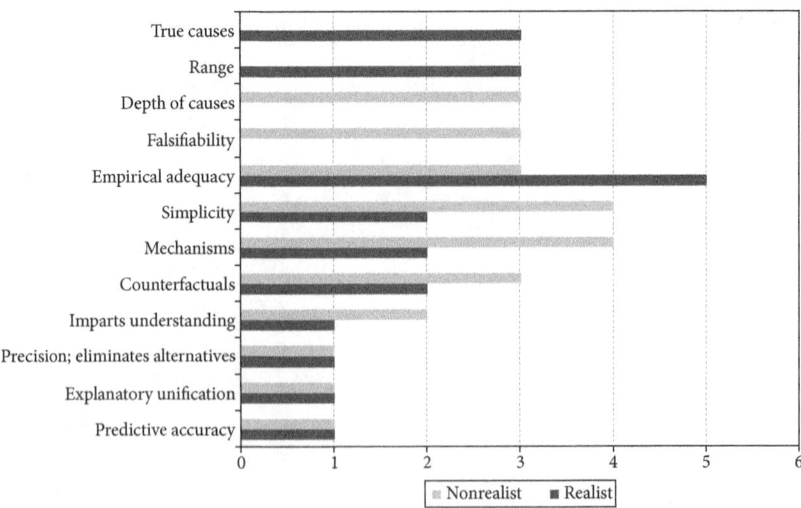

Figure 6.1 Nuclear proliferation (in descending order of differences of uses)

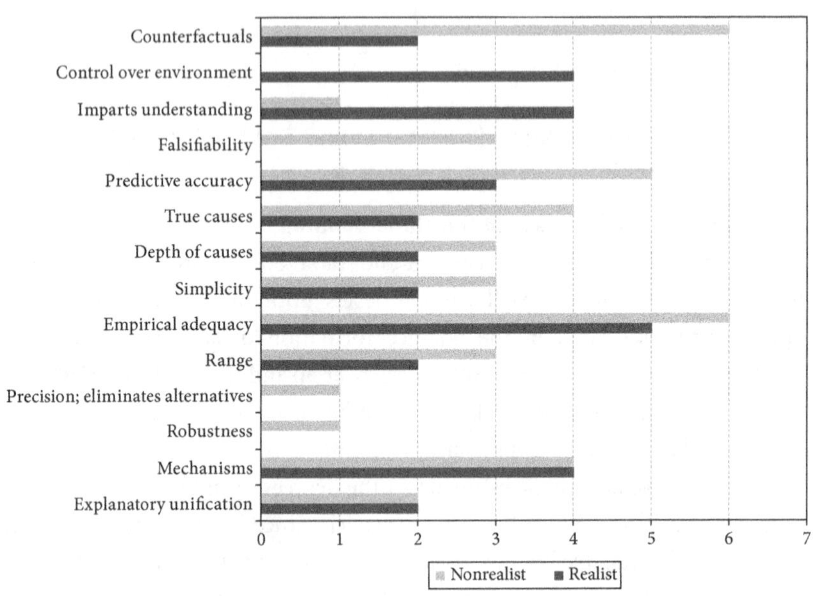

Figure 6.2 Alliance formation (in descending order of differences of uses)

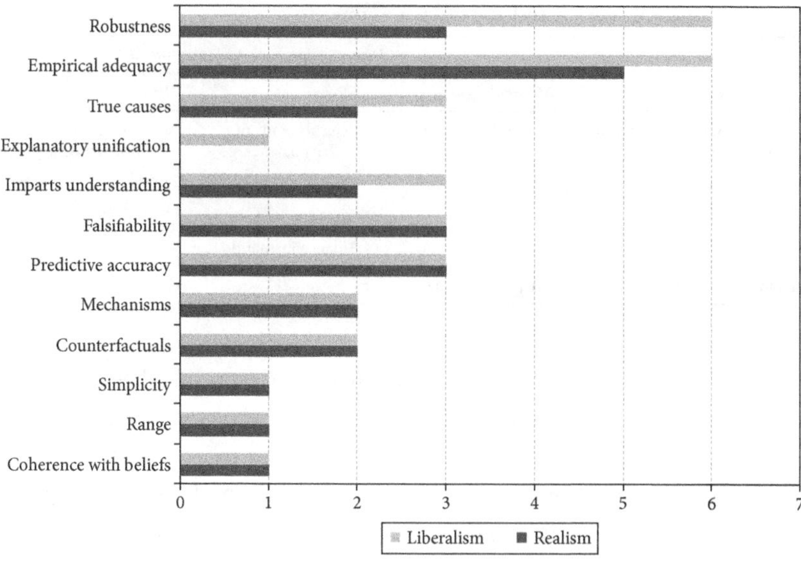

Figure 6.3 Democratic peace (in descending order of difference of uses)

Alliance formation debate		*Nuclear proliferation debate*		*Democratic peace debate*	
Realist explanations	Alternative explanations	Realist explanations	Alternative explanations	Realist explanations	Liberal explanations
Low overlap of criteria		Greater overlap		Much greater overlap	

Figure 6.4 Criteria overlap and approach-to-consensus

The relationships illustrated in Tables 6.1–6.3 and shown in Figures 6.1–6.4, combined with the results of the discussion of degrees of agreement and disagreement in the debates, enable us to depict the relationships along the lines of Table 6.4.

The relationships shown in Table 6.4 between overlap of criteria used by different theoretical schools and approach-to-consensus of their explanations

Table 6.4 Criteria overlap and approach-to-consensus

	Degree of approach-to-consensus		
	Minimal	*Modest*	*High*
Criterial difference between opposing theorists	Very little agreement	Rejection only of strict balancing	Agreement that liberal democracy is a cause
Low difference (0.061)			Democratic peace
Medium difference (0.141)		Alliance formation	
High difference (0.222)	Nuclear proliferation		

support both H_1, that differences in the criteria that opposing theorists rely on might be part of the reason theorists continue over time to disagree on explanations, and H_2, that agreement on criteria permits more consensus. Where the criterial overlap is least and the use of criteria is most skewed (i.e., in the nuclear proliferation debate), the persistence of disagreement is greatest. And where the use of criteria is most consistent between opposing realist and liberal schools, on DP issues, there is significant movement toward consensus, both negatively that realism cannot explain the peace between mature democratic states and positively that some aspect of liberalism can.[2]

This relationship that is evident between criterial choices and approach-to-consensus progress has thus far gone unnoticed in debates over theory and metatheory in international relations (IR). While H_1 and H_2 are supported by the evidence in Chapters 3–5 and the analysis here, a truly persuasive argument for H_1 and H_2 requires, in addition to the patterns just illustrated, further considerations showing that the present book satisfies the criterion of elimination of alternative explanations, as Chapter 1 stated that this is one of the criteria that this study relies on to show a superior explanation. To establish the value of the criterial explanation for H_1 and H_2 defended in this book, it is necessary to discuss alternative explanations. For each alternative explanation, we can then reject it, accept it in place of H_1 and H_2, or conclude that it constitutes an additional factor working along with criterial overlap. The next four sections compare alternative explanations to H_1 and H_2.

2. ALTERNATIVE ACCOUNTS—QUANTITATIVE VERSUS QUALITATIVE DEBATE

One attempt to formulate an alternative explanation for the pattern evident in section 1 is to claim that there is a relevant difference between quantitative and nonquantitative studies in the social sciences. Those who propose this alternative explanation would contend that quantitative studies are more precise than others, and the democratic-dyad debate was the most quantitative of the three, which would explain the greater progress in that debate.

Enthusiasts of quantitative IR and the Correlates of War project argued that even though IR had been studied for centuries, the discipline was moving in circles rather than forward. In their view, the reason for this was that scholarship was subjective, qualitative, and value laden; the only way to make progress was to reorient IR and other social sciences to emulate the natural sciences by making them objective, quantitative, and value-free. J. David Singer, perhaps the most influential figure in the behavioral movement in IR, published a widely read paper in 1969 in which he laid out the core argument of the behavioral approach (see also Singer 1965, 1966). In that paper, a reply to Hedley Bull's (1966) attack in *World Politics* on quantitative IR, Singer addressed each of Bull's criticisms. Singer argued that the advancement of knowledge in IR was to be found in the adoption of quantitative methods. Studying IR focusing on "history and philosophy" is not fruitful because "we probably have little more to learn from them in terms of method or concept. . . . These disciplines have gone almost as far as they can go in adding to social science knowledge in any appreciable way" (1969, 82). In naturalist fashion, Singer refers to the behavioral approach as "science" and describes the competition between traditional and behavioralist styles of scholarship as constituting a "war" that, as Singer saw it, the behavioralists were winning; their domination of IR faculty in political science departments, in Singer's view, had been limited only by the slow increase in the supply of properly trained quantitative scholars (1969, 85). The quantitative-qualitative alternative explanation can be stated as follows: progress in IR can occur only when scholarship takes the form of quantitative studies; and since the DP debate was the most quantitatively oriented of the three, its quantitative character accounts for the approach-to-consensus in that debate.

There are three principle responses to this proposed alternative to H_1 and H_2. First, the quantitative-qualitative argument is right in claiming that published works, especially prominent works, in the DP debate were more consistently statistical in nature than similarly high-profile works in the other two debates. There are indeed clearer guidelines for statistical research design and clearer tests to show when one statistical model is best. However, even in quantitative studies scholars must decide on trade-offs among criteria. Once the trade-offs and priorities are set, the results are clearer, and there is less interpretation required to determine which criteria are being used. As a result, there is more overlap between contending scholars' uses of criteria. These features do facilitate readers' ability to spot inferior explanations.

A second response is that progress in quantitatively oriented debates constitutes merely a special case of the general claims of H_1 and H_2 regarding the relationship of criterial overlap and consensus. The claim that quantitative studies have greater criterial clarity is consistent with H_1 and reinforces rather than contradicts the view that progress has been hampered by the inadvertent application of different criteria of explanatory superiority by contending explanatory schools.[3] And a third response is that, from the claim that quantitatively driven debates produce more consensus, one need not accept Singer's behavioralist conclusion that only quantitative work will exhibit progress. Rather than eliminating from IR those areas that are not amenable to quantitative argument, we should adopt the methods appropriate to those other sorts of IR inquiry. A strong case can be made for methodological pluralism by noting that IR scholars pose a variety of legitimate policy-oriented and theoretical questions, and not all of them can be answered quantitatively (see Chernoff 2005, 2007a, 2007b).

Consider mainstream questions such as the following: Is a bipolar system more stable than a multipolar system? Was the US nuclear alert in 1973 intended as a warning signal to Brezhnev? Is the use of nuclear weapons ever justified? Not all of these can be answered quantitatively. Questions like the first one are clearly best answered by methods that would include an examination of many cases, possibly with statistical tests of associations among variables. But questions like the second one are most effectively answered by means of interpretive methods. And questions like the third are best answered by analysis of concepts and application of moral theory. There is, moreover, no single, unified theory of IR into which all theories and laws of the social world must ultimately be made to fit. Because the social world is complex and multifaceted, IR and security studies must acknowledge that there are various orthogonal and crosscutting theoretical approaches and research methods, which cannot be aggregated into a single grand theory (Chernoff 2005, 20–21; 2007b, 123). And indeed the claims made in this book regarding the enhanced possibility of approach-to-consensus when criteria are explicitly acknowledged is not intended to apply to all IR debates, or even to all security studies debates (see Section 5 of the introduction to this book 5). Some questions—for example, is the use of nuclear weapons ever justified?—are of a different nature.

3. ALTERNATIVE ACCOUNTS—THE MEASURE-STIPULATION

Another way one might try to explain the high level of approach-to-consensus in the DP debate draws on the view of science of Pierre Duhem, an early twentieth-century French physicist and philosopher. Some of Duhem's highly original and far-reaching empiricist views of science have been rejected, but many have gained near-unanimous acceptance, one of which is the principle of the conventionality of the measure-stipulation, which states that science unavoidably makes use of measure-stipulation assumptions that cannot be based purely on observation and/or logic.[4] This principle might be used to propose another alternative to H_1 and H_2.

A rough idea of Duhem's measure-stipulation argument may be gained by imagining that scientists from our world visit a two-dimensional universe where they perform experiments and take measurements. They conclude that all their observations are consistent with two beliefs: (A) the surface of the universe is flat and Euclidean (parallel lines are always equidistant at their closest points) and there is a force operating in the universe that compresses all physical objects at a certain rate as they are moved away from the center of the universe; and (B) the geometry of the universe is curvilinear (i.e., non-Euclidean), and there are no such forces in effect. A and B are mutually exclusive, yet they both conform to all of the scientists' observations, and indeed to all possible observations in that universe.

If the scientists believe that an object is shrinking when moved in a particular direction, someone might suggest that they take a rigid measuring rod and measure the object before and after it is moved to see if the length changes. But of course the same forces would be shrinking the measuring rod. If a second measuring rod is suggested, the same problem arises. Ultimately, the scientists must decide whether they are to accept one stipulation or the other—either the object remains the same length both before and after it is moved, or alternatively, an unseen force shrinks as it is moved in a particular direction. Duhem argues that even though the measure-stipulation choice cannot be made based solely on pure logic and observation, it is nevertheless nonarbitrary, since it may be grounded on rationally defensible philosophical arguments about knowledge and science. Once the measure-stipulation is widely accepted, regardless of whether it is A or B, the scientific community can build a theory making use of it and then advance progressively to solve new, increasingly complex problems. But scientists cannot move forward if there is no conventional agreement on the measure-stipulation.

This alternative explanation suggests that the approach-to-consensus in the DP debate is a result not simply of the criterial overlap but also of the presence of a Duhemian measure-stipulation in that debate.[5] Unlike the alliance formation and nuclear proliferation debates, the DP debate had two progress-enhancing features that conferred advantages to it: there was a clear focus on two variables, democracy and peace, and its most intense phase began after there were widely accepted databases and measures for the variables, especially Correlates of War, Freedom House, and Polity. While scholars may have an unconscious tendency to define variables and code cases in ways that fit with their own hypotheses, scholars in the DP debate did not have a free hand to do either.

Those engaged in the nuclear proliferation and alliance formation debates thus had more latitude to define key terms (e.g., *national interest, symbolic gain, polarity, hegemony*) in ways that worked well for their own theories. The key terms in the other two debates were much less clearly defined than those in the DP debate. Does the concept of democracy, like the rigidity of the measuring rod, remain constant when moved across space, from Europe to North America, to Asia, and so on, and through time, from the clash between Athens and Sparta to the Anglo-Icelandic cod dispute? Or must the idea be adjusted for time and place? A reasonable argument can be made for either stipulation. We see that there was a single answer to the question "How should the cases be coded?" because DP researchers had a measure-stipulation in place before the debate gained full force.

The comparison of authors' freedom to define variables in the three debates is stark when we recall Levy's (2003, 145) argument, discussed in Chapter 4, that rival theorists in the alliance formation debate made use of different measures of power: hegemonic stability theorists use financial and trade measures, whereas balance-of-power theorists emphasize military capabilities. Levy views this as an obstacle to agreement on how to explain alliance formation. Such obstacles were absent in the DP debate, since there were already widely accepted databases, which meant that few authors used their own codings, and when they did, they were subject to careful scrutiny and required thorough defenses. Thus, it makes sense that community-wide agreement on the measure-stipulation will advance movement toward agreement by opposing sides.

There seem to be two appropriate responses to this proposed alternative explanation for the DP consensus. One is to concede that it is indeed very plausible as an explanatory factor. And the second is to reiterate that H_1 states that criterial overlap is one element that affects scientific progress in security studies; H_1 and H_2 do not claim, nor would it be plausible to claim that criterial overlap or divergence is the sole reason for the different degrees of progress in security studies debates. The measure-stipulation alternative is not inconsistent with the criteria-focused account in this book. And because progress in the studies of democratic dyads is so much more pronounced than in either of the other two debates surveyed, it is reasonable to expect that at least several factors combined to produce this singular pattern.[6]

4. ALTERNATIVE ACCOUNTS: EACH PHILOSOPHICAL SCHOOL EMPHASIZES PARTICULAR CRITERIA OF EVALUATION

The fact that there are different schools in the philosophy of science, and by implication in naturalist philosophy of social science, might be suggested as an alternative explanation for the pattern of progress and stalemate, namely that political realism is grounded in a different philosophy of science doctrine than opposing theories. As Chapter 2 noted, empiricism and scientific realism are the broadest descriptions of the opposing schools, though there are many variations (e.g., internal realism, causal realism, instrumentalism, constructivism empiricism, operationalism). According to this alternative, the criterial differences that this book has emphasized are simply a special case of broader differences between realists and opponents.

Empiricism and scientific realism differ over core issues, like the status of the entities to which theoretical terms refer and the "truth status" of assumptions. With regard to the former, the empiricist and scientific realist schools agree that nontheoretical terms typically refer to things that are observable. But the two schools differ on terms that refer to unobservable theoretical entities. Scientific realists regard all terms employed in accepted theories as referring to real entities, whether the terms are nontheoretical, like *water*, *silver*, or *penguin*, or theoretical, like *electron*, *genome*, or *gravitational force*, whereas empiricists do not infer the real existence of the referents of purely theoretical terms, even in accepted theories. With regard to the latter, empiricism and scientific realism also differ on "truth," in that scientific realists believe the best theories to be true, whereas empiricists generally accept that scientists may to hold varying degrees of belief in scientific theories, depending on the strength of the scientific warrant for the theories' acceptability. Empiricists do not accept that all theoretical scientific propositions warrant "full belief": theoretical propositions may be accepted in an only provisional way.

There are two significant counterexamples to this proposed alternative. One is that many security studies authors are too vague about where they stand on philosophical issues, like the status of assumptions or the "reality" of theoretical posits, to be classified in a way that would allow this factor to explain the pattern of stalemate and progress that has been observed. Chapters 3–5 demonstrated what a difficult task it is to identify even several of the key criteria authors use. Moreover, when authors state the criteria they use, as Solingen and Sagan did, the criteria often do not match any set of criteria that would be emphasized in one or another school in the philosophy of science.

A second counterexample is that those who can be classified show beyond any doubt that realists and their opponents do not line up on opposite sides of the philosophical divide. The most dramatic illustration of this is that Waltz and Mearsheimer are the two most prominent realists; indeed, both are structural realists, yet they disagree on metatheory. Waltz is clearly an empiricist, while Mearsheimer, who endorses the "truth" of theoretical assumptions, is a scientific realist.[7] This should not be viewed as counterintuitive, since philosophers of science who hold very different doctrines quite often can agree on how to evaluate empirical cases. It was noted earlier that all philosophical schools agree that Einstein's general theory of relativity is a scientific advancement over Newton's theory, that Harvey's theory was superior to Galen's, and so on. Indeed, they agree on almost all cases. Scholars' applications of diverse metatheories may well lead to the same conclusions about the best explanatory theories.

The ways in which different philosophical schools see science, and how they understand and characterize a "good" theory, affect how they prioritize different criteria of theory choice. We have noted a dozen or so criteria that are invoked by scientists and endorsed by philosophers of science. When one theory exceeds all others in terms of all criteria, such as simplicity or explanatory unification, there is no question that all investigators will prefer it. However, the real world of scientific debate is rarely so tidy. Most often in the natural sciences one theory will rate as best according to some criteria and as inferior according to others. But decisions must still be made about trade-offs and priorities among conflicting criteria. Which criteria are ranked ahead of which others will depend upon the metatheoretical and philosophical doctrines that one accepts. For example, if one explanatory theory is superior to another on grounds of simplicity and empirical adequacy but another fares better on grounds of depth of causes and mechanisms, the former will be preferable to empiricists and the latter to scientific realists. But what we have seen in security studies publications is that the criteria used do not match any consistent doctrines in the philosophy of science. Political realists do not adopt a set of priorities that differs in any consistent way from the set adopted by liberals or others.

5. ALTERNATIVE ACCOUNTS: RIVALS THAT ARE NOT TRULY RIVALS, BUT ANSWERS TO DIFFERENT QUESTIONS

A related objection would arise if someone proposed *question ambiguity* as a better explanation for the pattern than of stalemate and consensus in the three debates that H_1 provides. The present section sketches the case for this alternative. This is an important and plausible claim but a full probe into its explanatory power is beyond the scope of the present study.

Context and the Questioner's Intent

The lack of clarity about what particular question the explanatory answer in fact answers can stem from various sources, such as the intent of the questioner, the background knowledge and beliefs of the audience, and the area of greatest interest or concern to the audience. Various authors in IR and in the philosophy of science hold that an explanation does not exist in a vacuum but is developed to solve a particular puzzle or answer a particular question. The questions can be misunderstood if questioners and audiences do not pay sufficient attention to several key factors.

Suganami. Suganami, as noted in Chapter 2, has developed one of the most subtle and insightful accounts of causation in IR. He examines debates about the causes of war in a way parallel to the inquiries of Chapters 3–5 in this book. Suganami makes several important points connected to the present inquiry about the possibility of progress in security studies. First, Suganami argues there are different questions that one might have in mind when asking why wars occur. What would count as an acceptable explanation for war depends on which of the questions is intended. Suganami (1996, 33; 2002, 308) distinguishes the following questions: What conditions must be present for there to be war at all? What conditions are likely to give rise to war? How did this particular war come about? As he sees it, Waltz makes the case that anarchy is the most fundamental cause of war by failing to separate different questions that, at different times, Waltz's theory appears to be designed to treat.

In Suganami's (1996, 34) view, had Waltz consistently separated the first and the third questions, Waltz "would have hesitated to place together in the first level of analysis such incongruous items as . . . human nature . . . , the personality traits of key decision-makers, and . . . their specific thoughts and acts under specified circumstances." Furthermore, had Waltz separated them, "he would not have treated a historical interpretation that a tense and unstable situation among particular states at a given time was the system-level cause, for example, of the First World War as though it were the same kind of assertion as his central thesis that the fact that there is nothing in the international system to prevent war was the permissive cause of war as such" (1996, 34). Suganami says that the precise formulation of questions (which should reflect exactly what the questioner means by the question) will have a determinative effect on the sort of explanation that will provide an appropriate answer to the question. The meaning of a sentence, whether it is a description, explanation, command, or question, is affected by the context.

Van Fraassen. Although Suganami does not cite Van Fraassen, the latter developed an argument in the 1980s with which Suganami's has much in common. Van Fraassen explicitly rejects the idea that an explanation can be anything other than pragmatic. Consider a security studies scholar writing (to use Achinstein's 1984 example) about the War of 1812. Such a scholar might raise a question about the observation of the American flag flying over Fort McHenry after the British assault on the fort. For Van Fraassen an explanation is an answer to a question; thus, one would need to pose a question to which an explanation of the flag's presence would constitute answer, such as, "Why is our flag still there?"

However, on Van Fraassen's account, this question, phrased as it is, does not tell us all we need to know about what is being asked: knowledge of the context is essential. The questioner might be asking why our flag is still there (1) in contrast *to some other flag* being there, (2) in contrast to our flag being *somewhere else (or nowhere)*, or (3) in contrast to why is our flag there *instead of some other sort of object* being there. Which proposition forms the proper contrast to "Why is our flag still there?" determines just what that question is asking, which in turn determines what would count as an appropriate explanation of why our flag is still there. According to Van Fraassen, the proposed explanation is only an appropriate explanation (and still may or may not be successful) when it is clear what the *contrast class* is, which the context will supply. Wendt (1999, 88) also alludes to this element of explanation (see also Garfinkle 1981; Woodward 2003).

The questioner also may be asking for a sequence of events that led up to our flag still being there, or he or she may be asking for the function or purpose of the flag being there. These two questions would then call for different types of explanations—historico-genetic and functional, respectively. Thus, we also need to know the relevance relation of the question in order to know what would qualify as an explanation of "our flag still being there." Van Fraassen (1980, 130) holds that there must be several other elements beyond mere description for any set of statements to qualify as an explanation: "The description of some account as an explanation of a given fact or event is incomplete. It can only be an explanation with respect to a certain relevance relation and a certain contrast-class. These are contextual factors, in that they are determined neither by the totality of accepted scientific theories, nor by the event or fact for which an explanation is requested." In the DP debate there was a clear and delimited contrast class consisting of answers drawn from liberal theory and power-based realist alternatives.

Importance of the Audience's Background Knowledge and Interests

A reader must attend to several factors in order to understand just what a question is intended to convey and thus to know what would count as an explanatory answer. Suppose we compare a hypothetical academic conference in Chicago in 1998 to one in Beijing at the same time, where the scholars at either site consider the question, "How do we explain that the very heated dispute between the United Kingdom and Iceland in the 1970s over fishing rights did not result in war?" The idea that both the United Kingdom and Iceland are mature liberal democracies would be well known by both audiences, but the two audiences would regard this as an explanatory factor in different ways. The audience in Chicago would not believe that there is much of a reason for the two democracies to go to war, given that it is common knowledge to the audience and to the publics in either country that the United Kingdom and Iceland are mature democracies. However, in Beijing, scholars might not accept as part of their background beliefs that democracies like the United Kingdom and Iceland, which are developed capitalist states, almost never go to war with one another. The Chinese scholars are well aware that capitalist states do go to war with one another; in fact, such states might be even more inclined to do so because of the very fact of their being capitalist. The background beliefs of the target audiences form the context out of which a question gains specific meaning.

This should not be construed as a way in which naturalism fails and that the social sciences are less "scientific" than the natural sciences. Achinstein argues for context relevance and pragmatics of explanation universally, in physics and in all scientific contexts.[8] He presents an example of the context dependence of answers to a question about atomic theory, namely the Rutherford experiment in 1911. For Achinstein (1984, 286), "Rutherford's explanation is good . . . because it answers a causal question about the scattering [of alpha particles] . . . in a way that physicists at the time were interested in understanding the scattering." The specific aspects of the process in which the community of investigators is most interested affect the appraisal of competing explanatory theories. Thus, when Rutherford presented his explanation the audience (the scientific community of 1911) had specific interests in specific aspects of scattering. And those interests were part of the context of the explanation and formed a part of the framework for what would constitute a superior explanation.

Context Dependence, Progress, and the Democratic Peace Debate

The precise meaning of the question, in ways beyond those that Suganami (1996, 2002) emphasizes, can make a difference in the meaning of the question and thus in the sort of explanation that would be regarded as sufficient by the community to which the question is posed. The fact that the democratic-dyad debate was so intense over such a short period of time increases the chances that the aspect(s) of democracies' behaviors that the investigating community was most interested in would overlap to the greatest extent. In contrast, the nuclear proliferation debate took on a new form after the Non-Proliferation Treaty was signed, but there was still a steady stream of major works throughout the period. Quester was the only author who published one of the works surveyed prior to 1980; the works by Potter, Meyer, and Waltz appeared in the 1980s; and the remaining five were published within a ten-year period. And in the case of the alliance formation debate discussed in Chapter 4, the bulk of the writings are spaced out somewhat evenly over seven decades: with works by Morgenthau and Organski in the 1940s and 1950s; works by Claude, Bull, and Waltz the 1960s and 1970s; works by Walt, Mearsheimer, and Schweller in the 1980s and 1990s; and the next five surveyed were published in the 2000s.

The democratic peace debate is much more like the nuclear proliferation debate in terms of the condensed timing of the publication of the most often-read works: ten of the twelve works were published in just fourteen years. Only the earliest, Small and Singer, and the most recent paper included, Gartzke, are outside of the 1983–96 period. It may be that when authors are writing in such close proximity to one another, the context in which they are writing is most likely to be unchanged and thus they are more likely to be interested in the same aspect(s) of the explanandum phenomenon, and more likely to interpret the explanandum phenomenon (alliance formation, acquisition of nuclear weapons, peace within democratic dyads) in the same way. At the time of the Rutherford experiment, the scientific community of particle physicists had a particular interest, which may have made it more likely that members would agree on the superiority of one explanation. So the closer temporal sequence of works in the DP debate may have enhanced a similarity of focus and framework, which may in turn have helped greater consensus develop as compared to the other debates.

Suganami and the philosophers mentioned make a good case for question ambiguity as an explanation for the stalemate in some of the debates. Space considerations prevent further discussion. But as noted in connection with some of the other alternative explanations, H_1 states that criterial disagreement is one factor, perhaps among several. We may conclude, however, that any explanation in IR is an attempt to answer a question. But progress in debates over the "best" explanation requires that authors are extremely clear in how they formulate and explicate the central focus and meaning of any question they purport to be answering.

6. HOW MUCH METATHEORY IS ENOUGH?

If the central hypothesis of this book is right, namely H_1—that progress in security studies has been slowed because different scholars use of different notions of explanation or explanatory progress—it follows that authors pay too little attention to metatheory, in particular to criteria of explanatory superiority. It is then logical to return to the question posed in Chapter 1: how much metatheory and methodology is enough? There is no universally applicable answer. Rather, given the discussion of the previous section, it should not be surprising that the answer depends on context, in particular, on the nature of the intended audience, the type of publication, the particular debate to which the work is a intended to contribute, as well as on the nature of the claims being advanced. These must be taken into account for authors to be able to make their cases as persuasively as possible.

Starting Points Are Unavoidable

Every study must start at a starting point, as discussed in Chapter 1. Authors in the social sciences must build upon philosophical and logical assumptions, like the veracity of direct empirical observation, the validity of indirect proof (i.e., that P follows if not-P yields a contradiction). So, even though IR authors must rely on many philosophical and metatheoretical claims in presenting their arguments, it is impossible—and certainly unnecessary in most cases—to attempt to defend of all of them. Some starting point must be chosen. Published works in other fields, with other audiences, use different starting points. In an article submitted to a journal of philosophical logic, indirect proof and the law of excluded middle may be the subject of debate and, if so, the law of excluded middle could not be used as a starting point. Similarly, a contribution to metaphysics or epistemology might question the veracity of direct empirical observation, or the claim that there exists a mind-independent world of material objects. But no IR audience expects an author to prove them; any such attempt would be wasteful, merely taking up space in a book or article that could be used much more effectively by citing evidence or advancing the methodological and theoretical arguments. Thus, which starting points will be effective depends on the context of audience, publication, and so on.

Authors in IR and security studies are in the same boat with natural scientists, in that all are committed to a variety of different kinds of propositions, though they may not always realize it, and they certainly do not always acknowledge it. In IR an argument for an explanatory theory, T, would typically rely on different sorts of premises, which may be summarized in the following schema:

Schema Σ

1. P (metaphysical or epistemological claims, such as the veracity of direct observation; these are usually suppressed in IR publications)
2. Q (methodological claims and criteria of explanatory superiority—sometimes suppressed in IR publications)
3. R (defense of research design)
4. S (empirical evidence)

∴ 5. T (explanatory theory)

Anyone presenting an explanatory theory T in the natural or social sciences must be committed to claims of type P, Q, R, and S.

For all statements that are elements of P, Q, R, and S, every author must choose one of three options:

(i) To offer an explicit defense of the statement
(ii) To note explicitly that the argument depends upon the statement but not to present a defense
(iii) To leave the statement entirely implicit, as a suppressed premise

The choice of how to treat each of the statements in categories P, Q, R, and S should be made in a way that maximizes the rhetorical and persuasive effects, given the intended audience, and the space available to make the case for T. That is, in a book more attention should be given to some of the types of claims than in a journal article, and more should be given in a full-length journal article than in a published discussion note. And more attention should be given to some types of claims than to others; how much is most effective depends, for example, on whether the audience of that journal or that sort of book is generally accustomed to accepting the intellectual value of the P-type or Q-type statements. Examples would include the audience's acceptance of the intellectual value of statistically oriented explanations versus the value of comparative case studies, or its acceptance of constructivist principles of the nature of social reality.

Another aspect of P-R (and possibly S) is that the theory T is more persuasive the less vulnerable P-R are, and P-R are less vulnerable the less the totality of the content they convey. If someone advances an IR argument that relies on methods consistent with a range of philosophers, such as Kuhn, Lakatos, Popper, and Quine (i.e., any of those philosophers or their followers will accept the starting point), it will be less vulnerable, and thus more persuasive, than an argument that requires a stronger, more content-rich, or more specific, set of premises; for example, that Kuhn is right and the others wrong. To cite an extreme example, consider the following pair of propositions that state both mechanisms and outcomes: "Democratic dyads have greater structural constraints on crisis escalation than other sorts of dyads, which leads them to be less war-prone than other types of dyads" and "The political institutions realized through the unfolding of Absolute Spirit will exhibit perfection." The former is compatible with a wider range of principles in set P (premise 1) from schema Σ; the latter would be accepted only by those who endorse the metaphysics of Hegelian idealism (Dudley 2009, 12). Thus, it is unwise to adopt metatheoretical tenets that are not clearly necessary to derive the explanatory, theoretical, or descriptive inference that an author seeks to draw. We see, then, that that starting points are unavoidable in any empirical or philosophical argument. Authors in IR and security studies, just as natural scientists, are committed to a variety of different kinds of proposition, whether they acknowledge them or not. They should therefore choose the widest range of premises with which the argument will be consistent.

The recommendation of this study is that security studies researchers identify the criteria they rely on. This adds a step to, and slightly complicates, research and writing. But it is justifiable in view of the much greater scholarly progress for which it lays a foundation; it will increase direct engagement of scholarly works and explanatory progress. Some things are, by custom and norm, expected to be included in explicit form in scholarly publications. And just what is expected is a result of evolution based on a form of cost-benefit reasoning. In security studies publications authors are expected to cite sources of data, provide page references for quotations, identify the particular statistical tests that have been performed and the specific results obtained (rather than simply reporting that the author has conducted statistical tests and that the hypothesis has been corroborated by significant results), and so on. But other things are not expected, such as the height of the author who checked the reference for the quotation cited or the operating system—Windows or Mac—of the computer(s) on which the statistical tests were performed. The reason that some things are expected to be included is that the effort involved in including them is justified by the importance of the audience's need to be able to be clear on just what those are, in part so replication is possible, and these are justified by the ways they might enhance understanding within the scholarly community. Even though it is theoretically possible that some computer operating systems are less reliable than others, the difference is so small that it is not worth the extra effort and space for authors to report it.

It is important to note that what is expected by an audience or community changes over time. Some publication outlets now expect web citations to include the universal resource locator (URL) of the cite and the date it was accessed, because this could make a difference. This norm has evolved because websites, unlike books, may change over time. As more security studies researchers and other social scientists become aware that explanatory disagreement may result from uses of different sets of criteria, the inclusion of an explicit list of criteria could and should become a part of high-quality published work.

7. CONCLUSIONS—MANY SECURITY STUDIES DEBATES CAN MOVE TOWARD AGREEMENT

This book began by posing the question of whether the failure of security studies authors to move toward accepted best explanations of phenomena results, possibly in addition to other factors, from their use of divergent sets of criteria for the "best" explanation. The study investigated H_1, which proposes the affirmative answer, and H_2, which states that when authors do agree on criteria of evaluation, approach-to-consensus is more likely.

The Central Question Answered

Chapter 1 developed a method for selecting the key works that are most likely to form scholars' understanding of how good explanatory arguments are formulated in any particular issue area. Chapter 2 focused on the nature of scientific explanation and the criteria investigators use to choose one explanatory theory over others. It examined competing philosophical views of science (scientific realism, empiricism, pragmatism), the different kinds of things that these schools claim constitute a scientific explanation (e.g., speech act, formal argument), and various criteria of explanatory superiority (e.g., simplicity, explanatory unification, empirical adequacy, range of domain). Agreement on the best explanation would be much more difficult if the principal works in a field took explanation to be very different kinds of things. But we noted all of the published works that fit the criteria of "most influential" in the three debates conceived of explanation in a broadly similar naturalist way. With these clarifications we have conducted an inquiry that has shown that H_1 and H_2 are consistent with the evidential patterns in the three debates.

Chapters 3–5 sought to identify the specific criteria used in each of the ten to twelve works in the three security studies debates. Section 1 in this chapter provided an analysis of the results with the goal of identifying relationships, if any, between shared use of criteria and explanatory progress, as H_1 and H_2 claim. The conclusion of the analysis was that one debate, over the nuclear proliferation, had little overlap of criteria and little progress; the second, over alliance formation, had more overlap and more approach-to-consensus; and the third, over democratic peace, had significant overlap of criteria and comparatively much more approach-to-consensus. Sections 2–5 in this chapter considered a range of attempts to provide alternative explanations for this pattern. Some of the alternative explanations appear to have merit as (e.g., the measure-stipulation), some actually reinforce H_1 and H_2 by providing specific ways that criteria come to be shared by most or all prominent authors on an issue (the qualitative-quantitative argument, and question-ambiguity), and some are dubious (that realist and liberals endorse distinct sorts of criteria of explanatory merit). While these might deserve further discussion, none of the alternatives was clearly compelling enough to supplant or dispel the emphasis on criteria of H_1 and H_2.

Obstacles to Progress Can All Be Overcome

This chapter has noted several obstacles to progress. One is that the context is required to make clear a "relevance relation." Another is that the explanation must be relativized to a "contrast class." One might think that these two admissions lead to incommensurability-based pessimism about progress in security studies because opposing authors will unavoidably talk past one another rather than directly engage one another's arguments. But accepting pragmatic requirements, like acknowledging the crucial role of a contrast class and relevance relation, does not justify any such skepticism because there are specific measures that security studies authors can take to satisfy the requirements and surmount the obstacles. Certainly, when Van Fraassen proposes these as elements of explanation, he is in no way suggesting that these factors render progress impossible in the natural sciences.

One step that security studies scholars can take to improve the chances of progress is to pay more attention to stating their research questions with care and to offering clarifications of each research question's meaning, including some discussion of possible misinterpretations. This would entail authors making explicit the particular context in which the question is posed and providing detail that is sufficient to remove any likely ambiguities. Another sort of measure that would help would be to specify one's metatheoretical commitments, even though, as discussed in Chapter 1, defenses of those commitments are generally not required. And this book has made the case that authors should take the fairly simple step of thinking through and acknowledging explicitly which criteria they invoke as they compare their preferred explanations to their rivals' purportedly weaker explanations. This is not particularly onerous, and it would spare readers the trouble—and potential mistakes—that can arise from the sort of fallible interpretive exercise required in Chapters 3–5.

Finally, we are justified in optimism about approach-to-consensus progress, at least in the areas that are not primarily normative, because there has in fact been real progress of that sort in the study of democratic dyads. Chapter 5 showed that there was much greater similarity in the sets of criteria used by the two chief opposing schools of thought as compared with what was seen in the other two debates. The fact that democratic peace studies exhibited progress is powerful evidence against Kuhnian-inspired skepticism or other forms of reluctance to accept the possibility of progress.

Explicit Statements of Criteria of Appraisal Can Spur Future Progress in IR

As stated earlier, authors have three choices with respect to every step of an argument: to offer an explicit defense, to note explicitly that the argument depends upon that step but not to present a defense, and to leave the statement entirely implicit as a suppressed premise. With respect to the criteria that authors regard as most important for evaluating competing security studies explanations, the second choice is the most appropriate one. Only in rare cases is there a good reason to choose the first, and thus commit oneself to the defense of a criterion; there are works in other fields that may be cited for this purpose. And choosing the third option opens up the debate to miscommunication in ways that are unnecessary and that undermine progress. Thus, it would benefit engagement of different views for authors to state the criteria on which they judge their explanations to be preferable. In keeping with the goal of explicit statements of the criteria that are used as this book's explanation of stalemate and success in Chapters 3–6, at the close of Chapter 2 there is an explicit discussion of the criterial trade-offs.

Social scientists appropriately produce social science. There is no need for them to defend positions and advance debates in the philosophy of social science. It is up to philosophers to do so. However, it is essential for social scientists to have enough training in the latter to be able to understand their own methods and to advance research in their own substantive area so that they can develop their explanatory arguments within an intellectually coherent framework. They must recognize that the strength of their own explanations can be sapped by problems at the methodological and metatheoretical levels. They should try to draw on the broadest and least-likely-to-be-overthrown premises possible. And they should seek to make as explicit as possible the philosophical and methodological school they embrace including, at the very least, the specific criteria they draw on in arguing for their preferred explanatory answers.

With the relatively simple adjustment of making explicit the criteria on which security studies and IR authors rely when they lay out the framework, research design, and assumptions of their arguments, the prospects for progress in security studies will be significantly brighter than they are in the absence of these measures.

Reference Matter

NOTES

Chapter 1

1. There are also other sorts of interpretive circularity. Bohman (1993, 110) argues that there are at least five types, since theoretical descriptions are always subject to problems of selectivity, perspective, incompleteness, unspecified assumptions, and parts-whole circularity. See also Chernoff (2005, chap. 5 and 225n5).

2. Consider the following: (A) When we use the word *red* we apply it to the same sorts of things that we were taught that it applies to when we first learned the word *red.* (B) When we apply a word correctly, we follow the rule of applying it to the same sorts of things to which we were taught it correctly applies. (C) But consider that we must know the meaning of the statement (B), and that entails that we must know the meaning of the word *same.* (D) Substitute *same* for *red* in statement (A). The interpretivist may conclude that, since the example of this footnote is completely general with regard to the use of language, linear causal reasoning is unjustifiable anywhere, not excluding the social sciences and the natural sciences.

3. For a different sort of reason drawing on the origins of our notion of cause, see Chernoff (2005). Also we note that in the IR literature Alex Wendt (1999, 82) has sought to clarify the relationship between reasons, causes, and action by stating, "Norms are causal insofar as they regulate behavior. Reasons are causes to the extent that they provide motivation and energy for action."

4. Once the research design was concluded in 2010, adjustments based on the influence of subsequent publications were avoided, as they could not be done entirely consistently and ad hoc adjustments would produce biases.

5. "The term 'prediction' may be defined as follows: A rationally based expectation of the future, or prediction, in the natural or social sciences is a singular or general proposition which i) is indexed to the future relative to the moment of its utterance

ii) is based on a rationally justifiable body of theory, broadly construed iii) may be based on imperfect evidence iv) may be either deterministic or probabilistic and v) may be conditional, i.e., of the form, 'if conditions C obtain, then result E will follow'" (Chernoff 2005, 8).

6. The Lakatosian approach has support from many of the major figures in IR and the study of War. Vasquez (1998, 28), for example, endorses the Lakatosian view according to which the superior theory (1) has excess empirical content (i.e., can predict novel facts); (2) explains unrefuted content of the older theory; and (3) includes excess content, some of which is corroborated. He endorses the criteria of accuracy, falsifiability, explanatory power, progressive research program, consistency with other fields of knowledge, and parsimony and/or elegance (1998, 230).

7. In Kuhn's later statement on the subject, he endorses "accuracy, scope, simplicity, fruitfulness, and the like" (2000, 157). The discussion here offers some perspectives on the meaning of the notion of progress. As noted earlier, it is assumed that one of these or some other can be formulated in such a way as to provide a coherent concept of progress.

8. The author has addressed this other places (e.g., Chernoff 2005, 180–83; 2009, 163–64).

Chapter 2

1. Van Fraassen (1980, 13–19, 64–69) argues that the distinction between theoretical terms and observation terms is different from that between observables and unobservables. This allows him to acknowledge the theory-ladenness of observation without admitting the collapse of the distinction between theoretical and observation terms.

2. Empirical adequacy is a key criterion for empiricists. But empiricists recognize that other criteria are essential, since Duhem (1954) has shown that there will never be a single theory that is uniquely consistent with all observation statements. The Duhem thesis states that there are always many other theories that are consistent with the evidence, even if no one has yet formulated them. When a competing theory does arise, other criteria will be needed to make a choice.

3. Leibniz and Newton, on opposite sides of many issues, agreed on the primacy of simplicity (Leibniz, *Monadology* secs. 1–2; Newton, *Principia* 2:398). And according to Einstein (Barnett 1950, 22), "[T]he grand aim of all science . . . is to cover the greatest possible number of empirical facts by logical deductions from the smallest possible number of hypotheses or axioms." The role of simplicity in the philosophy of science cannot be overemphasized, especially when endorsed by Newton, Leibniz, and Einstein.

4. For Hempel (1965) an explanation consists of a set of propositions Pa_1, Pa_2 . . . Pa_n, which states relevant general laws (laws of nature); a set of propositions Pb_1, Pb_2, . . . Pb_n, which states the relevant initial conditions of the event to be explained;

and a proposition Q, which is the statement of the event or process to be explained. The propositions Pa_1, Pa_2, . . . Pa_n, Pb_1, Pb_2, . . . Pb_n jointly entail Q. If Q is the event of a car radiator cracking, then the laws deal with the properties of water, such as its expansion in volume as it freezes, the properties of the copper of the radiator, and so forth. The initial conditions state the material out of which the radiator is constructed, the presence of water in the radiator, the temperature of the water in the radiator when the car was parked in the garage during the night, the lowest temperature reached in that location on that night, and so forth. Together the Pa_1–Pa_n and Pb_1–Pb_n logically imply the cracking of the radiator.

5. Strictly speaking, the symmetry was not exact because the full deductive argument of an explanation (or at the very least, its premise set) constituted the explanation, whereas in the case of prediction, the prediction was only the conclusion of the deductive argument.

6. Hempel's (1942) famous paper can be interpreted as arguing that narrative-style explanations, despite interpretivist assertions, manage to explain only if they include I-S covering laws.

7. No assumption is made in the following chapters that the authors accept a set of criteria that form a coherent set, in the sense that they fit into one or another school of thought in the philosophy of social science. Some may do so, but given that so many authors implicitly rely on criteria, it is not a justifiable interpretive principle to assume that they adopt sets of criteria that fit together in a philosophically neat way that would be more justifiable to expect if they were explicitly endorsing criteria and using terminology like *scientific realism*, *constructive empiricism*, and so on.

8. To cite an IR application of this issue, Dessler (2003) argues that the "deeper" theoretical beliefs about structure do the explanatory work. Laws explain other laws by virtue of either a genus-species relationship or a part-whole relationship; in the latter, a regularity is a "manifestation of several other regularities" (Kinoshita 1990, 301, cited by Dessler 2003, 393). Consider also Jack Snyder's (1990) genus-species explanation for the end of the Cold War. One might respond by noting that how "deep" and how "far back" or "far down" one must go is context dependent. Dessler does not know of any part-whole explanations in IR; however, "democratic peace" explanations may come to be such.

9. We should add that while this is sometimes regarded as a criterion of theory acceptance, the widely accepted Duhem thesis (sometimes known as the Duhem-Quine thesis) tells us that it is impossible for the elimination of alternatives to be absolute, since some assumptions are made to carry out empirical tests, and there are always other possible theories that have not yet been proposed (see Gillies 1993; Chernoff 2012).

10. Reichenbach (1971) proposed that such an association is spurious provided that there is a factor C such that P(A/B&C) = P(A/C).

11. A number of philosophers have argued that the ability, at least in principle, to control or manipulate the world is a hallmark, and perhaps part of the correct analysis, of "causation." See, for example, Woodward (2003, 2006).

12. One listing of principle criteria is offered by Hands (1990, 77–78), who says that in "humankind's greatest scientific accomplishments . . . [researchers] choose theories because they are deeper, simpler, more general, more operational, explain known facts better, are more corroborated, are more consistent with what we consider to be deeper theories, and for many other reasons."

13. Vasquez (1998, 230) endorses the criteria of accuracy, falsifiability, explanatory power, progressive research program, consistency with other fields of knowledge, and parsimony and/or elegance. We noted earlier (in note 7 in Chapter 1) that Kuhn (2000, 157) endorses the criteria of "accuracy, scope, simplicity, fruitfulness, and the like."

14. Fetzer (2000, 113–14) argues that Hempel's account fits neatly with Aristotle's four causes: material (scientific laws), efficient (antecedent conditions), formal (logical relation between the explanans and the explanandum), and final (explanandum).

15. Sometimes norms and values are contrasted with rationality as a basis for explanation. But we should note that norms may be derived through rational philosophical inquiry, so what is actually contrasted with norms and values is the rational pursuit of material gain or self-interest.

16. If researchers say that putative explanations that meet a set of conditions are genuine explanations and that anything that does not meet those conditions is not a genuine explanation, then they should have some reason for saying that all of the conditions that are members of the set are required for something to be an explanation. Otherwise, they are offering merely a stipulative definition of the term *explanation.*

17. Many of the most influential social theorists, including Durkheim (1897), Malinowski (1942), Merton (1968), Parsons (1969), and Radcliffe-Brown (1965), rely extensively on functional explanation.

Chapter 3

1. In 2008 three kilograms of weapons-grade uranium were smuggled out of Russia. The Russian Oleg Khinsagov and three Georgians were arrested, and one hundred grams of 90 percent–enriched, weapons-grade uranium was found. Michael Bronner, "When the War Ends, Start to Worry," *New York Times,* August 16, 2008.

2. Waltz (1990, 731) acknowledges that some political leaders have spoken publicly about their aim of winning a nuclear war, but such rhetoric is only sporadic and never sustained over time.

3. Wohlstetter led a team for the US Arms Control and Disarmament Agency and produced a report that made some similar points; the study is not included in the analysis of this chapter because, despite its length and intended policy recommendations, it

makes no claims as to "explanation" (Wohlstetter et al. 1976). Hence, it would be unfair to include it in a study of agreement and disagreement on how to explain proliferation (see also US Department of State 1946).

4. In the twenty years preceding the publication of Meyer's (1984) book, and despite predictions to the contrary, only one new state (North Korea) had exploded a nuclear device, and even that test, for what it is worth, was claimed to not be a weapons test. Before writing *The Dynamics of Nuclear Proliferation*, Meyer had conducted considerable research on states' capabilities to conduct nuclear energy research, to construct power plants, and to build nuclear weapons. Meyer's book thus discusses in detail the attempts of advanced industrial states to limit proliferation by cutting off the supply of technology and fissile materials, notably by means of the London Suppliers Group and the US-sponsored International Fuel Cycle Evaluation conference.

5. In the context of a study in which proliferation decisions, as noted earlier, are the central focus, Meyer says, "Political and military variables appear to explain about 69 percent of the variation in the proliferation decision variable" (1984, 105–6).

6. Meyer refers to a specific, and policy-relevant, type of prediction as "forecasting" (1984, 145).

7. Meyer talks about different "interpretations" of models. But he appears to mean simply different specific claims consistent with the basic outlines of the model. So one interpretation or version of his technological imperative model III is that "the strength of the technological imperative grows in direct relation to the size of the nuclear establishment in any country" (1984, 84). However, "a somewhat different interpretation of model III is possible. . . . [T]he technological momentum toward nuclear proliferation is generated at the system level" (1984, 87).

8. In discussing the value of pursuing security by means of an alliance with great powers rather than developing one's own nuclear weapons, Solingen (2007, 13) says, "The domestic argument provides a *deeper* understanding of nuclear preferences insofar as it can also explain why alliance was chosen to begin with" (emphasis added).

9. Elsewhere in her book Solingen makes use of the causal-explanatory value of "necessary and sufficient conditions." For example, she rejects the liberal emphasis on democracy as an adequate explanation because "democratic regimes appear neither necessary nor sufficient for denuclearization" (Solingen 2007, 297).

10. To put it another way, the NPT clearly created another factor that scholars could use in trying to explain states' decisions; so as we examine the scholarly debate, it is reasonable to focus just on the period when that factor was available to them. But whether the formation of the NPT regime actually affected states' decisions is an empirical question that can be better understood by comparing cases with the pre-NPT cases when it was unquestionably not a factor.

11. With respect to the terminology employed, Singh and Way (2004, 879) say, "Existing arguments about the determinants of nuclear weapons proliferation do a

reasonable job of accounting for the data." They are arguing in such a way that the terms *accounting for* and *explain* are interchangeable.

12. This is an unusual use of *nationalism* in political science (Hymans 2006, 13, 24; and *Routledge Dictionary of Politics*).

13. Hymans acknowledges that what it takes for a state to acquire nuclear weapons is complex and has many steps. As a result, there are coding ambiguities regarding the dates at which states make the crucial decision to go nuclear. When is India properly said to have made the decision? Was it the decision to move toward the 1974 "peaceful" nuclear test, or was it the later decisions to weaponize that were crucial to the "weapons" test in 1998? In a latter publication, Hymans (2010) moves away from this benchmark.

14. Interestingly, in a 2008 paper Hymans regarded North Korea as a country that had been unsuccessful with its nuclear program, despite a test detonation in 2006. Following the 2008 tests, he said in 2010 that North Korea still lacked the "capacity to . . . produce reliable, deliverable nuclear warheads (2010, 171).

15. Jo and Gartzke (2007, 187n1) say in particular that Singh and Way (2004) do "not address the conditionality of nuclear weapons possession based on the presence of a nuclear weapons program."

16. Jo and Gartzke (2007, 169–70) add that pariah states also need the sense of security that they lose by becoming pariah states, especially since they do not have allies on whose conventional or nuclear weapons support they can rely.

17. The last measure is a log transformation of time trend since 1938—as newer proliferators benefit from all past knowledge and developments.

18. Jo and Gartzke describe one of the biggest surprises of the study—that facing a nuclear threat decreases the chance of a state instituting a nuclear weapons program and of acquiring nuclear weapons—which the authors say "may be because of the fear of preventive war" (2007, 184). But the negative association between the two factors needs explanation. Another instance is their observation that regional powers are at least slightly more likely to institute nuclear weapons programs than are nonpowers, but oddly, they are not really more likely to acquire nuclear weapons than are nonpowers who have weapons programs. The "disparity between the effect of status on major power and regional powers at the weapons proliferation stage . . . seems difficult to explain in terms of nominal prestige" (2007, 185). The statistical results need explanation, and in this case, none is readily found in the published literature.

19. The explanatory variables certainly could be divided into finer-grained categories, but it would be very difficult to see patterns. The survey makes clear where each author stands on the causal forces and actors.

Chapter 4

1. Richard Little (2007, 3) begins his most recent book by saying, "It is no surprise . . . that ever since the end of the Second World War a succession of key theorists in iconic

texts have attempted to demonstrate that the balance of power provides the foundations on which any overall understanding of international relations must start to build."

2. Morgenthau refers to the results of the Nye Committee's investigation (1934–36) of the US entry into World War I, which identified the role of business interests that profited from the war.

3. Organski (1958, 325) speculates about China surpassing the Soviet Union in a peaceful way, as it would be a result of the latter aiding the former's industrialization.

4. Virtually all of his critics, and especially Senator Taft, accused Wilson of militarism. Theodore Roosevelt was a rare exception who saw Wilson's policies as underestimating the necessity to wield power.

5. While Claude uses the term *balance of power* in his analysis of governance systems, he is, like other theorists, critical of the careless use of the term *balancing*. Like Morgenthau and Organski, Claude (1962, 17–18) argues that authors, though unconsciously, fail to use the term *balance of power* consistently, and that the equivocation leads not only to confusion but also, as in the case of A. J. P. Taylor, to invalid inferences (1962, 23–25). Claude even criticizes Morgenthau for inconsistent usage, despite the fact that Morgenthau is one of the few authors who is careful to distinguish the different meanings (1962, 26).

6. Surprisingly, Schweller does not note that his reference to the US presidential nomination uses *bandwagoning* in both a metaphorical and a nonmetaphorical manner, since the political parties used *physical* bandwagons.

7. Suppose an author divided states into those adept at the use of force, empathizers, those that use reason for problem solving, and the purely ideal oriented. To offer characterizations for the categories of state in the typology, the author chose names of Christian saints—George, Francis, and Thomas Aquinas, and Thomas More. Even though they were representing tendencies of social or political units, the connotations attached, and motivations ascribed, to those saints would create a certain sort of image of the system—and it would be quite a different image from that created by the use of wild animals like wolves, lions, and jackals.

8. Levy has also written important papers on preventive war, regime-type and war, diversionary war, prospect theory, and political psychology.

9. One difficulty here is that the United States is a hegemon across the board in military and economic measures. To sustain his point, Levy must emphasize the land-versus sea-based character of balance-of-power theories rather than the "overall military" versus naval assets of a hegemon. We should note that Levy adds the significant point that financial hegemons have different interests from continental hegemons; only the latter seek political control of other states and so are more threatening than financial hegemons.

10. When the theories are applied to smaller powers in regional contexts, the application may be impeded by the fact that the pure self-help principle does not fully hold,

as regional and small states can sometimes avoid balancing with other regional actors by appealing to outside great powers for security assistance.

11. In a footnote Levy (2004, 49n21) adds a fourth possibility, that no state has an interest in dominating the system. But Levy does not claim that it is advanced by actual theorists; even the arch-idealist Kant held that states seek power until the power is checked from the outside.

12. Although Levy is citing the difference in the threat level of land- versus sea-based hegemons, he does not cite Walt in this connection.

13. It is not clear in what "analytical power" consists. From the context, it may be the ability to explain and to predict strategies and behavioral outcomes. Levy invokes greater scope and specificity as criteria.

14. Brooks and Wohlforth (2005, 73n3) regard Pape's work as "the most ambitious theoretical effort to fully develop the soft-balancing concept."

15. Pape (2005, 29, citing Tertrais 2004) reports a French adviser saying, "The implementation of the U.S. strategy . . . tends to favor, rather than reduce, the development of the principal threats to which it is addressed: terrorism and proliferation." This might lead to objections to Pape's soft-balancing argument, since many states support the US nonproliferation and counterterrorism goals but perhaps believed that the Iraq invasion undermined those goals. Thus, opposition to the US policy was not a matter of soft balancing but rather was a helpful process aiming to advance the United States' own goals that the invasion would undercut (see Brooks and Wohlforth 2005; see also the discussion of their work in section 11 of this chapter).

16. Pape (2005, 24–25n31) criticizes Brooks and Wohlforth on this point, claiming that their evidence does not support their claims about those two factors. Prior to the Iraq War, other states talked about balancing measures, but they took no action: "Counterbalancing was limited to rhetoric" (Pape 2005, 21).

17. In discussing the trend away from a focus on power as the key variable in purportedly realist theories, Legro and Moravscik (1999, 6) say, "Many among the most prominent and thoughtful contemporary realists invoke instead variation in other exogenous influences on state behavior—state preferences, beliefs, and international institutions—to trump the direct and indirect effects of material power. Such factors are consistently treated as *more* important than power."

18. The widespread acceptance of the claim about the absence of counterbalancing alliances is not as straightforward as it might seem. Chapter 2 noted that theorists use various stratagems to avoid rejecting or altering their theories when predictions appear to be wrong (Tetlock 2005).

19. There are fourteen criteria, sixty-three total uses, and two groups of theorists. So the difference of two is a reasonable first cut at analysis, since the average use of each criterion by each school is two and a half.

20. All authors presumably endorse logical consistency as a criterion, though few say so explicitly. It is taken for granted in this study.

21. This latter point is less compelling given that empirical studies cannot execute ideal research designs; the reality of page limits and finite time intrude. Of course it would be possible to survey more authors within a given space if one were willing to cut back detailed explications of the coding decisions regarding authors' theoretical balancing stance and their uses of criteria. We might instead triple the number of authors on a single issue debate rather than study three debates. But that would yield very little perspective on levels of progress on answers and convergence on criteria. Consequently, the present research design considers ten to twelve authors on three different security issues. (Because there are five balance-of-power realist explanations and six alternative explanations, one might suggest adjusting the smaller group by one-fifth to get a more accurate comparison. However, because of the size of the differences just cited, a one-fifth adjustment will not alter any conclusions.

Chapter 5

1. This paper and Bremer's (discussed in Section 5) are among the five most cited ever in that journal.

2. In a later commentary, Doyle (2006) refers to his 1986 paper in the *American Political Science Review* that similarly regards claims about rational incentives as the driving forces for war and peace. Doyle (2006, 684) remarked that the last of the three 1980s papers on liberalism "bridged methodological divides. It reflected my long fascination with Carl Hempel's (1942) 'The Function of General Laws in History' and yet it gave a central place to interpreted, inter-subjective ideas and norms as causal factors. It lent itself to both quantitative and qualitative assessment. It argued that significant insights could be produced by the combination of institutions (representative republics), ideas (human rights), and interests (commerce, investment)."

3. Because the variables he uses have nonnegative integer values (0 is the minimum), Bremer uses an exponential Poisson rather than standard regression analysis.

4. Bremer compares the coding of the two data sets for the 6,675 cases in which they were values in both data sets; there was a very high level of similarity between them. There was a "Yule's Q coefficient of correlation" of +0.93" (Bremer 1992, 324n25).

5. The term *because* is used in this way on five different pages; references to *effects* are found on eleven of the forty-three pages. Bremer uses *condition* on six pages and in the subtitle of the paper.

6. Lake's paper is ranked the ninth most cited article among all IR articles in the top rated journals.

7. Kuhn contrasts these heuristic models with ontological ones.

8. In *Triangulating Peace* (2001), Russett and John Oneal offer statistical and theoretical support for the three hypotheses, the "legs" of the "Kantian tripod." In so doing, they explain why democracies do not fight wars against one another and why a system of democracies would be peaceful. Through the 1990s Russett and coauthors produced what Gartzke (2000, 192) says is "widely regarded as the leading quantitative research program in support of the democratic peace thesis." Russett, Oneal, and other coauthors discuss two counterarguments in detail: the DP phenomenon is an artifact of the Cold War, and it can be explained by the fact that liberal democracies' simply lack conflicting aims and have similar preferences.

9. It is not clear, however, in Owen's writings what exactly a causal mechanism must be like to be deemed "theoretically compelling."

10. The quotation here—"Democratic peace theory . . . also purports to explain . . ." (1994, 13)—contradicts Layne's comment that DP studies do not constitute a "theory" because the causal relationship is "neither proven nor . . . adequately explained" (1994, 5n1).

11. The fallacy, of affirming the consequent, is the invalid derivation of P from the premises "If P, then Q," and "Q."

12. Interestingly, this criticism seems to draw on the logic of Hempel's (1945) "paradox of the ravens." Spiro's inclination is to reject the view that the observation of a yellow tennis ball can confirm the hypothesis that all ravens are black. But he does not discuss this or consider the solutions that philosophers have offered to the paradox.

13. Elsewhere Spiro (1994, 60) seems to say that if the explanation does no better than randomness, we cannot reject the null hypothesis, and thus we cannot accept the explanation. Another counterexample to Spiro's position is that one can make up a highly ad hoc, unparsimonious, and patently false theory of explanatory principles—call it TC—that "predict" all past cases. The explanatory theory TC would be "untrue" but nicely predictive; in these two ways, it would parallel the randomness explanation for democratic-dyadic peace. Nevertheless, because of TC's abject failure to score well on any other important criteria of explanatory superiority, we would not use TC's excellent record of predictive success of past cases as a standard by which to reject all of the other explanations that are both serious and plausible, even if they do not predict quite as perfectly.

14. We also note that a recent *Teaching, Research, and International Policy* survey (Jordan et. al 2009) indicates that there are roughly equal numbers of academic liberals and realists in the United States and also in the English-speaking world overall, though there are small advantages for liberals in all groups (Jordan et al. 2009; Maliniak, Peterson, and Tierney 2012).

15. In all, Farber and Gowa coauthored three papers (1995, 1997a, 1997b) and wrote a fourth with Charles S. Gochman (Gochman, Farber, and Gowa 1996–97), and Gowa published single-author papers in 1995 and 1998 and a book *Ballots and Bullets*, in 1999.

Among the most often cited responses were those of Thompson and Tucker (1997) and Ray (1998).

16. See the context-dependence discussion in Chapter 2.

17. Farber and Gowa (1995, 137) cite Russett (1995, 172), who says that using lower levels of conflict as the indicator "constitutes a logical extension of the [DP] research program."

18. It is worth noting that Doyle describes various warfare "near misses" among liberal states (e.g., the United States and United Kingdom in the American Civil War, the Fashoda crisis) (216) and regards their jointly liberal character as what kept them from open warfare. Thus, given the mechanism he outlines, Doyle would regard the Correlates of War measure as the appropriate one.

19. Whether it is properly construed as a puzzle depends on the context and background beliefs, as discussed in Chapter 2.

20. We recall that according to Bremer's dyadic study of predictors of war, economic development ranked lower than democracy.

21. Gartzke does refer to necessary and sufficient conditions for war (in particular, to necessary conditions) in a more explicit way than other authors. But he does go beyond this purely extensional necessary-and-sufficient analysis.

22. Gartzke identifies coefficients by applying logit tests, although other tests are performed but not reported in the paper.

23. The five are *International Organization, International Security, International Studies Quarterly, Journal of Conflict Resolution,* and *Security Studies*. The *American Political Science Review* published a theoretical critique of the arguments for the dyadic hypothesis just over a decade ago (Rosato 2003), and in the next several years it published several short replies by Doyle (2005), Kinsella (2005), Rosato (2005), and Stantchev, Alexandrova, and Gartzke (2005). The *American Journal of Political Science*, not primarily an IR journal, published the Gartzke paper discussed earlier.

24. Further discussion of this sort of objection is taken up in Section 5 of Chapter 6, as is the specific issue of a specific set of "reference class" alternative answers that arises from the context.

25. The seven are as follows: (1) Democracies are not at all immune from fighting wars with nondemocracies. (2) Democracies tend to win a disproportionate share of the wars they fight. (3) When disputes do emerge, democratic dyads choose more peaceful processes of dispute settlement than do other pairings of states. (4) Democracies are more likely to initiate wars against autocracies than are autocracies against democracies. (5) In wars they initiate, democracies pay fewer costs in terms of human life and fight shorter wars than nondemocratic states. (6) Transitional democracies appear more likely to fight than stable regimes. (7) Larger democracies seem more constrained to avoid war than do smaller democracies (Bueno de Mesquita et al. 1999, 791).

26. These include works on democracy and terrorism by Abrahms (2007) and Brooks (2009), and on democracies and covert war by Downes and Lilley (2010). *International Security* has published works relating to DP but not questioning the dyadic hypothesis, such as Goldsmith (2008) on the relation of "full democracies," of the sort the dyadic hypothesis deals, to that of "partial democracies"; Downes on the claim that democracies are especially efficient in winning wars; Caverley (2010) on democracies' difficulties in winning small wars; and Kupchan and Trubowitz (2010) on whether Americans hold a liberal internationalist view.

Chapter 6

1. The aim of this comparative magnitude method is to reflect the logic of chi-square tests as closely as possible in the absence of data that satisfy the assumptions of the chi-square tests. (Chi-square tests for the three debates are not possible since such tests are invalid if any of the expected values is less than 5; and in these debates all of the expected values are less than 5.)

2. There is no meaningful association between authors' or schools' choices of criteria and the degree of agreement between proponents and opponents of balance-of-power explanations.

3. Philosophically empiricist social scientists make the trade-offs differently than scholars inclined toward scientific realism, as described in Section 4 of this chapter. It is possible that, for different sorts of questions, different prioritization among criteria is appropriate. Although this study adopts a set of criteria for finding the best explanation for patterns of progress, it does not endorse any universally applicable set of criteria or trade-offs for all problems.

4. In addition to the principle of measure-stipulation, other widely accepted principles of Duhem's are the principle of underdetermination of theory by data—which identifies limits on corroboration on the basis of the claim that a finite set of observations can never prove a particular theory (because there are always other theories, perhaps not yet formulated, that are also fully consistent the observations)—and Duhemian holism, which revolutionized the concept of "crucial experiment" and limited falsificationism by demonstrating that scientific theories can be tested only in conjunction with a set of auxiliary hypotheses and background beliefs (see Chernoff 2012). Duhem's view that explanation is primarily a psychological concept and not properly a part of physical science has generally been rejected.

5. I have offered this as a factor facilitating approach-to-consensus in the case of DP studies in other works (Chernoff 2004, 2005).

6. A caveat should be added in this connection. To investigate H_1 and progress in security studies, this study had to start from the very beginning to develop a database, which required choosing criteria for inclusion in the ranks of "most influential" works

in a debate (in Chapter 1), identifying the most common naturalist criteria in the philosophy of natural and social science (Chapter 2), and coding the works with respect to those criteria of theory choice (Chapters 3–5). While the criteria for choosing the publications that would be regarded as "most influential" were set out before analysis of the works was performed, which should thereby remove any conscious selection bias, it is possible that other scholars might produce different measures for "most influential," thus possibly leading to different results. The absence of a preexisting, widely accepted database constitutes a potential point of vulnerability of the present study.

7. Waltz has almost universally been interpreted as an empiricist, and the most relevant passages justify an interpretation of his position as empiricist and instrumentalist. But there have been some in recent years who dispute it; see Wæver (2009), Joseph (2010), and Humphreys (2013).

8. The context dependence of explanatory questions is not a uniquely "subjective" aspect of the social sciences that reveals its inferiority to the natural sciences. But Achinstein, like Hempel and Van Fraassen, is principally a philosopher of natural science, and as discussed in Chapter 2, all three specifically say that these pragmatic considerations hold of both the social and natural sciences. The importance of contrast classes is what makes memorable the (famous, apocryphal) answer the bank robber Willie Sutton offered when asked why he robbed banks: "That's where the money is."

REFERENCES

Abrahms, Max. 2007. "Why Democracies Make Superior Counterterrorists." *Security Studies* 16: 223–53.

Acheson, Dean. 1955. *A Democrat Looks at His Party.* New York: Harper.

Achinstein, Peter. 1971. *Law and Explanation: An Essay in the Philosophy of Science.* London: Oxford University Press.

Achinstein, Peter. 1977. "What Is an Explanation." *American Philosophical Quarterly* 14: 1–15.

Achinstein, Peter. 1984. "The Pragmatic Character of Explanation." *PSA: Proceedings of the Biennial Meeting of the Philosophy of Science Association* 2: 275–92.

Angell, Norman. 1933. *The Great Illusion.* New York: Putnam. London: Simpkin, Marshall, Hamilton, Kent & Co. First published in 1909 as *Europe's Optical Illusion.*

Armitage, Richard and Joseph S. Nye, Jr. 2004. "Introduction" *Securing a More Secure World.* (21 December): 1.

Aron, Raymond. 1968. *Peace and War.* New York: Praeger.

Austin, J. L. 1962. *How to Do Things with Words.* Cambridge, MA: Harvard University Press.

Babst, Dean. 1964. "Elective Governments: A Force for Peace." *Wisconsin Sociologist* 3: 9–14.

Babst, Dean. 1972. "A Force for Peace." *Industrial Research* 14 (April): 55–58.

Barnett, Lincoln. 1950. "The Meaning of Einstein's New Theory. *Life Magazine* (9 January): 22–25.

Barnett, Michael. 1996. "Identity and Alliance in the Middle East." In *Culture of National Security: Norms and Identity in World Politics,* edited by Peter J. Katzenstein, 400–431. New York: Columbia University Press.

Bayes, Thomas. 1764. "An Essay Toward Solving a Problem in the Doctrine of Chances." *Philosophical Transactions of the Royal Society of London* 53: 370–418.

Blainey, Geoffrey. 1973. *The Causes of War*. New York: Free Press.

Bloor, David. 1976. *Knowledge and Social Imagery*. London: Routledge.

Bohman, James. 1993. *The New Philosophy of Social Science: Problems of Indeterminacy*. Cambridge, MA: MIT Press.

Boyd, Richard. 1973. "Realism, Underdetermination, and a Causal Theory of Evidence." *Noûs* 7: 1–12.

Braithwaite, Richard B. 1953. *Scientific Explanation*. Cambridge: Cambridge University Press.

Brecher, Michael, and Jonathan Wilkenfeld. 1989. *Crisis, Conflict, and War*. Oxford, UK: Pergamon Press.

Brecher, Michael, Jonathan Wilkenfeld, and Sheila Moser. 1988. *Crises in the Twentieth Century: Handbook of International Crises*. 2 vols. Oxford, UK: Pergamon Books.

Bremer, Stuart A. 1992. "Dangerous Dyads: Conditions Affecting the Likelihood of Interstate War, 1816–1965." *Journal of Conflict Resolution* 36: 309–41.

Bridgman, Percy Williams. 1938. *The Logic of Modern Physics*. New York: Macmillan.

Brito, Dagobert L., and Michael D. Intriligator. 1996. "Proliferation and the Probability of War: A Cardinality Theorem." *Journal of Conflict Resolution* 40: 206–14.

Brodie, Bernard. 1946. "The Weapon: War in the Atomic Age and Implications for Military Policy." In *The Absolute Weapon*, edited Bernard Brodie, 70–110. New York: Harcourt, Brace.

Bromberger, Sylvan. 1966. "Why Questions." In *Mind and Cosmos*, edited by Robert G. Colodny, 86–111. Pittsburgh, PA: University of Pittsburgh Press.

Brooks, Risa. 2009. "Researching Democracy and Terrorism: How Political Access Affects Militant Activity." *Security Studies* 18: 756–88.

Brooks, Stephen G., and William C. Wohlforth. 2005. "Hard Times for Soft Balancing." *International Security* 30: 72–108.

Brooks, Stephen G., and William C. Wohlforth. 2008. *World out of Balance: International Relations and the Challenge of American Primacy*. Princeton, NJ: Princeton University Press.

Bueno de Mesquita, Bruce. 1981. *The War Trap*. New Haven, CT: Yale University Press.

Bueno de Mesquita, Bruce, and David Lalman. 1992. *War and Reason*. New Haven, CT: Yale University Press.

Bueno de Mesquita, Bruce, and William H. Riker. 1982. "An Assessment of the Merits of Selective Nuclear Proliferation." *Journal of Conflict Resolution* 26: 283–306.

Bueno de Mesquita, Bruce, James D. Morrow, Randolph M. Siverson, and Alastair Smith. 1999. "An Institutional Explanation of the Democratic Peace." *American Political Science Review* 94: 791–807.

Bull, Hedley. 1966. "International Theory: The Case for the Classical Approach." *World Politics* 18: 361–77.

Bull, Hedley. 1977. *The Anarchical Society: A Study of Order in World Politics.* New York: Columbia University Press.

Bush, George, and Brent Scowcroft. 1998. *A World Transformed.* New York: Knopf.

Carnap, Rudolf. 1950. *Logical Foundations of Probability.* Chicago: University of Chicago Press.

Carr, E. H. 1939. *The Twenty Years' Crisis: An Introduction to the Study of International Relations.* London: Macmillan.

Caverley, Jonathan D. 2010. "The Myth of Military Myopia: Democracy, Small Wars, and Vietnam." *International Security* 34: 119–57.

Chan, Steve. 1984. "Mirror, Mirror on the Wall . . . Are Democratic States More Pacific?" *Journal of Conflict Resolution* 28: 617–48.

Chernoff, Fred. 2002. "Scientific Realism as a Metatheory of International Relations." *International Studies Quarterly* 46: 189–207.

Chernoff, Fred. 2004. "The Study of Democratic Peace and Progress in International Relations." *International Studies Review* 6: 49–77.

Chernoff, Fred. 2005. *The Power of International Theory: Reforging the Link to Foreign Policy-Making Through Scientific Enquiry.* London: Routledge.

Chernoff, Fred. 2007a. "Methodological Pluralism and the Limits of Naturalism in the Study of Politics." In *Theory and Evidence in Comparative Politics and International Relations*, edited by R. N. Lebow and M. Lichbach, 107–41. New York: Palgrave Macmillan.

Chernoff, Fred. 2007b. *Theory and Metatheory in International Relations: Concepts and Contending Accounts.* New York: Palgrave Macmillan.

Chernoff, Fred. 2009. "Conventionalism as an Adequate Basis for Policy-Relevant IR Theory." *European Journal of International Relations* 15: 157–94.

Chernoff, Fred. 2012. "The Impact of Duhemian Principles on Social Science Testing and Progress." In *The Oxford Handbook of the Philosophy of the Social Sciences*, edited by H. C. Kincaid, 229–58. New York: Oxford University Press.

Chernoff, Fred. 2013. "Science, Progress, and Pluralism in the Study of International Relations." *Millennium: Journal of International Studies* 42: 346–66.

Choi, Seung-Whan. 2011. "Re-Evaluating Capitalist and Democratic Peace Models." *International Studies Quarterly* 55: 759–69.

Chubin, Shahram. 1994. *Iran's National Security Policy: Intentions, Capabilities, and Impact.* Washington, DC: Carnegie Endowment for International Peace.

Claude, Inis L. 1962. *Power and International Relations.* New York: Random House.

Cobden, Richard. 1836. *Russia.* Edinburgh, UK: William Tait.

Cobden, Richard. 1903. *Political Writings of Richard Cobden, Volume I.* London: T. Fisher Unwin. Originally published in 1867.

Copeland, Dale. 2000. *The Origins of Major Wars.* Ithaca, NY: Cornell University Press.

Crabb, Cecil V., and June Savoy. 1975. "Hans Morgenthau's Version of Realpolitik." *Political Science Reviewer* 5: 189–228.

Cummins, Robert. 1975. "Functional Analysis." *Journal of Philosophy* 72: 741–65.

Dafoe, Allan, John R. Oneal, and Bruce Russett. 2013. "The Democratic Peace: Weighing the Evidence and Cautious Inference." *International Studies Quarterly* 57: 201–14.

Davidson, Donald. 1980. *Essays on Actions and Events.* Oxford, UK: Clarendon Press.

Dessler, David. 2003. "Explanation and Scientific Progress." In *Progress in International Relations Theory: Appraising the Field*, edited by C. Elman and M. F. Elman, 381–404. Cambridge, MA: MIT Press.

de Vattel, Emmerich. 1916. *The Classics of International Law*, edited by James B. Scott. Washington, DC: Carnegie Institute.

DiFinetti, Bruno. 1972. *Probability, Induction and Statistics.* New York: Wiley.

Downes, Alexander, and Mary Lauren Lilley. 2010. "Overt Peace, Covert War? Covert Intervention and the Democratic Peace." *Security Studies* 19: 266–306.

Doyle, Michael. 1983a. "Kant, Liberal Legacies, and Foreign Affairs: Part 1." *Philosophy and Public Affairs* 12: 205–35.

Doyle, Michael. 1983b. "Kant, Liberal Legacies, and Foreign Affairs: Part 2." *Philosophy and Public Affairs* 12: 323–53.

Doyle, Michael. 1986. "Liberalism and World Politics." *American Political Science Review* 80: 1151–61.

Doyle, Michael. 2005. "Three Pillars of the Liberal Peace." *American Political Science Review* 99: 463–66.

Doyle, Michael. 2006. "Top Twenty Commentaries." *American Political Science Review* 100: 683–84.

Dray, William H. 1957. *Laws and Explanation in History.* London: Oxford University Press.

Dudley, Will. 2009. "Introduction." In *Hegel and History*, edited by Will Dudley, 1–14. Albany: State University of New York Press.

Duhem, Pierre. 1954. *The Aim and Structure of Physical Theory.* Translated by Philip P. Wiener. Princeton, NJ: Princeton University Press.

Durkheim, Émile. 1897. Review of *Essais sur la conception matérialiste de l'histoire*, by A. Labriola. *Revue Philosophique* (December): 200–205.

East, Maurice A., and Phillip M. Gregg. 1967. "Factors Influencing Cooperation and Conflict in the International System." *International Studies Quarterly* 11: 244–69.

Elster, Jon. 1979. *Ulysses and the Sirens: Studies in Rationality and Irrationality.* Cambridge: Cambridge University Press.

Elster, Jon. 1983. *Explaining Technical Change: A Case Study in the Philosophy of Science.* Cambridge: Cambridge University Press.

Elster, Jon. 1993. *Political Psychology.* Cambridge: Cambridge University Press.

Farber, Henry S., and Joanne Gowa. 1995. "Polities and Peace." *International Security* 20: 123–46.

Farber, Henry S., and Joanne Gowa. 1997a. "Building Bridges Abroad." *Journal of Conflict Resolution* 41: 455–56.

Farber, Henry S., and Joanne Gowa. 1997b. "Common Interests or Common Polities? Reinterpreting the Democratic Peace." *Journal of Politics* 59: 393–417.

Fearon, James D. 1998. "Domestic Politics, Foreign Policy, and Theories of International Relations." *Annual Review of Political Science* 1: 289–313.

Fetzer, James H. 2000. "The Paradoxes of Hempelian Explanation." In *Science, Explanation, and Rationality: Aspects of the Philosophy of Carl G. Hempel*, edited by James H. Fetzer, 111–37. Oxford: Oxford University Press.

Feyerabend, Paul. 1975. *Against Method: Outline of an Anarchistic Theory of Knowledge.* London: NLB; Atlantic Highlands, NJ: Humanities Press.

Finnemore, Martha. 1993. "International Organizations as Teachers of Norms: UNESCO and Science Policy." *International Organization* 47: 565–98.

Friedman, Michael. 1974. "Explanation and Scientific Understanding." *Journal of Philosophy* 71: 5–19.

Gaddis, John Lewis. 1987. *The Long Peace.* Oxford: Oxford University Press.

Garfinkle, Adam. 1981. *Forms of Explanation: Rethinking the Questions in Social Theory.* New Haven, CT: Yale University Press.

Gartzke, Erik. 1998. "Kant We All Just Get Along? Opportunity, Willingness and the Origins of the Democratic Peace." *American Journal of Political Science* 42: 1–27.

Gartzke, Erik. 2000. "Preferences and the Democratic Peace." *International Studies Quarterly* 44: 191–212.

Gartzke, Erik. 2001. "Democracy and the Preparation for War: Does Regime Change Affect States' Anticipation of Casualties?" *International Studies Quarterly* 45: 467–84.

Gartzke, Erik. 2007. "The Capitalist Peace" *American Journal of Political Science* 51: 166–91.

Gartzke, Erik, and Alex Weisiger. 2013. "Permanent Friends? Dynamic Difference and the Democratic Peace." *International Studies Quarterly* 57: 171–86.

Geller, Daniel S. 1990. "Nuclear Weapons, Deterrence, and Crisis Escalation." *Journal of Conflict Resolution* 34: 291–310.

George, Alexander L., and Andrew Bennett. 2005. *Case Studies and Theory Development in the Social Sciences.* Cambridge, MA: MIT Press.

Gibler, Douglas. 2007. "Bordering on Peace, Democracy, Territorial Issues and Conflict." *International Studies Quarterly* 51: 509–32.

Gibler, Douglas. 2012. *The Territorial Peace: Borders, State Development, and International Conflict.* Cambridge: Cambridge University Press.

Giere, Ronald. 1979. *Understanding Scientific Reasoning.* New York: Holt, Rinehart, and Winston.

Gillies, Donald. 1993. *The Philosophy of Science in the Twentieth Century: Four Central Themes.* Oxford, UK: Blackwell.

Gilpin, Robert. 1981. *War and Change in World Politics.* New York: Cambridge University Press.

Gochman, Charles S. 1990. "The Geography of Conflict: Militarized Interstate Disputes Since 1816." Paper presented at the thirty-first annual meeting of the International Studies Association, Washington, DC, April 10–14.

Gochman, Charles S., Henry S. Farber, and Joanne Gowa. 1996–97. "Democracy and Peace." *International Security* 21: 177–87.

Gochman, Charles, and Zeev Maoz. 1984. "Militarized Interstate Disputes, 1816–1976: Procedures, Patterns, and Insights." *Journal of Conflict Resolution* 28: 585–615.

Goertz, Gary, and Paul F. Diehl. 1993. "Enduring Rivalries: Theoretical Constructs and Empirical Patterns." *International Studies Quarterly* 37: 147–71.

Goldschmidt, Pierre. 2004. "Future Challenges for Nuclear Non-Proliferation." *IAEA Statements of the Deputy Directors General,* March 17.

Goldsmith, Arthur A. 2008. "Making the World Safe for Partial Democracy? Questioning the Premises of Democracy Promotion." *International Security* 33: 120–47.

Goodman, Nelson. 1947. "The Problem of Counterfactual Conditionals." *Journal of Philosophy* 44: 113–28.

Gowa, Joanne. 1995. "Democratic States and International Disputes." *International Organization* 49: 511–22.

Gowa, Joanne. 1998. "Politics at the Water's Edge: Parties, Voters, and the Use of Force Abroad." *International Organization* 52: 307–24.

Gowa, Joanne. 1999. *Ballots and Bullets: The Elusive Democratic Peace.* Princeton, NJ: Princeton University Press.

Haas, Michael. 1974. *International Conflict.* Indianapolis, IN: Bobbs-Merrill.

Hacking, Ian. 1983. *Representing and Intervening: Introductory Topics in the Philosophy of Natural Science.* Cambridge: Cambridge University Press.

Hands, D. Wade. 1990. "Second Thoughts on 'Second Thoughts.'" *Review of Political Economy* 2: 69–81.

Hanson, Marianne. 2002. "Nuclear Weapons as Obstacles to International Security." *International Relations* 16: 361–80.

Hanson, Norwood Russell. 1961. *Patterns of Discovery: An Inquiry into the Conceptual Foundations of Science.* Cambridge: Cambridge University Press.

Hempel, Carl G. 1942. "The Function of General Laws in History." *Journal of Philosophy* 39: 35–48.

Hempel, Carl G. 1945. "Studies in the Logic of Confirmation I." *Mind* 54: 1–26.

Hempel, Carl G. 1950. "Problems and Changes in the Empiricist Criterion of Meaning." *Revue Internationale de Philosophie* 41: 41–63.

Hempel, Carl G. 1965. *Aspects of Scientific Explanation and Other Essays.* New York: Free Press.

Hempel, Carl G., and Paul Oppenheim. 1948. "Studies in the Logic of Explanation." *Philosophy of Science* 15: 135–75.

Hintze, Otto. 1975. "The Origins of the Modern Ministerial System: A Comparative Study." In *The Historical Essays of Otto Hintze*, edited by Felix Gilbert, 216–66. New York: Oxford University Press.

Hirschman, Albert O. 1970. *Exit, Voice, and Loyalty: Responses to Decline in Firms, Organizations, and States.* Cambridge, MA: Harvard University Press.

Hobson, John A. 1926. *Free Thought in the Social Sciences.* New York: Macmillan.

Hollis, Martin, and Steve Smith. 1991. *Explaining and Understanding International Relations.* Oxford: Oxford University Press.

Humphreys, Adam R. C. 2013. "Waltz and the World: Neorealism as International Political Theory?" *International Politics* 50: 863–79.

Huth, Paul, and Todd L. Allee. 2002. *Democratic Peace and Territorial Conflicts in the Twentieth Century.* Cambridge: Cambridge University Press.

Hymans, Jacques. 2006. *The Psychology of Nuclear Proliferation: Identity, Emotions, and Foreign Policy.* Cambridge: Cambridge University Press.

Hymans, Jacques. 2008. "Assessing North Korean Nuclear Intentions and Capacities: A New Approach." *Journal of East Asian Studies* 8: 259–92.

Hymans, Jacques. 2010. "When Does a State Become a 'Nuclear Weapon State'? An Exercise in Measurement Validation." *Nonproliferation Review* 17: 161–80.

International Atomic Energy Agency. 1970. "Treaty on the Nonproliferation of Nuclear Weapons." Informational circular. April 22.

Jervis, Robert. 1978. "Cooperation Under the Security Dilemma." *World Politics* 30: 167–214.

Jervis, Robert. 1982. "Security Regimes." *International Organization* 36: 357–78.

Jo, Dong-Joon, and Erik Gartzke. 2007. "Determinants of Nuclear Weapons Proliferation." *Journal of Conflict Resolution* 51: 167–94.

Jordan, Richard, Daniel Maliniak, Amy Oakes, Susan Peterson, and Michael J. Tierney. 2009. *Teaching, Research, and International Policy: TRIP Project.* Williamsburg, VA: Institute for the Theory and Practice of International Relations, College of William and Mary.

Joseph, Jonathan. 2010. "Is Waltz a Realist?" *International Relations* 24: 481.

Kahn, Herman. 1962. *Thinking the Unthinkable.* New York: Horizon Press.

Kant, Immanuel. 1939. *Perpetual Peace.* New York: Columbia University Press. Originally published, Konigsberg: Friedrich Nicolovius, 1795.

Kant, Immanuel. 1963. "*Idea for a Universal History from a Cosmopolitan Point of View.*" In *On History*, translated by Lewis White Beck. Indianapolis, IN: Bobbs-

Merrill. Originally published in 1784 as "Idee zu einer allgemeinen Geschichte in weltbürgerlicher Absicht," *Berlinische Monatsschrifte* 4.

Kaplan, Morton. 1957. *System and Process in International Relations.* New York: Wiley.

Kapur, Ashok. 1979. *International Nuclear Proliferation.* New York: Praeger.

Karl, David J. 1996. "Proliferation Pessimism and Emerging Nuclear Powers." *International Security* 21: 87–119.

Katzenstein, Peter J. 1996. *The Culture of National Security: Norms and Identity in World Politics.* New York: Columbia University Press.

Kegley, Charles W., Gregory A. Raymond, and Richard A. Skinner. 1980. "A Comparative Analysis of Nuclear Armaments." In *Threats, Weapons, and Foreign Policy*, edited by Pat McGowan, and Charles W. Kegley Jr., 231–58. Thousand Oaks, CA: Sage Publications.

Keohane, Robert O., and Joseph S. Nye. 1975. "International Independence and Integration." In *Handbook of Political Science*, edited by Nelson W. Polsby and Fred I. Greenstein, 8: 363–414. Reading, MA: Addison-Wesley.

Keohane, Robert O., and Joseph S. Nye. 1977. *Power and Interdependence: World Politics in Transition.* Boston: Little, Brown.

Keynes, John Maynard. 1929. *The Treatise on Probability.* London: Macmillan.

Kim, Jaegwon. 1993. *Supervenience and Mind.* Cambridge: Cambridge University Press.

Kim, Jaegwon. 1999. "Making Sense of Emergence." *Philosophical Studies* 95: 3–36.

Kincade, William H. 1995. *Nuclear Proliferation: Diminishing Threat?* Colorado Springs, CO: Institute for National Security Studies, US Air Force.

Kincaid, Harold. 1996. *Philosophical Foundations of the Social Sciences: Analyzing Controversies in Social Research.* Cambridge: Cambridge University Press.

Kinoshita, Joyce. 1990. "How Do Scientific Explanations Explain?" *Royal Institute of Philosophy Supplement* 27: 297–311.

Kinsella, David. 2005. "No Rest for the Democratic Peace." *American Political Science Review* 99: 467–72.

Kitcher, Philip. 1981. "Explanatory Unification." *Philosophy of Science* 48: 507–31.

Kuhn, Thomas S. 1970. *The Structure of Scientific Revolutions.* 2nd ed. Chicago: University of Chicago Press.

Kuhn, Thomas S. 2000. "Reflections on My Critics." In *The Road Since Structure: Philosophical Essays, 1970–1993*, edited by James Conant and John Haugeland. Chicago: University of Chicago Press.

Kupchan, Charles A., and Peter L. Trubowitz. 2010. "The Illusion of Liberal Internationalism's Revival." *International Security* 35: 95–109.

Kyburg, Henry E., Jr. 1990. *Science and Reason.* Oxford: Oxford University Press.

Lakatos, Imre. 1978. *The Methodology of Scientific Research Programmes.* Vol. 1 of *Philosophical Papers.* Cambridge: Cambridge University Press.

Lake, David A. 1992. "Powerful Pacifists: Democratic States and War." *American Political Science Review* 86: 24–37.

Lane, Frederic C. 1979. *Profits from Power: Readings in Protection Rent and Violence-Controlling Enterprises.* Albany: State University of New York Press.

Layne, Christopher. 1994. "Kant or Cant? The Myth of Democratic Peace." *International Security* 19: 5–49.

Legro, Jeffrey W., and Andrew Moravscik. 1999. "Is Anybody Still a Realist?" *International Security* 24: 5–55.

Leibniz, Gottfried Wilhelm, Freiherr von. 1930. *The Monadology of Leibniz.* Introduction and commentary and supplementary essays by Herbert Wildon Carr. Los Angeles: School of Philosophy, University of Southern California.

Leon, David Pak Yue. 2010. "Reductionism, Emergence, and Explanation in International Relations Theory." In *Scientific Realism and International Relations*, edited by Jonathan Joseph and Colin Wight, 31–50. New York: Palgrave Macmillan.

Leplin, Jarrett. 1997. *A Novel Defence of Scientific Realism.* Oxford: Oxford University Press.

Levy, Jack S. 1985. "Theories of General War." *World Politics* 37: 344–74.

Levy, Jack S. 2003. "Balances and Balancing: Concepts, Propositions and Research Design." In *Realism and the Balancing of Power: A New Debate*, edited by John A. Vasquez and Colin Elman, 128–53. Upper Saddle River, NJ: Prentice Hall.

Levy, Jack S. 2004. "What Do Great Powers Balance Against and When?" In *Balance of Power: Theory and Practice in the 21st Century*, edited by T. V. Paul, James Wirtz, and Michel Fortmann, 29–51. Stanford, CA: Stanford University Press.

Lippmann, Walter. 1955. *Essays in the Public Philosophy.* Boston: Little, Brown.

Liska, George. 1962. *Nations in Alliance: The Limits of Interdependence.* Baltimore: Johns Hopkins University Press.

Little, Daniel. 1991. *Varieties of Social Explanation.* Boulder, CO: Westview Press.

Little, Richard. 2007. *Balance of Power in International Relations: Metaphors, Myths and Models.* Cambridge: Cambridge University Press.

Locke, John. 1952. *An Essay Considering the True Original Extent, and End, of Civil Government: The Second Treatise of Government*, edited with an introduction by Thomas Peardon. New York: Liberal Arts Press.

MacIntyre, Alasdair. 1967. "The Idea of a Social Science." *Proceedings of the Aristotelian Society* (41, suppl.): 95–114.

MacIntyre, Alasdair. 1971. *Against the Self-Images of the Age: Essays on Ideology and Philosophy.* London: Duckworth.

Maliniak, Daniel, Susan Peterson, and Michael J. Tierney. 2012. *Teaching, Research, and Policy Views of International Relations Faculty in 20 Countries.* Williamsburg, VA: College of William and Mary.

Malinowski, Bronislaw. 1942. *Magic, Science and Religion, and Other Essays*. Boston: Beacon Press.

Mansfield, Edward D. 1988. "The Distribution of Wars over Time." *World Politics* 41: 21–51.

Mansfield, Edward D., and Jack Snyder. 1995a. "Democratization and the Danger of War." *International Security* 20: 5–38.

Mansfield, Edward D., and Jack Snyder. 1995b. "Democratization and War." *Foreign Affairs* 74: 79–97.

Mansfield, Edward D., and Jack Snyder. 2005. *Why Democracies Go to War*. Cambridge, MA: MIT Press.

Maoz, Zeev, and Bruce Russett. 1993. "Normative and Structural Causes of Democratic Peace, 1946–1986." *American Political Science Review* 87: 624–38.

Maxwell, Grover. 1962. "The Ontological Status of Theoretical Entities." In *Scientific Explanation, Space, and Time*, vol. 3 of *Minnesota Studies in the Philosophy of Science*, edited by H. Feigl and G. Maxwell, 3–15. Minneapolis: University of Minnesota Press.

MccGwire, Michael. 1994. "Is There a Future for Nuclear Weapons?" *International Affairs* 70: 211–28.

Mearsheimer, John J. 1990. "Back to the Future: Instability in Europe after the Cold War." *International Security* 15: 216–22.

Mearsheimer, John J. 1994–95. "The False Promise of International Institutions." *International Security* 19: 5–49.

Mearsheimer, John J. 2001. *The Tragedy of Great Power Politics*. New York: W. W. Norton.

Mearsheimer, John J., and Stephen M. Walt. 2007. *The Israel Lobby and U.S. Foreign Policy*. New York: Farrar, Straus, and Giroux.

Mearsheimer, John, and Stephen Walt. 2012. "Mr. Obama Must Take a Stand Against Israel over Iran." *Financial Times*, March 4.

Merton, Robert K. 1968. *Social Theory and Social Structure*. New York: Free Press.

Meyer, Stephen M. 1984. *The Dynamics of Nuclear Proliferation*. Chicago: University of Chicago Press.

Mill, John Stuart. 1998. *Utilitarianism*. Oxford: Oxford University Press. First published in 1861.

Morgenthau, Hans J. 1954. *Politics Among Nations: The Struggle for Power and Peace*. New York: Knopf.

Morgenthau, Hans J. 1961. *Purpose of American Politics*. New York: Knopf.

Morgenthau, Hans J. 1972. *Politics Among Nations: The Struggle for Power and Peace*. 5th ed. New York: Knopf.

Most, Benjamin A., and Harvey Starr. 1989. *Inquiry, Logic, and International Politics*. Columbia: University of South Carolina Press.

Mousseau, Michael. 2003. "The Nexus of Market Society, Liberal Preferences, and Democratic Peace: Interdisciplinary Theory and Evidence." *International Studies Quarterly* 47: 483–510.

Mousseau, Michael. 2009. "The Social Market Roots of Democratic Peace." *International Security* 33: 52–86.

Mousseau, Michael. 2013. "The Democratic Peace Unraveled: It's the Economy." *International Studies Quarterly* 57: 186–97.

Mueller, John. 1973. *War, Presidents, and Public Opinion.* New York: Wiley.

Mueller, John. 1986. "Containment and the Decline of the Soviet Empire: Some Tentative Comments on the End of the World as We Know It." Paper presented at the International Studies Association Convention, Anaheim, CA, March 28.

Nagel, Ernest. 1961. *The Structure of Science: Problems in the Logic of Scientific Explanation.* New York: Harcourt, Brace, and World.

Nexon, Daniel. 2009. "The Balance of Power in the Balance." *World Politics* 62: 330–59.

Nizamani, Haider K. 2000. *Roots of Rhetoric: Politics of Nuclear Weapons in India and Pakistan.* Westport, CT: Praeger.

Nye, Joseph S. 2004. *Soft Power: The Means to Success in World Politics.* New York: Public Affairs.

Oneal, John R., and Bruce M. Russett. 1997. "The Classical Liberals Were Right: Democracy, Interdependence, and Conflict, 1950–85." *International Studies Quarterly* 41: 267–93.

Oneal, John R., and Bruce M. Russett. 1999. "Is the Liberal Peace Just an Artifact of Cold War Interests? Assessing Recent Critiques." *International Interactions* 25: 1–29.

Oneal, John R., and Bruce M. Russett. 2001. "Clear and Clean: The Fixed Effects of Democracy and Economic Interdependence." *International Organization* 55: 469–85.

Oren, Ido. 1995. "The Subjectivity of the 'Democratic' Peace: Changing U.S. Perceptions of Imperial Germany." *International Security* 20: 147–84.

Organski, A. F. K. 1958. *World Politics.* New York: Knopf.

Organski, A. F. K., and Jacek Kugler. 1980. *The War Ledger.* Chicago: University of Chicago Press.

Owen, John. 1994. "How Liberalism Produces Democratic Peace." *International Security* 9: 87–125.

Pape, Robert. 2005. "Soft Balancing Against the United States." *International Security* 30: 7–45.

Parsons, Talcott. 1969. *Politics and Social Structure.* New York: Free Press.

Paul, T. V. 2000. *Power Versus Prudence: Why Nations Forgo Nuclear Weapons.* Montreal: McGill-Queen's University Press.

Paul, T. V. 2003. "Systemic Conditions and Security Cooperation: Explaining the Persistence of the Nuclear Non-Proliferation Regime." *Cambridge Review of International Affairs* 16: 135–55.

Paul, T. V. 2004. "Introduction: The Enduring Axioms of Balance of Power Theory and Their Contemporary Relevance." In *Balance of Power,* edited by T. V. Paul, James J. Wirtz, and Michel Fortmann, 1–25. Stanford, CA: Stanford University Press.

Payne, Keith B. 1997. *Deterrence in the Second Nuclear Age.* Lexington: University Press of Kentucky.

Perkovich, George. 1999. *India's Nuclear Bomb: The Impact on Global Proliferation.* Berkeley: University of California Press.

Pomper, Gerald. 1963. *Nominating the President: The Politics of Conventional Choice.* Evanston, IL: Northwestern University Press.

Popper, Karl R. 1959. *The Logic of Scientific Discovery.* New York: Basic Books. First published in 1935.

Popper, Karl R. 1965. *Conjectures and Refutations: The Growth of Scientific Knowledge.* New York: Harper and Row.

Potter, William C. 1982. *Nuclear Power and Nonproliferation: An Interdisciplinary Perspective.* Cambridge, MA: Oelgeschlager, Gunn, and Hain.

Putnam, Hilary. 1962. "What Theories Are Not." In *Logic, Methodology, and Philosophy of Science,* edited by E. Nagel, P. Suppes, and A. Tarski, 240–51. Stanford, CA: Stanford University Press.

Putnam, Hilary. 1982. "Three Kinds of Scientific Realism." *Philosophical Quarterly* 32: 195–200.

Quester, George. 1973. *The Politics of Nuclear Proliferation.* Baltimore: Johns Hopkins University Press.

Quine, Willard van Orman. 1951. "Two Dogmas of Empiricism." *Philosophical Review* 60: 20–43.

Quine, Willard van Orman. 1969. *Ontological Reality and Other Essays.* New York: Columbia University Press.

Quine, Willard van Orman, and J. S. Ullian. 1978. *The Web of Belief.* New York: Random House.

Radcliffe-Brown, Alfred Reginald. 1965. *Structure and Function in Primitive Society: Essays and Addresses.* New York: Free Press.

Ramirez, Francisco O., and John Boli. 1982. "Global Patterns of Educational Institutionalization." In *Comparative Education,* edited by Philip Altbach, Robert Arnove, and Gail Kelley, 15–38. New York: Macmillan.

Ramsey, F. P. 1990. "Truth and Probability." In *Philosophical Papers,* edited by D. H. Mellor, 52–96. Cambridge: Cambridge University Press. Original work published in 1926.

Ramsey, F. P. 1931. "Truth and Probability." In *The Foundations of Mathematics and Other Logical Essays,* edited by R. B. Braithwaite, 156–98. London: Kegan, Paul, Tranch, Trubner & Co.

Ray, James Lee. 1990. "Friends as Foes: International Conflict and Wars Between Formal Allies." In *Prisoners of War,* edited by Charles S. Gochman and Alan Ned Sabrosky, 73–92. Lexington, MA: Lexington Books.

Ray, James Lee. 1998. "Does Democracy Cause Peace?" *Annual Review of Political Science* 1: 27–46.

Ray, James Lee. 2013. "War on Democratic Peace." *International Studies Quarterly* 57: 198–200.

Reichenbach, Hans. 1971. *The Direction of Time.* Berkeley: University of California Press.

Reiter, Dan, and Allen C. Stam III. 2002. *Democracies at War.* Princeton, NJ: Princeton University Press.

Resnik, David. 1994. "Methodological Conservatism and Social Epistemology." *International Studies in the Philosophy of Science* 8: 247–64.

Richardson, Lewis F. 1960. *The Statistics of Deadly Quarrels.* Pittsburgh, PA: Boxwood.

Rohrlich, Fritz. 2001. "Cognitive Scientific Realism." *Philosophy of Science* 68: 185–202.

Rosato, Sebastian. 2003. "The Flawed Logic of Democratic Peace Theory." *American Political Science Review* 97: 585–602.

Rosato, Sebastian. 2005. "Explaining the Democratic Peace." *American Political Science Review* 99: 467–72.

Rosenau, James. 1980. *The Scientific Study of International Relations.* London: Pinter.

Rothstein, Robert L. 1968. *Alliances and Small Powers.* New York: Columbia University Press.

Rummel, Rudolf J. 1968. "Domestic Attributes and Foreign Conflict." In *Quantitative International Politics: Insights and Evidence,* edited by J. David Singer, 187–214. New York: Free Press.

Rummel, Rudolf J. 1975–81. *Understanding Conflict and War.* Beverly Hills, CA: Sage Publications.

Rummel, Rudolf J. 1979. *National Attributes and Behavior: Dimensions, Linkages and Groups, 1950–1965.* Beverly Hills, CA: Sage Publications.

Rummel, Rudolf J. 1983. "Libertarianism and International Violence." *Journal of Conflict Resolution* 27: 27–71.

Russell, Bertrand. 1918. "On the Notion of Cause." In *Mysticism and Logic and Other Essays.* New York: Longmans, 132–51.

Russett, Bruce M. 1990. *Controlling the Sword: The Democratic Governance of National Security.* Cambridge, MA: Harvard University Press.

Russett, Bruce M. 1993. *Grasping the Democratic Peace: Principles for a Post–Cold War World.* Princeton, NJ: Princeton University Press.

Russett, Bruce M. 1995. "The Democratic Peace: And Yet It Moves." *International Security* 19: 164–75.

Russett, Bruce M., and John R. Oneal. 2001. *Triangulating Peace: Democracy, Trade and International Organization.* New York: W. W. Norton.

Sagan, Scott. 1996–97. "Why Do States Build Nuclear Weapons?" *International Security* 21: 54–86.

Sagan, Scott, and Kenneth N. Waltz. 2003. *The Spread of Nuclear Weapons: A Debate Renewed.* New York: W. W. Norton.

Salmon, Wesley C. 1971. *Statistical Explanation and Statistical Relevance.* Pittsburgh, PA: University of Pittsburgh Press.

Salmon, Wesley C. 1984. *Scientific Explanation and the Causal Structure of the World.* Princeton, NJ: Princeton University Press.

Scheinman, Lawrence. 1965. *Atomic Energy Policy in France Under the Fourth Republic.* Princeton, NJ: Princeton University Press.

Schelling, Thomas C. 1963. *The Strategy of Conflict.* Cambridge, MA: Harvard University Press.

Schelling, Thomas C. 1966. *Arms and Influence.* New Haven, CT: Yale University Press.

Schweller, Randall L. 1992. "Domestic Structure and Preventive War: Are Democracies More Pacific?" *World Politics* 44: 235–69.

Schweller, Randall L. 1994. "Bandwagoning for Profit: Bringing the Revisionist State Back In." *International Security* 19: 72–107.

Schweller, Randall L. 1996. "Neorealism's Status-Quo Bias: What Security Dilemma?" *Security Studies* 5: 90–121.

Schweller, Randall L. 2006. *Unanswered Threats: Political Constraints on the Balance of Power.* Princeton, NJ: Princeton University Press.

Scriven, Michael. 1959. "The Logic of Criteria." *Journal of Philosophy* 56: 857–67.

Sellars, Wilfred. 1956. "Empiricism and the Philosophy of Mind." In *Minnesota Studies in the Philosophy of Science*, edited by H. Feigl and M. Scriven, 253–329. Minneapolis: University of Minnesota Press.

Sen Gupta, Bhabani. 1978. "Dilemma Without Anguish: India, Morarji and the Bomb." In *Perspectives of India's Nuclear Policy*, edited by T. T. Poulouse, 224–39. New Delhi: Young Asia Publications.

Sheikh, Ali. T. 1994. "Pakistan." In *Nuclear Proliferation After the Cold War*, edited by Mitchell Reiss and Robert S. Litwak, 191–206. Cambridge, MA: Ballinger.

Simpson, E. H. 1951. "The Interpretation of Interaction in Contingency Tables." *Journal of the Royal Statistical Society B* 13: 238–41.

Singer, David J. 1965. "Introduction." In *Human Behavior and International Politics: Contributions from the Social-Psychological Sciences*, edited by David J. Singer, 1–20. Chicago: Rand McNally.

Singer, David J. 1966. "The Behavioral Science Approach to International Relations: Payoff and Prospect." *SAIS Review* 12: 12–20.

Singer, David J. 1969. "The Incomplete Theorist: Insight Without Evidence." In *Contending Approaches to International Politics*, edited by K. Knorr and J. N. Rosenau, 62–86. Princeton, NJ: Princeton University Press.

Singh, Sonali, and Christopher Way. 2004. "The Correlates of Nuclear Proliferation: A Quantitative Test." *Journal of Conflict Resolution* 48: 859–85.

Small, Melvin, and J. David Singer. 1976. "The War-Proneness of Democratic Regimes, 1860–1965." *Jerusalem Journal of International Relations* 1: 50–69.

Smart, J. J. C. 1990. "Explanation—Opening Address." In *Explanation and its Limits*, edited by Dudley Knowles, 1–19. Cambridge: Cambridge University Press.

Snyder, Jack. 1990. "Averting Anarchy in the New Europe." *International Security* 14: 5–41.

Snyder, Jack L. 2000. *From Voting to Violence: Democratization and Nationalist Conflict*. New York: W. W. Norton.

Solingen, Etel. 1994. "The Political Economy of Nuclear Restraint." *International Security* 19: 126–69.

Solingen, Etel. 2007. *Nuclear Logics: Contrasting Paths in East Asia and the Middle East*. Princeton, NJ: Princeton University Press.

Spiro, David E. 1994. "The Insignificance of the Liberal Peace." *International Security* 19: 50–86.

Stantchev, Branislav L., Anna Alexandrova, and Erik Gartzke. 2005. "Probabilistic Causality, Selection Bias, and the Logic of the Democratic Peace." *American Political Science Review* 99: 459–62.

Strevens, Michael. 2009. *Depth: An Account of Scientific Explanation*. Cambridge, MA: Harvard University Press.

Suchman, Marc C., and Dana P. Eyre. 1992. "Military Procurement as Rational Myth: Notes on the Social Construction of Weapons Proliferation." *Sociological Forum* 7: 137–61.

Suganami, Hidemi. 1996. *On the Causes of War*. Oxford, UK: Clarendon.

Suganami, Hidemi. 2002. "Explaining War: Some Critical Observations." *International Relations* 16: 307–26.

Tertrais, Bruno. 2004. *War Without End: A View from Abroad*, translated by Franklin Philip. London: New Press.

Tetlock, Philip E. 2005. *Expert Political Judgment: How Good Is It? How Can We Know?* Princeton, NJ: Princeton University Press.

Thayer, Bradley A. 2000. "Bringing in Darwin: Evolutionary Theory, Realism and International Politics." *International Security* 25: 124–51.

Thayer, Bradley A. 2004. *Darwin and International Relations: On the Evolutionary Origins of War and Ethnic Conflict*. Lexington: University Press of Kentucky.

Thompson, William R., and Richard Tucker. 1997. "A Tale of Two Democratic Peace Critiques." *Journal of Conflict Resolution* 41: 428–54.

Toulmin, Stephen. 1963. *Foresight and Understanding: An Enquiry Into the Aims of Science*. New York: Harper and Row.

Toulmin, Stephen. 1977. "From Form to Function: Philosophy and History of Science in the 1950s and Now." *Daedalus* 106: 143–62.

US Department of State, Committee on Atomic Energy. 1946. *A Report on the International Control of Atomic Energy*. Garden City, NY: Doubleday.

Van Fraassen, Bas C. 1980. *The Scientific Image*. New York: Oxford University Press.

Van Fraassen, Bas C. 2002. *The Empirical Stance*. New Haven, CT: Yale University Press.

Van Fraassen, Bas C. 2008. *Scientific Representation: Paradoxes of Perspective.* Clarendon, UK: Oxford University Press.

Vasquez, John A. 1993. *The War Puzzle.* Cambridge: Cambridge University Press.

Vasquez, John A. 1997. "The Realist Paradigm and Degenerative Versus Progressive Research Programs: An Appraisal of Neotraditional Research on Waltz's Balancing Proposition." *American Political Science Review* 91: 899–912.

Vasquez, John A. 1998. *The Power of Power Politics: From Classical Realism to Neotraditionalism.* Cambridge: Cambridge University Press.

Vasquez, John A., and Douglas Gibler. 2001. "The Steps to War in Asia: 1931–1945." *Security Studies* 10: 1–45.

Von Mises, Richard. 1964. *Mathematical Theory of Probability and Statistics.* New York: Academic Press.

Von Wright, G. H. 1971. *Explanation and Understanding.* Ithaca, NY: Cornell University Press.

Wæver, Ole. 2009. "Waltz's Theory of Theory." *International Relations* 23: 206–9.

Walt, Stephen M. 1985. "Alliance Formation and the Balance of World Power." *International Security* 9: 3–43.

Walt, Stephen M. 1987. *The Origins of Alliances.* Ithaca, NY: Cornell University Press.

Walt, Stephen M. 1998. "International Relations: One World, Many Theories." *Foreign Policy* 110: 29–47.

Waltz, Kenneth N. 1959. *Man, the State and War.* New York: Columbia University Press.

Waltz, Kenneth N. 1964. "The Stability of a Bipolar World." *Daedalus* 93: 881–909.

Waltz, Kenneth N. 1979. *Theory of International Politics.* Reading, MA: Addison-Wesley.

Waltz, Kenneth N. 1981. *The Spread of Nuclear Weapons: More May Be Better.* London: International Institute for Strategic Studies.

Waltz, Kenneth N. 1990. "Nuclear Myths and Political Realities." *American Political Science Review* 84: 731–45.

Waltz, Kenneth N. 1996. "International Politics Is Not Foreign Policy." *Security Studies* 6: 54–57.

Waltz, Kenneth N. 1997. "Evaluating Theories." *American Political Science Review* 91: 913–17.

Watkins, J. W. N. 1973. "Ideal Types and Historical Explanation." In *The Philosophy of Social Explanation*, edited by Alan Ryan, 82–104. Oxford: Oxford University Press.

Weber, Max. 1947. *The Theory of Social and Economic Organization*, translated by A. M. Henderson and Talcott Parsons. New York: Oxford University Press.

Weede, Erich. 1984. "Democracy and War Involvement." *Journal of Conflict Resolution* 28: 649–64.

Wendt, Alexander. 1999. *Social Theory of International Politics.* New York: Cambridge University Press.

Wilkenfeld, Jonathan. 1968. "Domestic and Foreign Conflict Behavior of Nations." *Journal of Peace Research* 1: 55–69.

Winch, Peter. 1958. *The Idea of a Social Science.* London: Routledge and Paul.

Wittgenstein, Ludwig. 1953. *Philosophical Investigations,* translated by G. E. M. Anscombe. Oxford: Blackwell.

Wohlforth, William C. 1999. "The Stability of a Unipolar World." *International Security* 24: 5–41.

Wohlstetter, Albert, Thomas A. Brown, Gregory Jones, David McGarvey, Henry Rowen, Vincent Taylor, and Roberta Wohlstetter. 1976. "Moving Toward Life in a Nuclear Armed Crowd?" Pan Heuristics/Science Applications report for the US Arms Control and Disarmament Agency. ACDA/PAB-263, December 4, 1975, revised April 22, 1976.

Wolfers, Arnold. 1952. "'National Security' as an Ambiguous Symbol." *Political Science Quarterly* 67: 481–502.

Woodward, James. 2003. *Making Things Happen: A Causal Theory of Explanation.* Oxford: Oxford University Press.

Woodward, James. 2006. "Sensitive and Insensitive Causation." *Philosophical Review* 115: 1–50.

Wright, Larry. 1973. "Functions." *Philosophical Review* 83: 139–68.

Wright, Quincy. 1942. *A Study of War.* Chicago: University of Chicago Press.

INDEX

Abrahms, Max, 282n26
Acheson, Dean, 137–38
Achinstein, Peter, 258; on contextual factors in explanation, 260, 283n8; on explanation and causality, 43–44; on ontology, 48
Alexandrova, Anna, 281n23
alliance formation debate. *See* balance of power
ambiguity of questions, 30, 257–61, 266. *See also* Suganami, Hidemi; Van Fraassen, Bas C.
American Civil War, 137–38, 210, 214, 281n18
American Revolutionary War, 127
Angell, Norman, 225
approach-to-consensus as indicator of progress, vii–viii, 3, 7, 8, 33, 70, 177, 180, 232, 233–37, 241–47, 249, 250–54, 265–66, 282n5
Arab-Israeli 1967 War, 191
Argentina, 76, 92, 97–99
Aristotle, 14, 70; on causal explanation, 38, 50–51, 274n14
Aron, Raymond, 192
Athens, 254
Austin, J. L., 34. *See also* speech acts
Austria, 163, 166
Austria-Hungary, 141, 157, 163

Babst, Dean, 182, 186
Bacon, Francis, 16, 28
balance-of-interest theory, 157, 160. *See also* Schweller, Randall L.
balance of power: analysis of results of debate, 244–45; approach-to-consensus of theories of, 175–77; core principles and standard claims of theory, 124–25; debate over, 123–80; meanings of by different authors, 10, 125; overlap of criteria of explanatory superiority and of consensus, 177–80; summary of criteria used by authors in debate over, 62–122, 129, 134, 138, 141–42, 145, 151, 155–56, 160, 166, 170, 174, 177–80. *See also* soft balancing
balance of threat theory, 147–50, 160, 161, 168, 175–80. *See also* Walt, Stephen M.
bandwagoning strategy, 123–24, 147–48, 151, 156–60, 161, 277n6
Barnett, Michael, 161
Bayesian interpretation of probability, 52
Bennett, Andrew, 86
Bhutto, Zulkifar Ali, 75
Blainey, Geoffrey, 123
Bloor, David, 29
Bohman, James, 11, 271n1
Boli, John, 94
Boyd, Richard N., 35
Boyle, Robert, 241
Braithwaite, Richard B., 39, 59
Brazil, 73, 76, 92, 97–99
Brecher, Michael, 206
Bremer, Stuart A., 279n1; on democratic peace, 197–202
Bridgman, Percy Williams, 44
Brito, Dagobert L., 63
Brodie, Bernard, 62
Bromberger, Sylvan, 41–42
Bronner, Michael, 274n1
Brooks, Risa, 282n26

Brooks, Stephen G., 160; on balance of power, 170–74, 278n14, 278n15, 278n16
buck-passing strategy, 124, 156, 159, 160, 168, 169, 221
Bueno de Mesquita, Bruce, 63, 198, 206, 208, 236, 246, 281n25
Bull, Hedley, 162, 176, 260; on balance of power, 142–46; on methodology debate, 251–52
bureaucratic politics explanation, 53, 65–66, 75, 78, 91–95, 97, 98, 112, 114, 116, 141
Bush, George H. W., 172
Bush, George W., 63, 166, 168–70, 172

Canada, 76, 96, 216
Carnap, Rudolf, 51–52. *See also* logical positivism
Carr, Edward Hallet, 156, 175
Carter, Jimmy, 108
Carthage, 145
causal mechanisms: identification as a criterion of scientific explanation, 38, 44, 48, 53–57. *See also* balance of power, summary of criteria used by authors in debate over; democratic peace, summary of criteria used by authors in debate over; nuclear proliferation, summary of criteria used by authors in debate over
causation, 17, 38–39, 41, 44–45, 50, 82–83, 99, 100–101, 106, 110, 114–15, 140–41, 144–45, 163, 169, 201–2, 257, 274n11; causal-conventionalism, 60; conventionalism, 16, 29, 253–55; reverse causation, 58. *See also* Duhem, Pierre
Caverley, Jonathan D., 282n26
chain-ganging strategy, 123–24
Chan, Steve, 182, 200
Chernoff, Fred: on causal-conventionalism, 60; on defining prediction, 272n5; on methodological pluralism, 24, 252; on scientific progress, 24, 241; on underdetermination thesis, 282n4
Chile, 210
China, 10; balance of power and, 145, 159, 170, 172–73, 192, 277n3; nuclear proliferation and, 52, 64, 66, 75, 77, 80, 85, 93, 99, 104, 108, 117
Chubin, Shahram, 112
civil war, 137. *See also* American Civil War
classical realism. *See* realism
Claude, Inis L., 124, 125, 164, 176, 260; on balance of power, 134–38, 277n5
Cobden, Richard, 124, 225
Cold War, 62–63, 80, 98, 124, 125–26, 127, 136, 145, 151–54, 159–61, 166, 171, 173, 175, 196, 224, 245, 273n8, 280n8
collective security, 134–37, 193
constructive empiricism, 29, 35, 42–43, 273n7. *See also* Van Fraassen, Bas C.
constructivism in international relations, 10, 29, 35, 86–88, 91, 107, 121, 124, 152, 161, 179, 183, 263
context-dependency, 44, 210–11, 234–36, 257–61, 266, 273n8, 275n5, 281n16, 281n19, 281n24, 283n8
Correlates of War database, 9, 183, 187, 193, 206, 215, 216, 221, 230, 251, 254, 281n18
Costa Rica, 163
counterfactual support as a criterion of scientific explanation, 40. *See also* balance of power, summary of criteria used by authors in debate over; democratic peace, summary of criteria used by authors in debate over; nuclear proliferation, summary of criteria used by authors in debate over
covering law model of explanation, 17, 34, 38–39, 46, 213, 220, 273n6. *See also* Hempel, Carl G.
Crabb, Cecil V., 129
criteria of explanatory superiority used in this study, 60–61
criteria to identify most influential publications, 3, 5–6
criteria of scientific progress, 2; convergence and divergence on, 118–22, 177–80, 237–40, 247–50; pragmatism and, 49–50. *See also* empiricism; scientific realism
Cummins, Robert, 59
Czechoslovakia, 183

Darwin, Charles, 45, 46, 47, 241
Davidson, Donald, 54
deductive-nomological (D-N) model of explanation, 35, 38–42, 44, 47–48, 133. *See also* Hempel, Carl G.
de Gaulle, Charles, 74, 95
degenerating research program, 31, 134. *See also* Lakatos, Imre
democracy. *See* democratic peace
democratic peace: academic debate on, 181–240, 24; analysis of results of debate, 245–47; summary of criteria used by authors in debate over, 185–86, 189, 196,

197, 201–2, 203–4, 207–8, 211, 214–15, 220, 224, 229, 237–40
Denmark, 161, 188
depth of causes as a criterion of scientific explanation, 22, 38. *See also* balance of power, summary of criteria used by authors in debate over; democratic peace, summary of criteria used by authors in debate over; nuclear proliferation, summary of criteria used by authors in debate over
Descartes, René, 28
descriptive versus normative accounts of science, 2, 3, 11–12
Dessler, David, 273n8
de Vattel, Emmerich, 143
Diehl, Paul F., 98
diFinetti, Bruno, 52
Downes, Alexander, 282n26
Doyle, Michael W., 6, 182; on democratic peace, 189–96
Dray, William H., 40, 44
Dudley, Will, 263
Duhem, Pierre, 27, 48, 241; conventionalism and, 29, 253–54; Duhem Thesis, 37, 272n2, 273n9, 282n4
Durkheim, Emile, 274n17
dyadic hypothesis, 33, 181, 184–86, 190, 193, 195, 201, 205, 223, 224, 228–29, 230–36, 238, 245, 281n23, 282n26. *See also* democratic peace

East, Maurice A., 182
Ecuadorian-Peruvian War, 191
Einstein, Albert, 241, 256, 272n3
Eisenhower, Dwight D., 66
elimination of alternatives as a criterion of scientific explanation, 48, 60. *See also* balance of power, summary of criteria used by authors in debate over; criteria of explanatory superiority used in this study; democratic peace, summary of criteria used by authors in debate over; nuclear proliferation, summary of criteria used by authors in debate over
Elman, Colin, 161
Elster, Jon, 58, 210
empirical adequacy: as a criterion of scientific explanation, 38, 60. *See also* balance of power, summary of criteria used by authors in debate over; criteria of explanatory superiority used in this study; democratic peace, summary of criteria used by authors in debate over; nuclear proliferation, summary of criteria used by authors in debate over
empirical fit. *See* empirical adequacy
empiricism, 16, 18, 28, 35–38, 265; types of, 18, 25, 29, 255; contrast with realism in metaphysics, 18; contrast with scientific realism as explaining stalemate, 255–57; criteria of theory choice and, 256; logical empiricism, school of, 29; scientific realism and, 35–37; theoretical truth and, 255; Waltz on, 139
exemplar publications and socialization of researchers, 3, 5–6, 13, 24
explanation: balance of power and, 126–29; meaning of, 2–3. *See also* balance of power, summary of criteria used by authors in debate over; criteria of explanatory superiority used in this study; democratic peace, summary of criteria used by authors in debate over; nuclear proliferation, summary of criteria used by authors in debate over
explanatory unification: as a criterion of scientific explanation, 38, 45–47. *See also* balance of power, summary of criteria used by authors in debate over; democratic peace, summary of criteria used by authors in debate over; nuclear proliferation, summary of criteria used by authors in debate over
Eyre, Dana P., 94

falsifiability as a criterion of scientific explanation, 17, 18, 30, 33, 50, 60. *See also* balance of power, summary of criteria used by authors in debate over; democratic peace, summary of criteria used by authors in debate over; nuclear proliferation, summary of criteria used by authors in debate over
falsificationism, 17–18, 189, 282n4
Farber, Henry S., 6, 228, 280–81n15, 281n17; on democratic peace, 220–24
Fearon, James D., 70
Fetzer, James H., 274n14
Feyerabend, Paul, 11, 18
Finland, 185, 216
Finnemore, Martha, 94
France, 10; balance of power and, 141, 158, 171–72, 174; democratic peace and, 190,

France (*continued*)
193, 197, 209, 224; nuclear proliferation and, 67, 74–77, 78, 80, 95–96, 109, 117
Franco-Thai War of 1940, 200
Frederick I of Prussia, 163
Freedom House, 187, 254
Friedman, Michael, 40; on explanatory unification, 45–46
functional explanation, 57–60, 91, 144, 162, 203, 259, 274n17

Gaddis, John Lewis, 62, 125
Galileo, 70
Garfinkle, Adam, 258
Gartzke, Erik: on democratic peace, 224–32, 242, 246; on nuclear proliferation, 111–15
Geller, Daniel S., 63
George, Alexander L., 86, 108
Gibler, Douglas, 230–31
Giere, Ronald, 52
Gillies, Donald, 273n9
Gilpin, Robert, 123, 273n9
Gochman, Charles S., 198, 206, 280–81n15
Goertz, Gary, 98
Goldschmidt, Pierre, 64
Goldsmith, Arthur A., 282n26
Goodman, Nelson, 40
Gorton, John, 109
Gowa, Joanne, 6, 228, 280–81n15, 281n17; on democratic peace, 6, 220–24
Great Britain: balance of power and, 74, 131–32, 137; democratic peace and, 193–94, 197, 209, 224. *See also* United Kingdom
Gregg, Philip M., 182
Grotius, Hugo, 143

Haas, Michael, 193
Hacking, Ian, 29
Hands, D. Wade, 274n12
Hanson, Marianne, 63
Hanson, Norwood Russell, 18, 47
Harvey, William, 11, 241, 256
Hempel, Carl G., 17, 41–42, 133, 241, 272–73n3, 273n14, 280n12; on functional explanation, 59; on logical empiricism, 29; on prediction and control, 27, 50, 219, 220; on psychological aspects of explanation, 44; on verification criterion, 35. *See also* deductive-nomological (D-N) model of explanation
hermeneutic tradition of scholarship, 18–19, 26
Hintze, Otto, 213
history of science as evidence for philosophical doctrines, 37–38
Hitler, Adolf, 157–58, 163–64
Hobbes, Thomas, 16, 142–43
Hobson, John A., 32
Hollis, Martin, 26, 53
Hume, David, 17, 28, 124, 145
Hymans, Jacques: nuclear proliferation, 106–11, 117, 242, 276n12, 276n13, 276n14
hypothesis H1: defined, 8; support for summarized, 265–66
hypothesis H2: defined, 8; support for summarized, 265–66
hypothetico-deductive (H-D) method, 28, 80, 146, 147, 220

ideal types and explanation, 56–57
imparting understanding as a criterion of scientific explanation, 41, 47, 60. *See also* balance of power, summary of criteria used by authors in debate over; democratic peace, summary of criteria used by authors in debate over; nuclear proliferation, summary of criteria used by authors in debate over
India, 51, 170, 200; nuclear proliferation and, 66–68, 75–80, 86, 93, 96, 100–108, 112, 276n13
International Atomic Energy Agency, 65, 66
interpretivism in the social sciences, 18–23; rules and, 21–22. *See also* MacIntyre, Alasdair; Winch, Peter
Intriligator, Michael D., 63
Iran: balance of power and, 170, 172–73; nuclear proliferation debate and, 85, 95
Iraq: nuclear proliferation debate and, 63–64, 73, 79, 85, 95, 102; US-led invasion of, 163, 166–67, 169, 171–74, 278n15
Iraq War, 169, 171, 278n16
Israel: balance of power debate and, 150; democratic peace debate and, 188, 191; nuclear proliferation debate and, 64–66, 73, 79–86, 100–102, 109, 110, 150, 188

Jefferson, Thomas, 209
Jervis, Robert, 100, 108, 192
Jo, Doon-Joon: on nuclear proliferation, 111–15, 276nn15–16, 276n18
Jordan, Richard, 5, 13, 25, 219, 280n14
Joseph, Jonathan, 283n7

Kahn, Herman, 62
Kant, Immanuel, 10–11, 28, 38, 142–43, 181, 186, 189–90, 194–95, 205, 211–12, 234–35, 278n11, 280n8
Kaplan, Morton, 73, 125
Kapur, Ashok, 76
Karl, David J., 113
Katzenstein, Peter J., 112
Kegley, Charles W., 101
Kennedy, John F., 66
Keohane, Robert O., 145
Keynes, John Maynard, 51
Kim, Jaegwon, 54, 139
Kincade, William H., 112
Kincaid, Harold, 57, 58
Kinoshita, Joyce, 45, 273n8
Kinsella, David, 281n23
Kitcher, Philip, 45–47
Kuchma, Leonid, 94
Kugler, Jacek, 123
Kuhn, Thomas S., 202, 263, 272n7, 274n13, 279n7; on exemplar works, 12–13; on incommensurability, 14, 29–30; on scientific paradigms, 29–32; on scientific revolutions, 13, 15; on socialization of researchers, 3, 5, 13–14, 24–25
Kupchan, Charles, 282n26
Kyburg, Henry E., 51

Lakatos, Imre, 30–32, 134, 263; on scientific progress and the growth of knowledge, 50, 272n6
Lake, David A., 206, 208, 215, 216, 279n6; explanation for democratic peace and, 202–4
Lalman, David, 206, 208
Lane, Frederic C., 202
Layne, Christopher, 216, 217, 223, 225, 240, 280n10; on democratic peace, 211–15
League of Nations, 134, 135, 143
Legro, Jeffrey W., 175, 278n17
Leibniz, Freiherr Gottfried Wilhelm von, 233, 272n3
Leon, David Pak Yue, 54
Leplin, Jarrett, 35
Levy, Jack S., 124, 125, 221, 254, 277n8, 277n9, 278nn11–13; on the explanation of balance of power, 160–66
liberalism, 3, 10–11, 33, 64, 66, 81, 97–116, 126, 147–53, 246, 250, 257, 259, 266, 275n9, 279n2, 280n14, 281n18, 282n26; democratic peace debate and, 181–240
liberal trade and economic explanations, 84–85, 87, 104, 106, 121, 153, 178, 196, 224–29, 231, 236, 246. *See also* Gartzke, Erik; Solingen, Etel
libertarian states, 186–89, 215. *See also* Rummel, Rudolf J.
Libya, 63, 64, 68, 79, 85, 95, 102
Lilley, Mary Lauren, 282n26
Lincoln, Abraham, 211
Lippmann, Walter, 184
Liska, George, 123
Little, Daniel, 53–55, 57
Little, Richard, 124, 276–77n1
Locke, John, 142–43
logical empiricism, 18, 29, 35, 42
logical positivism, 17–18, 35. *See also* Carnap, Rudolf
Louis XIV of France, 145
Lydia, Royal Mark Lady, 41

Machiavelli, Niccolò, 181
MacIntyre, Alasdair, 22–23
Madison, James, 209
Maliniak, Daniel, 5, 13, 25, 219, 280n14
Malinowski, Bronislaw, 274n17
Mansfield, Edward D., 104, 191, 212, 220, 224
Maoz, Zeev, 182, 212, 215, 216, 220, 246; on the explanation for democratic peace, 204–8
Maxwell, Grover, 35
MccGwire, Michael, 63
Mearsheimer, John J., 60, 127, 157, 160–61, 167, 176, 212, 215, 256, 260; explanation of balance of power and, 151–56; explanation of democratic peace and, 196–97
Merton, Robert K., 274n17
methodological conservatism as a criterion of scientific explanation, 50. *See also* balance of power, summary of criteria used by authors in debate over; democratic peace, summary of criteria used by authors in debate over; nuclear proliferation, summary of criteria used by authors in debate over
methodological individualism, 49, 52–57
methodological pluralism, 9, 24, 252
Meyer, Stephen M., 85, 101, 260, 274nn4–7; explanation of nuclear proliferation and, 79–84
Militarized Interstate Dispute (MID) dataset, 206, 230
Mill, John Stuart, 225

Minorities at Risk dataset, 230
Montmorency J. Littledog, Royal Mark, 235–36
Moravscik, Andrew, 175, 278n17
Morgenthau, Hans J., 156, 162, 164, 165, 175–76, 260, 277n2, 277n5; on the explanation of balance of power, 126–29
Morrow, James D., 236, 246, 281n25
Mueller, John, 151, 184
Mussolini, Benito, 157

Nagel, Ernest, 39, 40, 59
Napoleonic Wars, 135
national identity conception, 108–11
naturalism: as a philosophy of social science, 15–21, 24, 51, 61, 121, 179, 180, 188–89, 202, 228, 232, 251, 255, 260, 265, 282–83n6; definition of, 15–16
natural order, 47
neoclassical realism. *See* realism
Newton, Sir Isaac, 11, 12, 14–15, 28, 45–46, 55, 70, 233, 256, 272n3
Nexon, Daniel, 160
Nizamani, Haider K., 112
nonstate actors and nuclear proliferation, 63, 77
normative versus descriptive inquiry in the social sciences, 11–12
norms: democratic regimes and, 204–8, 210–11, 212–13, 217, 221, 222, 224, 236, 246; international relations theory and, 86–90, 100, 105, 108, 112–14, 124, 127, 144, 158, 162, 189, 192, 195, 271n3, 279n2; models and nuclear proliferation and, 93–98; of scholarship, 264
North Atlantic Treaty Organization (NATO), 67–68, 171
North Korea, 68, 80, 85, 88, 95, 98, 275n4, 276n13
Nuclear Nonproliferation Treaty (NPT), 10, 65–66, 75–76, 77, 85, 88, 89, 91, 94, 95, 97–100, 111–14, 117, 275n10
nuclear proliferation: agreement and disagreement on explanations of, 115–18; analysis of results of debate, 242–44; debate over, 62–122; summary of criteria used by authors in debate over, 67, 71, 78–79, 84, 89, 96, 101, 108, 110–15, 118–22
Nye, Joseph S., 63, 145, 155; soft power and, 159, 161

Oakes, Amy, 5, 13, 25, 219, 280n14
Obama, Barack Hussein, 54
Oneal, John R.: and democratic peace debate, 182, 204, 223, 226, 227, 229, 230–32, 280n8. *See also* Russett, Bruce M.
ontological commitment, 36, 47–49; methodological individualism and, 52–53
Oppenheim, Paul, 39
Organski, A. F. K., 123, 174, 176, 260, 277n3, 277n5; on explaining balance of power, 129–34; on power transition theory, 131–32
Owen, John, 212, 214, 215–16, 280n9; on explaining democratic peace, 208–11

Pakistan, 51, 64, 66, 68, 75–76, 78, 93, 101–7, 109–10, 112, 200
Pape, Robert, 160, 278n14, 278n15, 278n16; on soft balancing and alliance formation, 166–70
Parsons, Talcott, 278n17
partial entailment. *See* Carnap, Rudolf
Paul, T. V., 106, 123, 126; on the explanation of nuclear proliferation, 96–101
Payne, Keith B., 63
Peirce, Charles Sanders, 36–37, 241. *See also* pragmatism
Peloponnesian War, 181
Perkovich, George, 112
Peterson, Susan, 5, 13, 25, 219, 280n14
Philip II, 145
Poincaré, Henri, 241
political realism, 86, 88, 90, 92, 96, 97, 101, 117, 126, 174–75, 183, 184–85, 197, 212–15, 217–19, 230, 233, 244, 250, 255; defensive, 156–57; offensive, 152–53
Polity dataset: version II, 200–201, 206, 215, 220, 221, 254; version IV, 226, 230
Polybius, 124, 125, 145
Pomper, Gerald, 159
Popper, Karl R., 17–18, 28, 30–32, 39, 50, 134, 215, 226, 241, 263. *See also* falsificationism
Potter, William C., 260; explanation for nuclear proliferation, 71–79, 260
power transition theory, 131–32. *See also* Organski, A. F. K.
pragmatism, 30, 38, 42–44, 258–60, 265, 266, 283n8. *See also* Van Fraassen, Bas C.
prediction defined, 27
predictive accuracy as a criterion of scientific explanation, 36, 37, 38, 47. *See also* balance of power, summary of criteria used by authors in debate over; democratic peace, summary of criteria used by authors

in debate over; nuclear proliferation, summary of criteria used by authors in debate over
preventive war, 73, 113, 164, 276n18
process-tracing method, 158, 208, 212
progress, scientific, 1–2, 28–32; security studies and, 1–4, 32–33; traditions of explanation and, 8–33
proliferation of nuclear weapons. *See* nuclear proliferation
Prussia, 163, 166
Ptolemy, Claudius, 11, 14, 31
Putnam, Hilary, 35

quantitative versus qualitative debates as an explanation for progress, 250–52
Quester, George: on explaining nuclear proliferation, 65–67, 260
Quine, Willard van Orman, 35, 45, 263; Duhem-Quine thesis, 273n9

Radcliffe-Brown, Alfred Reginald, 274n17
Ramirez, Francisco O., 94
Ramsey, Frank Plumpton, 52
range of phenomena covered as a criterion of scientific explanation, 60. *See also* balance of power, summary of criteria used by authors in debate over; democratic peace, summary of criteria used by authors in debate over; nuclear proliferation, summary of criteria used by authors in debate over
Ray, James Lee, 198, 230, 232, 280–81n15
Raymond, Gregory A., 101
realism: as a philosophical contrast to empiricism, 18; as a theory in international relations. *See* political realism
Regan, Ronald, 108
Reichenbach, Hans, 49, 273n10
Richardson, Lewis F., 182, 183
Riker, Willian H., 63, 150
robustness as a criterion of scientific explanation, 49. *See also* balance of power, summary of criteria used by authors in debate over; democratic peace, summary of criteria used by authors in debate over; nuclear proliferation, summary of criteria used by authors in debate over
Rohrlich, Fritz, 29
Rome, 185
Rosato, Sebastian, 281n23
Rosenau, James, 53
Rothstein, Robert L., 158
Rummel, Rudolf J., 182, 197, 201, 206, 208, 211, 215, 232; on the explanation for democratic peace, 186–89
Russell, Bertrand, 48
Russett, Bruce M., 6, 182–83, 211–12, 215, 216, 222–32, 240, 246, 280n8, 281n17; on the explanation for democratic peace, 204–7
Russia, 64, 94, 111, 141, 163, 170–73, 274n1

Sagan, Scott, 98, 104, 107, 110, 111–13, 116, 256; on the explanation for nuclear proliferation, 89–96
Salmon, Wesley C., 44, 48–49
Saudi Arabia, 85
Savoy, June, 129
Scheinman, Lawrence, 74
Schelling, Thomas C., 90
Schweller, Randall L., 88, 161, 176, 208, 260, 277n6; on the explanation for balance of power, 156–60
scientific-causal tradition in the social sciences, 15–18. *See also* naturalism
scientific explanation, 17, 21–22, 34–61, 265; causation and, 50–52; contending views of, 34–38; criteria of described, 45–50; familiarity account of, 44; pragmatic theory of, 42–44
scientific realism, 28, 35–38, 265; contrast with empiricism as explaining stalemate, 255–57; criteria of theory choice and, 256; the D-N model and, 47–48; empiricism as an alternative explanation for disagreement, 255–57; theoretical truth and, 255; types of, 255
Scowcroft, Brent, 172
Scriven, Michael, 40–41
security model as an explanation for nuclear proliferation, 67, 84, 90–91, 94, 107. *See also* Sagan, Scott
security studies: central questions in, vii–viii, 9–11
Sellars, Wilfred, 18
Sen Gupta, Bhababi, 75
Sheikh, Ali. T., 112
simplicity as a criterion of scientific explanation, 38. *See also* balance of power, summary of criteria used by authors in debate over; democratic peace, summary of criteria used by authors in debate over;

simplicity as a criterion (*continued*)
nuclear proliferation, summary of criteria used by authors in debate over
Singer, J. David, 182, 188, 189, 195, 251, 261; explanation of democratic peace and, 183–86; methodology debate and, 251–52
Singh, Sonali, 114, 115, 275–76n11, 275n15; explanation for nuclear proliferation and, 101–6
Siverson, Randolph, 236, 246, 281n25
Small, Melvin, 182, 189, 195, 261; explanation of democratic peace and, 183–86
Smart, J. J. C., 45
Smith, Alastair, 236, 246, 281n25
Smith, Steve, 26, 53
Snyder, Jack L., 104, 112, 191, 212, 224, 273n8
soft balancing, 125–26, 161, 166–69, 278n14, 278n15. *See also* Brooks, Stephen G.; Pape, Robert; Wohlforth, William C.
soft power, 159, 161
Solingen, Etel, 93, 98, 104, 106, 107, 117, 242, 256, 275n8, 275n9; on nuclear proliferation, 84–89
South Africa, 74, 80, 84, 90–91, 92, 101, 102
South Korea, 76, 79, 87, 101
Soviet Union. *See* Union of Soviet Socialist Republics (USSR)
Spain, 200, 210
Sparta, 181, 254
speech acts, 43–44, 265. *See also* Austin, J. L.
Spiro, David E., 212; explanation for democratic peace and, 215–20, 223, 225, 240, 280n12, 280n13
Stantchev, Branislav L., 281n23
structural realism. *See* political realism
Suchman, Marc C., 94
Sudan, 87
Suganami, Hidemi: causes of war and, 29–30; contextual and causal explanation and, 44–45, 257–58, 260–61
Sweden, 97, 99, 102, 130, 161, 188
Switzerland, 97, 99; Swiss Cantons and Confederation, 190, 215
Syracuse, 145
Syria, 73, 79, 85, 87, 106

Tetlock, Philip E., 100, 108, 278n18
Tertrais, Bruno, 278n15
Thayer, Bradley A., 59–60
theoretical terms in scientific explanation, 36, 70, 255, 272n2
Thompson, William R., 223–24, 280–81n15
Thucydides, Son of Olorus, 124, 181, 211
Tierney, Michael J., 5, 13, 25, 219, 280n14
Toulmin, Stephen, 29, 40; natural order and, 47
Treaty of Utrecht, 145
Trent crisis, 210–12
Trubowitz, Peter, 282n26
true causes as a criterion of scientific explanation, 38. *See also* balance of power, summary of criteria used by authors in debate over; democratic peace, summary of criteria used by authors in debate over; nuclear proliferation, summary of criteria used by authors in debate over
Tucker, Richard, 223–24, 280–81n15

Ukraine, 94–96, 101–2
Ullian, Joseph S., 45
understanding versus explanation, 26
Union of Soviet Socialist Republics (USSR), 10; balance of power and, 124–26, 131, 142, 145, 148, 151–52, 159, 160, 163–64, 171, 172, 176; democratic peace and, 183, 224, 277n3; nuclear proliferation and, 62, 63, 64, 66, 71, 73–75, 77–79, 90, 91, 94, 96, 115
United Kingdom, 10; balance of power and, 133; democratic peace and, 163, 188, 259, 281n18; nuclear proliferation and, 67, 77, 79–80, 93. *See also* Great Britain
United Nations (UN), 64, 107, 143, 166, 171, 172, 227, 229
United States, 10, 25, 54, 58; balance of power and, 124–26, 130–32, 133, 142, 145, 148, 161, 163, 166–67, 169–73; democratic peace and, 190, 193, 197, 200, 210, 215, 216, 224, 276n15, 277n9, 280n14, 281n18; nuclear proliferation and, 62–64, 66, 68, 71–72, 73–77, 79, 93–95, 108

Van Fraassen, Bas C., 29, 35, 42–44, 241, 266, 272n1, 283n8; context, pragmatism and, 258–59. *See also* constructive empiricism; empiricism
Vasquez, John A., 50, 86, 161, 221, 230, 272n6, 274n13
Vietnam, 52, 66, 171, 192
Von Mises, Richard, 51
Von Wright, G. H., 26

Wæver, Ole, 283n7

Walt, Stephen M., 1, 154, 156, 161, 167, 176, 260, 278n12; balance of threat explanation of balance of power and, 146–51
Waltz, Kenneth N., 25, 53, 60, 63, 89, 113, 125, 135, 152, 154, 156, 157, 159, 160, 164, 165, 167, 175, 176, 212, 217, 228, 256–58, 260, 274n2, 283n7; explanation for balance of power and, 138–42; explanation for nuclear proliferation and, 67–71
War of Spanish Succession, 145
Warsaw Pact, 172, 183
Watkins, J. W. N., 53; methodological individualism and, 55–56
Way, Christopher, 114, 115, 275–76n11, 275n15; on explanation for nuclear proliferation, 101–6
Weber, Max, 26, 56
Weede, Erich, 182
Wendt, Alexander, 112, 258, 271n3
Wilhelm II, Kaiser, 191, 196–97, 214, 217
Wilkenfeld, Jonathan, 182, 206
Wilson, Woodrow, 135, 205, 277n4
Winch, Peter, 20–22; critique of MacIntyre and, 22–23
Wittgenstein, Ludwig, 20–21
Wohlforth, William C., 160, 278n14, 278n15, 278n16; on explanation of balance of power, 170–74
Wohlstetter, Albert, 274–75n3
Wolfers, Arnold, 125, 227
world government, 134–37
World War I, 82, 124, 130, 135, 140, 149, 150, 153, 157, 191, 192, 194, 197, 209, 214, 220–23, 258, 277n2
World War II, 29, 67, 74, 76, 79, 82, 90, 95, 96, 112, 115, 117, 130, 135, 149, 153, 196, 198, 220–23, 276n1
Wright, Larry, 58
Wright, Quincy, 143, 182, 183

Yugoslavia, 183